D1563165

LOVING GOD WITH OUR MINDS

Wallace M. Alston

LOVING GOD WITH OUR MINDS

The Pastor as Theologian

⸸ ESSAYS IN HONOR OF WALLACE M. ALSTON ⸸

Edited by

Michael Welker and Cynthia A. Jarvis

WILLIAM B. EERDMANS PUBLISHING COMPANY
GRAND RAPIDS, MICHIGAN / CAMBRIDGE, U.K.

© 2004 Wm. B. Eerdmans Publishing Co.
All rights reserved

Wm. B. Eerdmans Publishing Co.
255 Jefferson Ave. S.E., Grand Rapids, Michigan 49503 /
P.O. Box 163, Cambridge CB3 9PU U.K.

Printed in the United States of America

09 08 07 06 05 04   7 6 5 4 3 2 1

ISBN 0-8028-2857-4

www.eerdmans.com

Contents

Contents

Preface

In 2003 Wallace Alston had served the church and the academy for forty years. In 2004 he celebrates his seventieth birthday. Pondering this, friends and colleagues from the church and from the academy have contributed to a Festschrift in his honor.

I first knew Wallace as the Pastor of Nassau Presbyterian Church in Princeton and was deeply impressed with him. His pastoral energy and spirit radiated throughout the whole congregation. When he left to assume the office of the director of the Center of Theological Inquiry (CTI), the church had a very difficult time finding a successor. One day a member of the church said laconically: "We'll have to wait for the second coming of Jesus Christ to find a suitable successor to Wallace."

With Wallace the CTI turned into a theological "powerhouse." The international scope of the scholars in residence increased; female scholars and younger scholars of high quality joined the circle. Instead of one multi-year international and interdisciplinary consultation, Wallace launched four consultations simultaneously which covered a broad range of topics: Science and Theology on Eschatology; Globalization; The Common Good; Faith and Reason; The Identity of Jesus; Human Personhood and Dignity — these were treated by teams of high-profile scholars from all over the globe. With his quick eye for academic and theological quality Wallace accompanied all of these research processes. Relentlessly he pushed the groups for results that would serve both the church and the academy.

As a great missionary entrepreneur Wallace also organized consultations in parts of the world which are religiously and academically in crucial transitions: South Africa, Middle and Eastern Europe, and India. The topics chosen were meant to invigorate theological research in these countries. Theologians from different nations were invited to create a conference that would stimulate substantial theological thinking about crucial current issues: pluralism, globalization, the mission of the church, the potentials of 'public theology'.

I was privileged to join several of these events, including three consultations on "Reformed Theology: Identity and Ecumenicity." One consultation was with primarily systematic theologians, another with mostly biblical scholars, and a third one with ethicists and practical theologians from many countries. It was a joy to harvest the richness of current theological thinking in this tradition of faith. It was a particular joy working with Wallace to look for coherences and promising perspectives in this discourse, to "weave" contributions into a tapestry, and to discover potentials which will open the Reformed tradition to constructive dialogue with other Christian traditions of faith that would provide ecumenical orientation and theological leadership.

However, Wallace's main concern has been to launch the pastor-theologian project and to see it flourish. This project has never been a mere annex to the program of the CTI. It has served as the dialogue between theological, international, and interdisciplinary research and the theology cultivated and practiced in the church. Wallace was pleased to see how readily scholars from the academic consultation agreed to join the meetings of the pastors and how well the cooperation worked in general.

This book unites voices from the various enterprises of the CTI; voices from different churches, from different theological and academic disciplines, and from different countries across the globe. The book is thus a bouquet of diverse perspectives which try to mirror what is so central and admirable in Wallace, and also what is so dear and desirable for him to see among his fellows when we all work together and hope for the coming reign of God: to love God not only with one's heart, but also with one's mind — to live and think as pastor-theologians.

Without multifarious support this volume would not have come together. We thank, above all, Kathi Morley for her great support and never-ending patience in collecting the contributions. We thank Joshua Jeffers for his careful editorial support and Bill Eerdmans for the excellent cooperation.

MICHAEL WELKER
Heidelberg

Introduction

Wallace Alston attended seminary on a dare. George Buttrick, then minister of Harvard Memorial Chapel, threw down the gauntlet before a young naval officer stationed in Boston, challenging him to investigate intellectually what reason had led him to believe he was so against. Years later, having placed himself under the tutelage of some of the greatest theological minds of the last century, he accepted a call to a small church in Wadesboro, North Carolina.

There the rigor and relevance of his theological training came to the fore as he set out to engage the church he served on the side of justice in the struggle for civil rights. Later in the Epilogue to *The Church of the Living God*, his observations upon those times confirmed the theological instincts with which he had engaged his ministry from the beginning. He writes, "The church was wrong when it justified slavery and segregation with *fatally flawed theology*. It was wrong when it fought scientific judgments concerning human origins with *obscurantist biblical interpretation.*" Armed with the reasonable faith at which his mind had arrived in the classroom, he was relentless in the pulpit and the public square as he pressed the consequences of loving God with the mind upon the church and the world.

The boldness of his witness cut short his first call and sent him to the pulpit once occupied by his own professor of theology. It was while serving the First Presbyterian Church in Auburn, Alabama, that the influence of this young pastor-theologian began to be felt upon the next generation. Associate ministers on his staff, seminarians in the course of their summer placement, as well as the brightest and best young people in his congregation (heading toward seminary at his urging) were pressed to think critically and theologically about the substance of the church's witness. They were privileged to observe in this mentor how one's theological perspective affected every aspect of the practice of ministry.

Wallace's commitment to the theological formation of young ministers expanded to the classrooms of Duke Divinity School as he taught homiletics while serving the First Presbyterian Church in Durham, North Carolina. Whether in the classroom or in the congregation, no doubt Wallace's unique influence on succeeding generations of ministers was due to his relentless expectation that those with whom he worked also do business with, in his words, "those sources and practices which historically have enabled people to encounter and to be encountered by 'the grace of our Lord Jesus Christ, the love of God, and the communion of the Holy Spirit.'" By the time he reached Nassau Presbyterian Church in Princeton, the list of able pastor-theologians spawned by his ministry had grown long.

As one privileged to be on that list, I remember the evenings he would arrange in New York with Paul Lehmann for theological conversation; the monthly meetings in his office with Seward Hiltner so that we could discuss the theological dimensions of pastoral care; the staff meetings which would adjourn to the Nassau Inn for further reflection on some issue facing the church; the week-long staff retreats at the Alstons' cottage on an island in Maine where Ted Gill (our theologian-in-residence) and Wallace would reminisce about the heyday of theological education. Though I had been ordained for seven years when I joined the staff of Nassau Church, in many ways my theological education began in earnest under Wallace's wing. I listened and learned as he filtered every aspect of the church's ministry through the history of Christian doctrine, the theological minds of Karl Barth, Reinhold Niebuhr, Dietrich Bonhoeffer, or John Calvin, to name a few, and always through the theological complexity of the biblical witness.

The most vivid memory I have of those years happened in Maine on a staff retreat. We were returning from a visit to the other side of the island in a Boston Whaler and night had fallen. Wallace suddenly cut the motor in the middle of the sea and let us drift in silence for what seemed like an eternity. Then, looking up at the stars on a perfectly clear night, he began to muse: "Could it be that this is the only visited planet? Has God come only to us or are there others?" Quietly we began to talk about both the arrogance of answering in the affirmative and the humbling truth if we, alone, were the creatures by whom God had chosen to be known. Thus we came to breathe the air of theological reflection.

When in the spring of 1996 the opportunity to direct the Center of Theological Inquiry presented itself, Wallace did not hesitate. Though his absence from the pulpit week in and week out continues to be a loss for those whose faith grew under his substantive preaching, his vision for the intersection of the church and the academy has been a tremendous gift to both. Only months after assuming the position, he began to discuss the possibility of a program that would connect the reality of the church's ministry with the theological resources of CTI for the mutual enrichment of each. Soon the proposal for a Pastor-Theologian Program was on the desk of Craig Dykstra of the Lilly Foundation Inc.

As we look forward to our third round of three-year seminars, the identity of the ordained minister or priest as theologian and scholar has been lifted up in congregations throughout the nation and even internationally. Founded on the conviction, in Wallace's words, "that in all denominations there are pastors and priests of extraordinary intellectual ability, equally as capable of theological scholarship as academic theologians, who lack only the time, context, and encouragement for such pursuits, and that on their emergence as a formative influence the renewal of the church depends," the program will continue under his leadership as he retires from the position of Director of CTI.

In sum, there are more of us than even Wallace knows who could testify that, because he has loved God so faithfully with his mind as a minister of the church of Jesus Christ, "the God who said 'Let light shine out of darkness'" has shone in the hearts and minds of countless pastor-theologians "to give the light of the knowledge of the glory of God in the face of Christ."

CYNTHIA A. JARVIS
Philadelphia

I Cultural, Social, Political, and Ethical Challenges

"Who Is the Other?":
Embodying Difference through Belonging

Denise M. Ackermann

A Fragment from South African Church History[1]

The Dutch Reformed Church in the Cape Colony was faced with a dilemma in the early nineteenth century. Differences of race, history, and social circumstances created tensions in its ranks. In 1829 this church had resolved that Holy Communion was to be administered "simultaneously to all members without distinction of colour or origin." Sadly, the rift between the settler community and the indigenous people, many of whom were slaves, eventually caused the church to bow to social pressures. Race proved to be stronger than religion. In 1857 the synod of the Dutch Reformed Church passed the following resolution:

> The Synod considers it desirable and scriptural that our members from the Heathen be received and absorbed into our existing congregations wherever possible; but where this measure, *as a result of the weakness of some* [my italics], impedes the furtherance of the cause of Christ among the Heathen, the congregation from the Heathen, already founded and still to be founded, shall enjoy its Christian privileges in a separate building or institution.

This paper picks up on themes in an address given at the Lambeth Conference of the Anglican Communion, England, July 1998.

1. Taken from John W. de Gruchy, *The Church Struggle in South Africa* (Cape Town: David Philip, 1979), pp. 8-9.

3

For "the weakness of some," read the racism of some white settlers. Thus the separation of believers along race lines began, a separation which ultimately led to the theological justification of apartheid.

This snippet of history is more than a tragic racist incident. It reveals our human inability to deal lovingly and justly with difference across race, ethnic, and class lines. Cultural ideologies become more powerful than the demands of the gospel. The Synod's decision shows quite nakedly how the divide between "us" and "them" serves the powerful "us" at the expense of the "them" or the "other."

Why Difference, Why Otherness?

Why write about difference and otherness in a Festschrift of this kind? Quite simply because few issues have exercised so powerful a hold over the thought of this century as that of 'the other' or what is known as 'the problem of difference'.[2] To speak of difference and otherness is immediately a problem of language. Other than whom? Different from what? Am I the norm and those who do not confirm to my norm 'the other' or 'different'?[3] Today this problem has taken a prominent place in philosophy, theological ethics, and anthropology and has penetrated deeply into our reflections on our religious practices.

As a white South African who has lived through decades of apartheid in a multi-cultural, ethnically and religiously pluralistic society and who has known the sweet smell of democracy only very recently, I know both the promise and the potential of difference as well as the horror of otherness as exclusion. As a woman I have experienced the exclusionary tactics of patriarchal traditions, structures and practices. At the same time I have learned that the view from the margins of church structures brings its own kind of clarity. As a person living in this present age, I witness intolerance, ethnic hatred, and

2. Jacob Neusner, "Thinking about 'The Other' in religion: It is necessary, but is it possible?" in *Lectures in Judaism in the History of Religions* (Atlanta: Scholars Press, 1990), p. 17, writes: "The single most important problem facing religion for the next hundred years . . . is . . . how to think through difference, how to account, within one's own faith and framework, for the outsider, indeed for many outsiders."

3. See Collette Guilaumin, *Racism, Sexism, Power and Ideology* (London: Routledge, 1995), p. 250, who points out that "*difference* comes from a Latin verb *(fero)* which means 'to carry', 'to orient'. Dif-ference adds the idea of dispersion *(di)* to this orientation; we say 'to differ *from*'. What is important is the little *from*. . . . The kernel of the meaning is the distance from a centre, the distance from a referent (still *fero*)."

modern versions of tribalism nurtured in social and political conditions of appalling imbalances of power and wealth. As a citizen of Africa living through the greatest pandemic history has known, I see daily how stigmatizing people who are living with HIV/AIDS, how making them an unclean 'other', denies their human dignity and deprives them of care and comfort.

My prime concern in this contribution is, however, the manner in which difference and otherness is played out in the Christian church. I know churches who judge AIDS sufferers as sinners. I see others who exclude men and women from exercising their calling to ministry on grounds of their sexual orientation and whose communities are threatening to split asunder on this issue. I experience male hierarchical power exercised in discriminatory practices as endless. I cannot avoid placing difference and otherness at the center of my theological reflection. As a tribute to Wallace Alston whose heart rebels against exclusion on these kinds of grounds, I want to explore how the Body of Christ, instead of perpetuating exclusionary practices, can nurture *an ethic of difference through belonging.*

Thinking about Difference and Otherness

Difference is a reality that elicits at least four problematic responses. The first simply sees the other as a *tabula rasa,* a person with no story, no selfhood, no history. This response was common in certain missionary endeavours in the past. Many intrepid souls came to "darkest" Africa to bring the light of the gospel and then, on encountering the indigenous people whom they clearly found to be very 'other' — that is other than themselves — sadly failed to understand local stories, cultures, and traditions to such an extent that they did not truly see the selfhood of these people. Difference was made over into sameness, in this case into the image of the missionary colonist, in the cause of the moment. The underlying text is: "You should be like me. But, as you are not like me, remember that I am the center, the fixed point by which you and 'the rest' will be defined." This is the language of dominant power. In reality, there is no one center. There never was — except in the delusions of certain dominant philosophies and political systems. There are many centers.[4] To acknowledge, to accept, and to be willing to live with difference and otherness is to admit that there are a myriad of centers.

A second response is a familiar one in today's world. The other is expe-

4. David Tracy, *On Naming the Present: Reflections on God, Hermeneutics, and the Church* (Maryknoll: Orbis Books, 1994), p. 4.

rienced as a threat. The poisonous *apartheid* mentality of Afrikaner national-ism, the genocidal activities of the Nazis and the Hutus, the intransigent otherness of the Serbs, Bosnians, and Croats, and all racist and sexist attitudes, are contemporary examples of otherness as threat. Those in power say: "Only we have the truth and those who are different are our enemy." When the other is a threat, the strategy is to separate people and then, increasingly, to dominate and to demonize them.

There is a third response which is manifested in two distinct yet similar ways: The other is either seen as some exotic, romantic being who does not have to be taken seriously since she or he is so different, or the other is seen as a universal category of person with no particularity. The nineteenth-century western idea of the "noble savage," or the unthinking assumptions in the early days of the women's movement that saw "women" as one large, unspecified category of human beings, are examples of this kind of thinking. Both are pernicious and unacceptable. In failing to acknowledge difference and otherness, we make the other into a romantic ideal or a universal category, rather than regarding them as specific persons. In so doing we never afford the other the dignity of being engaged as a real person in all her or his difference.

A last response to difference and otherness which is particularly prevalent in today's world is that of indifference followed by abandonment. Those of us living in the developing world are stunned by the indifference of the rich nations to the poor and the diseased of the world. If we, who are different and other, do not have the goods or perform the services required by those who live in rich countries, we are simply treated with indifference and finally excluded by abandonment. As Miroslav Volf points out: "Especially within a large-scale setting, where the other lives at a distance, indifference can be more deadly than hate."[5] He argues that whereas hatred flares up in the proximity of the other and then dies down, cold indifference can be sustained over long periods of time. I become wrapped up in my political, social, and cultural system and exclude those who are other. I turn my eyes away from suffering, either because I am numbed or because I justify such turning away as necessary for my survival in an unfriendly world.

These responses are common to all. We exclude the other when our boundaries and our identities are threatened, when we feel discomfort as our symbolic world is impinged upon, and we reason that we need protection from the onslaughts of difference and otherness in order to be who we are.

---

5. Miroslav Volf, *Exclusion and Embrace: A Theological Exploration of Identity, Otherness, and Reconciliation* (Nashville: Abingdon Press, 1996), p. 77.

"Who Is the Other?"

Given our problematic responses to difference and otherness, the need arises for a more profound understanding of difference and otherness in all their complexity, ambiguity, and possibility. There is a liberal assumption that if we were to "treat everyone alike," the problem of difference and otherness would be dealt with. This view is deeply troubling. It assumes, as Rowan Williams points out, that there is "a basic 'inner' humanity, beyond flesh and skin pigmentation and history and conflict, which is the same for all people."[6] Of course we are all *biologically* the same. But the point is that to be properly human is not confined to our biology. Life is unavoidably cultural and diverse. Contexts are being made and remade unendingly. When we stress that we are all the same "under the skin" we risk making "the stranger the same as me" — itself a subtle way of defining the other.

> But human existence is precisely life that is lived in speech and relation, and so in history: what we share as humans is not a human "essence" outside history, but a common involvement in the limits and relativities of history. The only humanity we have in common is bound up in difference, in the encounter of physical and linguistic strangers.[7]

Who is the other? To speak of the other is to speak of space, boundaries, time, difference, our bodies, cultures, traditions, ideologies, and beliefs. To speak of the other is to speak of that other human being whom I may mistakenly have assumed to be just like me and who, in fact, is not like me at all. To speak of the other is to be open to otherness within myself, to the possibility of a foreigner within my own unconscious self.[8] To speak of the other is to speak of poverty and justice, of human sexuality, of gender, race, and class. To speak of the other is to acknowledge that difference is problematic, often threatening, even alienating, and that we do not always live easily or well with it.[9]

---

6. Rowan Williams, *On Christian Theology* (Oxford: Blackwell, 2000), p. 282.

7. Williams, *On Christian Theology*, p. 282.

8. See Julia Kristeva, *Strangers to Ourselves*, trans. L. S. Roudiez (New York: Columbia University Press, 1991).

9. M. Shawn Copeland, "Difference as a category in critical theologies for the liberation of women," in *Feminist Theology in Different Contexts*, ed. E. S. Fiorenza and M. S. Copeland, Concilium 1996/1 (London: S.C.M. Press, 1996), p. 143, writes: "Difference insinuates not merely variance, but deviation, division, discrepancy, discord, incongruity, incompatibility, inconsistency, anomaly, contrariety, aberration, and misunderstanding." She adds: ". . . difference carries forward struggle for life in its uniqueness, variation, and fullness; difference is a celebrative option for life in all its integrity, in all its distinctiveness."

To speak about the other is to speak about the nature of the church, the one body of many parts, challenged to unity in Jesus Christ (1 Cor. 12:12-13). Christianity is a pluralistic experiment because Christians are drawn from a myriad of cultural and historical contexts. Pluralism is inherently part of our canon, expressed in our doctrinal foundations[10] and in the very nature of ecumenism which seeks to draw very different community-oriented forms of Christianity into dialogue with one another. The church is thoroughly pluralistic. Difference matters. To link difference and otherness is to be truthful about the social and theological reality of the church. It is a Body whose fundamental vocation should be to make a place for the immense diversity of human beings who give their allegiance to Jesus Christ.

To speak of the Other is to speak about the ambiguity of God, the One who is Wholly Other and Wholly Related.[11] To speak of the other is to assume always that the strange other may be an angel of God bearing words that we need to hear.

We must always be alert to the reality of difference. It will not go away, neither should it.[12] It is who we are. We live our lives within the reality and the challenge of difference and otherness. As we struggle to live fruitfully with difference, we realize that we no longer have "one language and the same words" (Gen. 11:1). Alerted to the reality, as well as to the demands and the possibilities of difference, what are we to do? Instead of difference and otherness descending into a chaotic relativism, how can we deal with the vulnerability of our differences in such a way that the Body of Christ can flourish? What is the basis for a creative ethic of difference?[13] I suggest that *an embod-*

10. Raimundo Panikkar, quoted by Williams in *On Christian Theology*, p. 167, says: "The mystery of the Trinity is the ultimate foundation for pluralism."

11. Williams, *On Christian Theology*, p. 160, notes: ". . . we should not delude ourselves that God's difference is merely that one thing from another: we need to put down those formal markers (immutable, impassible, omnipotent, etc.) as a way of insisting that we cannot write a biography of God. As has already been said, his history is Jesus."

12. Paul Varo Martinson, "What then shall we do?" in *Lutherans and the Challenge of Religious Pluralism*, ed. F. W. Klos, C. L. Nakamura, and D. F. Martensen (Minneapolis: Augsburg, 1990), p. 179, warns: "We must always be alert to difference. The common makes relationship possible, difference makes it significant. Generally people do not give their lives for that upon which we all agree or find we have in common. People give their lives because of that which is different. Difference is fraught with significance."

13. In a lecture entitled "Christianity and structured pluralism" given at the Center for Theological Inquiry, Princeton in 2000, Michael Welker argued for a "structured pluralism drawn from the Christian trinitarian understanding of God." He recommends that the church should understand "the pluralism of the ecumene as the unity of different confessional modes of learning from scripture," as the biblical canon itself has a pluralistic texture.

ied ethic of difference through belonging can contribute to debates on the issues raised by these questions.

An Embodied Ethic of Difference through Belonging

The title of this section raises questions: Why embodied? Why an ethic? What is belonging? Before attempting to deal with these questions, it is necessary to "come clean" about my hermeneutic in regard to the church, the world, and the issue of belonging. Our inability to deal constructively with difference is not exclusive to the Christian church. It is a universal human problem. The use of the word "belonging" is itself not unproblematic. It can smack of a selective clan, a group of insiders who are in some way or other superior to those outside. In order to dispel any notions of restriction or privilege, it is necessary to say that I do not understand Christ's ministry, death, and resurrection as the private domain of the Christian church. Christ is for all humanity, for all creation, for all time. The entire human race belongs to God in Christ, whose eternal love and concern embraces all of creation. Belonging to the church acknowledges Christ's claims on us, his followers, in a particular way. We are to discern the activity of the Trinity in the world and to learn to live faithfully and well with it. When we, the church, fail to practice loving and just discipleship, we fail God's work in the world. This is the central concern of this paper — that the church, as the Body of Christ, should live up to its calling so that our Christian witness can be acceptable to God and compelling to the societies in which we live. Living well with difference is simply a test case for this resolve.

First, the ethical: dealing with difference and otherness is profoundly a question of ethics. I accept the Pauline basis for ethics in the church — that which is "for the common good" (1 Cor. 12:7). Our relationship with one another should be one of building up, not of excluding, stigmatizing, or discriminating. As Williams puts it:

> . . . we are engaged, in Christ, in *constructing* each other's humanity, bringing one another into the inheritance of power and liberty whose form is defined by Jesus. . . . There is a quite proper circularity to the ethics of the Christian community: I am called to use the authority given me by Christ (by Christ's *giving away* of power conceived as control and security) so as to nurture that authority in others, so that they may give it away in turn — to me and to others.[14]

---

14. Williams, *On Christian Theology,* p. 232.

9

Christ's reconstruction of human community is about a vision of human belonging that is more comprehensive than any existing form of human relationships. The church claims to show the world a new way of belonging made possible by God's creative power to break down our human barriers and prejudices. It is about building Christ-like persons. The church's good news is that a truly pluralistic human community is possible beyond what Williams calls mere "amiable mutual toleration."[15] Such a church witness knows only one boundary, Christ. Any action, any teaching, any attitude that detracts from or works against the common good of this radically pluralistic Body is judged to be unethical.

Second, what does an "embodied" ethic mean? To begin with, ethical concerns are expressed in embodied ethical acts, not merely in abstract ideas or theories that are divorced from practice. Theological ethics are embodied in acts performed in service of a way of life which embodies core Christian beliefs. Our actions are those of a people who see themselves as God's agents and who temper all they do by what God has done, is doing, and will do. For ethics to be embodied in this sense means that they are shaped, expressed, and tested in acts of justice and charity. We are ethical (or not) as embodied people because our bodies encompass all of who we are — our thoughts, emotions, and our acts.

The most compelling reason for ethics to translate into embodied acts lies in the embodied nature of the Christian faith. The story of the man Jesus of Nazareth, his identity in the framework of a reality whose whole structure is held to be significant, his place in a story of the world as coming from God and relating to God, lies at the heart of our faith.[16] Furthermore, through his body on the cross, all bodies, no matter how different they are, are united into one body. When Paul writes: "We who are many are one body for we all partake of the one bread" (1 Cor. 10:17), this bread is the suffering body of Jesus — the one body given for many. Many we remain, and Christ's offering does not obliterate our differences. It offers to break down the divides between us, to do away with exclusion, discrimination, and prejudice. We become "the body of Christ" — that one body with many members each one equipped with gifts for the common good by the Holy Spirit (1 Cor. 12:4-7). The Holy Spirit does not impose what Michael Welker calls "an illusory homogeneity." "The unity of the Spirit becomes a reality . . . by cultivating creaturely differences and by removing unrighteous differences."[17] Welker sees in the pouring out of the Spirit

15. Williams, *On Christian Theology,* p. 171.

16. See Williams, *On Christian Theology,* pp. 79-92.

17. Michael Welker, *God the Spirit,* trans. J. F. Hoffmeyer (Minneapolis: Fortress Press, 1994), p. 25.

on all flesh the promise of heightened awareness, of greater sensitivity about the effects of our exclusions and unjust relations.

> When the Spirit of God is poured out, the different persons and groups of people will open God's presence with each other and for each other. With each other and for each other, they will make it possible to know the reality intended by God. They will enrich and strengthen each other through their differentiated prophetic knowledge.[18]

Through deliberate, embodied acts of acceptance and care, destructive differences which separate Jew from gentile, female from male, slave from free, black from white, and gay from straight, are overcome. Difference is accepted as God-given. Then we can be set free together to accomplish God's will in this world.

Third, why belonging? Be-longing — to be in a state of longing — is intrinsic to being human. We long for closeness and intimacy, security, and nourishment, for a life in which justice and love flourish. "It is human to want things to be different."[19] Human longing and godly longing are found throughout scripture. The psalmist knew this longing.

> O God, you are my God,
> I seek you,
> my soul thirsts for you;
> My flesh faints for you,
> as in a dry and weary land
> where there is no water.[20]

In John 17 (particularly verses 20-24) Jesus, in one last powerful prayer, envelops both his longing "that they may be one, as we are one" and the essence of belonging: "Father, I desire that those also, whom you have given me, may be with me where I am, to see my glory, which you have given me because you loved me before the foundation of the world." Grace Jantzen notes that "Throughout Scripture, God is portrayed as a God of longing love, whose desire for the people of Israel is urgent, who is pained at their apostasy with the searing pain of a rejected lover, and who exults in their response with the exultation of reciprocated desire."[21] So the church prays "May your reign

---

18. Welker, *God the Spirit*, p. 151.
19. Peter Selby, *Belonging: Challenge to a Tribal Church* (London: SPCK, 1991), p. 1.
20. Psalm 63:1.
21. Selby, *Belonging*, p. 67.

come," the longing that God's will will triumph. This must be so as "The Church is the first fruit of God's longing."[22]

All human communities define themselves by the boundaries they draw and by knowing who does not belong and what defines those who do. Belonging presupposes not belonging and by drawing boundaries attention is drawn to those who are "out there" as compared to those who are "in here." Thus belonging is generally achieved at the expense of those who do not belong. Belonging to the church is, however, radically different from belonging to other groups or communities, such as family, club, race, gender, or class.[23] The church, as the first fruit of God's longing, does not depend on excluding people but should give witness to God's longing that the entire creation be transformed into the beauty and harmony for which it was intended. God's concern is such that it even includes the sparrow that falls to the ground. God's longing tugs at the hearts of the excluded, of those who are different, who are on the margins beyond the boundaries of exclusion we create. God's activity is constantly inclusive and a church that practises exclusion cannot thrive. It will remove itself from the source of grace and hope from which it draws life.[24] Ultimately only persistent self-exclusion can separate us from God's longing.

I am arguing that, given the reality of our pluralistic world in which difference and otherness is simply a fact, a sense of our common belonging to the Body of Christ achieved through Christ's ministry, death, and resurrection, can militate against experiences of exclusion, rejection, and abandonment in the church.

The Church and the Practice of Belonging

The notion of practice is at the heart of living the gospel.[25] "Practice is . . . the medium through which we act out our moral values and by which they are evaluated."[26] Christians act so that realities are "transformed, transfigured,

22. Selby, *Belonging*, p. 3.

23. It is interesting to note that there is an African saying which declares: "A person is a person through other persons." This articulates what we call *ubuntu*. This traditional African philosophy and way of life sees all of creation as sacred. Humanity is part of a vast interrelated web. As John Mbiti has put it so strikingly: "I belong therefore I am."

24. Selby, *Belonging*, pp. 1-4.

25. See Elaine L. Graham, *Transforming Practice: Pastoral Theology in an Age of Uncertainty* (London: Mowbray, 1996), pp. 112-41.

26. Alasdair MacIntyre, *After Virtue: A Study in Moral Theory* (Notre Dame, IN: University of Notre Dame, 1984), p. 187.

revolutionised, converted, transfigured."[27] Christian practices should not be narrowly individualistic, but be understood in the context of the church and in the cause of the coming of God's reign on earth. Faithful Christian practice that is ethical, effective, and relevant takes seriously the challenge of our common belonging in all our differences to the one Body.

How is it that we can so effortlessly avoid the compelling but simple truth that belonging to the one Body under the headship of Christ calls us to live well with difference? How can we practice belonging in our differences? Why not start by confessing and lamenting our failure to deal justly and lovingly with neighbours who are different? We have certainly failed to welcome one another as Christ has welcomed us, for the glory of God (Rom. 15:7). Each day we disobey the command to love our neighbour, the 'different other', as ourselves. Too often we stigmatize the other and thus refuse to be in relationship with her or him. Is the gay person, the ideologically "different" person, the woman claiming authority to preach and teach, the recent immigrant, the poor even uneducated person, the recently released convict, the refugee, the street child, the beggar, or the mentally disabled person equally valued in my church, as those who have the trappings of "belonging"? If not, confession, repentance, and lament are called for in order to restore ourselves to being a community of grace. That is in essence who we are — a community which exists by grace alone.

If this sounds easy, let me assure you that it is not. For those of us who have been used to dominant power or whose souls and minds are closed by rigid ideologies and fear of the other, an epiphany is needed.[28] Without an epiphany we may continue in a state of solipsism — quite literally as the sun of our own individual universe. Reality is merely and only the reality of my own consciousness.[29] The habit of putting the injunction "to love your neighbour as yourself" through hoops of devious reasoning, is deeply embedded. We forget that Jesus taught us that our neighbour is the radically other who is also the radically related. We forget that our neighbour has inviolable claims on us to be welcomed as Christ has welcomed us. There are of course no recipes for making epiphanies happen. But when we are surprised by an epiphany, we are caught in "a traumatism of astonishment"[30] and radically trans-

---

27. Duncan B. Forrester, *Truthful Action: Explorations in Practical Theology* (Edinburgh: T&T Clark, 2000), p. 27.

28. See Paul Ricoeur, *Oneself as Another,* trans. K. Blamey (Chicago: University of Chicago Press, 1992), p. 189.

29. See Edward Farley, *Good and Evil: Interpreting a Human Condition* (Minneapolis: Fortress Press, 1990), pp. 34-36.

30. Emmanuel Levinas, *Totality and Infinity: An Essay in Exteriority,* trans. A. Lingis (Pittsburgh: Duquesne University Press, 1969), p. 74.

formed practices become conceivable. Then belonging, no longer an abstract theological truth about the Body of Christ, draws us into a web of relationships with God and with one another.

Although relationship is central to our being and to our well-being, it is not easy to define. It is easier to say what relationship is not: it is not alienation or apathy, isolation or separation. For relationships to be loving and just they have to be reciprocal and mutual. The concept of mutuality in relationship is the touchstone against which the quality of our relationships is tested. Mutuality is concerned with the feelings, needs, and interests of each other. Mutuality spells out forbearance, generosity, kindness, forgiveness, considerateness — virtues often neglected. Mutual relationship does not do away with difference. Each person is a distinct individual. Respect for the other, or lack of it, is a matter of choice. You choose whether you will respect me despite our differences across race, ideology, sexual orientation, and culture; I choose whether I will respect you. Our qualities as people are the qualities of our relationships and our communities.

If we do not practice relationship there is no hope for building up the Body of Christ (1 Cor. 12). The Body is the result of the practice of mutual relationship, as well as the place where these relationships are put to the test. Being a "community in differences is a hard-won achievement."[31] The practice of mutual relationship is both profoundly simple and formidably demanding. We are innately relational beings. We are also congenitally antagonistic. Failure and betrayal threaten the health of the Body. They make a mockery of our common belonging. The well-being of the Body does not just happen. It takes the recognition of our interdependence and willingness to carry our differences into what Shawn Copeland describes as "deep-going conversion and serious honest conversation — speaking with head and heart and flesh; listening with head and heart and flesh."[32]

Mutual relationship which springs from our common belonging to the Body of Christ compels me to turn my gaze from myself and *"look"* into the face of the other. It is you and I, they and we, seeing and being seen.[33] In the face of the other I see a true and authentic human being. We both reflect something of the image of God.[34] The practice of belonging in the Body means that I acknowledge that I am not complete unto myself. I see myself in

31. Copeland, "Difference as a category," p. 149.

32. Copeland, "Difference as a category," p. 149.

33. I am aware of the fact that not everybody can see or hear physically. Insight and knowledge are, however, not just or primarily physical.

34. Ricoeur, *Oneself as Another,* p. 9, writes: ". . . the idea of God is in me as the very mark of the author upon his work, a mark that assures the resemblance between us."

the face of the other. I am not fully myself until I can see "me" in your face. You are the mirror of myself. I am the mirror of your self. Only when we can see ourselves and each other are we fully ourselves in all our differences.[35] As Edward Farley says: "The other, then, is what I do not and cannot experience in the mode in which I experience myself. It is an 'I' which is not I."[36] At the moment of truly seeing the other and being seen, surprised and illuminated, I am converted to an authentic existence and I can begin to fathom the claims that justice and love make on me.

Now the ground is ready for the seeds of ongoing conversation. "Conversation in its primary form is an exploration of possibilities in the search for truth," writes David Tracy.[37] We dare not cease the conversation because as Tracy reminds us, hope ". . . is grounded in conversation. . . ."[38] In South Africa, this truth is ever before us as we struggle to transform our society. Disagreements, incompatible interpretations of what truth is, even conflict, should not deter us. Without conversation we retreat into our solipsisms, the "enemy of conversation."[39] We become unable to respond to the call to love our neighbour. At best all we have is a 'learned ignorance' of what it means to be a human being. To counter this danger, we do have the one certainty that our differences are simply a fact of being human and that our membership of the One Body affirms the dignity and worth of all who belong. And we keep on talking. These conversations reach out beyond the boundaries of our communities to others who share our faith, to those of different religious persuasions, and to all who are concerned for a better world.

From "The Weakness of Some"[40] to Hope in Belonging

Finally, I cannot forget what the "result of the weakness of some" has done for "the cause of Christ" in my own country. The tragedy of unreconciled difference and otherness played out over centuries in South Africa has not only been costly in terms of human well-being, but it has also been a betrayal of

35. Ricoeur, *Oneself*, p. 3, where Ricoeur describes this experience as follows: ". . . the selfhood of oneself implies otherness to such an intimate degree that one cannot be thought of without the other, that instead one passes into the other. . . ."

36. Farley, *Good and Evil*, p. 35.

37. David Tracy, *Plurality and Ambiguity: Hermeneutics, Religion, Hope* (Chicago: University of Chicago Press, 1987), p. 20.

38. Tracy, *Plurality and Ambiguity*, p. 78.

39. Tracy, *Plurality and Ambiguity*, p. 25.

40. See the story from South African church history at the beginning of this paper.

the gospel in the heart of the Christian church itself. Separating believers at the table, using holy communion as a means of exclusion, makes a mockery of Christ's death on the cross and its intention of reconciling. It is also a denial of mutual relationship in the community of faith. It is unjust and unloving. We are reminded that "all who eat and drink without discerning the body, eat and drink judgment against themselves" (1 Cor. 11:29).

For the Eucharist to have meaning in our lives and to be a rite of hope, we need to feel its powerful pull to the radical activity of loving relationships with those who are different. The One who calls us to the table knows our differences. The One who issues the invitation and asks us to make peace with one another when we come, knows full well just how difficult that can be. Belonging to the Body of Christ is nothing less than the hope-filled daily grappling with the challenges, implications, and surprises of seeking to be in relationship with each other in all our difference and otherness for the sake of the One who makes belonging possible.

"A City upon a Hill"?
The Religious Dimension of
American Self-Understanding
and Its Crisis Today

Gerhard Sauter

The self-understanding of the American nation is grounded in the conviction of the Puritan settlers, who thought that the new community was going to be a city upon a hill. This city, they thought, would entrust itself to Divine Providence and place itself under God's judgement. Later, this metaphor was conceived differently: the American nation was then seen as a shining example for other communities. Thus, America is subject to a rigorous moral demand and at the same time understands itself to be founded on grounds that are sounder than those of other peoples.

On September 11, 2001, this trust, which had held the security of the United States to be inviolable, was shaken to its roots. How does this affect the quest for God's action in history and for the manifestation of Divine Providence? Even though American society is secularised, it still holds religious convictions to be vital. It will be critical for America, in light of this dilemma, to recall and re-establish the intrinsic profoundness of talk about God: God should be addressed as the One who promised to judge and to save in reconciling the world.

This was a lecture delivered on November 13, 2001 as part of the series "America Under Attack" by the North American Program at the University of Bonn, Germany. This program provides students of different fields (American studies, political sciences, law, sociology, geography, history, art history, theology) with an integrated curriculum. They can take the M.A. or B.A. degree. In this program I teach "Christianity in the U.S." My public lecture was concentrated on basic information. It has been translated by Natascha Gillenberg (Bonn/Duke Divinity School, Durham, NC), and revised by Professor Arthur Sutherland, Ph.D. (Loyola College in Maryland, Baltimore, MD).

On September 11, 2001, I was in Switzerland at the Bossey Ecumenical Institute working on the topic of eschatology along with American ministers serving congregations in Europe and the Near East who were members of the Pastor-Theologian Program of the Center of Theological Inquiry in Princeton.[1] The conference was planned and led by Dr. Wallace M. Alston Jr., the director of the Center. Many of the pastors had relatives and friends living in New York, many of whom had jobs in or near the World Trade Center. When the shock of seeing the disturbing images on TV began to wear off, a period of self-critical reflection began.

One topic emerging from this reflection focused on America's new vulnerability. The American pastors commented that the Civil War brought destruction, but that was a war fought among fellow citizens. They observed that the illusion of inviolability leads to actions that can be extremely dangerous. They concluded that the events of September 11 no longer permit Americans to think of themselves as inviolable in their own country. Moreover, Americans now experience vulnerability already familiar to Europeans and persons living in Israel, in Palestine, and in other places of our endangered world. The pastors observed that the trusted government security measures formerly in place had been invalidated and the current administration's "Star Wars Program" rendered senseless by these events. Americans will now have to learn to live with vulnerability in a way that other countries have had to learn and have never been able to forget. Insecurity has become the key signature of the world and the United States is no exception.

The comments brought home to me the peculiar religious dimension of America's self-understanding. *Americans have the conviction that they are a chosen people with a unique destiny, that they enjoy the special protection of God's providence or of the other national god they call "Liberty."* Many Americans who live abroad for an extended period of time and do not flutter as tourists from blossom to blossom like butterflies but look critically at the history of their environment, perceive their country and its politics from a different perspective when they return, a perspective much different from that of the majority of their compatriots. For them a demythologizing of the American dream of exclusiveness takes place. They view September 11 in this regard, without easing the shock that was caused by this event. One of the pastors said to me, after having seen the first pictures of the ruins and the

1. The "Pastor-Theologian Program" was established in 1998 for ministers and priests of all denominations. It "seeks to address the crisis of faith in the contemporary church by focusing attention on the ordained ministry as a theological vocation and on the church as a theological community" (leaflet of the Center of Theological Inquiry), and runs for three years. During regional seminars, scholars working at the Center act as resource theologians.

people fleeing in bewilderment, "Does that remind you of what took place in World War II?" I answered, "Yes, but there was no television."

A few days later at the National Cathedral in Washington, D.C., the country's political elite proclaimed its deep emotional shock and assured itself of its hope. Representatives of different religious groups, including a chief Rabbi, led in prayer. Billy Graham, the Baptist evangelist, who from time to time is regarded as the senior pastor of the American nation, beseeched God's help for this crisis just as God had rescued America and granted it safety in earlier times. The notion that this might have been an affliction from God was totally out of the question. Then the President spoke and promised retaliation. Was that — so one would like to ask with all the caution that is due to a foreigner — really the voice of America?

The *Battle Hymn of the Republic* was sung. The National Cathedral actually is an Episcopal Church, but at the same time it is also a symbol of American *civil religion,* the oddity that results from concurring with the constitutional separation of Church and State.[2] I will say more about this later.

In any case, in this solemn ceremony one thing became clear: God, as called on at this occasion by some people, was the God of America, not the God of the world, Lord of all people. God was seen as the guarantor of American identity and the one who also ensures that this nation remains unharmed. Other nations, particularly Germany, have been cured of a religious guarantee of identity like this through the bitter experiences of the last century. Is that now in store for the United States? The answer to the question would not be found in the purification of the national consciousness from some religious remnant. Nor would it be about a total secularization of political life. Rather the question is: *can one talk of God* in regard to revolutionary political events concerning the way of the world and to events that result in so much loss of life? Many Christians in the United States raise this question and many sermons are devoted to it.

Was the solemn event in Washington really a worship service? Or was it a rite that sought to symbolize the cohesion of the American nation? Are both supposed to be separate in civil religion? Some of my American friends

2. The term "civil religion" was introduced by Robert N. Bellah. See *Religion in America,* ed. William G. McLoughlin and Robert N. Bellah (Boston: Houghton Mifflin, 1968); Robert N. Bellah, *The Broken Covenant: American Civil Religion in a Time of Trial* (New York: Seabury Press, 1975); Robert N. Bellah and Phillip E. Hammond, *Varieties of Civil Religion* (San Francisco: Harper & Row, 1980); Gail Gehrig, *American Civil Religion: An Assessment* (Storrs, CT: Society for the Scientific Study of Religion, 1981); *Civil Religion and Political Theology,* ed. Leroy S. Rouner (Notre Dame, IN: University of Notre Dame Press, 1986); *Civil Religion, Church and State,* ed. Martin E. Marty (Munich/New York: K. G. Saur, 1992).

watched the commemoration on TV with quite mixed feelings. It was noted that George W. Bush said that God would be present in the suffering of the people but by that he meant the "innocent victims" in New York and Washington, not the potential and also innocent victims of American retaliation. During the spontaneous worship of prayer in the chapel at Bossey, only a few hours after the attack, God had been called on as the Reconciler of the World. Can we speak of God in a way other than as the Reconciler of the World?

In October 2001, on a flight to Newark, I read in a newspaper (*USA Today*, if I remember it correctly) that President Bush keeps a Bible on his desk, from which he often reads, particularly during these days, in order to get directives for his decisions. Is that just part of a conservative American President's image that he puts on for a segment of his constituency? That would be a much too cheap suspicion. Bush does come from the deep south of the United States, from the *Bible Belt*. He belongs to the United Methodist Church, but he is less rooted in the Christian faith than his parents are.[3] How does he read the Bible? What does he gather from it? He prays, that is not just a show. But does he pray "Thy will be done, on earth as it is in heaven. Forgive us our trespasses, as we forgive those who have trespassed against us"? He could read this in the Lord's Prayer (Matt. 6:10-12). But would he conceive it differently? *How does it relate to his maxim that first evil has to be wiped out and then we can proceed to making peace?*

As I approached Newark there was an eerie gap in the skyline of New York City. It lacked the two bright silver towers. The whole view was different. There was another face: the nose was missing. The taxi driver told me, "I see that every day, but even now I cannot get used to it. The gap that has been torn there only allows us to take every day as it comes." The blaze of lights in Manhattan, weaker than before, reminded me of what an old American friend of mine, who has seen a lot of the world, once said to me, "The power consumption of Manhattan approximately corresponds to that of the whole African continent, perhaps excluding South Africa." There I was immediately facing the economic discrepancy of the United States compared to other countries. Is that supposed to mean that it is this discrepancy that was hit by the terrorists' attacks? Or was it an attack on an open society and its liberality? Or is it the case that one cannot be separated from the other? If so, that would be fatal!

These are four snapshots. Maybe they can offer an impression of the

3. For a religious profile of Governor George W. Bush, prior to his election as president in 2000, see the interview with *U.S. News*, "Running on his faith" (www.usnews.com/usnews/news/9911206/bushint.htm).

complexity of the emotions and thoughts that followed the World Trade Center bombing. Let us try to understand what is going on here. Even more complex is the political rhetoric that invokes and uses terms that arouse religious associations without really being rooted in the religious traditions of the country. One of these mistakes was, for example, when George Bush talked about the "crusade" the free world had to wage against terrorism. This term is used in the United States for evangelism; it means to win people over to the Christian message. It could have been this context from which the President spoke. But he did not take into consideration the fact that the term "crusade" had to bring back the worst memories for Muslims. Others quickly talked him out of using this language as well as his thoughtless talk about *infinite justice* as the title for the operation in Afghanistan. There was severe protest in America against this type of rhetorical *faux pas* and I was also told that even "Papa Bush" exercised his parental authority against this type of demagogy. But even if one avoids these types of rhetorical mistake, a certain pattern of thinking can remain obscured and unchallenged. *First, I would like to uncover what I call the religious dimension of the American self-consciousness, and then to seek to understand it.* I do not want to justify it, but to make clear that this is an important ingredient of American behavior and thinking. We have to take it into account if we want to comprehend fairly what has been going on.

In order to understand this, we have to go far into the history of North America, to some of its first settlers. The lay preaching done by John Winthrop in 1630, the English lawyer and first governor of Massachusetts, while crossing to Bay Colony on the "Arabella," the flagship of a little fleet of immigrants, is often regarded as path breaking. It is in his speech *A Model of Christian Charity* that the biblical metaphor first turns up that henceforth will accompany American history: *a city upon a hill.* This metaphor, like the term *manifest destiny* — the destination, even the obligation of the American people — has become the mark of the religious dimension of America's self-understanding.[4] Senator Albert Beveridge of Indiana (1900) stated:

> God has not been preparing the English-speaking and Teutonic peoples for a thousand years for nothing but vain and idle self-contemplation and

---

4. E.g., John Quincy Adams to John Adams, August 31, 1811: "The whole continent of North America appears to be destined by Divine Providence to be peopled by one *nation,* speaking one language, professing one general system of religious and political principles, and accustomed to one general tenor of social usages and customs. For the common happiness of them all, for their peace and prosperity, I believe it indispensable that they should be associated in one federal Union." *The Writings of John Quincy Adams,* vol. 4, ed. Worthington C. Ford (New York: Macmillan, 1913-17), p. 209.

self-admiration. No! He has made us the master organizers of the world to establish a system where chaos reigns. He has given us the spirit of progress to overwhelm the forces of reaction throughout the earth. He has made us adept in government that we may administer government among savage and senile peoples. Were it not for such a force as this the world would relapse into barbarism and night. And of all our race He has marked the American people as His chosen nation to finally lead in the regeneration of the world. This is the divine mission of America, and it holds for us all the profit, all the glory, all the happiness, possible to man. We are trustees of the world's progress, guardians of its righteous peace.[5]

The ideology of *manifest destiny* was formulated in 1846 by the journalist William Gilpin and soon afterward read to the U.S. Senate:

The *untransacted* destiny of the American people is to subdue the continent — to rush over this vast field to the Pacific Ocean — to animate the many hundred millions of its people, and to cheer them upward . . . to teach old nations a new civilization — to conform the destiny of the human race. . . .

Divine task! Immortal mission! Let us tread fast and joyfully the open trail before us! Let every American heart open wide for patriotism to glow undimmed, and confide with religious faith in the sublime and prodigious destiny of his well-loved country.[6]

But what was the context into which Winthrop had put the metaphor *a city upon a hill?*

Now the only way . . . to provide for our posterity is to follow the counsel of Micah: to do justly, to love mercy, to walk humbly with our God. For this end, we must be knit together in this work as one man. We must entertain each other in brotherly affection; we must be willing to abridge ourselves of our superfluities, for the supply of others' necessities; we must uphold a familiar commerce together in all meekness, gentleness, patience, and liberality. We must delight in each other, make others' conditions our own, rejoice together, mourn together, labor, and suffer together: always having before our eyes our commission and community in the work, our community as members of the same body. So shall we keep

5. Charles D. Ameringer, *U.S. Foreign Intelligence: The Secret Side of American History* (Lexington, MA: Lexington Books, 1990), p. 71.

6. Robert Hughes, *American Visions: The Epic History of Art in America* (New York: Alfred A. Knopf, 1997), pp. 189-90.

the unity of the spirit in the bond of peace, the Lord will be our God and delight to dwell among us, as His own people, and will command a blessing upon us in all our ways, so that we shall see much more of His wisdom, power, goodness, and truth than formerly we have been acquainted with. We shall find that the God of Israel is among us, when ten of us shall be able to resist a thousand of our enemies, when He shall make us a praise and glory, that men shall say of succeeding plantations: "The Lord make it like that of New England." For we must consider that we shall be as a city upon a hill, the eyes of all people are upon us. So that if we shall deal falsely with our God in this work we have undertaken, and so cause Him to withdraw His present help from us, we shall be made a story and a by-word through the world: we shall open the mouths of enemies to speak evil of the ways of God and all professors for God's sake; we shall shame the faces of many of God's worthy servants, and cause their prayers to be turned into curses upon us, till we be consumed out of the good land whither we are going.[7]

With this Winthrop alludes to Jesus' Sermon on the Mount, "You are the light of the world. A city built upon a hill cannot be hid" (Matt. 5:14). A person who has been to the Sea of Galilee might think of Safed, the little town above the lake whose white houses sparkle in the sunlight. This city on the hill later became the center of the Cabala, a Jewish mystical renewal of the perception of the mysteries of God, world, and humanity. Winthrop's speech also refers to other biblical expressions that outline the overall picture; it is interspersed with biblical allusions. The repetition of the exhortation of the Old Testament Prophet Micah (6:8) emphasizes the self-understanding of the settlers. They regard themselves as being the descendants of the people of Israel; they, too, are on their way to the "promised land." They are allowed to take the land, and the instructions of God make the social order obligatory. Their numerical inferiority reminds one of the story of Gideon, the spirited fighter for God. With ten other men he pulled down the idolatrous altars of his father who had come to terms with the country's customary religion (Judg. 6:25). And then, with three hundred men, he utterly destroyed an enormous army that lay "along the valley as thick as locusts, and their camels were without number, countless as the sand on the seashore" (7:12). The colonialists are elected in order to form a unity and are called to be united. They owe this unity to the Holy Spirit, who is the bond of peace. This means, according to

7. John Winthrop, "A Model of Christian Charity," in *The American Puritans: Their Prose and Poetry*, ed. Perry Miller (Garden City, NY: Doubleday, 1956), pp. 79-84; quotation is from p. 83.

the epistle to the Ephesians (4:3), that they are one Christian community, members of one body, of the body of Christ (1 Cor. 12:12). And to this community already is granted what in the Revelation of John, the last book of the Bible, is promised only for the last days: in the new world God will dwell among humanity, "they will be his people; and God himself will be with them" (21:3).

For Winthrop, the city upon a hill symbolizes the responsibility of a people's community and its accountability to God. That is why this community places itself under God's judgment right from the beginning. Winthrop could have pointed to 1 Peter 4:17: God's judgment begins with the house of God, not with its enemies. The "world" forms the audience of what is going on in the city of God and on behalf of it. The city of God is the stage of God's action towards humanity. Only in regard to this is it an exemplary community.

Yet, what remained of Winthrop's speech in the collective memory of the United States is the metaphor "a city upon a hill." The same is true also for academic publications where this metaphor is mentioned.[8] Often, the phrase is trimmed to "America shall be the shining example." For example on January 9, 1961, John F. Kennedy put it that way when he wanted to denounce political corruption before the Supreme Court of Massachusetts.[9]

The second part of Winthrop's sermon concerning God's judgment was repressed and because of that the meaning of the metaphor was changed: the city upon a hill with its constitution, with its rules, norms, and customs, becomes the *ideal society* instead of a community that can exist only under God's judging and saving action. This shift of meaning could take place only through amputation. The "jeremiads" that had accompanied American sermons on the city upon a hill throughout two centuries fell into oblivion. "Jeremiads" are sermons that call people to repentance and that seek to remind them of the lamentations of the prophet Jeremiah in the Old Testament. Under no circumstances are they whiny lamentations about bad times and increasing immorality. Lamentations 3:21-23 says, "But this I call to my mind, and therefore I have hope: the steadfast love of the Lord never ceases, his mercies never come to an end; they are new every morning; great is your faithful-

8. Even Sydney E. Ahlstrom in his standard survey *A Religious History of the American People*, vol. 1 (Garden City, NY: Doubleday, 1975), p. 193, quotes only excerpts of Winthrop's speech in a way that creates the impression that the city upon a hill is a communal task that has to be fulfilled.

9. Samuel Eliot Morison, *The Oxford History of the American People* (New York: Oxford University Press, 1965), p. 65 n. 1.

ness." The confidence that after every affliction one may experience the grace of God again turns the lament into prayer.

For Jonathan Edwards (1703-1758) it was crystal clear: one can rightly speak of the city of God only in regard to the judging and saving action of God. Edwards was one spokesman of the *Great Awakening,* the American revival and renewal movement (1723-44). He was also an important philosopher of religion and a leading theologian as well as one of the first presidents of Princeton University.[10] However, by the beginning of the twentieth century, at the latest, his point of view fell into oblivion. Only the metaphor *a city upon a hill* remained. Moreover, it was now said with a different meaning: America is the light and it shines into a dark world; everybody else is located in the shadow, if not in black darkness altogether. The visibility of God's city — not to be ignored because of what happens on behalf of it — is interchanged with its brightness, its function as an example, and its identification with the good, the just, with what is well pleasing to God.

The correct dilemma facing America's religious self-understanding can be traced to this interchange of meaning, this metaphor torn in half. The dilemma is not new; it is rather over a hundred years old. But now it breaks out again, and many, too many, try to cover it up, disguise it, or at least gloss over it.

These "jeremiads," even when they denounced a morally deplorable state of affairs, were not fixed on it, but viewed it in a larger perspective, like Winthrop with his reminder to turn to each other (to be devoted to one another, to care for each other), to take one another seriously in every distress and to help, to carry the burden together, to share joy, and to understand themselves as *community,* as *members of the same body.* They stressed a communitarian characteristic, which remained alive in the United States at least in smaller neighborhoods, and which has recently gained a renewed attention.

"Jeremiads" do not have anything in common with the sort of moralistic lectures that are given in the United States with pleasure when they are addressed to others. Recently, I heard a radio report of just such an example. On a television show Pat Robertson, a right-wing member of American Protestantism, declared that the destruction of September 11 was a divine judgment upon the immorality of the modern America, because of its abortion laws and the acceptance of homosexuality. Neither economic nor social policy was the topic, let alone the en-

---

10. See, among others: Robert W. Jenson, *America's Theologian: A Recommendation of Jonathan Edwards* (New York: Oxford University Press, 1988); Caroline Schröder, *Glaubenswahrnehmung und Selbsterkenntnis: Jonathan Edwards' theologia experimentalis,* Forschungen zur systematischen und ökumenischen Theologie, vol. 81 (Göttingen: Vandenhoeck & Ruprecht, 1998).

tanglements of America in world politics. Franklin Graham, son of Billy Graham, charged Islam as the "arch-enemy" of Christianity. But as this does not seem to go well with *political correctness,* Graham Jr. was brought back into line.

John Winthrop's sermon, one of the religious documents of American Puritanism, is indeed far away from that sort of moralism which wants to divide the "world" into good and evil and, by claiming God for the renewal of broken conditions, seeks to eradicate evil in order to realize the ideal society. Winthrop and all the others who followed him in thinking, speaking, and acting in the same spirit, conceived America as being under the sentence of God, not on God's side. This became apparent in other ways. One sees this, for example, in President Abraham Lincoln's last public speech on April 11, 1865, one day after the surrender of General Robert E. Lee. Lincoln felt that after the end of the American Civil War, with its devastating consequences for the South but also many wounds for the North, one should not speak of either victor or defeated.[11] As Lincoln had said earlier in his *Second Inaugural Address* on March 4, 1865, slavery was a sin against God's providence. Because of this the outcome of the war was some sort of trial by ordeal. It was not the partisanship of the Living God on behalf of one of the fighting parties, each of whom had called on God for victory. Both were placed under God's judgment: "The judgments of the Lord are true and righteous altogether." Lincoln quoted this from either Rev. 16:7 or 19:2 (the contexts speak about shed blood of the holy and the prophets!) and continued, "with malice toward none; with charity for all; with firmness in the right, as God gives us to see the right, let us strive on to finish the work we are in."[12]

That was spoken in a spirit of reconciliation which presupposed that none of the participants was innocent. That is why assignments of guilt did not occur: charge and revenge were out of place. A political scientist might read Lincoln's message as a document of unprecedented wisdom or maybe as a clever tactical turn. In my opinion, it is rather a symptom of American *civil religion,* the transfer of religious symbols into the national self-understanding. Lincoln's bond with the church was — in contrast to that of his wife — rather loose, but as a man who was well-versed in the Bible he was convinced that the nations were tools of the *Almighty,* and that this went especially for the United

---

11. Morison, *The Oxford History,* p. 703: "For Lincoln did not consider himself a conqueror."

12. Edwin Scott Gaustad, *A Religious History of America* (New York: Harper & Row, 1966), pp. 196-7; cf. also James M. McPherson, *Battle Cry of Freedom: The Civil War Era,* The Oxford History of the United States, vol. 6 (New York/Oxford: Oxford University Press, 1988), pp. 843-4. For a detailed analysis of Lincoln's Address and its context, see Ronald C. White Jr., *Lincoln's Greatest Speech: The Second Inaugural* (New York: Simon & Schuster, 2002).

States as *the chosen people*.[13] What could slap this "chosenness" harder in the face than this people's rupture? Lincoln might have asked himself secretly how a reconciliation that amounts to more than just repairing a disturbed social relationship could be possible, hoping, nevertheless, to get a positive response from the majority of his compatriots. This would have been an understanding that itself presupposed a prior experience with reconciliation.

After Lincoln's assassination many have regarded his understanding of reconciliation as a bequest for the arduous way towards national unity of the United States.

Maybe Lincoln's *Addresses* remain exceptions in the political history of the United States; after all, they were directed to domestic affairs, not to foreign politics. For the latter, as mentioned before, it was the splitting of Winthrop's metaphor "a city upon a hill" that resulted in one model for society and another model for the "world" of geo-political concerns. Sooner or later this split image can lead to an imperialism fed by religious roots and lived out in moralistic dualism. The desire to set the world in order might ultimately result in the subjugation of all of those who do not want to submit to the example of the shining city.

We might take the *just war theory* as an example of something that has become real after September 11. This theory has a long and tangled story within secular philosophy and Christian theology.[14] The limitations on what justifies war and on how far wars may be pursued were gradually increased in the era after the Enlightenment. Legitimate wars were made to face the test of justice. Wars of conquest were banned and martial law was put under the control of specified norms. But American voices of the twentieth century advocated military campaigns against "the evil" in the world. These campaigns were considered "just" when they were directed against unrestrained oppression, injustice, and the intention to exterminate. Under these ideas the United States considered itself to be the trustee of humanity and acted on behalf of all humankind. The American nation must — and can — prove "just cause" in intervening in world events. The turn to legitimacy is discernible with President Woodrow Wilson, a dyed-in-the-wool Presbyterian, when he asked the American Congress on April 2, 1917 to consent to the declaration of war against Germany[15] and in his "14 points" of the January 8, 1918, Peace

---

13. Ahlstrom, *A Religious History*, vol. 2, pp. 136-7; William J. Wolf, *The Almost Chosen People: A Study of Abraham Lincoln* (Garden City, NY: Doubleday, 1959).

14. Heinz-Horst Schrey, "Krieg. Historisch/Ethisch; 6. Die Rezeption des Krieges in der christlichen Moraltheologie," in *Theologische Realenzyklopädie*, ed. Gerhard Müller, vol. 20 (Berlin/New York: Walter de Gruyter, 1990), pp. 28-55, esp. pp. 35-41.

15. Woodrow Wilson, "War Message," in *Great American Speeches*, ed. Gregory R. Surioano (New York/Avenel, NJ: Gramercy Books, 1993), pp. 137-42.

Conference of Paris. He outlined in them that reconciliation between nations meant fighting for peace, relentlessly and until victory, just because one has to eradicate the reasons for war, root and branch.[16] Harry S. Truman was not self-critical either when he claimed international standing for the moral values of the American nation after the victory over fascism. Here, too, just war means, *to place oneself as justified in world society and in world history.*

Even the general condemnation of wars that was urged especially by the Americans in the Ecumenical Movement after the end of the Second World War shows ambiguous characteristics. The statement "War is not according to God's will" issued by the First Assembly of the World Council of Churches in Amsterdam (1948) "formulates not so much a consensus as the already achieved possibility of legitimizing future wars as just wars."[17]

This moralistic, nonpolitical, pragmatic intention for peace and readiness for war can, de facto, coincide when legally protected rights that are declared to be universal — human rights most of all — come into conflict with positive law (for example, international law). I can only hint here at this ethical dilemma and the political rhetoric that easily allies with it — the division of the world into good and evil.

Despite its appearance this division is not a religious one — at least not one based on Jewish-Christian grounds — but it happens through the confusion of religion and moralism. The moralist knows how to relate God to the world in every given situation, and knows how to quickly make "God" a component of the world order and its guarantor. In this way the moralist also is able to incessantly ascribe guilt to others when he wants to make sense of godlessness here.

It is not an accident that after September 11 the smoldering debate about "just war theory" has flared up again in the United States. I consider it to be a theologically promising sign.[18] Or perhaps it is a voice in the midst of a secularized world that speaks amidst the whirlwind of political instability:

> For the ignorant, the superstitious and me (and maybe you), the face of the Evil One was revealed, and died; for the ignorant, the superstitious and me (and maybe you), the cross survived. This is how God speaks to us. He is saying, "I am." He is saying, "I am here." He is saying, "And the

16. *Great American Speeches*, pp. 143-46, esp. p. 146.
17. Schrey, "Krieg. Historisch/Ethisch; 6," p. 41.
18. David S. Yeago, "Just War: Reflections from the Lutheran Tradition in a Time of Crisis," in *Pro Ecclesia: A Journal of Catholic and Evangelical Theology*, vol. 10 (Northfield, MN: Center for Catholic and Evangelical Theology, 2001), pp. 401-27; John L. Berquist, ed., *Strike Terror No More: Theology, Ethics, and the New War* (St. Louis: Chalice, 2002).

force of all the evil of all the world will not bury me." I believe this quite literally. But then I am experiencing Sept. 11 not as a political event but as a spiritual event.[19]

This leads us to another perception of providence, the old companion of American piety and politics. I will refer to some lines from John Irving's *A Prayer for Owen Meany,*[20] an exemplary literary account that, by the way, is based upon profound theological advice.[21] Young Owen Meany considers himself to be chosen as a tool for God. While acting in a drama he sees in his mind's eye his own gravestone. From then on he attempts to arrange his life towards this end even though his comprehension is fragmentary. He remains confident of God's providence, his providing, and of his care for him, though he can only catch a glimpse of this. He cannot avoid making plans but at the same time he realizes again and again in flashes of lightning that he is not able to plan his life and particularly not the heroic death of which he dreams. Again and again he experiences setbacks regarding his efforts to bring his plans into line with the vision of his death. Only at the end does Owen Meany, as well as the reader, get to see the connection. It happens through a sports exercise, a little detail, apparently without consequences and meaning, of which he could not in any way see the value. Yet, thanks to this exercise he can protect children from their would-be murderer, at the expense of his own life. The connection he had always been looking for in vain had been with him all the time without his knowing it. It was happening alongside him, simultaneously so to speak, without visible relation to everything he saw before him. Something done without purpose turns out to play a decisive role.

In a split second, Owen Meany had gotten an idea about when and how his life would end. But he does not let himself be fixed on this prognosis, even though it worries him a lot. He wants to believe: to hold on to God, to ask for God's will in the planning of his life, and to be dissuaded from the relentless self-doubts that are caused by circumstances. What he experiences with others and with himself, what he thinks and how he talks about it, does not add up. Nevertheless, the narrator succeeds in not letting the story fall apart into various fragments, nor does he interpret it in a psychologizing manner.

Gaps and inconsistencies obstruct every conclusive interpretation. Owen Meany's exaltations might be exposed as pathological narcissism, and

19. Peggy Noonan, "Welcome Back, Duke: From the ashes of Sept. 11 arise the manly virtues," in *The Wall Street Journal,* 12 Oct. 2001, editorial page.

20. John Irving, *A Prayer for Owen Meany* (New York: William Morrow, 1989).

21. Irving thanks his teacher Frederick Buechner in the acknowledgments of *A Prayer for Owen Meany.* See also Buechner's memoir *Telling Secrets* (San Francisco: HarperCollins, 1991).

the narrator indeed leaves it open whether this is possible from time to time. Or we might also read *Owen Meany* as an example of typical American consciousness of "chosenness" roused from its happy daydreams and prepared to die on behalf of others. "Chosen for suffering" — is this the new paradoxical message of success? The dying Owen Meany, after all, desires to be awarded a medal for his bravery.

Yet, this might only be another indication of the deeply entangled relationship between personal decision-making and a problematic political fate that has tormented Owen Meany for a long time. John Irving's *A Prayer for Owen Meany* belongs to the best tradition of American piety that is supported by theological depth.[22] It does not know simple answers to difficult questions. It is far away from the know-it-alls on the Internet who attempted to answer the absurd topic "Where *was* God on September 11?" It will be a long and arduous way to the question "What is God *like* in times of crisis?" and even more particularly, "*Who* is God, to whom we pray?"

---

22.   http://google.yahoo.com/bin/query?p=%22where+was+God%22%2c+september+11&hc=o and www.biblrytr.com/boston.htm.

We Are Not Our Own:
On the Possibility of a
New Christian Humanism

William Schweiker

It is with profound gratitude and genuine delight that I make a contribution to a volume dedicated to Wallace Alston. The man's energy, clarity of conviction, and passionate devotion to the community of faith and the life of the mind emboldens everyone fortunate enough to know him. In what follows I intend to advocate a version of Christian humanism as requisite for the life of faith in our time. Of course, Alston might find my advocacy of this position and its obvious concern for human freedom a bit too Arminian for his "reformed" taste. I am, after all, a Methodist of some sort![1] Yet by the end of the inquiry hopefully Alston will see some reflection of his own piety and vocation in this expression of the Christian tradition.

A caveat is in order. This inquiry into Christian humanism and also my advocacy of how best to carry on its legacy is historically informed. And yet, I cannot claim to be an expert in the history of humanism. The inquiry is decidedly systematic and ethical in style and intent. The basic claim is that the sensibilities and ideals found among Christian thinkers of a broadly humanistic bent must be reclaimed and yet revised in the light of the pressing challenges of the global age. No doubt a historian could challenge the details of the argument. Others who labor in different parts of the vineyard of Christian thought will simply reject the argument outright. All that one can do in this situation is to make one's case as best as possible and hope for a fair hearing.

---

1. I have made a case for theological humanism elsewhere. See William Schweiker, *In the Time of Many Worlds: Theological Ethics and Global Dynamics* (Oxford: Blackwell Publishers, 2003).

The Legacy of Christian Humanism

As far as I can see, the challenges of our age center on the power and dignity of human beings.[2] In a time of profound environmental endangerment wrought by the fantastic spread of technology and market-driven consumption, all life on this planet is bound to the destiny of the human adventure. In a similar way, we live in a time of incredible human suffering and travail when the most minimal needs of many people are denied and the dignity of many more demeaned. Here too the future is at stake, namely, the future of the human species. Finally, the present age is characterized by increasing religious, ethnic, and cultural conflict among peoples. If there is little or no way to conceive of human commonality beyond our tribal differences, then the fires of hate and fanaticism will eventually consume us all. In all these ways, it seems right to say that questions about human power and dignity are at the very center of contemporary, global challenges. We must fashion communities and ways of life dedicated to responsible existence. People are now called to respect and enhance the integrity of life. And that is why one ought at least to reconsider the legacy of Christian humanism.

The idea and history of Christian humanism is of course complex, much debated, and rich in thinkers and communities.[3] The origins of modern humanism are usually found in the Renaissance and the revival of interest in classical Greek and Roman writers as the backbone of education. But the legacy of humanism is long and varied, reaching into the distant past as well as the rise of the modern world. Consider just a few thinkers in order to grasp the range and reach of this legacy in the Christian tradition.

Clement of Alexandria, often considered the most learned of the Church fathers, drew on a wide variety of sources and continued to wear the philosopher's cloak. St. Augustine was a rhetorician and has been acknowledged as the last great Hellenistic philosopher. He penned what became the

---

2. On this see Hans Jonas, *The Imperative of Responsibility: In Search of an Ethics for the Technological Age*, trans. Hans Jonas and David Herr (Chicago, IL: The University of Chicago Press, 1984). Also see William Schweiker, *Power, Value and Conviction: Theological Ethics in the Postmodern Age* (Cleveland, OH: Pilgrim Press, 1998).

3. On the recent discussion about religious and non-religious humanism see Tzvetan Todorov, *Imperfect Garden: The Legacy of Humanism,* trans. Carol Cosman (Princeton, NJ: Princeton University Press, 2002); R. William Franklin and Joseph M. Shaw, *The Case for Christian Humanism* (Grand Rapids: Eerdmans, 1991); and also Timothy G. McCarthy, *Christianity and Humanism: From Their Biblical Foundations into the Third Millennium* (Chicago, IL: Loyola Press, 1996). For a brief study of the attack on humanism in a host of thinkers see Kate Soper, *Humanism and Anti-Humanism* (La Salle, IL: Open Court, 1986).

virtual manual for medieval education, his *De Doctrina Christiana.* John Calvin, as is well known, was steeped in humanistic education, wrote his first treatise on a work by Seneca, and also spoke of the philosophy and school of Christ. Philipp Melanchthon was steeped in humanistic learning and along with penning the Augsburg Confession, the first Protestant manifesto, also wrote on philosophy and education. Erasmus, the greatest of the sixteenth-century Christian humanists, presented a vision of the free unfolding of human life within a decidedly Christomorphic philosophy. He did so through satire, like *In Praise of Folly,* but also in dialogues, commentaries, and biblical translation. John Wesley, an Oxford Don, worked to revive vibrant faith, established schools, and sought to "reform the nation." Friedrich Schleiermacher engaged the whole compass of intellectual labor even as he worked to help found the University of Berlin. In the twentieth century, Paul Tillich spoke of an ecstatic humanism while Karl Barth finally came to insist on the humanity of God. Of course, for a variety of reasons not all of these thinkers would claim for themselves the name "Christian humanist" in any technical sense of the word. Yet the connection between the love of God and the life of the mind manifest in the labor of education and social transformation might best define the project of Christian Humanism.

Oddly, in our time Christian theologians too often and too glibly reject this proud heritage. They rush to embrace whatever purports to accent Christian uniqueness against other peoples and traditions. Anti-humanism has captured the minds of many theologians. There are many reasons for these developments. Why did the "rights of man" so hard won in the early modern turmoil of social and economic change prove powerless before the forces of hatred and death in the twentieth century? How did aspirations for valid knowledge and political self-government give way to the forms of scientism, fascism, and totalitarianism that scarred the past century? How has the modern celebration of human power manifest in the spread of technology led in our day to a worldwide environmental crisis? In the light of these failures, it is hardly surprising that many join the criticism of the historical legacy of humanism. Yet in the face of killing fields, gas chambers, and rape camps, there has also been resistance to intolerable horror in the name of our fragile shared humanity. The poor, suffering, and the oppressed rightly cry out for recognition of their human dignity. These events have led others to champion what the Jewish philosopher Emmanuel Levinas has called the "humanism of the other man."[4]

---

4. See Emmanuel Levinas, *Entre Nous* (Paris: Grasset, 1991). For an account of the "inhumane" that has sparked new reflection in ethics see Jonathan Glover, *Humanity: A Moral History of the Twentieth Century* (New Haven, CT: Yale University Press, 2000).

In many ways, we confront a profound and even troubling question. Given the sad legacy of inhumanity in the last century, the worldwide environmental threat brought on by the expansion of the human kingdom, but also the cries for human dignity, is it possible to forge a viable and vibrant Christian humanism that protects and promotes human dignity not against but within the wider compass of life on this planet? In many ways this is the basic question confronting the Christian community in the global era. Anything like a complete answer to that question is, of course, well beyond the bounds of one essay! But in order to begin to make some headway in answering it, one needs, first, some clarity about a set of convictions that define in a general way a humanistic outlook. And we will have to show how best to understand the distinctiveness of Christian humanism. With those ideals in mind, we can then turn to the most basic criticisms of Christian humanism and offer a response to them. I will conclude these reflections by trying to advance an argument capable of meeting the challenges of the present time.

Basic Humanistic Ideals

On several points all humanists agree: the importance of freedom or self-determination; human beings as fit objects of respect and esteem, the ends of action; the fundamentally social nature of human life and thus the importance of community; and, lastly, human fallibility and thereby the demand to test all claims to truth linked to a suspicion of authoritarianism. It is hardly surprising that humanists have advocated the ideals of liberty, human rights, democracy, general education, and the public scrutiny of opinions. Of course, how each of these ideals is understood is hotly debated. What is meant by freedom? Surely on that point Calvin and Wesley differ! Many contemporary thinkers also disagree about how to conceive of freedom. How best to define the boundaries of community and norms of justice? Here too theologians and Christian communities differ. What do we mean by an end of action, and who precisely is the fit end of human acts? Non-religious humanists insist that the well-being of other human beings is the sole end of right actions. A religious thinker, say, a Christian humanist, will argue for a richer conception of human transcendence and so the divine good as the ultimate end of action. As one might expect, there is constant debate about how rightly to articulate these shared humanistic ideals. But granting this debate, it is safe to say that humanists of all stripes desire to respect and enhance human existence within and not against the wider realms of life.

On my understanding, what distinguishes Christian humanists from those who share these ideals and yet reject religious belief is a conviction about how best to conceive the distinctiveness of human beings.[5] One can state this conviction by borrowing a phrase from John Calvin. In the midst of Book III of the *Institutes of the Christian Religion,* Calvin, in describing the Christian life of self-denial in all its joy and sorrow, hope and yet travail, raises his otherwise stark rhetoric to new and profound levels. St. Paul's words found in Roman 8 were probably in Calvin's mind. "Nothing can separate us from the love of God in Christ." Calvin writes a virtual hymn to the truth that in all things and in all ways we are not our own. The "hymn" progresses through a series of "stanzas" proclaiming that we are not our "own" at the level of reason or will, proposals for the end of action, and also possessions. And then he writes:

> On the contrary, we are God's; to him, therefore, let us live and die. We are God's; therefore let his wisdom and will preside in our actions. We are God's; towards him, therefore, as our only legitimate end, let every part of our lives be directed.[6]

We are God's. That is the most fundamental fact of human existence. Of course, this confession was partly meant by Calvin to draw a line between the church and those outside the body of Christ. He returns to the theme in discussing "predestination," hardly a humanist topic! And it is also true that many of his followers took the real point to be a division of humanity into the elect and the damned. These positions sadly pit theocentric faith against a humanistic sensibility. But Calvin's deeper insight, I submit, was that the defining fact of human existence, what bestows human life and freedom with purpose and dignity, is a relation to the divine. Human life is not defined by what we possess, even our dreams of self-possession or eternal election! It is defined by a relation to the living God. And that relation, when right, ignites a confident and ardent service with and for all mortal creatures.

Two recent authors have made virtually the same point, if in less moving language. "Christian humanism," they write, "bears witness to the crucial importance of insisting on the uniqueness of human nature. It claims that the human capacity for a relationship with God sets the human creature apart as possessing a special dignity not given to other beings within the created or-

---

5. Given the limitations of space, I cannot consider the relation between Christian and other forms of "religious humanism." That comparison would take different shape between theistic and non-theistic visions.

6. John Calvin, *Institutes of the Christian Religion,* 2 vols., ed. John T. McNeill and trans. Ford Lewis Battles (Philadelphia, PA: Westminster Press, 1960), III.7.1.

der."[7] Calvin's statement and this contemporary formulation no doubt stress too much the uniqueness of human beings over against other creatures and their possible relations to the divine.[8] Nevertheless, they are correct that the human relation to God in the name of Christ grounds Christian humanism. The question then becomes, how is that relation to be defined and lived? Interestingly enough, it is precisely on these points, that is, a conception of human distinctiveness and also the moral vocation of human beings, that one finds the deepest contemporary criticisms of Christian humanism. With some sense of the ideals of humanism in hand and also the marker of what is distinctive about classical Christian humanism, let us turn to these criticisms. Only if we can answer them will it be possible to outline a viable Christian humanism for our day.

Critics of Christian Humanism

Contemporary non-religious humanists as well as theologians and philosophers who advocate a "humanism of the other man" reject a specific conception of human existence and dignity that defines the central strand of classical Christian humanism. The issue is anthropological, that is, how to define and understand what it means to be a human being. Traditional Christian humanism, the detractor argues, entails a conception of the self that in principle excludes the claim of the other as radically other than self. It focuses on the self and its cultivation or perfection. The humanist commitment to education is seen in this light as grounded in a vision of human life aimed at the fulfillment of self. And behind the idea of fulfillment is really a deeper commitment to personal flourishing and happiness, what Greek and Roman Hellenistic philosophers called eudaimonia.[9]

---

7. Franklin and Shaw, *The Case for Christian Humanism*, p. 7. Also see Emil Brunner, *Christianity and Civilization* (New York, NY: Charles Scribner's Sons, 1949).

8. It is important, I judge, to draw a distinction between "uniqueness" and "distinctiveness." While every humanist insists that human beings are distinctive insofar as we are "moral creatures," this does not mean that we are utterly unique and without connection to other forms of life.

9. This *eudaimonistic* vision is found more readily in other strands of modern humanism. Montaigne writes, for example, "As much as I can, I employ myself entirely upon myself." And, again, in the *Essays*, "You have quite enough to do at home, don't go away." In other words, true freedom is self-labor removed from the tangle of cares that too easily and too often preoccupy us with matters of penultimate importance. See Michel de Montaigne, *The Complete Works: Essays, Travel Journal, Letters*, trans. Donald M. Frame (Stanford, CA: Stanford University Press, 1958), III, 10, 766-67.

If that is so about any form of humanism, what about the neighbor that the Christian is commanded to love? Is the living God nothing more than the end of human aspirations, the provider of our happiness? That hardly seems like the biblical vision of God. The God who thunders from Sinai or meets us in the Cross is a far cry from the joy of human natural desiring. As Luther might put it, a loving God is hidden under his opposite, command and Cross. The living God requires a radical care for the neighbor, even love of one's enemy rather than the search for happiness. The great Methodist ethicist Paul Ramsey insisted that Christian love has very little to do with consequential reasoning aimed at flourishing. Christian love is a duty of care for the other precisely because this and this alone is what the Lord requires of us.[10] In this respect, the very idea of Christian humanism is an oxymoron that inscribes a deep betrayal of biblical faith replacing it with the classical Hellenistic ideal of human flourishing and happiness. In the face of the twentieth century and the idolatries of state, race, and blood, Christians must insist on the radical freedom and sovereignty of God. What is needed is vibrant concern for the other and a profound awareness of the otherness of God.[11] Theocentrism seems to exclude the very possibility of humanistic sensibilities in the life of faith. One must thereby reject Christian humanism as a truthful expression of faith and life.

Another kind of critic admits that Christians are in fact responsible for the other precisely in the name of agapē and the demands of radical neighbor love even if this includes love of self. On this account, Christian faith is humanistic not in the sense of a classical vision of self-formation and fulfillment, but because it makes human well-being basic to a vision of faithful existence. After all, Jesus insisted that the Sabbath was made for man and not man for the Sabbath. The difficulty for this detractor of Christian humanism lies elsewhere. It focuses on the moral dimension of Christian humanism more than the underlying anthropology.

The Christian, the critic observes, is commanded to love everyone. Christian love is thereby non-discriminatory and necessarily abstract. One is

---

10. See Paul Ramsey, *Basic Christian Ethics,* The Library of Theological Ethics (Louisville, KY: Westminster John Knox Press, 1993). The point is often, but need not be, made in the form of the importance of divine command ethics. For a summary statement of this issue see William Schweiker, *Power, Value and Conviction,* esp. ch. 8. Also see Richard J. Mouw, *The God Who Commands* (Notre Dame, IN: University of Notre Dame Press, 1990); and also J. M. Idziak, *Divine Command Morality: Historical and Contemporary Readings* (New York, NY: Edwin Mellen, 1980).

11. On this see Orrin F. Summerell, ed., *The Otherness of God* (Charlottesville, VA: University of Virginia Press, 1998).

commanded to love an abstract other (the "neighbor") and do so through loving God. The "neighbor" is nothing more than a category for any human being stripped of all concrete particularity. Christian love, the detractor insists, is blind to the concrete other and in fact really loves the other as a means to loving God. Calvin's point, after all, was that God is the only legitimate end, and therefore all other ends, including human beings, are set against that ultimate, divine good. One is to love one's neighbor, but what is meant by the "neighbor" seems shorn of all reference to gender or class or race or language or cultural heritage. Stated otherwise, Christian love is otherworldly; it is really directed at God and not at other, concrete real persons. And given this, Christian faith cannot be a genuine form of humanism since it does not take human beings as the only fit end of action. Given the forms of tyranny and suffering in our world, especially those forms rooted in seeing human beings in abstract form (sexism, racism, etc.), one must reject all generalized claims about neighbor love. And one must reject religious conviction altogether in the name of a viable contemporary form of humanism. This is the tactic of neo-humanists.[12] They insist on "lateral transcendence" rather than any relation to the sacred as a divine good.

We have now isolated two kinds of current criticism of classical Christian humanism that have arisen out of the painful experience of the last century. Christian theologians have responded to the criticisms in a variety of ways and to various ends. Karl Barth, for instance, leveled the first charge against "liberal" theology, claiming that in its concern for human religious experience it subsumes the divine into the self. He argued that one must begin with the revelation of the Word of God that is totally other than the human self. The only true man is Jesus Christ; the rest of us are phenomenal men. What is more, the Word of God confronts one as permission and command to live in a specific time and place. Given this fact, Barth responds to the second criticism by insisting that the divine command is concrete and particular. The entire point of the divine command is to insure the freedom of God and the priority of God's will over generalizable moral maxims. Yet in the end, Barth advocated the "humanity of God" because he too was worried about otherworldiness.[13]

Other theologians respond differently. Some feminists, for instance, agree that Christian love is too often an abstraction from specific relations of

12. See Todorov, *Imperfect Garden;* Martha C. Nussbaum, *Women and Human Development: The Capabilities Approach* (Cambridge: Cambridge University Press, 2000).

13. Karl Barth, *Church Dogmatics* III/2 (Edinburgh: T&T Clark, 1957); *The Humanity of God* (Atlanta, GA: John Knox Press, 1982).

care and therefore must be refashioned in the direction of relationality rather than the duty to love. But these theologians often appeal to women's experience and thereby retain at least remnants of the basic anthropological claims attached by the first kind of detractor.[14] And, finally, there are ecological theologians who insist that the focus on human flourishing is wantonly anthropocentric. In an age of global environmental endangerment, the task before us to break free from anthropocentric ideals and seek to respond rightly to all realms of life, even when this might demand the sacrifice of distinctly human goods.[15] The point is that a "humanistic" outlook is driven by a faulty moral position centering on "human well-being" and this is backed by a specific anthropology. In this light, one must see human beings as part of the wider system of life on this planet and also expand the boundaries of the moral community.

So the criticisms go. A good deal of contemporary Christian theology and ethics is an extended response to these criticisms of Christian and humanist outlooks. Yet how might an avowedly Christian humanist address these matters? As the next step in my argument I want to turn to that question. My answer requires clarity about how best to formulate the anthropological point in light of the double love command as the summary of responsible existence. In doing so, I will be making some revisions in this grand legacy of thought while also, hopefully, retaining and advancing its spirit.

Rethinking Christian Humanism

The first point to make is that for the Christian humanist what we have called the anthropological and moral dimensions are inseparable. And this is so even though many Christian humanists were not as clear about the point as one might wish. In the classical formulation, true self-knowledge is bound to the love of God. But what does that mean? To love God is to know one's self truly, or, conversely, to have a true apprehension of one's self is to grasp the

---

14. For example, see Beverley Harrison, *Making the Connections: Essays in Feminist Social Ethics,* edited by Carol Robb (Boston, MA: Beacon Press, 1985). Also see Cristina L. H. Traina, *Feminist Ethics and Nature Law: The End of Anathemas* (Washington, DC: Georgetown University Press, 1999); Darlene Fozard Weaver, *Self Love and Christian Ethics* (Cambridge: Cambridge University Press, 2002).

15. For the most trenchant position see James M. Gustafson, *Ethics from a Theocentric Perspective,* 2 vols. (Chicago, IL: The University of Chicago Press, 1981, 1984). For a radically anti-humanist position see Peter Singer, *Unsanctifying Human Life: Essays on Ethics,* ed. Helga Kuhse (Oxford, UK: Blackwell, 2002).

ultimate object of one's desiring, one's love. What is more, there is testimony to the relation between God and self in each and every human heart. This relation to the divine constitutes human existence as such.

The point was made by some of the classical Christian thinkers. Erasmus, for instance, claims, in his *Enchiridion Militis Christiani* (1503), that God simply is the life of the human soul. John Calvin opens *The Institutes of the Christian Religion,* easily the most comprehensive statement of Protestant faith in the Reformation era, with the claim that true and sound wisdom consists of knowledge of God and knowledge of self. He even goes on to claim that these two are bound together so closely that it is difficult to say which brings forth the other. Does knowledge of God lead to right self-understanding? Is the inverse the case? Much earlier, St. Augustine, in the *Confessions,* articulated the principle that both Erasmus and Calvin explore, namely, that God is always nearer to us than we are to ourselves. God's closeness finds witness in the human heart. The very core of our being is restless until it rests in God.

This claim about the relation of God and self continues into the modern world. John Wesley, who insisted on vital, living faith, proclaimed that "true religion, or a heart right towards God and man, implies happiness as well as holiness. . . . [T]he Spirit of God bearing witness with the spirit of a Christian, that he is 'a child of God.'"[16] Friedrich Schleiermacher, another "reformed" theologian and the great translator of Plato, claimed that the immediate self-consciousness is itself a testimony to one's relation to the divine. And in the twentieth century, Paul Tillich talked about "ultimate concern" and the experience of being grasped by the Word of God, an ecstatic relation in the depths of human beings.[17] As they are created and redeemed, the presence of the divine life is manifest within consciousness, the spirit, self-knowledge, or the restless heart. Granting the fault and fallibility that riddles human life, God is not without witness in the rough and tumble of human existence.

However, it is also the case that these thinkers, and others as well, were not always clear about the causal relation between the human heart and the living God. For Christian humanists what it means to be a self, an actual living individual, cannot mean that somehow we first come to self-awareness and then in a subsequent act decide to love God! Knowledge of self does not

16. John Wesley, "The Way to the Kingdom," in *Sermons on Several Occasions,* First Series (London: Epworth Press, 1944), p. 77.

17. Paul Tillich, *Systematic Theology,* 3 volumes in 1 (Chicago, IL: The University of Chicago Press, 1967); also see his *Morality and Beyond,* Library of Theological Ethics (Louisville, KY: Westminster John Knox Press, 1995).

lead to or cause the knowledge of God. The knowledge of self and love of God arise simultaneously or they do not arise at all. One does not peer inside of oneself somehow to find God. This is not a version of religious narcissism or bland natural theology. What is more, an unfaithful or distorted relation to the living God means that the self, despite its illusion to existence, is not really alive. Outside of a right love of God we do not and cannot truthfully know ourselves. There is, we might say, a kind of living death in which the self, while biologically alive, is nevertheless spiritually dead. Not surprisingly, one can diagnose various moods or states that manifest the right or distorted relations between self, God, and others — moods like a guilty conscience, holy sadness, as Schleiermacher calls it, the restless heart, human folly, or, conversely, real joy in a life of love. Christian humanists examine "moods" because they disclose the condition of our lives within the defining relations to the living God. However, the state of the "soul" and its signifying moods (guilt, joy, sadness, hope) does not cause a relation to the divine.

The depth of the human plight on this account is that we are not aware of ourselves precisely because we do not love God. We exist in a haze, a profound sleep or spiritual death unmindful of our condition or the actual depths of our existence. As the Protestant reformers put it, we must be shocked into self-awareness through the convicting power of the "law" to expose our misdirected loves. One then looks to where God and human existence are disclosed in proper relation, one looks to the event of the Christ and the witness of scripture to that event.[18] This means, ironically enough, that selfhood or individuality is not a brute given. We do not "own" ourselves. Our true selfhood is received from God in grace and achieved through the cultivation of Christian character.

A good deal of misunderstanding is found on this point about the non-causal relation between God and self, even among theologians. For instance, when Schleiermacher argues that human consciousness always entails a "feeling" *(Gefühl)* of absolute dependence on a "whence," he means this in a very formal way. For any actual human beings, their existence is and always will be shaped by the beliefs and practices of some community. Schleiermacher's point is simply, theologically considered, that human existence is never self-explanatory.[19] We are not trapped within the confines of our wants, desires, and imaginings. Our "feeling" is not a causal form of knowing God. Likewise, Erasmus, against Luther's more strident formulations, asked "What good is

---

18. For the classic statement see Luther's Lectures on Galatians (1535) in *Luther's Works,* vols. 26-27 (St. Louis, MO: Concordia Press, 1963).

19. Friedrich Schleiermacher, *The Christian Faith* (Philadelphia, PA: Fortress Press, 1976).

man if God acts on him as a potter acts on the clay?"[20] Erasmus is not saying that we make ourselves! As children of Adam we are made of "clay." Yet our character is not only received, it is also something we must freely achieve. In other words, there is a double transcendence of the self: one always and already exists in relation to the other who is God, and, what is more, genuine life is a constant struggle of self-overcoming, an achievement, to have right relations to others. Causal language is then simply inadequate: we are not just "clay pots" in the hands of an otherworldly craftsman, and the living God is not a product of human wants.

With respect to the anthropological criticism, the detractors are simply wide of the mark. To be a self, on this distinctly Christian humanist account, is to find oneself in another, in God, and always to surpass self in the free struggle for the cultivation of character marked by love of others.[21] This is hardly a veiled "Hellenistic outlook" centered on eudaimonia. In fact, what is meant by "happiness" has been radically changed through reference to the demands and possibility of "holiness," as Wesley put it. Holiness just is the life of love. And yet, it must be noted that precisely on this issue Christian humanists do differ from other versions of Christian faith. Knowledge of self and knowledge of God arise simultaneously and they do so in such a way as to affirm, rather than deny, distinct human capacities for action and free relations to others. Unlike some more strident forms of Christian faith, including Augustine and Calvin at certain points, that verge on necessitarianism in order to preserve God's sovereignty, the argument here protects and promotes the distinctiveness of human beings as moral agents. Stated differently, Christian humanists believe that theocentrism and humanist ideals must go together in an adequate account of faith and life.

This brings us to the second important insight or revision needed to meet current detractors. Not surprisingly, for this strand of tradition the connection between self-knowledge and love of God is a way to conceptualize the core of the Christian witness. Christian faith is, after all, a trust in and love of the living God who is manifest in Christ that ignites and emboldens service of all things in relation to God. What is more, Erasmus, Calvin, Augustine, Schleiermacher, and certainly Wesley, among others, grasped that the double

---

20. Erasmus, *Diatribe on the Freedom of the Will*, in *Luther and Erasmus: Free Will and Salvation*, ed. E. Gordon Rupp and Philip S. Watson, Library of Christian Classics (Philadelphia, PA: Westminster Press, 1969).

21. For an analogous argument made by a philosopher deeply indebted to Protestant thought, see Paul Ricoeur, *Oneself as Another*, trans. K. Blamey (Chicago, IL: The University of Chicago Press, 1992). Also see *Paul Ricoeur and Contemporary Moral Thought*, ed. John Wall, William Schweiker, and W. David Hall (New York, NY: Routledge, 2002).

love command, to love God and one's neighbor as oneself, expresses this connection between God and self-knowledge as a maxim for the conduct of life. That maxim finds testimony in each and every heart. In some way, every person has a grasp, no matter how tenuous or distorted, of the claim of others to respect and esteem as well as a longing for the divine. The task of the Christian community, as Wesley intimated, is to form and order personal and social existence so that people's actions and relations enact the ground and destiny of life in the living God. A life aimed at enacting that truth is in turn nothing other than the union of holiness and happiness, that is, the highest human good.[22]

For the Christian humanist, what defines the dignity of human life, a free relation to the divine as the very life of one's life, is specified in terms of the double love command, to love God and to love the neighbor.[23] But this means that the "self" is not some solitary "I" in relation to itself. There is no private community between self and God lodged in the deep interiority of the "I." The "self" is profoundly marked by otherness; God and neighbor inhere in the love that defines existence. As Luther put it in words that any Christian humanist can affirm, "a Christian lives not in himself, but in Christ and in his neighbor."[24] The Christian is caught up in God through faith in Christ and also poured out to the neighbor in love. Christian existence, in other words, does not rest or resolve itself in itself. The Christian self is in and for the other: the divine and the neighbor. What is more, the right intentionality of our lives appears to us under the form of the demand of love as itself the distinctly Christ-like path to the highest good. Who I am, what I can become, is

---

22. It is interesting to note that in analyzing the concept of the "highest good" in terms of the mutual infusion of happiness and holiness, this strand of thought not only draws on ancient themes in moral philosophy but also anticipates modern forms of thought running from I. Kant's ethics to recent discussions by theorists like Paul Ricoeur and others. It is also important to note that someone like Wesley saw the "Sermon on the Mount," rather than the Decalogue (Calvin) or the theological virtues and natural law (Roman Catholic ethics), as the sum of the Christian life. This requires linking happiness or blessedness (the Beatitudes) to the whole counsel and teaching of Christ.

23. On the importance of the love command see William Schweiker, "And a Second is Like It: Christian Faith and the Claim of the Other," *Quarterly Review* 20, no. 3 (Fall, 2000): 233-47; and also Paul Mendes-Flohr, "A Postmodern Humanism from the Sources of Judaism," *Criterion* 41, no. 2 (Spring, 2002): 18-23.

24. Martin Luther, "The Freedom of a Christian," in *Martin Luther: Selections from His Writings*, ed. John Dillenberger (Garden City, NY: Anchor Books, 1961), p. 80. For a recent statement of this claim in Christian philosophical theology see Robert P. Scharlemann, *The Reason of Following: Christology and the Ecstatic I* (Chicago: The University of Chicago Press, 1991); and William Schweiker, "The Reason for Following: Moral Integrity and the Christological Summons," in *Faith and Philosophy* (forthcoming).

specified in a project of increasing love for God and for others. The Christian "self," again, is not a brute given. It is not an origin but rather a project or task whose end is the God of life and the life of the neighbor. That is why Christian humanists speak of cultivation, education, and even perfection. Genuine formation is to bear the image of Christ in one's life through love of God and others.

In this vision of life, the "self" is not an abstract principle of identity. It is a concrete person in community with others seeking to live out a life of love within the complexities and realities of existence. But the self is also not lost in God or the neighbor. There is no "mystical" absorption of self into the divine nor is there a moral effacement of the worth and dignity of the individual person in praise of the priority of the "other." Rather, a person in her or his own dignity exists within a complex set of relations with the ability and task responsibly to orient life.[25] That is, again, why Christian humanism insists on the importance of freedom.

The same thing must be said about the neighbor. Since the love of God and true self-knowledge arise together, the command to love neighbor as self cannot mean, despite what the detractors think, that a Christian loves others in the abstract as a means to the divine. Insofar as the self is in God through faith and in the neighbor in loving acts, the same is true in principle of all other people. That is, any other actual living person exists in a complex web of interrelations with others and with the living God. Of course, how they live within that web can take almost infinite expression. Some live in hope and courage, others live in despair and anger, still other people struggle to be faithful parents and good citizens. The ways of life that people adopt are many and complex and part of the richness and poverty of human reality. The Christian humanist finds this variety of ways of life profoundly ambiguous. It is part of the comic, but also tragic, tapestry of existence. But this acknowledgment of the ambiguity of the human project does not entail an easy acceptance of all forms of life as equally good and true. No way, style, or path of life ought to be adopted that violates the double love command and thus effaces and distorts the life of others and the right intentionality of one's own life. In fact, human sin consists in a closure of the self on itself in which relations to God and others are denied and the intentionality of life to its highest good thereby thwarted. The life of faith is to awaken from that condition of spiritual death and to live in love.

It would seem, then, that a response is possible to very prominent criti-

---

25. For the moral theory that backs this reading see William Schweiker, *Responsibility and Christian Ethics* (Cambridge: Cambridge University Press, 1995).

cisms of the legacy of Christian humanism. Of course, I have not been able to outline in detail a robust revision of Christian humanism. My task is more modest. It is simply to make a case for the importance of such an agenda in Christian moral thinking. Yet even if this tentative case for a renewed Christian humanism is persuasive, other problems remain to be answered. What would a viable account of Christian humanism look like in an age of global dynamics and radical moral and religious diversity? These matters have not been addressed by thinkers standing in this legacy. I want to conclude this inquiry by turning to those matters and thereby round out my contribution to the renewal of Christian humanism in tribute to the work of Wallace Alston.

The Present Challenge

In many respects, the arguments made above in defense of Christian humanism are a bit too easy for our age. It may be that the root issues have not really been addressed. In order to make the anthropological and moral argument for this vision of Christian life one must in fact accept what can no longer be presupposed, namely, that there is a wide, if often tacit, acceptance of biblical and other Western ideals and values. Even the criticisms of classical Christian humanism seem to presuppose that background. What I have called the "anthropological" criticism presupposes that it is good to be a self. The issue that divides thinkers is how best to conceive of the self. The moral criticism likewise arises out of a shared presupposition about the nature of moral responsibility and hence the demand to respect and enhance not only one's own life but that of others. But the fact is that we increasingly live in a world in which the complex interactions of cultures and traditions manifest a lack of shared presuppositions. In some traditions and cultures the idea of a "self" is hardly a defining idea. It is seen as an imposition of "Western" modes of thought. Within the spreading global market, it is not at all clear that anything can trump the drive of consumption and the satisfaction of personal preferences. Everything can be seen as a commodity for the satisfaction of individual needs and wants. Even the moral life, it is argued, is simply a means to the end of personal satisfaction. How ought one to respond to this new, changed situation?

Ironically, it is precisely in this situation that a renewed Christian humanism is sorely needed. As we have seen, the core of this outlook is that human dignity is not a matter of self-possession. We are not our own, as Calvin put it. The drive for possession, the wanton lust for consumption and the clinging to whatever is believed to satisfy human longing, is in the final analysis destructive of the human spirit. This is not to say that everyone should take a vow of poverty! But it is to say that in a world of want and also gluttony, the profoundest message of the Christian witness is that while we live by bread we do not and cannot live by bread alone. A human life driven by unrestrained want is not really living; it is a mark of death within life. This insight combats the dulling and deadening forces of consumerism and might just as well enable Christian thinkers to engage representatives of traditions and culture less beholden to "Western" conceptions of the self. For if the argument above was in any way compelling, then a properly Christian conception of the human dislodges the "I" from the center of reflection. It shows that genuine existence is in love. The distortion and destruction of life lies in its closure driven by the desire to engulf all life in the self, what was traditionally called "concupiscence."[26]

Once we grasp the Christian conception of what it means to be a self, then two things follow. First, what it means to be a self is more complex and saturated with "otherness" than typical ancient and modern philosophical conceptions. Anti-humanists and the varied forms of neo-humanists simply have not grasped this point. The neo-humanist argument for "lateral transcendence" can too easily be implicated in the mad rush to fulfill all human desire. And, likewise, the modern anti-humanist attack on the self is off target since what the Christian humanist means by the "self" is not a being defined simply by its "self-relation." And we also see, second, that Christian humanist thinking is diagnostic. It aims less to explain "doctrines" and much more to analyze and articulate the structures of lived reality thereby to provide orientation and guidance for life. Doctrine is in the service of faithful living. The diagnosis shows, in part, that in order to preserve our humanity, one must have a trans-human good beyond the "self" in mind. Other forms of "religious" thought, like Buddhism, are also rigorously diagnostic in character while challenging a focus on the "self." They seek to isolate, articulate, and answer a range of human problems thereby better to orient and direct human life. A Christian humanist is, accordingly, able to see adherents of other reli-

---

26. Among twentieth-century theologians, it was Paul Tillich who correctly saw that in our time the problem of sin is most clearly manifest not just in "pride," the favored sin of most theologians, but in concupiscence. On this see his *Systematic Theology*. Also see William Schweiker, "Having@toomuch.com: Property, Possession and the Theology of Culture," *Criterion* 39, no. 2 (Spring/Summer 2000): 20-28; "Responsibility and the World of Mammon: Theology, Justice and Transnational Corporations," in *God and Globalization*, vol. 1, *Religion and the Powers of the Common Life*, ed. Max L. Stackhouse with Peter J. Paris (Harrisburg, PA: Trinity Press International, 2000). Likewise, see *Having: Property and Possession in Religious and Social Life*, ed. William Schweiker and Charles Mathewes (Grand Rapids: Eerdmans, 2004).

gious traditions who have undertaken diagnostic thinking as fellow travelers in a quest for what is good and right.

This brings us to another reason why a new Christian humanism is needed. I have just argued that one needs religious sources, a Christian humanism, to respond to the global spread of consumerism and with it the drive of technology to enfold all forms of life within the kingdom of human power. Yet in a world of increasing conflict and tribalism, one equally needs a robust Christian humanism. Since we are not our "own," that is, we are defined as human beings not just by the usual markers societies establish to divide the world into "us" and "them" but by a relation to the divine and the neighbor, then ethnic, political, gender, racial, and even religious differences cannot be ultimate. To be sure, those forms of identity are crucial and necessary in human life. As already argued, no one is an abstract "self" or an abstract "neighbor." We always live concrete, situated, embodied lives bearing various markers of identity. Yet while that is obviously true, the force of any kind of humanism, and especially Christian humanism, is that there is a bond between peoples as finite and fallible creatures within the community of life.[27] By insisting on this point one has the means to counter the viciousness and excessive tribalism of one's own home tradition. And one also has the means to appeal to the good will of others to inhabit their community with just that capacious sensibility.

There are signs, thankfully, that thinkers in other traditions and cultures are beginning to reclaim the best and most humane insights of their communities. And the reason for this ought to be obvious to everyone. In an age in which each and every religion has fostered the most fanatical and violent forms of fundamentalism, the resources of the religions must be bent towards humane purposes or they will surely feed global conflict. It is precisely because of one's belief in and dedication to a specific faith, says the Christian faith, that one can and must argue for its humanistic expression. Religious thinkers should find common cause not in terms of seeking some unified theological vision that will somehow cut across all of the religions. Rather, what can and must be sought is an internal renewal, a reformation, of each and every tradition to grasp the service they can render to life. For the Christian humanist this is simply living out the double love command mindful that we are not finally or ultimately our own.

---

27. There is little doubt that one of the major questions now facing us is how to carry on comparative religious reflection around widespread human problems. See Daniel C. Maguire, *The Moral Core of Judaism and Christianity: Reclaiming the Revolution* (Minneapolis, MN: Fortress Press, 1993); Michael J. Perry, *The Idea of Human Rights: Four Inquiries* (Oxford: Oxford University Press, 1998); *A Companion to Religious Ethics,* ed. William Schweiker (Oxford: Blackwell, 2004).

And this brings us to the last reason for taking the "cloak" of Christian humanism. Without doubt, one of the pressing issues of the twenty-first century is and will be the worldwide environmental crisis. In this light it might seem odd to insist on Christian humanism rather than, say, an ecological holism in ethics. And yet surely it is the case that the crisis we face is a crisis of the relentless spread of the human kingdom. The age of globality is nothing else than a time of unbridled human power operative in and through transhuman systems, the global market, media, and other technologies. It is also a cultural phenomenon in which human beings make meaning through symbolic representations.[28] The only way to orient these "agencies" toward what respects and enhances life is to insist that they are the working out of distinctly human choices and decisions. In this way, global agencies are made responsible even as people can be seen again as the makers, not the products, of those systems. That is to say, if we wish to avoid a runaway expansion of nonhuman agencies that too easily trammel rather than enrich life, we must humanize them and thereby set their actions and relations within a moral framework. But insofar as we do that, we must also labor for an expansion and education of human desires and hopes to include the awareness of the oft unheard cry of other forms of life. To do that requires, once again, a transhuman good, just the kind of good that invigorates the legacy of Christian humanism. The inner secret for meeting the ecological crisis might just be a renewed and robust understanding of the moral vocation of human beings to respect and enhance the integrity of all life before God.

Last Thoughts

In these pages I have tried to make a case for the possibility of a new Christian humanism. I have not been able to unfold in any detail the shape and content of that vision of faith and life. It is enough to meet some widespread objections to the idea and legacy of Christian humanism as well as indicate its need in the current world situation. In the end, it must be said that Christian humanism is more than a set of ideas or doctrines or moral ideals. It is a specific stance in life characterized by a deep and abiding trust in the living God, dedicated to respecting and enhancing the integrity of life, and moved by a love of life despite the folly and brokenness of human beings. The sensibilities of the Christian humanist are such that she or he wants to make life better,

---

28. For a helpful discussion of this see John Tomlinson, *Globalization and Culture* (Chicago, IL: The University of Chicago Press, 1999), p. 18.

richer, and deeper through dedication to social transformation, education, and an unceasing willingness to learn. One believes that these are the true marks of the life of faith, a devotee walking in the ways of the living God. And whether he takes the name or not, I judge that these sensibilities and commitments have been powerfully displayed in the life and work of Wallace Alston.

The Moral Roots of the Common Life in a Global Era

Max L. Stackhouse

Wallace Alston, through the Center of Theological Inquiry, has graciously supported the research and writing project now issuing in the four-volume set *God and Globalization*.[1] This project not only involved the development of a complex theological and ethical conceptual framework to order research and writing on such a vast topic, it involved the organization of a marvelous company of specialists in particular areas of social, cultural, and religious analysis of the forces that either are generating what we today call globalization or are manifesting or responding to it. Throughout this process, Wallace has been not only a generous supporter of the project but an enthusiastic encourager to it and an acute questioner of some points of view that appeared in the course of the study.

More widely, he has encouraged the Center itself to reach out beyond the Euro-American boundaries to which it was historically largely tied, and globalized the work and impact of the Center — both by drawing scholars from the "developing world" into conversations at Princeton, and by arranging for Western scholars to engage church and theological leaders in other

---

An earlier, briefer version of this argument appeared in *The Expository Times* (Scotland) 113, no. 5 (Feb. 2002): 157-61. The sources of the longer arguments can be found in Max L. Stackhouse, Dennis P. McCann, and Shirley J. Roels, eds., *On Moral Business: Classical and Contemporary Resources for Ethics in Economic Life* (Grand Rapids: Eerdmans, 1995); my *Publc Theology and Political Economy: Christian Stewardship in Modern Society* (Grand Rapids: Eerdmans, 1987); and my forthcoming bibliographical essay, *Capitalism, Civil Society, Religion and the Poor* (ISI Press).

1. Max L. Stackhouse, with Peter Paris, Don Browning, and Diane Obenchain, eds., *God and Globalization*, vols. 1-3 (Harrisburg, PA: Trinity Press International, 2000).

parts of the world. In brief, the Center is a more cosmopolitan place under his leadership than it has been at points in the past, and this reflects both an increased catholicity and ecumenicity of awareness in the theological enterprise and the realities of international and transnational life to which the term globalization points.

Indeed, these experiences seem to have challenged some ways of looking at the faith and ethics that he had developed, based on his deep appreciation of the theology of Karl Barth, and the profound friendship he had with Paul Lehmann. Wallace does not change perspectives easily. Thus, I have decided to present a particular set of observations in this forum, because the three central points I treat below are not matters that gained positive social or theological attention from either of these figures of the last century, and I suspect that Wallace is still suspicious on these matters. However, I hope to persuade him and the large number of scholars and pastors who share his suspicion, if not by this essay, then in due course as people ponder the studies coming out of these wider global encounters.

We can hardly read a newspaper or hear a news broadcast without having the term "globalization" thrown at us several times. Most people identify the term with the economy and, indeed, with the spreading influence of capitalism. Not a few presume that globalization is caused by the expansion of the global market and by the intrusions of transnational corporations into cultures around the world for the most crass of reasons. There is something to this view because the attempts of individuals to improve their economic well-being have prompted people from the wealthier parts of the globe to seek resources, labor, and markets wherever they can find them, now that the world is shrinking due to technological means of communication and transport. And people from the less developed regions are eager to get jobs, skills, and products from abroad to use for their own purposes (including the opportunity to participate in the wider-world's "good" life as quickly as possible). In fact, all can see that globalized business today is a major force. Every national economy must open its borders or become a backwater, and every significant business must be alert to global forces and opportunities or die. Thus, most leaders in most countries of the world eagerly offer incentives to corporations that will come into their lands — even though they are often disruptive of traditional ways of life. And, when they do come in, some parts of the population gain rapidly, others more slowly, and those least able to adapt suffer, thus increasing inequalities even if most improve.

But to view these matters as the most important realities of globalization is, I have come to believe, a very narrow view of what is going on. Economic expansion is, in fact, only the most obvious and most recent and most apparent corollary of a much more complex and lengthy historical process that is in substantive measure theologically, ethically, and ecclesiologically generated. What is happening, I think, is the formation of at least the material basis of a global civil society, one that involves as great a change as that from the Roman Empire to mediaeval Feudalism, from that to the Reformation-Renaissance period of urbanization, and from that to the Industrial Age. But if we want to understand why this latest change is so dramatic or, even more, if we want to shape the process and not only allow ourselves and our neighbors to be swallowed by it, or allow the weaker peoples of the earth to be crushed by it, we must recognize that a purely economistic way of interpreting social history is mistaken — although it is the way social changes have been largely interpreted both by Marxist socialists and Liberal capitalists for more than a century. Ironically, this materialist view has been largely adopted by radical Christians who saw Marxism as "prophetic" and by pietistic Christians who saw capitalism as worldly practicality and faith as private belief. Both are mistaken.

What appears to some to be an economic juggernaut without social boundaries or moral purpose may in fact be a set of ethical developments rooted in complex historic dynamics and spiritual developments, now out of control because they are not recognized as religiously-driven presuppositions that have become incarnated in the culture. Without theological tending, nurture, and guidance, they have become "powers, principalities, authorities, and dominions" that shape us in more ways than we want to be the case. Such powers may have been, in fact, divinely created potentialities that may be critical for the well-being of civilization, but the failure to nurture and guide these forces has allowed them to become autonomous in the sense that they have no consciousness of God, divine law, or moral purpose. Indeed, they are usually held to be "externalities" from an economist's point of view, but the neglect of them by theologians and Church leaders as well as by business leaders and economists, has meant that we cannot grasp what is driving the globalizing forces of today.

Three great themes seem to me to exemplify the issues: *the theological character of technology, the ecclesiological character of the corporation, and the vocational/professional character of management.* In preparation for taking up these themes, I want to mention a paradigmatic related area that may be familiar, but that needs wider application. It can be found in the work of Max Weber. We need not offer an extensive analysis, but it may be useful to review key elements of his classic argument. He claimed that a Protestant "this-worldly asceticism" gave rise to certain key aspects of modern economic life. This thesis has been under debate for a century. Although some revisions are needed, on the whole, I think, Weber was on the right track. The most important contribution is this: religious ideas have consequences, often unintended, in social life. And once we see this, clergy and theologians have to take responsibility for how they work and where they lead.

The Theological Character of Technology

One key theme that is decisive for globalization is the notion that "the world" is something that is real and, in the primal intent of God, good, that it is not ultimate reality but created, and that it has not only been in need of tending perennially, but has also fallen and thus is something to which we are not to conform. Indeed, it needs changing. Yet the world is something that God so loved that it is being redeemed, and those who know God are sent as agents into it to aid in the process of redemption and transformation, even as it groans in travail toward a new creation that hosts a new complex civilization, the New Jerusalem. Views such as this, which intellectual honesty demands that we trace to the power of religion in culture, invite a deeper view of globalization. Those who catch the vision of a promised reign of God that transforms the world toward justice, righteousness, peace, and bounty are to employ every moral means to make the vision actual, so far as possible in the limits of history — for all.

That is why, from early on, some strands of religious history have been pro-technological — willing to engage in the transformation of nature and of society, not because they are hostile to materiality and culture for the sake of spirituality, but to restore and then fulfill the potential of the creation and the promise of a new community. All salvation religions have a cosmic vision, a sense of time, and a hope for change to an altered state of being. In some religions — Christianity, especially — it is central. Thus, for those parts of the tradition that recognized this, technology and the intentional restructuring of the world, selves, and society became a duty.

Globalization could not take place without technology. It has revolutionized the family farm, the craftsman's shop, the local store, the government office, and the way we travel and do business. Why do we have this drive to change nature, to reorganize it so that it will do what we want it to? It is not a natural attitude. Most species and many societies want to adapt to their environment, not adapt their environment to them. Many cultures find the "right order" of things by studying nature and then seek to fit into it. But other traditions study nature to see how it can be changed to make the lot of humanity better. Against the "ontocratic" religions of the world, Christianity holds that nature does not rule life; the Creator God does, and we as God's creatures are given the freedom to have, under God, a dominion over the earth as a mark of obedience to God's will and way.

In a new study, David Noble begins his first chapter by stating that "the dynamic project of Western technology, the defining mark of modernity, is actually mediaeval in origin and spirit. . . . (It) was rooted in an ideological innovation which invested the useful arts with a significance beyond mere utility."[2] The ancient Greeks had a sophisticated science in some areas, and the ancient world shines with the products of subtle technique. But it was only later that technology, the product of technique and science, became combined with moral and spiritual meaning. Noble shows how "the mechanical arts" came to be identified with transcendence implicated as never before in the Christian idea of redemption. He writes: "The other-worldly roots of the religion of technology were distinctly Christian. For Christianity alone blurred the distinction and bridged the divide between the human and the divine." This development brought "the striking acceleration and intensification of technological development in . . . (mediaeval) Europe." This is clearly based on the view that humanity is created good, but is fallen. The fact of the goodness means that residual capacities to improve life are present; the fact of fallen-ness means that improvement is required.

I personally love the example of different attitudes toward technology illustrated by David Landis's book on the history of the clock.[3] He shows that the Chinese built accurate timekeeping devices long before the West thought of them. But he also points out that they did so because they wanted to know when to conduct the proper rituals that would integrate the Empire more perfectly into the harmonies of earth and heaven. They used their science to make humanity and society conform to the cosmic order. When these devices were brought back to the West, they were almost immediately developed for another purpose. They were applied to make the people conform to a supernatural purpose — the reordering of schedules for proper allocation of time to prayers and work, both to honor God and serve the neighbor. Thus, when the newly discovered time-keeping instruments were adopted, they were used to make the divisions of the day more rational, especially in the monastery. No longer did the monks wake at dawn, early in the summers, late in the winters, do their prayers then go to work until meals and prayers at the end of daylight. Clocks woke the monks at the same time, winter or summer, dark or

---

2. David Noble, *The Religion of Technology: The Divinity of Man and the Spirit of Invention* (New York: A. A. Knopf; Distributed by Random House, 1997).

3. David Landis, *The Wealth and Poverty of Nations* (New York: W. W. Norton, 1999).

light, for their prayers, and then followed a regimen of work, eating, prayer, and sleep that was on the clock schedule. In fact they set up bell systems to notify everyone. That is the origin of "Frère Jacques." The sleepy-head monk will not get up on time, even when the morning bells are ringing! These bells became the markers of time for the peasants in the fields and the merchants in the cities. The disciplined person and community are governed not by the urges and cycles of nature and the body's felt needs, but by proper obedience to the laws of prayer and work. Landis goes on to show why and how European watchmakers became the emblem of this, and how and why timing was essential to the assembly line, to industrial efficiency experts, and now to the speed of the microchip — all a direct result of this, although Silicon Valley knows little of the theological roots of what they do. Today, global technologies calculated to the nanosecond provide the basis of communications, trade, and much else.

Today, of course, there are new movements for eco-justice and eco-feminism within as well as beyond the Christian tradition, and many have taken their cues from the neo-naturalist traditions of the romantic, post-Enlightenment age, that ironically challenge the ways in which humanity has used ideas of "dominion" to disrupt Mother Nature and modulate the presumed "natural" relationship of humanity with the earth. Indeed, in some church calendars, Earth Day is celebrated as a Christian festival, not seldom with many overtones of neo-pagan assumption, as both Ronald Cole-Turner and Jürgen Moltmann have noted in our God and Globalization series in their ecologically-sensitive understanding of creation. They know that we should care for the world God has given us; but it is not at all clear that we can and should abandon the technological ethic of "dominion" that the deeper tradition has fomented. Brad Allenby has recently argued, quite compellingly in my estimation, that we already live in an "anthropogenic" world. No part of the earth's environment is not already influenced in some measure by human intervention, and there is no other way to preserve the resources of the earth wisely than by recovering, refining, and extending the theological ethic that generated the technology that now drives much of how humans relate to the bio-physical universe.

But, like the example of the work ethic, this is only an illustration, another feature of the complex of conditionalities that shape all that we are and do. A second major conditionality is rooted in the fact that the technological revolution which these classic theological views fostered needed an institutional home in which to operate. And, in many cultures, where technology is introduced, no proper institution is available to house technology and cultivate it except the government — a fact that reinforces statist governance of the whole of life. What kind of an institutional arrangement is necessary in a civil society if a modern economy is to flourish? Adam Smith thought it was the market and the division of labor; Karl Marx thought it was the control of the means of production and the division of the classes; and surely they saw parts of the process. But the metaphysical legitimacy of the transformation of nature was presumed by both, and neither saw that for a vibrant technology to generate new benefits that reduce drudgery on a world scale, a distinct institutional matrix has to be created.

The Ecclesiological Character of the Corporation

It is seldom recognized that most of the activities of human civilization (religion, nurture, education, production, distribution, consumption, the cultivation of the arts, medical care, defense, and legal enforcement) have been conducted by two centers of social organization — the family (which includes kinship organizations such as clan, tribe, or caste) and the regime (the council of elders, king, emperor, or republic). Trade, of course, existed between families or between regimes and between the household-based artisans and the palace commission. Moreover, the worship center, whether at the hearth or at the temple to the regime's deities, reinforced the supreme authority of familial or political loyalties.

In such a context, the birth and growth of the corporation, which is neither familial nor political, is an amazing event — one rooted in a deep history with striking implications. Indeed, from a socio-ethical point of view we should call what we now have a "corporate-technological economy" rather than simply a "market economy." Nothing is new about having markets, except their extent which is now largely a function of the fact that corporations have consolidated workers and leaders outside the family or political regime and consolidated technological resources not possessed by either to create both more for the market and more for what is wanted in and from the market. What is new is not only that the channels within which the market works have much to do with a sense of a work ethic being properly rewarded, and with a sense of all of life being conducted under a universal moral law, and with the legitimacy of the technological transformations of nature, but the fact that technologically-equipped corporations are now primary actors in the market and are able to sustain it around the clock and around the world. The laws of the market, if they are to be morally influenced, will be shaped not only by the familial patterns that cultivate the work ethic and political institutions that constrain corruption, but by technologically concentrated corporate organizations that produce goods and services that are desired by families and governments.

In the nineteenth century, corporations began their dramatic growth, but powerful forces in opposition were marshaled. For more than a century, many tried to mobilize political parties, class interests, national identity, and traditional loyalties against them. This opposition continues in many places in the anti-globalization movements, and almost always holds that more extensive state control is necessary. Still, efforts to rediscover a moral theory of the corporation are under way.

It has been amply documented but largely forgotten that the roots of the modern corporation are in the Church. Christians formed communities of faith distinct from the household or the regime out of the models they had at hand — the synagogue and the cult. Further, people joined the Church irrespective of familial or political connection. It is precisely in this independent social space that the Church grew as a *corpus Christi* anticipating a New Jerusalem. In fact, the life of Jesus transcended both family and state — he neither came from an ordinary family nor married to continue one; he was neither an heir to power nor an aspirant to political office. He promised a Kingdom of another order. Thus, the early Church established another center of human loyalty and activity. For the first time in human history, and with only some analogies to earlier monastic and mystery cult traditions, an enduring model of a third center of organization, what sociologists today call "voluntary associations" and political theorists today call, less elegantly, "NGOs" (non-governmental organizations), was formed. Indeed, the legal basis for the persecution of the early church was that it had no right to exist as a corpus, a charge made today in countries where Christians are still persecuted.

Over time, gradually demanding and getting the right to exist, to own property and to designate trustees and managers as a *persona ficta,* the church spawned independent religious orders, hospitals, and schools, all managing to secure a place for less patriarchal, certainly trans-familial and non-royal participation (although patriarchy, familistic duties and aristocracy persisted). Later, covenanted forms of these organizations became the basis for highly successful institutions in the "free cities" of the West and expanded steadily from then through the twentieth century. A dramatic growth came when the legal entity of the corporation converged with the technology of the Industrial Revolution, and the fruits of the "work ethic." These are among the decisive roots of the current globalizing economy — reinforced by legal provisions for limited liability, the "prudent man rule" for trustees, and the distinction between unjust usury and just interest (decisive for finance).

Today, the corporation is the basic organizing principle of complex societies — not only the for-profit businesses, but hospitals, universities, professional associations, unions, ecological advocacy groups, political parties, and singing societies. Civil society is, indeed, a consociation of incorporated bodies — ordinarily good citizens of political orders and sensitive to people's diverse familial, religious, and cultural involvements outside their work, but less and less identified with either any specific familial or any political connection. Those who think only in terms of kinship loyalty or political authority resent this fact, but it is arguably the great organizational change that allowed humans to cooperatively utilize their talents to form new technologies and to raise humanity out of subsistence and want toward the promise of affluence and plenty.

When developed, the business corporation continually alters its internal shape, sometimes in terms of hierarch-subsidiary and sometimes in more federal-pluralistic ways. Further, it continues to expand its operations to include people from families and nations that did not cultivate the social form, and to develop partners and branches, customers and suppliers around the world. This transforms familial and political life wherever it goes, establishing both a new pluralism in civil society and new transnational centers of production, finance, distribution, consumption, and technological development. Today, it is likely that no viable ethic for the future can be developed that does not wrestle with the presuppositions and social implications of these historic influences. They now join humanity together in a more unified economic destiny than has ever been the case where those who resist corporate organization most resolutely are most tragically left behind.

Of course, a corporation without theological and ethical guidance can become an evil instrument of oppression, as can technology. If it does not see itself under a more ultimate authority, if it is seen not as an interpersonal, cooperative endeavor called to increase the wealth of all stakeholders and host communities by providing goods or services that enhance the quality of life, but only as an efficient money machine devised to maximize gain by squeezing as much value out of the material resources and human labor as is possible irrespective of human rights, social consequences, or ecological damage, it comes to represent not a genuine "corpus" guided by ethical principle and purpose, but an artifact of dehumanized and dehumanizing exploitation that needs constraint or dissolution. The corruption in some mega-corporations has recently exemplified this dispirited option.

The Vocational-Professional Character of Management

Who runs these technological-corporative institutions of modernity? Who seeks the most creative interaction of technological resources and human agents in a cooperative effort? The answer, of course, is "managers," business professionals. However, business is not necessarily a "profession" in the classical sense. While clergy, lawyers, doctors, and teachers were long identified as "the professionals," and while architects, engineers, accountants, pharmacists, nurses, psychologists, and certain military or law enforcement officers have more recently been recognized as professionals also, this understanding of business is relatively new. Historically, professionals had to undergo specialized training, be admitted to associations by examinations on theoretical and practical matters, take oaths to standards of conduct, be certified by public agencies, and manifest a dedication to values (e.g., clergy to faith, lawyers to justice, doctors to health, teachers to wisdom, police to law and order, accountants to honesty, etc.) that were beyond material gain or worldly success. Business was at once more democratic and more pragmatic — whoever had the talent for success could do it. The development of graduate schools of business and management in the last century, however, demonstrates efforts to develop a new level of professionalism.

Yet, something is lost in what managers are called to do if we do not remember the deep roots of the idea of profession. It developed out of the proper response to a sense of a "calling," a notion derived from Biblical themes and cultivated in religious history. If one had a "vocation" to some function decisive for the well-being of humanity and the glory of God and was given the gifts to perform that calling well, one was expected to cultivate a disciplined profession. One might, of course, live "off it," but in another sense one was expected to live "for it." It was more than a job or a career or clever expertise. It involved treating what one did with a sense of duty and responsibility under God that brought with it an opportunity to serve humanity.

In spite of the fact that ideas of "job," "career," "status," "pay," or "achievement" have obscured this level of meaning for many in contemporary life, other contemporary pressures invite business leadership to recover the deeper vision of professionalism. The Business Schools now attract some of the most promising young talent of the future, and have begun to certify that well-trained business managers are equally qualified experts as those who graduate from a Divinity School, Medical School, Law School, or many doctoral programs. This new, professional degree marks a potential new chapter in the history of the professions, for it brings the prospect that business is developing internal standards of performance and excellence that were neither universally practiced nor widely recognized. It is unlikely that governments will or should conduct qualifying exams for top business executives, as doctors, lawyers, clergy, professors, architects, and others are required to take in order to practice their profession. Still the ripple effect of this development means that business, commerce, and management courses in colleges and universities are adopting standards of excellence that can also be found among those who are in pre-medical, pre-law, and other pre-professorial courses of study.

At the same time, the awareness of deep moral and spiritual values connected with the professions seems to be declining in many areas. Even in the growing number of courses in business ethics, it can scarcely be said that the fundamental questions of integrity, of principle, and of sacred responsibility are touched upon deeply. Only at some Christian and Jewish colleges and universities in the West does the deeper religious grounding shape questions of professional conduct overtly; yet in Christian colleges in many developing nations, value-laden studies in "commerce" are extending the attitudes and convictions that shaped the standards of earlier traditions — often among future business leaders who are members of other faiths.

And here the issues come down to very fateful ones for our global future. On one side are very personal issues. People in many professions are today frustrated with what they are finding in the secular professional schools (in the West or among the rest) and in their work places. They may, in a certain sense, love their work and appreciate the material rewards, but the moral and spiritual roots of why they do what they do are blocked from vision, and the temptations to cynicism invade consciousness and behavior. Justice, including the defense of human rights universally, is too often blocked out of the practice of Law, the health of the total person — mind, body, and spirit — is too often neglected by the cure orientation of modern Medicine, and Wisdom is often viewed as impossible or marginal to the central agenda of the contemporary, postmodern academia where even the quest for truth is considered impossible. Moreover, the transformation of nature as a quest for redemptive possibilities is hardly known by today's technology. Covenantal patterns of relationship are frequently lost in our view of the corporation, and the trustee-stewardship model of management is seldom discussed.

It is an open question whether the professions can cultivate an inner sense of meaning in our time, one that can guide the organized units of the common life as we move increasingly toward a global society, which has no overarching political order to coordinate its meanings and contain its potential perils. In this context, the question becomes decisive of whether the managers of today and tomorrow can capture a moral and spiritual vision of what they do, why they do it, under what principles of right and what vision of the good they may conduct their duties. Historically, it is evident that all these have been nurtured and shaped by religious traditions. It is not at all clear that a purely secular vision can guide in the changing circumstances of today.

In the final analysis, these themes are not only a matter of intellectual honesty about their roots, and not only a structural matter as to how they are cultivated in the professional schools and professional organizations, but they become also quite personal and quite collegial. What is the proper vocation of each one of us as we try to be faithful to our deepest convictions, excellent in what we do, responsible family and community members, and as global citizens? And what does it take to cultivate a company of the committed who will assist one another assume the responsibilities that are required by our own inner convictions and our present objective situation? Nothing will suffice but a solid moral and spiritual foundation. The clergy and the theologians of our new world have to do some deeper digging on these issues than has yet been done. A recovery and a recasting of key themes in our moral heritage seem to me to be necessary for tomorrow.

Theology in the Crisis of Humanity

Carver T. Yu

A Heap of Broken Images

In the present age, nihilism is no longer standing at our doorstep, but has pervaded into the very core of our being. We are not merely standing in the midst of spiritual ruin, our very being as the human person is threatened to be in ruin. Almost half a century ago, John Macmurray had already pointed out to us that "the cultural crisis of our time is the crisis of the personal."[1] The crisis has deepened and become much more pervasive, and the far-reaching implications have become much clearer.

Indeed, the twentieth century has seen a series of foundation-shaking deconstruction. The Marxian idea of truth as ideology opened the way. Then came logical positivism claiming to have demolished all metaphysical structures only to discover within three decades that its very foundation on which it launched critical attacks was nothing but quicksand. With the collapse of logical positivism, the pendulum swung from epistemological certainty to epistemological despair. Science then became the target of deconstruction. "Reality" as "discovered" by science was unmasked first as subjective constructions, then as social fabrication. Established values or structures of meaningfulness are reduced to figments either in personal world-making or social construction. Hermeneutics takes up the final round of deconstruction. The science of interpretation has now become a philosophical posture determined to eradicate any hope for objective truth and meaning. The true implication of hermeneutics, as philosophers like Gianni Vattimo put it, is ni-

---

1. John Macmurray, *The Self as Agent* (London: Faber & Faber Ltd., 1957), p. 29.

hilism. It is no wonder that some philosophers would talk about the "nihilistic vocation of hermeneutics."[2]

However, amidst all these, much more fundamental and devastating is the breakdown of the idea of the human person. The classical idea of the self as something with its inner nature, or the Kantian idea of the self as transcendental ego-subject, or the existentialist idea of the self as a momentary being-for-itself with absolute freedom, are all unveiled as illusion. The self, to the postmodern mind, is nothing but a bundle of socially constructed images. To put it more bluntly, the self is a collection of ever-shifting cultural codes. The human mind, which was formerly thought to be an independent entity endowed with the power to unlock the secret of the world, is nothing but a medium through which culturally fabricated images flow. The mind is not a mirror of reality, to use Rorty's imagery. It is merely a mirror that reflects mirrors of mirrors; and those mirrors keep being dashed to pieces only to be remade anew. The self is thus a heap of broken images, which T. S. Eliot long anticipated in *The Waste Land*. With the information age coming upon us like a tidal wave, we begin to see how real is the shattering of the self into a heap of broken images.

What is the condition of the human person in this information age? A portrait of information man was painted for us long before the arrival of the information age. In James Joyce's *Ulysses* we see exactly what an information man looks like in the main character of the novel, Leopold Bloom. According to Edmund Wilson, Joyce's modern Ulysses is a reversal of the classical hero. The Homeric hero is a venturous and strong-willed character, whereas our modern protagonist is passive and will-less. The Homeric hero lives in a world of action, but our modern protagonist lives in an inner world of consciousness. What constitutes the life of our modern Ulysses, instead of events, is merely a continuum of sensations and consciousness. Looking into his consciousness, what do we find there? There are nothing but piles after piles of information. From personal life history to the history of mankind, from astronomy to entomology, from geometry to physics, from physiology to psychology, Leopold Bloom has acquired information so exhaustive as to a comic degree. He knows something about the "cataclysmic annihilation of a planet" through collision with a "black sun"; he has the data about the most economical way of producing 500,000 W.H.P. of electricity; he can even furnish us with his budget for June 16, 1904. In such a piling up of information, the formlessness of his consciousness is evident. There is no magnetic center,

---

2. Cf. Gianni Vattimo, *Beyond Interpretation*, trans. David Webb (Cambridge: Polity Press, 1997), pp. 1-14.

no direction, and no differentiation of values. Everything is neutralized and de-orientated. No one piece of information is more important than the others. His mind does not draw distinction between major and minor matters. Saul Bellow points out what Joyce is trying to portray for us:

> Joyce is psychic junkman of our age, after Freud. For the last of facts may be the first. Thus we know the lining of Bloom's hat, and the contents of his pockets; one knows his genitals and his guts, and we are thoroughly familiar with Molly, too, how she feels before her period, and how she smells. And with so much knowledge, we are close to chaos. . . . *Ulysses* is a comedy of information. Leopold Bloom lies submerged in an ocean of random facts: textbook tags, items of news, bits of history, slogans, clichés. . . . Why is the diversity of data so dazzling and powerful in *Ulysses?* The data are potent because the story itself is negligible. . . . It is the absence of a story which makes Bloom what he is. By injecting him with a purpose, a story would put the world in order. . . . The plan of Bloom's life is planless. . . . The stream of consciousness flows full and wide through the will-less. . . . The truth of the present day is the little Bloom, whose will offers no hindrance to the stream of consciousness. And this stream has no story.[3]

What are absent in Bloom's life are not merely purpose, plan, and will, but also emotion and a sense of gravity for life. Bloom is basically a hollow man, a man with no inwardness.

German sociologist Wolf Dieter-Narr sums up the problem for us most vividly, "The change in behavior long observed by Riesman, Mitscherlich, Weber and many others consists in a destruction of 'inwardness', in a loss of the individual's mechanism for reflection and for the process of experience. . . . Our modern society has become a society of conditioned reflexes, a society where the individual is important only as a bearer of attributes — with reference to this or that attribute but not to what these attributes constitute: the person."[4]

Emptying the self of inwardness, it is inevitable that the self would be reduced to a mechanistic structure. It is therefore no surprise that there is a trend in postmodern psychology to see the human self as a mere bundle of

---

3. Saul Bellow, *Technology and the Frontiers of Knowledge* (New York: Doubleday, 1975), pp. 14-15.

4. Wolf Dieter-Narr, "Toward a Society of Conditioned Reflexes," in *Observation on the Spiritual Situation of the Age,* ed. Jürgen Habermas (Cambridge, MA: MIT Press, 1984), pp. 33, 36.

"desires" (instincts). Gilles Deleuze and Felix Guattari reject the psychoanalytic idea of seeing the self in terms of id, ego, and super-ego. The person is a machine, which is a collection of machines (organs are no more than machines). These machines, with all the necessary couplings and connections, are structured for production, the production of desires. "There is only desire and the social, and nothing else," and "desire production is one and the same thing as social production."[5] To talk about the self, one can only talk meaningfully about energy flow within the system of machines.

The Battle for the Human Person

It is therefore no exaggeration that the most urgent battle call in the present age is one that is for understanding of the human person. If theological anthropology is to make any meaningful contribution at all, it has to make available the spiritual resources of the Christian tradition to help the human person to regain her inwardness and come out from the narcissistic mode of being.

It is true that philosophical or theological anthropology since Descartes has to a large extent taken the human consciousness or human subjectivity as its starting point for developing an understanding of the human person. However, human consciousness and the inwardness of being human are two very different things. In fact, it is precisely in defining the human person in terms of the structure and content of human consciousness that the human self may be reduced to a bundle of sensations mediated through what we call the consciousness, or to a set of epiphenomena of bio-chemical reactions manifested physiologically in the form of consciousness, or a set of socio-cultural codes packaged in personal consciousness. The human self is then rendered into a system of conditioned reflexes, where her capability to experience (not to have experiences floating in her consciousness as content of the consciousness), to reflect, and to create meaning and values out of her inner activities, is negated. Postmodernist philosophers may have demolished the idea of the human person as subject, but they still operate in terms of the human consciousness. In fact, the whole postmodern discourse is grounded on the totalization of subjective consciousness. The human person from the postmodern perspective is consciousness without the subject. But what does

5. Gilles Deleuze and Felix Guattari, *Anti-Oedipus: Capitalism and Schizophrenia*, cited from *From Modernism to Postmodernism — An Anthology*, ed. Lawrence Cahoone (Oxford: Blackwell, 1996), pp. 414-5.

that mean? If we take a closer look at Hume's idea of the "I" as "a bundle of perceptions (or sensations)," we will be able to see what we mean by consciousness without inwardness.

It is well known that Hume renders the "I" as nothing but "a bundle or collection of different perceptions" in his oft-quoted argument:

> For my part, when I enter most intimately into what I call *myself*, I always stumble on some particular perception or other, of heat or cold, light or shade, love or hatred, pain or pleasure. I never can catch *myself* at any time without perception and never can observe anything but the perception. . . . I may venture to affirm of the rest of mankind that they are nothing but a bundle or collection of different perceptions, which succeed each other with an inconceivable rapidity and are in perpetual flux and movement.[6]

However, as soon as we replace the "I" with "a bundle of perceptions" in this very passage, the whole argument would sound rather strange, and a fundamental problem reveals itself. With the substitution, Hume's original argument would sound like this:

> When *the bundle of perceptions* enters most intimately into what it calls *itself, the bundle* always stumbles on some particular perception or other, of heat or cold, light or shade, love or hatred, pain or pleasure. *The bundle* never can catch *itself* at any time without perception and never can observe anything but the perception. . . . *It* may venture to affirm of the rest of mankind that they are nothing but a bundle or collection of different perceptions. . . .

Here, it seems that if Hume's argument is to make sense at all, the bundle, which is mistakenly identified as "I," has to be something more than just a summation of perceptions. The bundle reflects on itself as well as all the perceptions that constitute the very bundle itself. What exactly is this reflective activity? What reality does it point to? If the reflection belongs to the category of perceptions, then what sort of perception is it? If, however, it cannot be categorized as one of the perceptions, then the bundle has within itself something more than mere perceptions. Would it then mean that the "I" is more than just a bundle of perceptions? Right here, the meaningfulness of what we call "inwardness" becomes quite clear.

---

6. David Hume, *A Treatise of Human Nature,* ed. A. D. Lindsay (London: J. M. Dent & Son, 1934), p. 239.

The Responsive and Responsible Self

Where should we start? We have to start from the human presumptuousness that defines modernity. "Know then thyself, presume not God to scan. The proper study of mankind is man." This opening line from Alexander Pope's poem "Of the Nature and State of Man With Respect to Himself, as an Individual" in his *An Essay on Man*[7] reflects the modern ethos very well. It indicates not only a shift from the theological to the anthropological horizon, but also a purely humanistic understanding of the human person. However, this is where it goes wrong. "Know then thyself"? Can the human person ever truly know herself as a pure self? We are here reminded of Samuel Beckett's trilogy, *Molloy, Malone Dies* and *The Unnamable*. It describes a journey of the self in search of itself by peeling off layers of "external" relations, and going into the innermost of the self, hoping to find the pure self. It turns out to be a journey into total disintegration. The pure "I" in solipsistic monologue in *The Unnamable* is a completely dissolved personality speaking chaotic gibberish.

If the modern and postmodern path of understanding the human person is going in the wrong direction, we need to consider Calvin's prophetic insight seriously. Calvin warns us of our possible misunderstanding of ourselves: "it is certain that man never achieves a clear knowledge of himself unless he has first looked upon God's face, and then descends from contemplating Him to scrutinize himself."[8] According to him, any understanding of the human person is determined by the understanding or misunderstanding of God. What we need in philosophical/theological anthropology is something that approximates the Copernican Revolution, turning from anthropocentrism to a deeper form of humanism. The modern and postmodern culture needs to see humanity not as a ground in itself, but as a gift pointing to the reality of a realm much more profound. Any disregard of this "given-ness" is already a distortion of the nature of being human. For Christian theologians, there can be no starting point other than the belief that the human person is made in the image of God. That means the "signature" of God's being is written into the depth of human being. There is no such thing as the "pure self" in the human person, for with the "self," there is always the presence of the Other. It is this Other who gives Himself for the constitution of the human self. The reality of the human self points always to something other than itself.

7. Alexander Pope, "Of the Nature and State of Man with Respect to Himself as an Individual," in *An Essay on Man* (London: Methuen, 1950), Epistle 2.
8. John Calvin, *Institutes of the Christian Religion*, ed. John T. McNeill (Philadelphia: The Westminster Press, 1967), p. 37.

However, to respond to the anthropological misunderstanding, we need to go further. Here John Macmurray and Karl Barth provide insights that can heal the postmodern age of its narcissistic and nihilistic despair.

In his monumental work *The Self as Agent,* John Macmurray lays bare the problem of philosophical anthropology in the western tradition. Philosophical anthropology since the Enlightenment is individualistic and idealistic. The self is perceived as the subject conscious of herself as well as the object given to her thought. Consciousness is the beginning of everything. Self-consciousness is the center and foundation of the consciousness of the world. The self necessarily stands at the center of the world. Starting with consciousness, she is also contemplative, putting cognition, thinking, and knowing as the defining character of her being. Pure thought becomes the ultimate fulfillment of truth in human form. In Macmurray's own words:

> Modern philosophy is characteristically *egocentric.* . . . Firstly, it takes the Self as its starting-point, and not God, or the world or the community; and . . . secondly, the Self is an individual in isolation, an ego or 'I', never a 'thou'. This is shown by the fact that there can arise the question, 'How does the Self know that other selves exist?' Further, the Self so premised is a thinker in search of knowledge. It is presented as the Subject; the correlate in experience of the object presented for cognition.[9]

This is the ontological root of the spiritual crisis in the Western tradition. Macmurray proposes to turn away from the idea of "the self as a subject" to the idea of "the self as an agent," from the idealistic "thinking self" to a more holistic "acting self." In order to be fully human, the whole concept of being has to be changed. To be is to act; and to act is to engage, to respond, and to submit oneself to the objectivity of the other. In acting, the human person thinks. "The Self that reflects and the Self that acts is the same Self. . . ."[10] However, in thinking, the mind alone is active, whereas in action, the whole person, including the mind as well as the body, is active. In action, the self thinks with intention, with her will and emotion; and in action, she interacts with that which is other than herself. Each action is a thinking action in response to reality. She comes to know the world not in the abstraction of thought, but in engagement with demands coming from the reality of the real world in which the other is as real as the acting self. In self-awareness, in transcendental reflection of consciousness, one can in principle do so in isolation without the world and others. Yet, in action, one does not act in a

9. Macmurray, *The Self,* p. 31.
10. Macmurray, *The Self,* p. 86.

vacuum, in isolation. In action, one encounters the other as the irreducible center of will, emotion, and thought. One encounters the world as a stubborn reality that can call all human frameworks into question. Action bears within itself reciprocity, mutuality, and responsibility. In this being as being-in-one-act, one begins to comprehend the human person in its totality. In action, one confronts reaction, which may call one's action into question. One is called to be accountable and engage the other to be accountable at the same time. Such is mutual accountability and thus mutual engagement for unfolding. Reality and truth are revealed in such a dynamic way.

The human person conceived in such a way is at once a responsive and responsible self. The moral dimension enters into the picture in our perception of reality. The world is real in engaging the human person to respond to it, to reckon with the intrinsic structure and characteristics of its being. In responding to the various modalities of being of the world, the self "ek-sists" (exists) out of itself. It comes out of itself to unfold itself in and through the world. In such a way, the whole created realm is recognized to be hetero-centric in communion.

If John Macmurray's idea of the self as agent provides the philosophical pointer for turning away the idealistic narcissistic mode of anthropological thinking, then Karl Barth provides us with the theo-ontological grounding for this alternative perception of the human person. The human person's being in her act has its ontological ground in God's being in His act. Barth is extremely helpful here. The starting point for all theological statements is, according to Barth, "God is."[11] But God is who He is in His act, in His works. God of course is who He is even without His works. Yet, it is in His works, in His action toward human being that He reveals who He is as the One who is in His act.[12] In His act we see the actuality of God. First and foremost, we come to know God as the One who acts to reveal Himself. Without this very act of revealing, nothing "is." This act of revelation turns out to be at once an act of self-giving. God's revelation is not an objective manifestation or demonstration for spectacle. It is an act of creating covenantal reality. Revealing and giving is one and the same thing. This lays the foundation for the unity of the human person's being and knowing. In receiving the knowledge of God, the human person receives not merely an abstract detached knowledge, she receives God in His very act of giving Himself.

In God's act of revealing, we come to encounter the Being of God who

11. Karl Barth, *Church Dogmatics*, I/2, ed. G. W. Bromiley & T. F. Torrance (Edinburgh: T&T Clark, 1957), p. 257.
12. Barth, *Dogmatics*, pp. 260ff.

loves.[13] The very essence of His act is the act of self-giving. The center of God's revelation is the Incarnation. The Incarnation reveals God's unfathomable freedom. He is the subject of His Being, the subject of His act. God is the only Being that is truly a Subject. He is absolutely free, in the sense that when God is characterized as the Lord, He is first and foremost the Lord of His own living and loving.[14] He Himself is the ground and reason for His love. As He loves, and loves in the way of giving Himself totally, unconditionally, in Jesus Christ, He manifests His sovereignty. It is in the act of love manifested in the Incarnation that the full reality of God's sovereignty is revealed. So God's freedom is freedom in love, it is a freedom of giving up oneself. This is true self-determination. When one touches God's freedom, one touches the absoluteness of God, the transcendence of God in action.

His freedom to love takes a definite form of manifestation — the freedom in covenant. He bounds Himself to covenantal love, which is a responsive love. This love invites response and reciprocity. Love that is genuine does not monopolize the privilege of loving. It imparts a freedom to love in the covenantal partner.

God's act of revealing Himself, giving Himself, in short, His act in covenantal love defines the covenantal partners He creates for Himself. The human person is also one who shares these capabilities of self-revealing, self-giving, and bearing covenantal responsibilities. The human person is one who has the freedom to love.

Such a theological anthropology is no mere theoretical formulation. It calls for the discipline of life. Human reason has to be reoriented to acknowledging the absoluteness and the mystery of the other person under whom and above whom is the absolute Other. It also calls for the reshaping of human emotion. Human emotion has a clear directive, the directive of love. Truth also means truthfulness to the other. Theology can no longer be a mere academic exercise. It is an act of perceiving and proclaiming the truth of God in and through the total being of the one who does theology. Theology is therefore a spiritual discipline involving the heart, the mind, and even the body.

Possible Contributions from the Chinese Tradition

The battle for the human person has to be fought with all possible cultural resources available. Writing from a Chinese perspective, I believe that the Chi-

13. Barth, *Dogmatics*, pp. 272ff.
14. Barth, *Dogmatics*, p. 301.

nese spiritual tradition can have something significant to contribute in restoring the inwardness of the human person.

The Christian anthropological orientation that we have expounded above finds resonance with the Chinese humanistic tradition. Both the Christian and the Chinese tradition have a common language, the language for life-transforming truth, which is also a language for authentic humanity. For the Christian, the more we understand man, the more shall we grasp the heart of God. At the same time, to understand truth and to live out the truth in one's humanity is one and the same thing. In the Chinese tradition, man has a unique position, but never at the center of Reality. He is at once a partner and an expressive mode for the manifestation of Tao. "Participating in the transforming and nurturing process of Heaven and Earth" and "being in unity with Heaven and Earth" is one and the same thing as a central theme in the Confucian tradition.[15] Therefore, learning of the highest order is the learning for the fulfillment of humanity. As Yang Hung (one of the most influential philosophers in the Han Dynasty, 53 B.C.–18 A.D.) put it, the learning for the refinement of humanity is way above the learning to transform matters into gold.[16] Any genuine pursuit of knowledge should lead ultimately to the fulfillment of humanity as an unadulterated manifestation of Heaven and Earth. Or as the Christian sees it, all theological understandings lead to authentic humanity as the manifestation of the Divine Logos.

In the Chinese tradition, to be in unity with Heaven and Earth, man has to be fully authentic in being human, to develop his own nature fully.[17] To Mencius (372-289 B.C.), the "fulfillment of the heart of humanity" is the beginning of all understanding. "When one strives to fulfill, one knows the nature of humanity; when one knows the nature of humanity, one knows heaven. Thus cultivation of the heart of humanity is the fundamental."

In all philosophical reflections or quests for truth, the Confucian tradition concentrates on the cultivation of authentic humanity or self-knowledge. Such concentration on humanity in general and the self in particular aims precisely at exploding anthropocentrism. The Confucian masters are all too aware of the peril of the human heart being carried away by egoism

---

15. *The Doctrine of the Mean*, #22. "Only he who possesses absolute sincerity can give full development to his nature. He who is able to give full development to his own nature can give development to the nature of other men . . . he who can give full development to the nature of all beings can assist the transforming and nourishing powers of Heaven and Earth . . . he may with Heaven and Earth form a triad." Cf. *Sources of Chinese Tradition*, ed. Wm. Theodore de Bary (New York: Columbia University Press, 1960), pp. 134-5.

16. Yang Hung, "The Chapter on Knowing and Being," *Fayan*.

17. Hung, "Knowing and Being."

or desires prompted by fleeting external distractions. However, to avoid this, one has to dwell deep in the self's identity. In so doing, one begins to see the unity of the self with Heaven-and-earth and all things.[18] According to Chu Hsi (1130-1200 A.D.), quoting Master Shao Yung, "Man's nature is the concrete embodiment of the Way."[19] And that is why the *Doctrine of the Mean* would say, "to follow human nature is called the Way."[20] To grasp the Way of Heaven and Earth, the key is in grasping human nature. One concentrates on the self not to indulge in it, but through it one may hear the Way, for humanity is the "language" through which the Way speaks most clearly. One concentrates on the self in order to transcend it.

At the same time, the self is a great gift from Heaven and Earth. One has to recognize its givenness, and take it with a sense of gratitude and reverence *(Ching)*. *Ching* is a posture of taking Heaven and Earth with utmost seriousness. With that, one cannot but safeguard the integrity of humanity with a sense of gravity. Striving to preserve one's integrity and authenticity is the most fundamental attitude to life, undistracted by any anxiousness to prove oneself to be worthy. This attitude is called *Cheng*.[21] Yet, in striving to maintain one's true authenticity, one has to empty oneself of *self-centeredness* and desires due to "the distracting and disintegrating effect of uncontrolled exposure to external influences and sense-knowledge."[22] Only then can the self be filled with the "mind" of Heaven-and-Earth. "The mind that is empty can contain all principles," whereas a mind that is filled with external "impressions" has no room for true learning.[23] Thus "emptying" is a fundamental exercise in life. Such "emptying" leads to "having no mind." It is in such a state of being that the Will of Heaven-and-Earth is fully manifested in the self. *Self-concentration is the way to self-transcendence.* This is an antidote to the postmodern narcissistic disintegration of the self.

18. Wm. Theodore de Bary, "Neo-Confucian Cultivation and Enlightenment," *The Unfolding of Neo-Confucianism,* ed. Wm. Theodore de Bary (New York: Columbia University Press, 1975), pp. 173-6.

19. Chu Hsi, *Chin-ssu Lu,* #47, translation from Wing-Tsit Chan, *A Source Book in Chinese Philosophy* (Princeton: Princeton University Press, 1963), p. 617.

20. Chan, *Chinese Philosophy,* p. 620.

21. According to Ch'eng I, the student of truth "should hold fast to the mind with reverence. He should not be anxious. Instead he should nourish and cultivate it deeply and earnestly, and immerse himself [in the Way]. Only then can he have a sense of fulfillment and be at ease with himself. If one seeks anxiously, that is merely selfishness . . . ," cited from de Bary, *Chinese Tradition,* p. 168.

22. De Bary, *Chinese Tradition,* p. 167.

23. *Ming-Ju Hsueh An,* II, 7/10, cited from de Bary, *Chinese Tradition,* p. 186. Also refer to *Chin-ssu Lu,* 4/2a.

*   *   *

After three centuries of critical pursuit for fear of being marginalized by the Enlightenment, theology needs to recover the long forgotten practice of "emptiness, unity of knowing and being, quietude" in the Christian tradition. The Chinese tradition can be a wellspring of resources for Christian theologians to draw from. At the same time, both the Chinese and the Christian traditions should work together to respond to the loss of inwardness of the present age. Chinese theologians are well situated to make available those resources for a new direction in theological reflection worldwide.

Serving God in a Time
When a World-view Collapses:
The Pastor-Theologian at the Beginning
of the Third Millennium

Michael Welker

The office of the pastor has always been, and will continue to be, a difficult one. Pastors are expected to proclaim the word of God, the presence of Jesus Christ. They have to witness to the creative power of God, to the pouring of the Holy Spirit. They are to announce the coming reign of God, and they have to promise the forgiveness of sins. Any one of these is a task beyond the capacities of a human person.

Karl Barth's description of the dilemma the pastoral ministry faces is to the point: "As ministers we ought to speak of God. We are human, however, and so cannot speak of God. We ought therefore to recognize both *our obligation and our inability* and by that recognition give God the glory."[1]

To have to speak of God — and yet not to be able to do so: this is possibly still worse in times like ours which put an enormous trust in professional skills and grant credit only after having tested the competence of the person in office on a regular basis. In recent decades the loss of much of the aura of the pastoral office has intensified the difficulties and greatly increased the burden of the ministerial task. In many parts of the world, at least in the Protestant churches, the second half of the twentieth century brought a change in the common attitude toward the pastoral office. What had happened?

This contribution proposes that a complex change in the world-view is to a high degree responsible for this shift. We are witnessing the slow collapse

---

1. Karl Barth, "The Word of God and the Task of the Ministry," in *The Word of God and the Word of Man,* trans. Douglas Horton (1928; 1957; reprint Gloucester: Peter Smith, 1978), pp. 183-217; 186.

of an old and the emergence of a new world-view, which theology (both in the church and in the academy) has not yet fully diagnosed, but has described in misleading ways. "Breakup of tradition," "growing individualization," and "from unity to plurality" are formulas often applied to this change. This loss of the old world-view has meant that teaching and preaching in the church have indeed lost a complex basis, be it in terms of the worldly "foundations" they used to trust, be it in terms of the images of "reality" they used to oppose. Instead of concentrating on the main task of the pastor — namely to take up the challenge presented by the word and the Spirit of God — they were absorbed in fighting the change in the world-view. The following contribution will examine the misleading formulas and will try to show in what way they will have to be revised or at least qualified in order to avoid the traumatizing disturbance of the real pastoral and ministerial task.

Do We Suffer Only from "a Break in Tradition"?
How the "New World" of the Media Supplants
"Cultural Memory" and Religion Based on It

One of the often repeated diagnoses for the change in world-view is the following. The classical main-line churches of the Western industrialized nations, their theologies and their church life are in a crisis, because our cultures have experienced a "break in tradition." This diagnosis, however, actually veils the problems. In our cultures we experience breaks in tradition all the time. The post-war years, decolonization, the sixties, the Vietnam war, the oil crisis, the end of the cold war, the break-down of Marxist-Leninist socialism, September 11, 2001 — we have experienced the break of tradition in numerous complex events in the past years. Sometimes the break is accompanied by laments, sometimes by hopes for a better world. Breaks in tradition as such are a recurrent phenomenon in the world of the twentieth century and of our days. The diagnosis aims at something else, but does not name it. It aims at the problem that *in the past decades a radically transformed attitude towards the world has developed.*

This new attitude towards the world arises in tandem with the spread of the electronic media, especially in connection with the rapid and global spread of television and the internet. Attendant on this worldwide spread of television and of the internet is a *fundamental twofold devaluation of "cultural memory,"* of the hierarchy of the classics, of what is canonical, and of the idea that historical memory can provide orientation in contemporary crises. The first devaluation of cultural memory is connected with the fact that the new media are bringing the huge inflation of a river of data that constantly demands our attention. *The concentration required to grasp the world of today and of the proximate future is increasing enormously. The "inhabiting" of the past and the shared "bringing to life" of the past are diminishing drastically.* The individual and the shared activity of remembering and reconstructing the past, of citing traditional texts, and of working on a formative continuum are being replaced by another type of "world formation" and "self-formation." The formula "detemporalization of the world and spatialization of the world" has been used in an attempt to grasp this process.[2] The extremely intensified and exhaustive collective attention to the present and the proximate future is suppressing the cultivation of "cultural memory." A continuous stimulation and excitement go hand in hand with the requisite attention to the present and the proximate future. This stimulation masks the fact that *the suppression of shared remembrance and of cultural memory leads to a "cooling off" of human life together.* The Heidelberg Egyptologist Jan Assmann has further developed insights of Claude Lévi-Strauss and distinguished between "'hot' and 'cold' memory."[3] "Cold memories" remove what is unique and extraordinary from past events. They remove the history-shaping power from events, and from the society that both is affected by these events and attributes these events to itself. Or they do not even allow this power to be developed. History from the perspective of "cold memory" is no longer "inhabited." It no longer is a shared realm of experience amenable to ongoing formation. The media abound in stimulations for "cold" memory, since they are continually offering past events and interconnected sets of events to our attention. The abundance of memories, the way in which they are presented, and the dominance of attention to today and tomorrow are responsible for a continual cooling off of remembrance, indeed for a continual expulsion from "inhabited" history.

The second devaluation of cultural memory intensifies and accelerates the first, and is in turn intensified by the first devaluation. *The media's presentation of the world calls any naive view of the "unity of history" and the "unity of the lifeworld" radically into question.* Previously it was the preserve of science and art to call these cultural "self-evident assumptions" into question. Now so-called common sense also does so. The otherness, indeed the foreignness of forms of life, of holistic conceptions, and of appeals to tradition in other regions of the world, becomes strikingly clear on a daily basis. Wonder is becoming routine. We are becoming familiar with the experiences of foreign-

2. David Harvey, *The Condition of Postmodernity* (Cambridge: Blackwell, 1990).

3. Jan Assmann, *Das kulturelle Gedächtnis* (Munich: Beck, 1999); Claude Lévi-Strauss, *Das wilde Denken* (Frankfurt: Suhrkamp, 1970), p. 270.

ness, with lifeworlds that we ourselves cannot inhabit. The knowledge of the particular values and good impulses that emanate from foreign traditions and lifeworlds leads not only to the enrichment of one's own lifeworld, but also to broken and distanced attitudes towards one's own lifeworld. These effects are heightened by mass tourism.

The way in which the media sensitize us to foreign lifeworlds and traditions transforms not only our relation to the world as a whole, but also leads to human beings becoming sensitive to differences of lifeworlds and of ways of connecting to tradition within their own culture. In the midst of what seems to be familiar, that which is foreign becomes evident. The distance to "foreigners" can diminish, while the distance to some relatives, neighbors, and members of one's "own people" can increase. This differentiated and complicated view of the world requires a new orientation. It no longer seems advisable to let one's own tradition and one's own "classics" exercise a monopoly in providing orientation. The situation seems to call for uncertainty, experiments with one's identity, caution in making commitments, and in any case a rejection of overly strong attachments to every form of "cultural heritage." If memory is to be cultivated at all, then let it be as "cold" as possible!

This attitudinal change has repercussions for many other apparently self-evident cultural assumptions. And all of them affect religion deeply. The cultural evaluation of the relation between old and young is changing. The complex world with its rapidly changing "today and tomorrow" no longer requires primarily "life experience" and the calm, sober wisdom of maturity. It requires the ability to pick things up quickly and nimbly; it requires an intelligence capable of change and adaptation. The "old world" is relegated to specialists and museums. The real world belongs to youth!

But the concept of educational formation is also changing. *The educational ideal is shifting from the acquisition and cultivation of ordered knowledge to a skillful selectivity that is adequate to the situation and function in question.* The laptop with internet access seems to make it superfluous to have one's own familiar collection of books, and indeed for there to be libraries at all. When kindergarten and school — at least in Germany — expect children to memorize something, the requirement acquires a bad reputation as burdensome. Indeed it almost attains the level of bodily injury.[4] Flexibility of attention must not be disturbed by tying memory down.

The worldwide spread of the electronic media is transforming views of

---

4. For the American situation, see Allan Bloom, *The Closing of the American Mind* (New York: Simon and Schuster, 1988).

the world and perceptions of reality. These transformations go hand in hand with a worldwide intensification and acceleration in the transport of both freight and persons. The world's conversion to automobiles and paved roads, the intensifications of maritime shipping and of rail transport, but especially the explosive development of air travel run parallel to the development of the electronic media. The two developments are mutually reinforcing. Both lead to an acceleration, intensification, and globalization of economic developments. *The economy and the media appear as the leading factors in shaping the world and reality.*

The global spread of the electronic communications media and of the transportation system goes hand in hand with a triumphalistic development of new consumer technologies. New consumer technologies intensify the flow of economic communication, and at the same time increase the need for new economic goods. As economic communication intensifies, so does electronic communication, which in turn increases the need for new technologies and economic goods. *The political system, the education system, and the family must adjust themselves accordingly. Where they — with law and religion — oppose the dynamic of the market, they are put hopelessly on the defensive. A litany of laments has accompanied consumerism, the routinization of both parents working outside the home, and the attendant stress on families, the school system, and the health care system — all developments that would lead to the destruction of the nuclear family and to the functionalization of the education system.* Religion and churches, which had specialized in the stabilization of the nuclear family, its sexual morals, and its role structures, had depended on the support of the classical education system and tried helplessly to catch up with these developments. With each acceleration of the circulatory system of economy-technology-media, religion and churches — always a day late — lost influence and the possibilities to play a formative role in the development.

The global circulatory system of technology-economy-media is changing the world-view of individual human beings, along with their attention, their memory and their expectation, and their evaluation of tradition, age, and education. *This global circulatory system has also changed the fixed orientation of individuals and of societal subsystems towards the nation-state and towards politics.* Religion and churches, politics, and society have not only been required to experience the enormous weakening of historical orientation and of "hot" memory, but they have also lost the standardizing modern individualism important for the Protestant understanding of faith and freedom. And they finally lost the dual or dualistic world-view that had long been cultivated in phrases such as "church and state" or "church and society."

Do We Suffer Only from "Individualization"?
Why Western Cultures Look for Their Heroes and
Heroines in Competitive Sports and in Entertainment Music

The claim that the crisis of Christianity can be traced back to the "break in tradition" is superficial. The other frequently repeated statement that "individualization" initiated the crisis, is plainly deceptive. Most people connect or even identify "individualization" and "the development of personality." They think: if what the churches, theology, and the augurs of the spirit of the age claim is true, namely that individualization, read: the development of the personality, is connected to the break in tradition, then tradition has lost. (This seems a further reason for the relativization of history and cultural memory.)

Such an attitude is supported by a number of developments that hardly anybody would want to deny. In Western industrialized nations, we have experienced *an enormous explosion in education and the sciences* in connection with technological, economic, and media developments. This brought with it great possibilities for the *development of the individuality* which could be considered among the positive aspects of the growth of personality. This is true of the *emancipation of women,* particularly by their entrance into the complete education system, of the changes in the role behavior in the family, and of some changes in the sexual morals in the past decades. However, those who criticize "the individualization" aim at something different.

The formula "the break in tradition and individualization" is not really concerned with the development of personality, but rather it complains about the *systematic isolation of individuals. It laments the individualization and the loss of "connectivity."*[5] The lament is that in our contemporary Western industrialized nations life's powers of connectivity — bound to justice, caring, and truth — are being weakened, that the social loyalties and solidarity are being dissolved. The lament that human beings are becoming incapable or unwilling to enter into long-range obligations and commitments and that it is becoming increasingly unlikely that one can depend in an enduring way on such obligations and commitments, has many — far too many — empirical confirmations. The contemporary crises of religious communities and churches, of parties, unions, and many kinds of clubs, and above all the dissolution of the classical familial forms, confront us daily with the fact that we are in a problematic cultural situation. For many years now, politics, ecclesiastical and secular social services, cultural analysis, sociology, and psychology

---

5. Cf. Jan Assmann, *Maʿat. Gerechtigkeit und Unsterblichkeit im Alten Ägypten* (Munich: C. H. Beck, 1990), esp. pp. 283ff.

have used catch phrases like "breakdown of solidarity," "the autistic society," "from social state to social market," and "amusing ourselves to death" to issue warnings about the destructive consequences of this development.

But are the claims correct that people in the Western industrialized nations have lost all "connectivity," that they are on their way to becoming a horde of couch potatoes, web idiots, cyber sex freaks or bizarre, shrill, erratic types who seclude themselves more and more from the processes of communication of real life? These claims blur the search for new forms of connectivity and prevent their critical valuation.

Why is it that the electronic media in their connection with competitive sports and entertainment music get so much resonance? Why do sports and music take up so much social space alongside the picturing of "the world" in the news and commentaries, alongside the ever new stories of virtual families and outbursts of violence? The success of these forms teaches us something about the search of our cultures for "connectivity" and about the search for a picture of the human being *(Menschenbild)* that is generally convincing.

The new cultural fixation of individuals on the present and the near future as well as the constant cooling down of memory can be successful only if there is a continuous agitating of attention, a constant distraction. In their connection with competitive sports and electronic entertainment music, the media have found ways to guarantee this endless flux that accumulates attention and stimulates distraction. Countless ads connect media, market, and the persons and icons of sports and music. The connection of media with competitive sports and entertainment music appeals to the emotions and allows for many short-term connectivities and fleeting demarcations. With others I can admire some athletes, while I differentiate myself from them by my preference for different songs. But my musical tastes link me to still other people. A vast network of emotionally charged communalities and differences is thus easily built up and as easily altered.

It is still quite unclear what the inflation of electronic and globalized entertainment music means for mentalities, and, more specifically, for the cultural and ecclesial memory. Again and again we are assured that *sports are the backbone of our culture, since they concentrate people on fairness, justice, achievement, individual effort, etc.* This is quite correct. At the same time, however, *sports bring to bear in a society a Nietzschean ethos, an "olympic ethos,"*[6] which situates youth, the fit body, and competition within a knock-

6. Wolfgang Huber, *Die tägliche Gewalt. Gegen den Ausverkauf der Menschenwürde* (Freiburg: Herder, 1993); also W. Huber, "Den Menschen entdecken. Zukunftsaufgaben der Diakonie," in *Brennpunkt Diakonie: Festschrift für Rudolf Weth,* ed. M. Welker (Neukirchen-

out system, that is, an absolute will to succeed. Competitive sports, by pushing these demands into people's consciousness and unconsciousness, thus lend a hand in the brutalization of the ethos.

But why do competitive sports and electronic entertainment music gain such an enormous cultural influence? The observation is certainly correct that the media feed the need for the constant agitation of emotion without great demands of interpretation. Today people have access to a wild variety of entertainment, without having to leave their homes, without having to enter a real public, and without much effort. This possibly has a drug-like influence on many. But why? Why exactly these forms? Why exactly these heroines and heroes?

Competitive sports and entertainment music combine the universally possible identification with human actions and forms of expression with radical singularity, absolute individuality. Thus they seem to provide for an integration which is of top-most importance for people, namely *the connection of the radical uniqueness and the universal meaning of the individual.* In modern thought, basic concepts such as person, subject, individual, and the I also connect both aspects: "The I" is this singular human existence, but at the same time "the I" is a representative of the species. But there is an important difference between what the media offer as connectivity and the concept modern thought developed. The modern ideal of personality and education asked how people in their autonomy and their freedom could best express and realize what is general to the human species. In the suppression or at least control of the sensual inclinations the autonomous person grew as a rational and moral being. This need for an "elevation" of the person to a general reasonable and moral being has entered a deep crisis in the changes of the worldview described above.

Current culture searches for increased integration, for connectivity, but in a new way. The ideal is no longer the modern dream of a universally adapted rational and moral identity. Today's culture is obviously interested in *how people can express their radical singularity in a way that can be grasped universally.* At rock bottom, radical individuality seems to be situated in bodily existence and in the individual emotions. Body and emotions seem to provide the basis for what is "authentic." *Competitive sports and entertainment music are forms in which bodily existence and emotions can be grasped*

Vluyn: Neukirchener, 1997), pp. 39-47; and Hermann Barth, "Die Würde des Menschen kennt keine Einschränkungen. Wider den Götzendienst am Starken und Leistungsfähigen," in *Brennpunkt Diakonie: Festschrift für Rudolf Weth,* ed. M. Welker (Neukirchen-Vluyn: Neukirchener, 1997), pp. 65-82.

universally. The persons who successfully present themselves in these forms today offer models in the search for the ideal of humanity.

The countless talk shows in which people publicly open up their intimate lives as if they stood before God demonstrate that the publication of one's own body and emotions marks the area where current culture is directing its search for genuine human life. This diagnosis is supported by the fact that — considering what magazines, movies, and TV offer — there is an unbroken progress of Western societies in becoming more shameless. To be sure, ever more graphic depictions of sex and also the latent or open glorification of violence are means for the media to fight becoming stale. With ever cruder appeals and ever shriller stimulations the impression is countered that the media is only an apparatus which offers "second-hand life." In fact, the media is shaping our existence. The enormous attention on a world-wide level paid to media developments backs the judgment that here we can see a deeper human search for life which should be taken seriously. It is a matter of the human ideal, the depiction of the person, of her or his ennoblement that is at issue.

Why the Church Is No Longer Seen as the "Second Sovereign Power beside the State," and Why the "Aura of the Pastoral Office" Seems to Fade Away

Up to the time after the Second World War, the Western industrialized nations kept up what could be termed a Hegelian world-view. One's own history is the center (or at least one center) *of history. The state* is the highest secular instance of integration and dominance in the public sphere. To be sure, this was only a world-view. The arts had long known better. Sensitive scientists knew better. And the economy knew better. Really a proper biblically-oriented Christian theology should have known better, namely that this is only one form among others of the construction of the social world. It is a problematic one because it kept up an endless chain of wars. But the place the Church gave itself and which also was assigned to it was as the second sovereign power beside the state. "The church was understood to be a sovereign power analogous to the state and allied to the state in a partnership, a societal macro-institution" (Wolfgang Huber). *The presentation of the public sphere in terms of duals (church and state, church and society) was taken as a reality.* This construction may have helped moral renewal after fascism and after the derangement of the "family of peoples" in the world wars. Dense resonances for the church corresponded to this self-presentation and understanding of the church. The pastor's office profited from this situation. In smaller places the pastor held a position immediately after the Lord God and the Lord Mayor. There is no doubt that in the cities he belonged to the elite. He stood apart from the rest of the society: he wore a dark suit and had a slightly set off and renouncing smile. *In the pastor the aura of the "office" was visible and perceivable.* This aura was cultivated and strengthened week by week when the pastor entered the church — which, as a rule, was well attended — to serve God's word.

But it was not only the public power of "the Church" that provided the pastor's office with resonance. The aura of the office was also strengthened by the education the pastor had, by his personality, and his manner of living. The pastor knew about the depth of things. He had a way to grasp abstract and basic concepts: dignity and morals, the essence of the human being, the good and the true, and certainly faith and sin. Hardly anyone among the members of the bourgeois society would have publicly declared dignity to be a problematic concept, truth to be a chimera, and sin to be the invention of hypocrites. Nietzsche did not yet enjoy academia's consent, and the declared atheists who held a public office were known. The position of Christian religiosity and the churches was reinforced by the "Cold War" and the ideological opposition of Marxism-Leninism to capitalism. The "poor brethren and sisters in the zone occupied by the Soviets," as they were then called in West Germany, were more or less handed over to "the atheists" without protection.

The spiritual official owed his public respect not only to the fact that it was acknowledged that he knew about the abstract concepts and their spiritual foundations. Even the competence he had in the "old languages" (Hebrew, Greek, and Latin) was respected without fail although the public could only vaguely imagine its benefits. In the same way that most of the children stood up in trams to make room for the elderly, most of the parents would show reverence for the knowledge of the old languages, the old cultures, and traditional values. But not only did the aura of public resonance and classical education surround the pastor and his office. Also the vicarage was considered a protecting sphere where an exemplary family life and an exemplary married life were assumed to exist. The grace of the pastor's daughters and the easy education of his sons were proverbial. In those times the pastor's office seemed to offer a proof of the verse in the Bible that "all things work together for good for those who love God . . ." (Rom. 8:28). *A pre-pluralistic view of reality, structured by dualizing political mega-ideologies and not yet shaken by the electronic media and consumerism, was the basis for an effective and radiant interplay of tradition, classical education, the setting of moral standards in family life, and an impressive religiosity.*

In the past decades the aura surrounding the person and the office of the pastor in the Church service, in his/her public standing, and personal life has at least been diminished. As can be expected, this did not just happen from the outside. The pastors themselves got rid of their black suits and their renouncing smile. Confronted with the loss of the aura many sought refuge by engaging themselves in social agendas or in attempts to become knowledgeable in the variety of cultural innovations. Others turned to metaphysical and mystical forms of abstraction. Still others adopted a rhetoric of "Perhaps it is yet worth it" or "And yet. . . ." The defensive attitude in the face of a public that appeared more and more diffuse and had forever more disparate demands could frequently be observed.

Many pastors faced conflicting expectations in their congregations. Some now found the pastors far too human, others regarded them as still displaying their office's authority too much; some thought them too progressive, others too traditional; for some, they were too active in social concerns, for others, they were too much oriented on piety and liturgy. *The inflation of demands, and the conflicts between the expectations, rushed upon the office once the aura that had belonged to it was diminished or even eliminated.* To be sure, most of the pastors found their own way, their own form, style, and tone. But the awareness that a part of the congregation was "frustrated away" or could not be attracted into a vital faith life so that one had to live with a more or less small "clientele" has been distressing. Of course even in the time of the intact "aura of the office" not everything the parson did suited everybody. But there is a world of difference between the calm or slightly self-critical consciousness that what one does does not suit everybody, and the haunted consciousness that it really suits hardly anybody at all.

So, the complex interrelation between the nation state and the church has dominated much of the modern ministry. However, in many respects matters were different in countries without national churches.[7] During the eighteenth and nineteenth centuries in the United States, for instance, missions and immigrations from nations with State Churches, like the Methodist missionaries from the United Kingdom, German Protestants settling in the nation's heartlands, groups representing the so-called peace churches, found themselves in a radically different social environment. In this context churches organized themselves less on the model of the state and more in terms of civil associations.[8] This is to say, churches came to understand them-

---

7. I owe the following insights to conversations and cooperation with William Schweiker.

8. On this, see H. Richard Niebuhr, *The Kingdom of God in America* (Middletown, CN: Wesleyan University Press, 1988); James Luther Adams, *Voluntary Associations: Socio-Cultural Analysis and Theological Interpretation*, ed. J. Ronald Engel (Chicago: Exploration Press, 1986).

selves as voluntary associations and in the process developed the uniquely American phenomenon of "denominations."

This development placed specific pressures on the churches. On the one hand, it meant that each religious community was competing for membership, a competition that was often carried into the expansion of the Western frontier. Pastors had to be not only community organizers and bearers of tradition, but also missionaries and managers. This managerial self-understanding is currently seen in the demands for "church-growth." But, second, the existence of the churches as part of civil society meant there was a constant need to show the contribution of the community to the project of the nation. In this sense, the political force on the churches in terms of loyalty was often more extreme, but also more subtle, than in classical European churches. As the current debate in the U.S.A. about church and society shows, churches constantly worry about their social or public role. This has given rise not only to conflicts about the exact meaning of the non-establishment clause of the Constitution, but also to the development of "public theology."

Of course, all of these developments and the pressures they put on the churches had profound impacts on theology. *While European churches and theologians often worried about the threat of the political power and its claims to loyalty, in nations without an official State Church the socio-political problem centers on questions of diversity and moral relativism.* Because of this, pastors often became not simply managers but also the stewards of public morality and voices of understanding and mediation between diverse and often conflicting ethnic and racial groups. The social function of the churches was helping to preserve the peace of the civil order. This led to the search for "great ideas" at a level of abstraction that all could accept. Indeed, Walter Rauschenbusch and other Social Gospel theologians could speak of "Christianizing the social order." This meant, simply, the social embodiment of Christian "ideals." Yet these "ideals" were all too often indistinguishable from the purposes of democratic polity. Indeed, if the struggle for "justice" or "solidarity" or "health" becomes the message and mission of the church, who would not agree? These abstractions, these great concepts, provide the way to manage cultural, ethnic, and racial differences at the level of civil society. *Thus the search for great concepts in these churches contributed to the loss of their distinctive voice. With that loss the churches, like too many European churches, were in fact subsumed into the social and political agenda of the nation state.*

It would be too simple to ascribe the loss of the aura of the pastor's office only to the fact that the church is no longer seen as the second sovereign power beside the state or that the church can not keep a distinctive voice.

Along with the change of the world-view through the circulation of power of the media, technology and economy, beliefs about person and personality, as well as the notions of education in the sense of "paideia" *(Bildung)*, changed radically. How could Christianity in its theologies, its "paideia," its religious communication inside and outside of the churches respond to this challenge?

The Pastor-Theologian at the Beginning of the Third Millennium

It belongs to the many good insights and initiatives of Wallace Alston's to state publicly that the crisis of the churches in Western industrial societies is — not only but to a high degree — a theological crisis, and that consequences must be drawn. When theology loses its power to diagnose the current situation, when it looks for support from philosophers and theorists who themselves are helpless before the complexity of the contemporary situation, it is indeed bad enough. But the real trouble and agony of theology set in when its helpless wrestling with an inadequate world-view becomes confused and identified with the theological challenge presented by the word and the Spirit of God. When the wrestling with God's calling becomes confused with the wrestling with an outdated and fading world-view or with an unclear and seemingly threatening new world-view, or is even replaced by it, then theology is in deep trouble.

In this situation it is important to identify the structural and conceptual difficulties which led to the impression that classical theology was very well equipped to deal with monistic, dual, and dualistic world-views, but was not able to deal with structured pluralistic settings. Only a vague "plurality" (of persons, settings, contexts, mind-sets, and institutions) could then be conceived, which was to be integrated by conservative or liberal figures of thought. In dealing with such pluralities which operate like markets and are constantly changing, the media simply did much better than the academy and the church. Although certainly each and every teacher and pastor always has to do with a "plurality" of individuals and groups, the theological challenge is much more compelling — and promising. Starting from the community constituted by the pouring of the Holy Spirit with a specific constellation of gifts, and the church as the "body of Christ" with a specific constellation of members, through the biblical canon with a specific constellation of witnessing voices to the ecumene with a specific constellation of confessions and church-movements, theology has to face forms of spiritual life and orientation with a complex pluralistic structure. A structured complex, not a chaotic and relativistic ensemble, has to become focused. The same holds true for societal pluralism, rightly understood.[9]

To learn to decode these structured pluralistic forms, and to understand their inner dynamics seems crucial if we want to become familiar with the emergent new world-view which is polycontextual and polycentric. Above all, it is crucial to notice that theologians are not at a loss in this situation, because their very content of faith is simply not totally bound to monistic and dualized or dualistic world-views. To be sure, in the biblical traditions and in the dogmatic and religious-philosophical heritage there are many monistic and dual or dualistic forms of thought and orientation. But, as indicated, the biblical canon, the law traditions, and certainly most notions of the Holy Spirit, the notion of the body of Christ, the very texture of creation, and many other basic contents of faith exhibit a rich and pluralistically textured structure. Likewise, the trinitarian understanding of God (if not reduced to binitarian dualism or vague sociability) challenges and explodes conventional modes of understanding and discourse.

An analogous observation can be made on the level of anthropology. A long and influential philosophical and theological tradition feasted on the Cartesian concept of personhood and, when it turned religious, on an intimate relation to its "inner other" which it called "faith." This notion confused the typically modern "subjectivization" (with its standardized notion of reasonable and moral personhood "which all of us are," with its claim that we are all equal and near to our God), and the post-modern unique individual who tries to cultivate and live out his/her singular emotional-bodily existence. An escape from the highly reductionistic anthropology provided by the typically liberal modern mindset and an avoidance of the opposite danger of the illusionary postmodern self of "unlimited possibilities" and a "longing for ultimate fulfillment" (achieved by reaching the narcissistic peek) are equally important if theology is to witness the sustaining, rescuing, and ennobling God as the ground of human personhood. Thus in anthropology, too, the pastor theologian is directed back to the triune God, who is "a complex God" (Mark Heim), in order to discover in this light, what God in his divine glory has provided for us.

This is no easy task. Quite to the contrary. It is a most complicated, even an impossible task to speak of God and God's intention with his creatures when we know that we are humans and will never in this life be equipped to rise to this challenge. However, when despite this knowledge the pastor ap-

---

9. Cf. Michael Welker, *Christianity and Structured Pluralism* (Valparaiso, 2004); *Kirche im Pluralismus* (Gütersloh: Chr. Kaiser, 2000).

plies himself/herself to this task and really wrestles with God and God's word and guidance, without dismissing the task of critically evaluating coming and going world-views, serious attention, respect, and support will sooner or later be regained. To this end it is necessary to differentiate between the absolutely minor (though necessary!) task, namely to come to grips with past and present world-views, their emergence and their decay, and the primary task of the pastor-theologian to take up the challenge of God's word.

II Dialogue with the Sciences and the Humanities

A Scientist Looks at Theological Inquiry

John Polkinghorne

The central religious question is the question of truth. Religion can encourage one in life and support one at the approach of death, but it cannot validly do either of these things unless it is actually true. As an unrepentant critical realist[1] in this age of postmodernism, I reject any instrumental notion of religion as being merely a technique for living, or any relativistic notion of its being simply the chosen cultural practice of a particular community. Having thus nailed my epistemological colors to the mast, I must nevertheless acknowledge that religious belief that was without visible consequences for individual life and for communal responsibility, would be open to serious question. I must also agree that theology (the intellectual reflection upon religion) is inevitably affected by, and can benefit from, the cultural windows that are open at any particular period of history. This point is made clearly enough by recalling the influence of neo-Platonism on Augustine and of newly recovered Aristotelianism on Aquinas. At the present time, it can scarcely be doubted that the task of theological inquiry is influenced, among other factors, by the discoveries and the methods of discourse of the natural sciences.

The fact of the matter is that theological inquiry in any age faces a herculean task. In its attempt to speak of God, the One who is the ground of all that is, theology must in some fashion take account of all the forms of human inquiry into the nature of what is. Therefore it needs to consider the full range of investigation into the multidimensional reality of creation. Clearly

---

1. J. C. Polkinghorne, *Belief in God in an Age of Science* (New Haven: Yale University Press, 1998), chs. 2 and 5; *Faith, Science and Understanding* (New Haven: SPCK/Yale University Press, 2000), ch. 5.1.

such a task is beyond the unaided capacity of a single person. If it is to be adequately attempted at all, it will certainly require the assistance of well-conceived projects of interdisciplinary working.

The first Director of the Center of Theological Inquiry, Dan Hardy, was well aware of this necessity and he inaugurated the work of a group of scientists and theologians, convened to explore the interface between science and religion. I was privileged to be a member of that group. Our attention gradually came to be focused on questions of divine action and of God's relationship to time. We had just completed this project when Wallace Alston arrived to be the second Director of CTI. Not only did he support the continuation of this kind of activity, but he was also able to find the resources to expand it, so that at any time since then there have been a number of ongoing research projects of a multidisciplinary character, hosted and supported by the Center. As part of this continuing program, I was able to collaborate with Michael Welker as we shared in the chairing of a project engaging with eschatological questions.[2] Currently I am a participant in another project whose focus is on theological anthropology. Not only have these experiences been of the greatest stimulation to my own theological thinking, but I also feel that through this work I have come to gain some insight into the kind of methods of theological inquiry that can prove fruitful at the present time.

First, I have come to attach great importance to the *multidimensional character* of the inquiry. For the past twenty years I have engaged in thinking and writing about the interaction between science and religion. In consequence I have attended many conferences and working groups in which scientists and theologians have come together to talk to each other. Usually the scientists have been drawn from a fairly specific discipline that seemed to be the one most appropriate to the theological point under discussion, as when quantum theorists contribute to a consideration of how one might understand divine providential action operating in the world within the grain of physical process. Valuable though these activities have undoubtedly been, they have the character of bilateral conversations. For many purposes of theological inquiry, one needs a discourse with a wider embrace. One of the great strengths of the CTI projects has been precisely the multidisciplinary character of the groups of participants that have been assembled.

For example, in addition to systematic theologians there have been biblical scholars. I have to say that it seems to me still to be the case that the interaction of these two groups, within the broad setting of the religious academy,

---

2. See, J. C. Polkinghorne and M. Welker, eds., *The End of the World and the Ends of God* (Harrisburg, PA: Trinity Press International, 2000).

is not yet wholly satisfactory or adequate. There are honorable exceptions who rise above a restricted encounter, but often the intense specialization of contemporary academic life seems to encourage the experts to be wary of venturing even a little distance from the area of their particular competency. Biblical scholars, persuaded to collaborate in a wider-based project, often choose to make their contribution in the form of a detailed scholarly exegesis of a specific, quite narrowly selected, passage chosen from the relevant material. The depth of insight conveyed by this kind of tightly focused study is certainly highly illuminating to the more general reader, but there is surely also a need to have contributions that offer a wider survey of the concepts presented within the total scope of the biblical tradition. This is something that the experts often seem reluctant to undertake.

One has to recognize that multidisciplinary work is characterized by everyone engaging fields of knowledge of which they do not feel themselves to be fully the master. Of course, there is danger in such boldness, but there is also the prospect of beginning to achieve something of what the venture is actually all about. We have to be prepared to stick our necks out a little if we are to see somewhat further than we did before. Changing the metaphor, the members of the group have not been invited in order to sing a sequence of solos, but to form a choir, able to work together in harmonious polyphony.

It seems to a physicist that the relation between systematic theologians and biblical scholars is analogous to the relation between theorists and experimentalists in science. The two halves of the scientific enterprise certainly need each other and they must be in continuing dialogue. There are no scientific facts that are not already interpreted facts — and interpretation demands a theory-based point of view about exactly what is happening and what actually is being measured by the instruments used. Yet the theorists in their turn need the nudge of nature to encourage them to new feats of interpretative daring, for time and again we have found in science not only that nature is stranger than we thought, but that it is stranger than we would have been able to think without the prompting of its intransigent refusal to conform to our prior expectations.

The biblical scholars are the counterparts of the experimentalists, for they are dealing with the record of those fundamental events and insights that brought the Christian faith into being and on which the development of its tradition must always depend. Yet these scholars cannot do justice to the character of the material that they are handling if they confine themselves solely to the protocols of the secular historians. The latter base their judgments on a principle of uniformity, the dictum that the past, beneath the façade of its cultural difference, was very much in essence as the present is today. The whole claim of the New Testament, however, is that it records events that correspond to divine acts of startling novelty, without precedent in human history. Of course, that claim might be false, but its possibility and consistency cannot be prejudged by those investigating the evidence. Rationality is the attempt to conform our thinking to the nature of that which we are trying to think about, and so the rational New Testament scholar must be prepared to explore whether the radical claims of the apostolic writers have an interpretative consistency and an adequacy to the phenomena that can persuade us that they are, in fact, correct. The assessment of this intellectual possibility is a matter of theological judgment. In this task the biblical scholar needs the assistance of the insights of the theologian. Equally, the latter needs the insights of the biblical scholar if theological claims are to be exhibited as well-motivated by evidential and experiential considerations (what I have called the approach of "bottom-up thinking").[3] Therefore the enterprises of the theologian and the biblical scholar intertwine, just as do the enterprises of the theorist and the experimentalist in science. In the same way that science needs the nudge of nature, so theology needs the nudge of scripture. I also believe that it needs the liturgical nudge of the experience of the worshipping community, a point to which I shall return.

Of course, the need for "specialisms" is not removed. In science, theorists, on the whole, do not actually try to do experiments. Instead they seek to be informed of the character and quality of the results obtained by their colleagues. Experimentalists have to understand the nature of physical concepts and predictions, but they seldom try to construct whole theories themselves. There has to be mutual respect and mutual exchange. It is surely the same in theology between the systematicians and the exegetes.

The multidisciplinary groups at CTI have contained not only natural scientists but also social scientists. I have found it very fruitful in the projects in which I have participated, to be able to benefit from my colleagues' explorations of culture, while at the same time offering, on my part, some insights into the exploration of nature. There are also the human scientists, operating in a sense in the middle between the natural sciences and the social sciences. They represent an interdisciplinary interface with theology that so far has been insufficiently explored. I entertain the hope that the twenty-first century will soon remedy this defect. Of special value are likely to be the insights that psychology can provide, since it seems able to operate with concepts of a sufficiently general and overarching character to make the interaction with the-

---

3. J. C. Polkinghorne, *Science and Christian Belief/The Faith of a Physicist* (New Haven: SPCK/Princeton University Press, 1994).

ology particularly fruitful. This aspect of psychology contrasts with the current interdisciplinary potential of some more recently developed subjects in the area of human science, such as neuroscience and artificial intelligence. Understandably they are currently concentrating on very specific questions (such as the neural pathways for processing visual information) and lack widely-agreed, overall synthetic theories. A fruitful interchange with theology requires concepts of a more general range.

Truly multidisciplinary activity is complex and demanding. In consequence its pursuit needs *continuity of engagement and development*. Here is a point that from the start has been fully appreciated at CTI. I believe this to have been a very important ingredient in the success of the research projects that the Center has sponsored. Many interdisciplinary groups are formed by convening an appropriate collection of well-known scholars, meeting for the exchange of papers written beforehand. Often there is only one such encounter before someone edits the collected offerings to form a book. Just occasionally there might be a second meeting to tidy things up before publication. There is no doubt that valuable works have been created in this way, though it is also the case that such collections can sometimes seem so various in style, level, and approach that the outcome has rather a disjointed air about it. It has been an extremely fruitful aspect of the CTI projects that they have involved a sequence of meetings, often at six-month intervals and spanning three years or so. Papers are written and read beforehand, discussed, and critiqued at the meeting, then taken away for further work and elaboration in order to be considered again at the next meeting. These successive iterations of individual papers do more than simply improve the contributions themselves. They constitute an activity that gradually forms a group mind, ensuring that the final volume will prove to be more than the sum of its individual chapters. It may be difficult for those who have not actually had this experience to appreciate exactly how fertile it can be.

The first meeting or two of such a multidisciplinary group can often seem fragmented and perplexing. People come from their specialties with different concerns, different aims, and different methods for attaining those aims. One can easily find oneself wondering whether anything worthwhile could possibly come out of this bewildering diversity. Yet, given that the participants are truth-seeking persons willing to listen to their colleagues, after a while a fertile degree of mutual interaction and comprehension begins to occur. It is a most exciting and rewarding experience to be a part of this growth of convergence. The creative process is one that takes time and cannot be hurried. Very few institutions seem able to find the necessary patience and willingness to commit resources to this kind of middle-term group working, but

I believe that the experience of CTI shows clearly that this is a particularly fruitful method of theological inquiry. One must hope that it will become an increasing component in the theological explorations of the twenty-first century.

The kind of multidisciplinary work that I have been describing needs backing from those who are convinced of its value. All the time he has been Director of CTI, Wallace Alston has given that backing, not only with reliability and generosity, but also with a real interest in the subject matter of the groups. As someone who has a Ph.D. in New Testament studies and who also was for many years a greatly respected pastor, Wallace has had at least a toe in the academy and at least one foot in the Christian community of the Church. That combination is of great importance. The earliest meaning of the word 'theologian' was not simply someone who thought about God, but someone who was also a person of prayer to God. I have already suggested that theological inquiry needs not only the nudge of scripture, but also the liturgical nudge of the worshipping community. Its resources do not lie solely in the academy, but they are also to be found in the life of the whole Church. I have already lamented the contemporary degree of separation between systematic theology and biblical studies. More lamentable still is the contemporary tendency to maintain a divorce between the pulpit and the lecture hall. A division between the experiential life of the pastoral ministry and the intellectual pursuit of academic understanding is an impoverishment of both.

No one knows this better than Wallace Alston. One of the most successful initiatives he has taken at CTI has been the creation of the pastor-theologian program. This enables those with real theological interests, who are serving in the Church's front-line of parochial ministry, to meet together over a period of three years in regional gatherings for the study of the particular theme selected for each year, and then once during that year to meet nationally for a plenary session devoted to the chosen topic. Many of us engaged in CTI research projects have had the opportunity to play a modest part in this imaginative program, by acting as resource persons at a regional meeting or giving a lecture at a plenary session. I can say that these have been exceptionally enjoyable occasions for me. They have also been occasions of great encouragement, for I have been able to see something of the intellectual liveliness and scrupulous concern for the truth that are to be found among the serving clergy. It is not easy to find time for study and reflection amid the many demands of pastoral responsibility. Yet there are those whose commitment to theological inquiry is such that they are willing to do this. Something of the energy and interest of their activities can be gleaned from the collections of extracts from the essays that these pastor-theologians have written, which have recently been published.[4]

The Center of Theological Inquiry exists to foster pursuit of that central religious question of truth. There is much fideistic assertion in the religious world today. While no proper understanding of the nature of religion would want to deny that adherence to a faith tradition demands the committed allegiance of the whole person, this commitment properly takes place with the assent of the mind and not in separation from the intellectual search for truth. Of course, there is mystery in the infinite Reality of God that finite human minds will never adequately encompass. Yet we are called to love the Lord our God with our minds as with all the other parts of our being.

Faced with the created mystery of the physical universe, scientists do not simply ask the question of what is reasonable, for we know that the world is stranger than our a priori thinking can imagine. Instead, scientists ask the question: What makes you think that might be the case? I think that such an open, evidence-based approach to the search for truth is as natural to Christianity as it is to science. Theological inquiry is faith seeking understanding; it is the great quest for motivated belief about the truth of God. The Center of Theological Inquiry and its Director, Wallace Alston, have done much of great value in furthering that inquiry.

4. W. H. Lazareth, ed., *Reading the Bible in Faith* (Grand Rapids: Eerdmans, 2001); *Hope for the Future* (Grand Rapids: Eerdmans, 2002).

Open Order of the Natural World and Human Mind: Is There a Future for the Cooperation of Natural Sciences and Christian Theology?

Botond Gaál

"Teleological" Nature of the Laws of the Universe

Everyone can remember Edward Teller, world-famous nuclear physicist, saying at a lecture for scientists at the Debrecen Committee of the Academy of Sciences in 1996, "We must understand: modern science means that the world is open."[1] The same idea was emphasised by academician István Lovas when, explaining about the difference between common and deterministic chaos, he claimed: "Near future is predictable but the distant one isn't."[2] Both quotations urge one to think of this issue in deeper details and not just be satisfied with the way certain laws understood by the human mind describe the perceivable and visible world. That is, nature cannot be regarded as something whose understanding is merely knowledge limited by the "borders" of the mind; on the contrary, it should be taken as something with some kind of openness beyond its own self. This is the issue Einstein presented by asking his famous *"why"*-question when he saw that natural events had never been merely *incidental* or purely *necessary*. One cannot claim these events always take place in a blind and random way or that they must "obey" strict rules recognized by the mind. The former notion was commented on by Einstein, "God does not play dice,"[3] whereas, contemplating the latter one, he thought a scien-

---

1. Botond Gaál, *Edward Teller in Debrecen* [in Hungarian] (Debreceni Szemle, 1997/3-4), p. 540.

2. István Lovas, *Order and Chaos* [in Hungarian] (Debreceni Szemle, II, 1994/1), p. 40.

3. Although it is widely known as "God does not play dice," Einstein wrote it in German as "Der Alte würfelt nicht!" which would translate into English as "The Old Guy does not throw dice!" — Michael Welker, "Springing Cultural Traps," *Theology Today* 58, no. 2 (July 2001): 168.

tist "is activated by a wonder and awe before the mysterious comprehensibility of the universe which is yet finally beyond his grasp."[4] He got to the idea that "in its profoundest depth it is inaccessible to man."[5] He interpreted this idea in other words, saying, "God does not wear his heart on his sleeve."[6] Before Einstein, Max Planck also claimed that "to be functional," the laws of nature made use of some external power.[7] Einstein declared several times that he found the deepest secrets of nature amazing.[8] That is why he thought of the question of *"why"* so often. Why is the world as it is and why is it not different?

It is quite evident that neither Einstein nor any other scientist could give an answer to this *"why."* Nor can we expect to get a satisfactory and final answer to this question in the future. The answer can be satisfactory only if it is not aimed to be a final one. This is due to the inherent nature of the matter, as it was clearly recognized by Einstein and Planck,[9] let alone other scientists. They wanted to shape and direct approaches in a way that could raise something new; they expected some explanation about the secrets of unexplored fields. That is why some great scientists' ideas — such as Cantor's theories in mathematics, Planck, Einstein, Heisenberg, and Carl F. von Weizsäcker's theories in physics — often took a direction when, based on experience, these ideas presumed the logical necessity of God's existence. If one adopts the theological approach, he or she must say this interpretation or conclusion, i.e. "theologia naturalis"[10] derived from the so-called general revelation — although viable, or capable of representing some kind or certain level of faith — cannot serve as a source of the true knowledge of God, and no theology can be based on it in the Christian sense of the word. The object of Christian theology is God and his revelation.[11] The object of natural sciences is the uni-

---

4. Albert Einstein, *Out of My Later Years* (New York: Philosophical Library, 1950), pp. 30, 60.

5. Albert Einstein, *Ideas and Opinions* (New York: Crown Publishing, 1954), p. 49.

6. Thomas F. Torrance, "Einstein and God," in *Reflections*, vol. 1 (Princeton, N.J: Center of Theological Inquiry, 1998), pp. 14-16.

7. Cf. Max Planck, "Az egzakt tudomány értelme és határai" [in Hungarian], in *Válogatott Tanulmányok* (Budapest: Gondolat, 1965), pp. 301-4.

8. Cf. Albert Einstein, "Hogyan látom a világot" [in Hungarian] (Budapest: Gladiátor Kiadó, 1994), p. 16. This is just one of the many similar declarations by Einstein.

9. Among the great scientists, Max Planck was the one to discuss the matter in the clearest possible way. Cf. Planck, "Az egzakt tudomány értelme és határai," p. 302.

10. According to the representatives of "Theologia naturalis," God is recognisable from nature, history, or through logic without adopting the Christological approach.

11. The object of Christian theology is written in the Bible. However, the issue of what can be regarded as a source of revelation is still debated in Christianity. One of the greatest controversies of Protestant and Catholic theologies lies in this issue.

verse as a whole which is thought to be the world created by God in the Christian ideas. The way of thinking in exact sciences and Christian theology is uniform in one way: both search the final basis of the knowledge relevant to their own field. Both find it justified to raise the question of *"why,"* but neither thinks of "grasping" this final basis in its perfection. However, both fields of science can lay the right track of thinking after all. One should ask a question again: How can this way of thinking, resulting in the right approach, be characterized?

In this modern age of ours it was scientific thinking that used the age-old term of philosophy to characterize natural laws as being of "teleological" nature. They refer to a certain basis or goal outside and beyond themselves, representing the significance of their origin. The intention to search for the uniform theory of space is regarded to be "teleological" in this sense of the word, as the final basis of order is being sought. But the *anthropic cosmological principle*[12] can also be discussed in this sense. This is a kind of scientific effort to explore the deepest cause and basis of the order of nature. In this case, the association between the formation of the universe and life — more closely of the mind perceiving the world — serves as a source for answering the *"whys"* in the hope of finding unknown facts at the same time. A serious answer has been presented in the Big Bang model on behalf of the natural sciences, i.e. the world has its beginning in time and its creation is in a fine-tuned relationship with human existence. Christian theology has followed this approach since the beginning and, keeping the Jewish religious traditions, it has expressed its views in its teaching about Christology. "He is before all things, and by him all things consist" (Col. 1:17). The Apostle Paul understood the whole world was included in "all things." It can be seen that both the sciences and Christian theology offer a "teleological" way of thinking in mutual harmony to achieve their goal, i.e. scientific development. This goal, the so-called *telos,* cannot result in any kind of "proof of God," it can only help find the right approach.

---

12. Recently, several articles have been devoted to the anthropic principles of cosmology in both natural sciences and philosophy. In addition to translated works, in-depth Hungarian papers have covered the topic, too. Let us highlight László Végh, "Az 'életrevaló' világegyetem," *Élet és Tudomány* 10 (June 1988); László Végh, "Az antropikus világegyetem" (Fizikai szemle, 1989/4); László Székely, "Az 'antropikus elv' a kozmológiában" (Világosság, 1989/2); Gyula Dávid, "A lakható világegyetem" (Természet világa, 1990/7) — all in Hungarian. With respect to the theological answer to the questions of "how" and "why," two papers should be mentioned: Botond Gaál and László Végh, "A Szentírás és az antropikus kozmológiai elv," (Theologiai Szemle, 1991/4); Botond Gaál, "A Universe Fine-Tuned for Intelligent Life," *Perspectives* 10 (1995): 19-23.

Uniform Approach to the Universe

Christian thinking looks at the reality and order of the world partly from a Jewish-Christian monotheistic approach and partly from the incarnation of Christ, for the reality of creation is confirmed by incarnation itself; therefore a Christian would search for the basis and explanation of the world "outside" incarnation. In other words, the point in the world's existence is not in the world itself, but human intelligence comprehending it is still part of the immanent world. The question is: What rules govern this intellectual process? The Greeks were right to examine the world through "external" objectivity, utilizing intellectual power, almost "exceeding" that power. But they made a mistake when they thought that human intellectual activity and ideas of the world were of divine nature. It was also out of the question that man could completely melt into one with the universe — a typical oriental religious approach. Neither the stoic or pantheistic approach — uniting divinity and nature — nor any form of the *aprioristic* views offers a solution either. In contrast with them, *Christianity has always emphasized that the universe received its order — the basis of universal approach — from its Creator, and human intellect, a distinguishable but inseparable part of this created order, searches, comprehends, describes, and explains this order.* The rationalistic approach in the Enlightenment had different views; therefore, a gap developed between scientific thinking and the natural world, and only the scientific approach of the twentieth century could show the way out of this complicated situation. It is the laws of scientific thinking and intellectual approach that can be relevant for further thinking as far as our standpoint is regarded.

This kind of uniform approach to the world, which has been an inherent part of Christian thinking, will definitely result in changes in almost all fields of science. The amount of effort we should put in the individual fields is still to be seen. A correct approach may yield some result. Let us present a few examples as an illustration. In the first place, let us think of the still existing problem raised by Georg Cantor: *mathematical thinking* always works between the finite and Absolute, presuming the reality of the Absolute. In his famous theorem that various branches of mathematics are not provable within mathematics itself, Kurt Gödel, famous *logician,* suggested that thinking is open upward, toward a higher level of thinking. As for the natural laws of *physics,* discovered by systematic thinking and translated into the language of mathematics, they can never describe a real event or the reality of an event perfectly. This is best expressed by Einstein's famous statement: "As far as the propositions of mathematics refer to reality they are not certain; and as far as they are certain, they do not refer to reality."[13] So we never possess a "finite kind of order" or "absolute truth"; we are just at a landmark of the road leading to reality.

In an attempt to advance, mathematicians are searching for ways of creating a new kind of mathematics which can handle time in order to let us learn about nature more precisely or get closer to reality. If we could incorporate real time, instead of "Euclidean time," in laws written in the language of mathematics it would mean that history is embedded in these formulae. In 1989, this explicitness of mathematics beyond itself was summarised by John D. Barrow as follows: "If the universe is mathematical in some deep sense, then the mysterious undecidabilities demonstrated by Gödel and Turing are part of the fabric of the universe rather than merely products of our mind. They show that even a mathematical universe is more than axioms, more than computation, more than logic — and more than mathematicians can know."[14] When Márton Sain, a mathematician-historian, summed up these internal theoretical problems he had the presumption that ". . . this statement leaves the world of mathematics and connects mathematics with the reality out of mathematics."[15] This is also predicted by the second law of thermodynamics according to which entropy should increase, but, on the contrary, it is order which increases in macroscopic scales. An increase in entropy relates only to closed systems, but the vast domains of the universe, including our planet, too, belong to an open system. And if nature is like this, man, being a part of nature, cannot do anything but follow this law, due to his created intelligence. Based on the *categorical imperative* in Kant's moral law, this internal intellectual constraint was given a telling name, *"thermodynamic imperative,"* by R. B. Lindsay. Therefore, man can do nothing but explore the superior laws of the order of open systems against the entropic growth of closed systems, and use his "exploration" in science and technology so that it promotes order in any case. Similar conclusions can be drawn from the research of the non-balance thermodynamics by Ilya Prigogine, holder of the Nobel-prize.

Biology can also contribute to the solution of the problem if it assumes an approach reflecting that man — a living organism by itself — is an organic part of nature, in his completeness. Being an open system, a living organism serving as a functional whole should be incorporated in the surrounding

13. Einstein, *Ideas*, p. 233.

14. John D. Barrow, "The Mathematical Universe," *Natural Science* (May 1989): p. 311.

15. Márton Sain, *There Is No Royal Way!* [in Hungarian] (Budapest: Gondolat, 1986), p. 806.

world in a way that it is not treated as a "separate" part. Man and his environment are factors dependent on and belonging to each other. What man becomes is greatly decided by his environment. The opposite is also true. What the environment becomes can be decided by man and his technological activities. Man, therefore, is not just an individual organism in the world but an organically essential part of it, not only in its physical form but also in the intellectual sense. The above will obviously change the approach of *medical science* so several medical problems may expect an answer or solution. The human body is also part of the aforementioned open world and obeys similar laws. Let alone the fact, that the comprehending mind, with its openness, is exclusively characteristic of man.

Examples can be brought from other fields, as well. This approach is also expected to have an influence on the development of *history* as a science. The Enlightenment clearly distinguished between nature and man's intellectual activities; accordingly, mankind did his job as something "different," a "foreign body" in the course of history. Man had his own "necessarily immanent truths of the mind" whereas history, part of nature, had its "contingent historic truths." Lessing, referring to it as the greatest problem of contemporary philosophers, claimed that "contingent historic truths could never serve as proof for the necessarily immanent truths of the mind."[16] Therefore, neither history nor Christianity, a historic religion, could be treated in a way in which human intellect could fit in as an organic part. According to the approach of the era of the Enlightenment, the truths of the mind were separated from the course of history, society, and religious life. When Lessing realized it he cried out, "This is the ugly and wide ditch which I am trying to cross in vain. If someone could help me cross it, for God's sake, please, come and help me!"[17] This famous eighteenth-century philosopher could not consider that it was not only the historic events but also the scientific truths, created by the mind, that had an open structure. According to Christian thinking neither is absolute — which is different from the ideas of the mind in the Enlightenment — but both have their final and common basis in God, the Creator. The "ugly and wide ditch" was not created by nature but the mind, artificially and unnecessarily. If man is really placed in the order of nature, as its organic part, it can take us further on the way to notice that certain fields of *social science*, such as *law* or *ethics*,[18] are inherent parts of the open universe in the same way

16. *Lessings Werke*, Deutsche Verlags-Anstalt, Stuttgart, *Über den Beweis des Geistes und der Kraft*, 790. Cf. Sándor Czeglédy, *Hit és történet* [in Hungarian] (Budapest: Sylvester, 1936), p. 62.

17. Cf. Czeglédy, *Hit és történet*, p. 66.

18. Difficult questions requiring further study may emerge in connection with these

as man is with his open physical, biological, and intellectual faculties. Christian theology cannot be neglected in this development for the same reasons. If it wants to keep its original openness it cannot think in terms of "necessity" or "probability." Theological science should also be careful not to fall into a closed intellectual system, where it is determined "from above" how to think of things and what the limits of those thoughts are. But probability is not a solution for theology either if, arguing with the freedom of the mind, it wants to be a kind of theology, neglecting the disciplines of cultivating science. The former would exclude itself from development, the latter would result in disintegration.

The consideration of the idea of openness will certainly yield positive results in the *philosophy of science,* too. From this point of view, the uniform approach to the universe means much more than the ideas of the "structure of scientific revolutions" recently raised and discussed by Thomas S. Kuhn, an American philosopher and historiographer.[19] According to him, the history of sciences is a series of discrete scientific revolutions in which the old paradigms are always replaced by new ones. Kuhn discussed only the "ways" of the changes of paradigms, he had never investigated the reasons — that is why we do not know why one has different opinions of something that was thought about in a different way earlier. Michael Polányi explained the reasons in a more persuasive manner when discussing the relationship between personal knowledge and reality.[20] He pointed out that human intellectual activities always had a dimension pointing towards a more perfect truth, which, on one hand, resulted in and ensured openness upward, and, on the other hand, could act as a regulatory principle for the mind toward levels downward or backward. This is well illustrated by the relationship between Newtonian physics and Einstein's Theory of Relativity. From a scientific point of view, a higher level of knowledge is new in the sense that earlier it was thought to be impossible.[21] Thus, human intelligence can surprise us with unexpected new forms and structures of knowledge. So the "development-theory" of scientific

---

fields of science. For example, it is worth discussing the problems of order and disorder, and examining the relationship between social and moral entropies versus natural entropies. All this can take us further in the direction of ecological and medico-ethical questions. Research based on *contingency* may result in decisive answers in many cases, but they cannot be discussed in the frame of this article.

19. Thomas S. Kuhn, "The Structure of Scientific Revolutions" [translated into Hungarian] (Budapest: Gondolat, 1984).

20. Cf. Michael Polányi, *Personal Knowledge* (London: Routledge and Kegan Paul, 1983), pp. vii-viii.

21. Gaál, *Edward Teller,* p. 540.

revolutions discussed in Kuhn's way should not neglect the fact that the human mind which has created them is also open; i.e., these revolutions are the result of human intelligence with an open structure. The laws of nature are also open, and this explains why the order of the universe and the laws of human intelligence are in harmony.

The common historic development of exact sciences and Christian theology for two thousand years can have serious teaching for all fields of science. All parts of the universe have an immanent but open order, and because human intelligence is of a similar kind, it should be allowed to follow this order. Christian thinking has always represented this approach; therefore, I am convinced that the cooperation of sciences and Christian theology will yield further results.

Saint Gregory of Nazianzus as Pastor and Theologian

Brian E. Daley

For most modern students of Christian theology, a first encounter with those early theologians we call "the Fathers of the Church" can be somewhat surprising, if only because their concerns and their mode of expression may seem to us less theological than pastoral. Although the texts of the first four Christian centuries come in many literary genres — letters, sermons, commentaries, polemical tracts, histories, saints' lives, dialogues modeled on those of Plato — most of them have a strikingly oratorical character, a rhetorical style redolent of preaching and public discourse, rather than the more analytical, expository character we associate with systematic thought. For Christian readers since the time of the Reformation, trained to identify theology with the university and the seminary and to see it above all as a matter of the analysis of concepts and ideas in the scholastic mode, much of the writings of the Fathers can seem to lack the hard intellectual edge we have come to expect in theological argument.

In the last third of the fourth century, it is true — in the strident polemics of the final stage of the Arian controversy in the Eastern Church, when defenders of the Nicene confession pitted their intellectual and religious strength against Arian leaders, like the bishop Eunomius of Cyzicus and the philosopher Aetius — theology began to take on a new form, borrowed more from the philosophical lecture hall than from the pulpit. As representatives of this third generation of the Arian party began, in the late 350s, to develop a more aggressive and sharply articulated critique of the Nicene affirmation of the full divinity of the Son of God, their arguments were more often couched in the terse, "scholastic" form of logical debate than in the expansive, familiar style of epideictic, or "show" oratory. The Neo-Arians wrote in definitions and axioms, chains of syllogisms, questions and responses; theology had come within the realm of dialectics. Although this secular, dialectical style originally drew the contempt of pro-Nicene respondents such as Basil of Caesarea, his brother Gregory of Nyssa, and their friend and supporter Gregory of Nazianzus — the three seminal expositors of classical Trinitarian theology, known as the "Cappadocian Fathers" — it eventually came to dominate mainstream Christian theological argument as well, especially in the literature of Christological controversy that followed the contentious definition of the Council of Chalcedon (451).[1]

It seems all the more significant, then, that Gregory of Nazianzus, perhaps the most eloquent of early Christian orators, an accomplished and voluminous poet and letter-writer, who himself was frequently critical of those who are "too clever in argument,"[2] and who "philosophize about God"[3] in a spirit of prideful self-display, soon after his own death came to be known by the title he continues to bear in the Orthodox tradition: "Gregory the Theologian."[4] This title, which had been used widely in the secular Hellenistic tradition to designate those literary or philosophical writers who told the stories of the gods or reflected on the divine reality, was applied much more narrowly by Christian authors, as befitted Biblical monotheism: to Moses, for in-

---

1. For a discussion of this change in the form and literary style of theological argument in the fifth and sixth centuries, see Brian E. Daley, "Boethius' Theological Tracts and Early Byzantine Scholasticism," *Mediaeval Studies* 46 (1984): 158-91. See also Lorenzo Perrone, "The Impact of the Dogma of Chalcedon on Theological Thought between the Fourth and Fifth Ecumenical Councils," in *History of Theology. The Patristic Period*, ed. Angelo di Berardino and Basil Studer (Collegeville: Liturgical Press, 1996), pp. 414-60; and Basil Studer, "A Scholastic Theology," in *History of Theology. The Patristic Period*, ed. Angelo di Berardino and Basil Studer (Collegeville: Liturgical Press, 1996), pp. 473-81.

2. *Oration* 27 (= First Theological Oration).1 [*Sources Chrétiennes* (= SC), ed. J. Bernardi, J. Mossay, and P. Gallay (Paris: Éditions du Cerf, 1978), 250.70].

3. *Or.* 27.3 [SC 250.76].

4. Although the precise origin of this honorific title is unknown, Gregory — whose death is to be dated sometime around 390 — seems to have been identified this way by the time of the Council of Chalcedon in 451. In the dossiers of authoritative theological voices included in the acts of the abortive Council of Ephesus (431), excerpts from Gregory are attributed to "the great and most holy bishop Gregory, born at Nazianzus" (e.g., *Acta Conciliorum Oecumenicorum* [ACO] I, 1, 7, p. 93.2). Similar excerpts in the florilegia of Chalcedon, twenty years later, are ascribed to "Gregory the Theologian" (e.g., ACO II, 1, 3, p. 114.15). This remains his identifying nickname for Eastern Orthodoxy. Maximus Confessor, in the 640s (*Dialogue with Pyrrhus*, PG 91.316 C), and John of Damascus, in the first half of the eighth century, cite him by this title (PG 94.1068 A), and John twice introduces quotations from Gregory Nazianzen simply by saying *theologikōs eipein*: "to speak theologically" — which for him was apparently the same as "to speak as the Theologian" (PG 94.1237 C; 1328 B).

stance, by Clement of Alexandria,[5] or to Jeremiah by Gregory Nazianzen himself.[6] In the Greek Christian tradition, it came to be the peculiar nick-name of three writers of central importance for Byzantine theology: John the Evangelist,[7] Gregory of Nazianzus, and the early medieval mystical writer and hymnographer Symeon the Younger (949-1022), known more widely (possibly because his literary gifts were thought to match those of Gregory) as "the New Theologian." Each of these three Christian authors is labeled "Theologian" by Eastern Christianity because each of them was considered a classic example of one who knew how to "talk about God" in Christian accents; all of them provided the developing Christian doctrinal tradition with the vocabulary in which it could continue to articulate its faith in the one God who had chosen Israel as his people, and who had revealed the Trinitarian structure of his being in the person of Jesus and the Spirit-filled life of the church. Of the three, however, it is only Gregory who can also accurately be called a "pastor" — a bishop who not only held the cure, official and unofficial, of the faithful in a few remote villages in central Asia Minor, but who presided, at a crucial time in the church's history, over the orthodox Christian community in Constantinople, the capital of the Eastern Roman Empire.

Thanks to a well-developed penchant for self-revelation and self-promotion, usually spiced with a good mixture of self-pity, Gregory has left us far too much information on his own life to be easily summarized here.[8] He was a provincial aristocrat from the high plains of Hellenized Anatolia, born about 330 as the son of a Christian bishop and landowner and a wealthy, deeply religious Christian woman with wide-ranging family connections. Gregory received an education that was extraordinary even for a person of his

---

5. *Stromateis* 1.22 [GCS Clemens Alexandrinus 2, 93.11].

6. *Or.* 31 (= Theological Oration 5).16 [SC 250.306].

7. Origen seems to have been the first Christian writer to speak of the Evangelist John simply as "the Theologian": see, for instance, Fragment 1 on John (A. E. Brooke, ed., *The Commentary of Origen on S. John's Gospel* 2 [Cambridge: Cambridge University Press, 1896], 211.15, 212.8). In this same passage, Origen refers more generally to the Christian Scripture as "the theological writings" (*ai theologiai,* Brooke, *Commentary of Origen,* 213.11). Cf. Frag. 3 (Brooke, *Commentary of Origen,* 214.17), where the reference to light in John 1:5 is referred to as "the light spoken of by the Theologian" *(to theologoumenon phōs).*

8. A number of thorough biographies of Gregory of Nazianzus are available: see Paul Gallay, *La Vie de saint Grégoire de Nazianze* (Lyon: Vitte, 1943); Jean Bernardi, *Saint Grégoire de Nazianze* (Paris: Éditions du Cerf, 1995); John McGuckin, *Saint Gregory of Nazianzus. An Intellectual Biography* (Crestwood, NY: St. Vladimir's, 2001). McGuckin's book is especially notable as an example of exhaustive theological analysis and sympathetic, if critically acute, biographical reconstruction, in a lively and readable form. I follow most of his chronological suggestions for Gregory's life in this essay.

social class: after normal preliminary studies in grammar and rhetoric at Caesarea, the capital of the province of Cappadocia, he seems to have spent the better part of a year doing further rhetorical studies at Caesarea in Palestine and Alexandria, in 347-348, and then traveled — by a dangerously stormy sea-voyage of twenty days — to Athens, where he spent the next ten years studying rhetoric and philosophy in the company of some of the leading minds of his day, Christian and pagan. Gregory's companion, during much of his stay in Athens, was a fellow Cappadocian, Basil of Caesarea — himself a member of a large and influential Christian family that included Macrina, his eldest sister, a woman of learning and deep commitment to the ascetical life, Gregory, a younger brother who later became bishop of Nyssa, and five others. The friendship between Gregory of Nazianzus and Basil of Caesarea, forged in their student days and developed through later years by correspondence and a common interest in the works of Origen, eventually drew Gregory into the active work of pastoral leadership in ways he clearly both resisted and feared.

On his return to his family estate at Arianzus, near his father's episcopal town of Nazianzus, around the beginning of 359, Gregory seems to have planned to spend his days as a gentleman of cultured leisure, reading and writing *belles lettres* and philosophy in the classical tradition, and studying the Christian Scriptures. His father, however, who was elderly and needed assistance in caring for his people, strongly urged him to take seriously the pastoral responsibilities implied in his education, and eventually forced him to be ordained as a presbyter at Christmas, 361. Gregory seems to have reacted with a combination of panic before his new duties and resentment at his father's moral pressure, and fled within a few days to the estate of Basil's family in Pontus, where he spent the next few months with his friend in theological discussion and study. By the following Easter, however, he was back in Nazianzus, sharing his father's pastoral burdens. The first three of his collected orations — elaborate pieces that may never have been delivered orally, and were in any case carefully edited later on — are attempts to explain his flight from the call to ministry not as a refusal of responsibility, but as an acknowledgement of its immense personal challenges. Orations 1 and 3 are brief, occasional pieces, but Oration 2 is a long and elaborate reflection on the difficulties and the importance of Christian ministry, which had great influence on later Patristic treatments of the subject.

The rest of Gregory's life was largely defined by the tension between his personal desire for the quiet life of a comfortable, eremitical Christian man of letters — a desire doubtless reinforced by his own introspective, sensitive temperament — and the demands of the contemporary church that he exercise intellectual and pastoral leadership. When his friend Basil became bishop of the provincial capital, Caesarea, in 370, Basil found himself continually embroiled in theological controversy, mainly over questions of Trinitarian theology and the role of organized monasticism, and in the political struggles theology and religious practice were now beginning to generate in a Christian Empire. Both Basil and Gregory's father, Gregory the Elder, urged the younger Gregory to accept episcopal ordination himself, in order to reinforce the position of the defenders of Nicene orthodoxy with his own gifts of argument and persuasion. After a good deal of resistance, Gregory allowed himself to be ordained bishop of Sasima, a tiny mountain hamlet, in 372 — roughly the same time at which Basil's younger brother Gregory was ordained bishop of Nyssa, in the western part of the province. In his writings, Gregory of Nazianzus shows continuing resentment, both of the pressure Basil and his own father had used in persuading him to become a bishop, and of the insignificance of the see that was actually given him. Gregory's emotions were rarely simple, and usually mixed!

Gregory seems never to have resided in Sasima, or to have given the church there more than cursory attention. When he was not away pursuing ascetic and literary retirement — as he did in the politically tense years 375-378, when he lived with a women's monastic community in Seleucia, near the south coast of Asia Minor — Gregory assisted his father in shepherding the small community of Nazianzus, which was still more substantial than Sasima. Late in 378, however, the call to enter more centrally into the public life of the church was renewed, now at a much higher level. With the death of the anti-Nicene Emperor Valens in that year at the battle of Adrianople, the opportunity seemed to many Christians open again to promote the Nicene confession of the full and eternal divinity of Christ, as Son of God — along with the full divinity of the Spirit sent by Christ and his Father — as the normative faith of the imperial church. Nicenes in Constantinople invited Gregory to come and act as unofficial pastor of their community, and his cousin Theodosia, married to an influential senator, offered him one of her houses there as a place to live and work. Basil died January 1, 379, and the pro-Nicene party was sorely in need of wise leadership; a few weeks later, the Spanish general Theodosius, himself a devout Nicene Christian, was acclaimed emperor by the armies at Sirmium in the Balkans. To Gregory the time seemed right to accept the invitation, and in the autumn of 379, he took up residence in Constantinople, in effect bishop of the Nicene Christians there. Here his theological and rhetorical abilities rapidly raised him to further prominence; when Theodosius victoriously entered Constantinople in the autumn of 380, he confirmed Gregory's position as metropolitan of the imperial capital.

It was in this role that Gregory was called upon to preside at some of the early sessions of the council of Eastern bishops — known to the churches as the First Council of Constantinople — which met in the capital to deal with pressing issues of faith in June, 381. Characteristically, perhaps, his relations with the other bishops at the council were not easy. Gregory seems to have been urging them to issue not only a strong confirmation of Nicaea's teaching that the Son is eternally part of the substance of God, but to assert the share of the Holy Spirit, as a distinct *hypostasis* or individual, in that same divine substance: that both Spirit and Son, in other words, are "of the same substance" as the Father, and that the three *hypostases* encountered in the history of divine self-revelation constitute a single, indivisible Mystery. This position was clearly more explicit than the majority of bishops were prepared to endorse in Constantinople in 381; the profession of faith they did produce reaffirms the Nicene position on the Son, but stops short of proclaiming the Spirit "God" or identifying him directly with the divine substance. Though we know little of the debates and politics of the council, it is clear that Gregory felt himself both slighted and threatened by the opposition — some of whom questioned his credentials as bishop of Constantinople because of his earlier appointment as bishop of Sasima, on the grounds that the fifteenth canon of Nicaea had prohibited the "translation" of all ranks of clergy from one local church to another. Before the council was over, Gregory resigned both from its presidency and from the see of Constantinople, and by the end of 381 he had returned to Cappadocia, to the cultivated but austere retirement he had always sought. He spend the rest of his life, until his death sometime around 390, corresponding earnestly or wittily with friends, editing his old sermons and composing new ones, and writing a massive body of poems, mainly on Christian subjects, in the whole range of Greek classical meters. Freed from the burden of office in the church, he had become a man of letters once again.

In the context of the present volume, Gregory of Nazianzus is important, it seems to me, as one of early Christianity's clearest examples of one who was both pastor and theologian — one who struggled with the encroachments of the practical and the theoretical life on each other, but who still strongly affirmed and exemplified, in many of his works, both the essentially pastoral character of theological argument and reflection, and the centrality of theological understanding and discourse, when carried out in the tradition of Biblical and orthodox faith, to pastoral ministry.[9] A number of

---

9. For a thorough and perceptive treatment of the constant interweaving of the theological, pastoral, and spiritual dimensions of theology in all of Gregory's works, see Christopher A.

modern Western writers have criticized him as a theologian for his apparent lack of originality and depth,[10] but in doing so doubtless miss his central concern to see theology always as a form of preaching and persuasion, and church ministry as rooted in the thoughtful articulation of the Gospel.

What is pastoral ministry, in the view of Gregory of Nazianzus? Although he comments frequently on aspects of the pastor's task, his fullest and most characteristic treatment of the subject is the long, impassioned defense of his own reluctance to be ordained a presbyter, which comes down to us in the collected edition of his discourses as Oration 2.[11] Gregory here makes the remark, later echoed by Pope Gregory the Great in his *Pastoral Rule,* that it is hard to see why even the most virtuous person would feel qualified to assume such an office, "for in reality the guidance of the human person seems to me to be the art of arts and the science of sciences, since humans are the most changeable and diverse of all living beings."[12] In the course of the oration, which is really the first fully developed essay in the Christian tradition on the nature of ministry, Gregory describes a number of the elements he considers essential to serving the faithful as their official pastor. First, ministry is clearly *leadership,* in Gregory's view. It is a form of "rule" *(archē),*[13] an acquired self-

---

Beeley, *Gregory of Nazianzus: Theology, Spirituality and Pastoral Theory* (Dissertation, University of Notre Dame, 2002).

10. This judgment appears, for instance, in Frederic W. Farrar's delightful and informative sketches of the life and work of leading figures in the early church — a work first recommended to me by Wallace Alston. Farrar writes of Gregory: "His title — the Theologian — would be much more applicable in the modern sense of the word to Gregory of Nyssa. . . . As an original thinker, Gregory [of Nazianzus] was far less profound than his younger namesake . . ." (*Lives of the Fathers* 1 [Edinburgh: Adam and Charles Black, 1889], p. 576). More recently, Anthony Meredith echoes the same idea: "In many ways Gregory was an elegant, orthodox and unexceptional writer, more memorable for his powers of expression than for any strikingly new contributions to the history of theology" (*The Cappadocians* [Crestwood, NY: St. Vladimir's Press, 1995], p. 44). Both authors clearly value originality much more highly than it was valued in either Christian or pagan antiquity, but miss the importance of rhetoric in the theological enterprise.

11. The title given this oration in the Greek manuscripts varies considerably. The most common is some variant of the following: "An Apologetic Discourse of Saint Gregory the Theologian, on account of his Flight to Pontus and Return from There, because of his Ordination as Presbyter; in which the Subject is: What the Nature of Priesthood Is, and What Kind of Person a Bishop Should Be." Although undoubtedly the work of later Byzantine scribes, this title reveals how later tradition understood both the circumstances and the contents of the treatise.

12. *Or.* 2.16. Cf. Gregory the Great, *Pastoral Rule* 1.1: "How rash it is for an unskilled person to take on pastoral authority, since the government of souls *(cura animarum)* is the art of arts!"

13. *Or.* 2.3, 5, 8, 9, 10, 15, 28, 56, 78, 113. For a discussion of the many ways in which Gregory speaks of ministry as leadership in this oration, see the introduction of Jean Bernardi to his edition and translation of the work, SC 247.45-48.

discipline — a "philosophy," in his terminology — that consists in "taking on the leadership of souls and authority over them."[14] The role of the pastor is first of all to bring order *(taxis)* into a human community disordered by sin and individual self-promotion; a community without order, he observes, is incapable of worshipping God.[15] In one passage, Gregory compares the minister's role in the community to that of an animal-tamer, struggling to domesticate not just an ordinary beast, but a kind of mythic monster: "an animal composed of many kinds of beast, with many forms and shapes, large and small, tame and wild," calling for all kinds of behavior from its tamer to keep it in control.[16]

A second theme in Gregory's description is the *therapeutic* aspect of ministry. The pastor must be "a physician of souls," all the more skilled in his practice than an ordinary doctor is required to be, because the soul is itself imperishable and called to eternal union with God.[17] Gregory conceives of the human person, here and throughout his works, in the classic terms of Christian Platonism: as an immortal and self-determining creature, mysteriously embodied among the opaque things of this lower world in order to test and purify its desires by struggle; the goal of life is "that [the soul] might draw its lower element [the body] towards itself and elevate it, freeing it gradually from its coarseness, so that what God is to the soul, the soul might become to the body."[18] So he proposes that

> the objective of our art is "to give wings to the soul,"[19] to snatch it from the world and to give it to God, to preserve what is made in God's image if it has remained so, and to lead it back when it is in danger, but also to repair what has fallen into ruin, by causing Christ to dwell in human hearts through the Spirit; above all, it is to make it divine, to give that which belongs to the ranks of heaven a share in heaven's blessedness.[20]

14. *Or.* 2.78.

15. *Or.* 2.4. The notion that order, within a varied and dynamic creation, is the underlying principle of life, given by God, and that self-willed disorder is the origin of corruption and death, is also a theme in the works of Athanasius: see, for example, *Against the Pagans* 41-43 (on the role of the Logos in maintaining the order and life of the universe); *On the Incarnation* 4-8 (fall and redemption by the incarnation of the Logos); *Letter to Marcellinus on the Psalms* (singing the Psalms as a means of restoring God-given order to the soul).

16. *Or.* 2.44.

17. *Or.* 2.16.

18. *Or.* 2.17.

19. This phrase, familiar in Greek antiquity, is an allusion to Socrates's description of the philosopher's task in Plato, *Phaedrus,* 249a.

20. *Or.* 2.22. This allusion to salvation as "divinization" is repeated in *Or.* 2.73, and ap-

This interior rescue operation, which Gregory describes largely as a healing of our present condition of sensuality and alienation from God, calls for a physician's skills: the ability to read symptoms and to prescribe remedies appropriate to individual needs, and the ability even to adapt one's personal style, in dealing with "patients," to motivate their cooperation in an appropriate way.[21]

In a few passages in Oration 2, Gregory speaks of the minister's role also in liturgical terms, as one who has a distinctive, mediating "place" between God and the people, between the dazzling brilliance of the heavenly realm and the darkness of earth.[22] Yet he makes it clear that this "priestly" role is a share in the priesthood of Christ, not to be understood apart from him.[23] So the more dominant liturgical emphasis of the work is on the ministry of the word, which he calls "the first of our duties."[24] Gregory goes on to describe this as essentially a theological task, requiring a daunting degree of intellectual responsibility and self-control: "to give each person his measure of the food of the Word in due season (see Luke 12:42), and to manage the truth of our own opinions by good judgment,"[25] whatever the subject might be. Gregory goes on to list the main subjects of theological discourse, as he sees them: the nature of the visible and invisible worlds, the human person as spiritual and material, divine providence in history, our original creation and final end, the course of salvation history as told in the Biblical narrative.[26] The "chief point" of theology, however — as well as the aspect of theology most challenging to human thought, most fraught with the danger of error and exaggeration — is "what we are to understand of the blessed Trinity, the source

---

pears frequently in Gregory's works; it is understood as the final stage in a process of re-creation by grace that involves the individual believer more and more intimately in the holiness and Sonship of Christ, by the power of the Holy Spirit. In Or. 2.77, Gregory seems to allude to the same idea by saying that the minister's role is "to lead souls to their espousal, and to be their marriage-broker"! A classic treatment of the theme of divinization in Greek Patristic theology, recently translated into English, is Jules Gross, *The Divinization of the Christian according to the Greek Fathers,* trans. Paul A. Onica (Anaheim, CA: A & C Press, 2002); for Gregory's use of the theme, see pp. 193-7.

21. *Or.* 2.26-34.
22. *Or.* 2.74-75.
23. *Or.* 2.73.
24. *Or.* 2.35.
25. *Or.* 2.35.
26. *Or.* 2.35-36. For a similar outline of the "content" of Christian theology, see the end of his "First Theological Oration," *Or.* 27.10. The list is clearly borrowed from the preface to Origen's treatise *On First Principles,* which outlines both the topics on which the rule of faith lays down clear norms for faith, and those which call for further investigation.

of all things."[27] The proclamation and interpretation of the word of the Gospel, in fact, which forms the center of Gregory's view of ministry, seems to be nothing more or less than the continuing attempt to articulate the inseparable, single Mystery of God's involvement in time, and of God's involvement of the creatures of time in his own eternal life: the Mystery of God's life-giving, saving presence which the church still articulates — especially thanks to the efforts of Gregory and his fellow Cappadocians — in terms of the twin doctrines of the Trinity and the Incarnation.

These two doctrines, which Gregory rightly sees as simply two aspects of one reality larger than thought and speech, recur in most of his works, as a kind of refrain, a signature tune; God's self-communicating reality as Trinity, he remarks at the close of his farewell address to his community at Constantinople, is for him "my theme for meditation and my source of pride."[28] Gregory's five "Theological Orations," which come down to us as Orations 27-31, are perhaps Christian antiquity's most dense and most thoroughly developed treatise on the human ability to know God in history, and on God's being as Father, Son, and Holy Spirit; they bring Christian *theologia* to its classical expression. But Gregory articulates his understanding of the Mystery in other places — in Oration 20, for instance, significantly titled *On Theology and the Appointment of Bishops,* a shorter sketch of the same classical vision presented in the Theological Orations, where an orthodox understanding of God as Trinity is seen as both the product of intense moral and intellectual purification and as the prerequisite for church leadership; in Oration 43, his *Panegyric on Basil,* where Basil's Trinitarian Orthodoxy is described as a central part of his leadership as bishop;[29] and in the triad of sermons for Christmas and Epiphany (Orations 38-40), where the Mystery of the Trinity, and of the redeeming Incarnation of the Son which has revealed it to us, is repeatedly presented as the real "message" of the season.[30] Many of Gregory's theological poems, written presumably during his retirement in the hope of providing young Greek readers with a new corpus of Christian literature in the best classical style,[31] celebrate these same mysteries.[32] *Theologia,* understood

27. *Or.* 2.36.

28. *Or.* 42.27.

29. *Or.* 43.30, 68.

30. *Or.* 38.8-9, 13-15; *Or.* 39.11-13; *Or.* 40.5.

31. See his reflections on why he writes poetry, in the poem "To His Own Verses" (Poems II, 1, 39, esp. ll. 9-15, 37-41, 90-97).

32. See, for instance, the first three of his so-called *Poemata Arcana,* which portray Father, Son, and Holy Spirit in the splendor of Homeric terminology, dialect and meter; also Poems I, 1, 29-34 (hymns to the Triune God); Poems I, 1, 10-11 (on the Incarnation); Poems I, 1, 19-28 (on passages from the Gospels).

as Christian talk of God, as the constant repetition of the church's proclamation of God's full reality, made visible in Jesus and communicated as transforming life in the Holy Spirit — a body of doctrine adapted to the needs of every individual and group, yet consistent in its content and practical implications[33] — is for Gregory clearly the central, unceasing task of the pastor.

How does one prepare for this daunting task? Without doubt, Gregory and his fellow Cappadocians were convinced of the importance of a humanistic education — of the linguistic, critical, and philosophical training so highly developed in Hellenistic antiquity — as laying the foundation for understanding and preaching the Word in terms that could convince the mind and move the heart. He writes in his panegyric on Basil:

> I think that everyone endowed with reason will agree that education *(paideusis)* is the foremost blessing we possess. I do not mean simply the noble education which we [Christians] cultivate, which has no respect for simply verbal elegance and magnificence, but values only the salutary effect and beauty of the ideas. I mean also secular education, which most Christians erroneously hold in contempt as subversive and dangerous, and tending to drive us far from God.[34]

Gregory himself, like his younger contemporary Augustine, was a specialist in the use of words; "I cleave to the word alone," he writes in his first oration *Against Julian*, "and I make no complaints about the labors I have undergone, on land and sea, that procured me the chance to make it mine!"[35]

But the acquisition of the verbal and speculative skill needed to communicate the Trinitarian Mystery of salvation in Christ called, in his view, for more than simply secular study and immersion in the Christian Scriptures and tradition. It called for "philosophy" in the broader sense cultivated in late antiquity by pagans and Christians alike: control and gradual restriction of our physical drives and sensual gratifications, withdrawal from the distractions of the world and the possibilities of recognition available to the articulate and the powerful,[36] the purgation of the intellect, the quest for purity of heart,[37] continual growth in virtue and spiritual focus.[38] So Gregory writes in

33. See *Or.* 2.44-46, on the need to "feed" each believer what he or she needs to grow towards graced perfection in Christ.
34. *Or.* 43.11.
35. *Or.* 4.100.
36. See *Or.* 2.6-7.
37. *Or.* 2.39, 74.
38. *Or.* 2.14. For a seminal treatment of the practical, "pastoral" aspect of most ancient

383 to Eudoxus, a young professor of rhetoric in Cappadocia, who seemed to have an aptitude for philosophy in its ascetic and pastoral, as well as its speculative sense:

> Far from us be thrones, power, wealth, distinction, promotions and falls, or that cheap and detestable thing, reputation, which leads rather to the disgrace of the one who seeks it and does not laugh at the farce and pretension of this great theatrical show! But let us concern ourselves with the Word alone,[39] and let us choose to put God before all things, the one sufficient Good available to us.[40]

The "philosophy" required of the theologian, in fact, must be more thorough-going and transforming than any simply intellectual or dialectical discipline, because its theoretical object is nothing less than God. So in his First Theological Oration, Gregory urges that we always be mindful of God, but that we remain modest and self-restrained in what we attempt to say of him, always conscious of the danger of vanity inherent in clever speech; theology done without virtue, especially theology done by a theologian who lacks the humility of Christ, always runs the risk of becoming simply an academic show (which Gregory compares to professional wrestling!), and, in the process, of cheapening its subject beyond recognition.[41]

When all the Platonic imagery and allusions to the culture of his day are set aside, what can Gregory of Nazianzus have to say to pastors and theologians of our own time who desire, like him, to convey the Christian Mystery in all its immediacy and power to the world they serve? A few themes stand out, perhaps, in what we have so briefly said:

(1) Christian pastoring is always theology first of all: speaking about the God revealed by Jesus, the God involved personally in created history as Father, Son, and Holy Spirit, the God who shapes us and draws us not just to know him, but to participate in his life. To speak rightly of God, to avoid the danger of self-promoting "babble" in our preaching, requires that the pastor's speech be unmistakably centered on the news of Jesus, divine and human, as

---

philosophy, and its parallel aspects both to the ascetical understanding of Christian "philosophy" of the fourth century and to modern forms of the quest for inner transformation, see Pierre Hadot, *Philosophy as a Way of Life*, ed. and trans. Arnold I. Davidson (Oxford: Blackwell, 1995).

39. Gregory seems to be cultivating ambiguity here: the *logos* he recommends to Eudoxus's concentration can mean Scripture, the things of the mind, the use of words, or simply the divine Logos who is the ultimate meaning and revelatory source of all of them.

40. Letter 178, to Eudoxus the Younger.

41. *Or.* 27, esp. sections 5, 2, 7-9.

it is contained in the Scriptures, the rule of faith, and the church's confessions. Theology of any kind is always dialogue: bringing these traditional sources for speech about God into conversation with the scientific, philosophical, and cultural concerns of each new age. But the pastor who attempts to carry out her or his tasks of leadership or sacramental ministry or therapeutic engagement apart from this theological, kerygmatic center is like someone leading an expedition in the dark or operating without surgical training — the exercise soon becomes aimless and empty.

(2) Christian theology, if authentic, is always pastoral in its purpose and its effects, because it is always an attempt to bring to human words the glimpse of the divine Mystery given to us by Jesus, which Christians believe transforms our lives and our hopes. It is never simply dialectical speculation; it is a call to live in God, a reflection on all that has happened "for us and for our salvation." Theology cannot survive and be itself, apart from the faith a pastor proclaims. As Gregory writes, at the end of his Third Theological Oration:

> When we put our primary emphasis on the power of reason, letting go of faith, and destroy the plausibility of the Spirit by our questioning, and when reason is then overwhelmed by the greatness of the subject — overwhelmed, surely, because it sets out simply by using the weak instrument of our intelligence — what happens? The weakness of reason appears as a weakness of the Mystery. And so the cleverness of reason lays open the "self-emptying of the cross," as Paul discovered. For faith is the completion of our human reason.[42]

Without the faith of the whole church, theology remains without content.

(3) If a pastor is to communicate this faith with theological sophistication, he or she needs a wide range of human skills: education, cultural sensitivity, eloquence, personal skills, the confidence to lead with authority, the wisdom to adapt to his or her audience. The pastor needs to be a poet as well as a therapist, a teacher as well as an animal trainer.

(4) But the pastor also needs to be a "philosopher" in the ancient sense: one whose life is simplified and largely purified from the dominant needs proposed by a consumer culture, whose inner drives are in control, whose priorities are single-mindedly centered on the quest for God. As Gregory puts it:

> Before one has mastered this [sensual aspect] as far as possible, and has sufficiently purified one's understanding, before one has moved far be-

---

42. *Or.* 29.21.

yond the rest in nearness to God, I think it is unsafe for him [or her] to receive authority over souls, or to be made a mediator between God and other people — for this, perhaps, is what a priest is meant to be![43]

Wallace Alston once described the purpose of his program for Pastor-Theologians as a seeking for ways to let the best theological research and thought of our time find its way "into the bloodstream of the Church." The astonishing success of the program thus far witnesses to a certain theological anemia all of us feel, who are involved in the ministry of talking about God. Gregory Nazianzen, in the fourth century, and Wallace in our own — different as they are in personality, and in theological and pastoral style — have both recognized, more deeply than many in the church, the inseparability of humanistic culture, discipline of life, and thoughtful, learned, Scriptural piety from any fruitful form of Christian leadership. The church stands deeply in debt to them both, as men who have succeeded, genuinely and publicly, in living the Mystery.

43. *Or.* 2.91.

"... The Doing of the Little Righteousness":
On Justice in Barth's View of the Christian Life

Dirk Smit

Reading Barth in South Africa?

From afar, at least from the perspective of several South Africans who came to know him, Wallace Alston has the reputation that he reads Karl Barth, that he is committed to the Reformed faith and the ecumenical Church, and that he is deeply concerned with issues of justice.

For many of us, these commitments do not appear as separate or diverse interests, but as one, as a single commitment. Many of the respected and influential South African theologians in the struggle against the ideology, theology, and practices of apartheid were inspired by precisely this kind of understanding of the Christian faith. They held a deeply Reformed vision of the Christian life — already represented by Calvin and some early Reformed confessions — concretely expressed in their commitment to the unity of the church in its faith and order, its life and work, and its mission and witness, and theologically informed by a Barthian reading of this tradition.

Well-known theologians like Willie Jonker,[1] David Bosch,[2] Jaap

---

1. W. D. Jonker, without a doubt the most widely respected theologian of the Dutch Reformed Church over several decades, and also a leader in the struggles against the influence of apartheid theology in church and society, was not only steeped in the theology of Calvin and the Reformed Confessions, but also deeply influenced by Karl Barth. For his respect for the Reformed tradition, see his study *Bevrydende Waarheid. Die Karakter van die Gereformeerde Belydenis* (Wellington: Hugenote Uitgewers, 1994), and for his engagement with Barth, see, e.g., his autobiographical "Some remarks on the interpretation of Karl Barth," *NGTT* 29 (1988): 29-40, and his *Selfs die kerk kan verander* (Kaapstad: Tafelberg, 1998). His contributions to the series of systematic theological works which he wrote with Jaap Durand, called *Wegwysers in die Dogmatiek*, were finally all attempts to come to grips with Barth's views — on Jesus Christ, on the Holy Spirit, and on election and covenant.

2. Missiologist David Bosch, tragically killed in a car accident in 1992, was arguably the

Durand,[3] John de Gruchy,[4] Allan Boesak,[5] Takatso Mofokeng,[6] and Russel

best-known Dutch Reformed theologian of his generation outside South Africa. In both ecumenical and evangelical circles his impact has been remarkable. He is probably best known for his magnum opus, *Transforming Mission. Paradigm Shifts in Theology of Mission* (Maryknoll, NY: Orbis, 1991), but he also published many other influential and popular books and read many papers over several decades. In almost all of these, the influence of Barth is not only pervasively present, but most of the time also explicitly acknowledged. See e.g. also *Witness to the World* (Atlanta: John Knox Press, 1979).

3. Jaap (J. J. F.) Durand, both a missiologist and a systematic theologian, was widely respected for his clear and prophetic witness and his courageous, also public commitment to unity, peace, reconciliation, and justice over several decades. Not only did he often engage with Barth's theology and write insightfully about Barth's reception in South African Reformed churches, but he also clearly acknowledged Barth's crucial influence on his own life and work. See for example his autobiographical essay "Hoe my gedagtewêreld verander het: van ewige waarhede tot gekontekstualiseerde metafore," *NGTT* 43 (2002): 64-70, abridged as "When theology became metaphor," *JTSA* 111 (Nov. 2001): 12-16.

4. John W. de Gruchy, from the United Congregational Church of Southern Africa, has significantly contributed to church and society issues in South Africa, in the spirit and tradition of Barth and Bonhoeffer. In August 2000, he deservedly received the Karl Barth Prize in Berlin, as acknowledgement of this. Many of his publications over several decades bear witness to this influence, from his doctoral thesis on the ecclesiology of Barth and Bonhoeffer, to popular works, like *Cry Justice. Prayers, Meditations and Readings from South Africa* (London: Collins, 1986), and scholarly works, like *Liberating Reformed Theology. A South African Contribution to an Ecumenical Debate* (Grand Rapids: Eerdmans, 1991). See also for some reflections on this influence, Dirk J. Smit, "Seeing Things Differently: On Prayer and Politics," in *Theology in Dialogue. The Impact of the Arts, Humanities, & Science on Contemporary Religious Thought: Essays in Honor of John W. de Gruchy*, ed. Lyn Holness and Ralf K. Wüstenberg (Grand Rapids: Eerdmans, 2002), pp. 271-84.

5. Allan A. Boesak played a major role, both in Reformed and in ecumenical church circles, both within South Africa and internationally, and in diverse capacities as church leader and pastor, theologian and scholar, and social activist. He often appealed to both Calvin (and the Reformed tradition, including Abraham Kuyper) and Barth, both in his more popular sermons and pastoral work and in his more scholarly work. See the volume of essays, *Black and Reformed. Apartheid, Liberation, and the Calvinist Tradition*, ed. Leonard Sweetman (New York: Orbis, 1984), for such references to both Calvin and Barth. In his "Foreword" for *On Reading Karl Barth in South Africa*, ed. Charles Villa-Vicencio (Grand Rapids: Eerdmans, 1988), he explains: "I have often recognized in Barth's writings a strangely contemporary ring, and have used them in my own theology," and then couples this with the influence of Paul Lehmann on his life and thought, "Professor Lehmann's theology has had a profound influence on my theological pilgrimage, and I rate his *Transfiguration of Politics* among the most formative theological studies I have ever read."

6. Takatso A. Mofokeng, one of the most respected South African Reformed systematic theologians and scholars, dealt extensively with Barth in his doctoral dissertation, *The Crucified among the Crossbearers. Towards a Black Christology* (Kampen: Kok, 1983). As motto, he used Barth's words: "In each age and by each responsible theologian the best definitions, combina-

Botman,[7] albeit in diverse ways and with different emphases and influences in their own lives and work, are in the final resort all best described by this Reformed and ecumenical vision, inspired by Calvin, read through Barth's eyes. Central in this vision is a deep commitment to justice.[8]

The Struggle for Human Righteousness

In 1962, at the end of his academic career, Barth gave the Warfield Lectures at Princeton, on "evangelical theology."[9] In a simple way the 76-year-old theologian drew together the most fundamental convictions and concerns of his work and life. He concluded these lectures with a final question and answer session in the Princeton University Chapel, just a stone's throw from the

---

tions and conclusions must always be sought and found afresh in dogmatics with a continually new desire for obedience." However, he explicitly wanted to move "Beyond Barth," pp. 222ff., because, according to him (and in the spirit of Dutch theologian Noordmans), Barth did not "succeed to provide a satisfactory answer to those people 'whose entire life seems to be a long Good Friday.'" And yet, precisely this move "beyond Barth" was doing what Barth called for, according to his own motto.

7. Russel H. Botman, another leading Reformed theologian and scholar, both in South Africa and ecumenically, and particularly also in the circles of the World Alliance of Reformed Churches, did his doctoral work on Dietrich Bonhoeffer (his unpublished thesis from the University of the Western Cape is called *Discipleship as Transformation? Towards a Theology of Transformation,* 1994). He has, since then, often read and published papers on Barth and his role in South Africa. See e.g. his recent "Belhar and the white DRC: Changes in the DRC: 1974-1990," *Scriptura* 76 (2001): 33-42, for a much discussed, challenging and influential analysis.

8. For Barth's own reception of Calvin, see e.g. his early lectures, *The Theology of John Calvin* (Grand Rapids: Eerdmans, 1995), in which his appreciation for Calvin's social and moral vision plays a central role (particularly pp. 48ff.), as well as the short but instructive "Thoughts on the 400th Anniversary of Calvin's Death," in his *Fragments Grave and Gay* (Glasgow: Collins, 1971), pp. 105-10. Several valuable essays on the theme are to be found in Hans Scholl, ed., *Karl Barth und Johannes Calvin. Karl Barth's Göttinger Calvin-Vorlesung von 1922* (Neukirchen: Neukirchener Verlag, 1995). Recently, Cees van der Kooi published a very instructive comparison of Calvin and Barth, focusing on the knowledge of God in their thought, *Als in een spiegel. God kennen volgens Calvijn en Barth* (Kampen: Kok, 2002). John Webster aptly comments: "Barth is evidently drawn to the Calvin whom he portrays as the theologian of the Christian life and obedience," *Barth's Moral Theology* (Grand Rapids: Eerdmans, 1988), p. 3. Later he concludes: "It would not be too much to claim that in the Calvin lecture cycle Barth already and very quickly formed some of the basic lines of his later ethical thinking: the picture of God and humanity as agents in relation; the irreversibility of gospel and law; and the coinherence of dogmatics and ethics," p. 34.

9. Karl Barth, *Evangelical Theology. An Introduction* (1963; reprint, Grand Rapids: Eerdmans, 1980).

church where Wallace Alston would spend an important part of his life. "Would you elucidate how 'evangelical theology' is related to politics?" someone asked. "How are eschatology and sanctification related to political action?"

"What do we mean when we speak of politics?" Barth responded, and provided his own, seemingly simple answer:

> Politics is an aspect of what we have just called culture. Politics means the human attempt to create and uphold some sort of order and peace in the world. Even at best, politics will create only *some* sort of order or *some* peace, no more. The purpose of politics is to realize in some degree something like a human commonwealth. Now since 'evangelical theology' deals with God's justice (God has revealed the justice of the covenant in Jesus Christ), it confronts all human attempts to create justice, order, peace, and so on with this superior justice. Thus there is an encounter here and to this extent 'evangelical theology' has to do with politics. Now, we also say that Jesus Christ is a King who came once and who will come again. If we look at the fact that he came — we then understand our sanctification. He came; and since he came, we are sanctified for the service of this King. But he will come again — here we then have eschatology. Christians look forward in hope to the new coming of the same King. So from both sides — from sanctification completed in Jesus Christ's death and resurrection on to eschatology or his second coming in glory — Christianity has to do with politics. If Christians serve the King of Kings, then politics is something straightforward. Thus theology is itself political action. There is no theological word, no theological reflection or elucidation, there is no sermon and even no catechism for children which does not imply political meaning and as such enter into the world as a little bit of political reality. You cannot believe in the Kingdom which can and will come without also being a politician. Every Christian is a politician, and the church proclaiming the Kingdom of Jesus Christ is itself a political reality.[10]

Behind this deceptively simple answer lies Barth's whole career. Careful exegesis will find almost every central theme in his oeuvre resonating here beneath the seemingly quiet and peaceful surface. Perhaps a useful way to approach this answer could be to read it against the backdrop of his last lecture series, which he completed shortly before he went on the tour to the United

---

10. Karl Barth, "A Theological Dialogue," *Theology Today* XIX, no. 2 (July 1962): 171-7, specifically pp. 175-76.

States, and in particular the very last paragraph of his posthumously published, unedited lecture fragments from his ethics of reconciliation, §78.4 of the *Church Dogmatics,* with the heading *fiat justitia.* It may even be plausible to imagine that he still had these last lectures in mind that evening in Princeton when he heard this question and responded in this fashion!

In these lectures, thinking about "the command of God the Reconciler,"[11] Barth considers — in typically Reformed way — the Christian life. He finds the heart of the Christian life in prayer, in invocation, in calling upon this God, and therefore discusses this life by reflecting on the different petitions of the Lord's Prayer. Unfortunately, he finds time to deal only with the first petition, hallowed be thy name, under the heading "Zeal for the honor of God" (§77),[12] and the second petition, thy kingdom come, under the heading "The struggle for human righteousness" (§78).

In the opening sentences, where Barth paraphrases in his usual way the thrust of what is to follow, he already makes the point very clearly: "Christians pray to God that he will cause his righteousness to appear and dwell on a new earth under a new heaven. Meanwhile they act in accordance with their prayer as people who are responsible for the rule of human righteousness, that is, for the preservation and renewal, the deepening and extending, of the divinely ordained safeguards of human rights, human freedom, and human peace on earth."[13]

He develops these ideas in four paragraphs. Under "revolt against disorder," he argues that the genuineness of human zeal for God and accordingly of the passion with which we pray the first petition has to be tested (§78.1). This testing brings us within the sphere of ethical discussion, he says, and in particular within the ethical struggle for human righteousness. "Zeal for God's honor can be good, obedient, and full of promise only when it is directly accompanied by the struggle for human righteousness" (p. 206). He then describes this struggle in terms of revolt, conflict, warfare — however, not against people, but against a plight. "The militant revolt demanded of Christians — and this distinguishes it from all kinds of other revolts — is not directed *against* [Barth's italics] any people . . . not even the wicked on ac-

---

11. Every volume of the *Church Dogmatics* ends with a section on ethics, but according to Barth this part, the ethics of reconciliation, forms the heart of everything.

12. Eberhard Busch took this notion as title for his very helpful introduction to Barth's own work, particularly the *Church Dogmatics,* namely *Die grosse Leidenschaft. Einführung in die Theologie Karl Barths* (Gütersloh: Kaiser, Gütersloher Verlagshaus, 1998); for the ethics, see specifically pp. 161-83.

13. Karl Barth, *The Christian Life: Church Dogmatics* IV/4 (Grand Rapids: Eerdmans, 1981), p. 205 [references to these pages now follow in brackets].

count of their wickedness and oppression or on account of what Christians have to suffer at their hands in coarser and more refined forms." Instead, "they rebel and fight *for* [Barth's italics] all people, even, and in the last resort precisely, for those with whom they may clash" (pp. 210-1). Ultimately, all people together are suffering from a common plight, which is the real enemy, "a disorder which both inwardly and outwardly controls and penetrates and poisons and disrupts all human relations and interconnections" (p. 211).

How do Christians revolt and struggle against this plight? Their decisive action, which, correctly understood, includes all other possible forms of action, is their calling upon God in the second petition of the Lord's Prayer, says Barth. Christians have the freedom to pray that God's kingdom, Godself in this act, will appear and come. Their use of this freedom, their sighing, calling, and crying "Thy kingdom come," is the revolt demanded from them against this disorder and human plight (p. 212). However, given the nature of prayer, he continues,

> Invocation of God in and with this prayer, obedient human action in this vertical direction, implies (as the same obedient human action) the horizontal of a corresponding human, and therefore provisional, attitude and mode of conduct in the sphere of freedom. . . . To pray the prayer does not excuse them from provisionally rebelling and battling the disorder in their own human thoughts and words and works. On the contrary, they cannot pray the prayer aright without in so doing being projected into this corresponding action of their own which is provisional but nonetheless serious in this particular sphere.

He is careful to prevent possible misunderstandings of this "corresponding human action, provisional yet serious." What kind of seeking first God's kingdom and righteousness would that be, he asks rhetorically, what kind of hungering and thirsting after it, what kind of waiting for the new heaven and the new earth in which it dwells, what kind of praying that prayer, if we were not motivated thereby to do resolutely what we can here and now on this side in orientation and with a view to God's side, without claim or illusion, not trying to anticipate what only God could begin and only he can finish, but rising up for righteousness and order in the midst of disorder and opposition to it? He answers his own rhetorical questions without any hesitation:

> Where free praying of the second petition is a living and powerful event in the great hope of God's future, there the vitality and force of little hopes for the present of a person and a people will not be lacking: the free

and responsible advocacy, actualized in little steps, of that which in the light of the act which God has commenced and will complete can be called human right, human freedom, and human peace, of that which very provisionally and incompletely can already be these things.

This leads him to consider what he calls the ethical implications of this petition in a second paragraph, on "the lordless powers" (§78.2). Here he speaks "more closely and more precisely" about the enemy, the great disorder, the plight, the forms of human unrighteousness that contradict and oppose the salutary order and righteousness of God. This involves not only human rebellion against God, but also the many rebellions unleashed by that rebellion, namely those of human abilities, exalting themselves as lordless powers, turned against human beings themselves (p. 215). Barth's innovative and often fascinating description of several of these powers — the demonism of politics; the very mobile demon called Mammon; the intellectual constructs called ideologies and -isms; what he calls *chthonic* forces, from the physical spheres of the created cosmos, including technology, fashion, sport, pleasure, transportation! — is probably the part of the ethics of reconciliation that has received most attention from commentators. These powers, Barth concludes, disrupt life, rob people of freedom, oppress them, afflict them, and harass them. Under their lordship, people become "people of disorder," estranged from God, from themselves and from others. As these powers tear apart the individual, they tear society apart also. They destroy and ruin both individual and society. Their dominion reveals, though it does not constitute, the plight of humanity, "the profound unrighteousness in which we people exist — each alone and in mutual relation — because of the basic unrighteousness of our relationship to God, the unrighteousness in which, each for themselves and all for others, we inevitably make life more or less difficult" (p. 233).

Over against this kingdom of human disorder, however, stands the kingdom of divine order, says Barth, and discusses this in a third paragraph called "thy kingdom come" (§78.3). What do Christians pray for when they call upon God in this way? he asks, and answers that this kingdom "defies expression" (p. 237). All errors at this point have their source in the idea that we are able by analogy to get some picture and concept of the kingdom of God, thinking we know what is meant by the terms God, kingdom, or coming (p. 237). It "escapes all intellectual systematizing," it is "independent of human will and act and different from all the human works and achievements into whose sphere it enters" (p. 240). Again, he is clearly at pains to protect what he has to say against widespread misunderstandings and false interpretations. Human beings "cannot bring in the kingdom of God." It is "not a kind of continuing, prolonging, excelling, and completing of what people may, as commanded, attempt and undertake in a more or less rich understanding of their relationship to it or in some other form of reflection on what is good. It is instead the new thing." It is "not a refining or strengthening or intensifying or qualifying of such action." It is instead "God's own action, which does not merge into the best of human action" (p. 240).

On this point, Barth is convinced that he is parting company with Reformation exegesis, which has, remarkably, remained normative in modern theology until his own time. His strong eschatological understanding once again causes a major crisis for ethics, as has been the case in his early period of *Romans,* and he is fully aware of this. "If we cannot say something about this, what have we been talking about all this time? And should we not be left in darkness as to the extent to which, as we pray for the dawning of God's righteousness, we find ourselves summoned to take up resolutely, if relatively, provisionally, and feebly, the struggle for human righteousness too?" He admits that with this strictly eschatological meaning of the prayer "its ethical relevance is at stake, which leads to a further question" (p. 246).

Where does Barth find an answer to this question? In the fact that according to the New Testament this future, this coming kingdom, this strictly eschatological act of God has also already taken place, in a definitive event within history, in a specific, once-for-all and unique history within that history, namely in Jesus Christ. In Him we receive knowledge of this kingdom, of this new thing of God, and precisely on the basis of this knowledge we call upon God for its manifestation (p. 247). Speaking about God's kingdom could only mean telling his story (p. 253), the story of the center, the whence and whither, the basis, theme, and content of all the New Testament sayings (p. 248). It means telling the history of Jesus Christ, of his words, deeds, suffering, death, resurrection, and gift of the Holy Spirit (pp. 248-9). Jesus is the kingdom, and therefore Christians know something of what they pray for when they pray for the coming of this kingdom.

Fiat Iustitia?

Finally, these thoughts bring Barth to the fourth and last paragraph of his final lectures, called *"fiat iustitia"* (§78.4). Victims of the ongoing course of the world, those suffering under the many and complex forms of human unrighteousness and disorder, have seen Him, *Yahweh tsidkenu,* "the Lord our Righteousness." They have the freedom and joy, but also hear the command, to lift up their heads and call upon Him to come. Their obedience to this command, their humble but vigorous use of the freedom to call upon God in this way, is their true and essential revolt against unrighteousness and disorder (pp. 260-61).

For Barth, praying this prayer is of extreme importance. It is the fundamental human, ethical activity, "the core and star of the very modest contribution that can be made on the human side in the battle against disorder." In all its modesty, he says, "this is the most authentic, powerful, and effective thing that can be done on the human side." All else that might be considered and done "does not reach up to Christian expectation and prayer because even at best it can be aimed only at shifts of emphasis within the world, at contestable, partial, and provisional corrections of the human situation."[14] Again he deliberately uses rhetorical language to underline the point:

> The prayer which this King himself has laid on the lips of Christians, even as and though it too is a wholly human and therefore feeble action, surpasses all other possibilities of human revolt against disorder. As Christians call upon God with this petition, they do what is qualitatively more and better than the best that all other movements for the establishment of human righteousness can do, their own efforts included. If only they knew what a task and what power were entrusted to them when as children of God they are freed and summoned to hasten to their Father with this prayer to him! If only they knew what a debt they incur to him and themselves and the whole world which they have to represent with this petition if they neglect to do this! If only they knew finally with what profoundest rest and joy they can withstand the inner and outer assaults of the course of the world with all things that are so unseemly and intolerable and monstrous and impossible in it when they do not grow indolent and slothful but persist cheerfully and industriously in the by no means heroic action of praying "Thy kingdom come."

14. An early but still very helpful introduction to Barth's view of the centrality of calling on God for Christian life remains Eberhard Jüngel's essay "Anrufung Gottes als Grundethos christlichen Handelns. Einführende Bemerkungen zu den nachgelassenen Fragmenten der Ethik der Versöhnungslehre Karl Barths," in *Barth-Studien* (Gütersloh: Gütersloher Verlagshaus Gerd Mohn, 1982), pp. 315-31. According to him, this in fact represents the final point, summary, and challenge of the whole *Church Dogmatics:* "Barths Entwurf versteht die Anrufung Gottes als das dem Menschen gebotene Tun, als Aktion im strengen Sinne. . . . (Hier haben wir zu tun) mit dem pointiertesten Ausdruck jener Grundentscheidung der Theologie Barths, die die Kirchliche Dogmatik innerhalb und ausserhalb der Theologie zur Provokation werden liess. . . . Mit dem Verständnis der Ethik als Unterweisung im Beten ist noch einmal der genuine Ansatz der ganzen Kirchliche Dogmatik, ist insofern aber auch die Fülle ihrer Probleme auf das pointierteste zur Stelle," pp. 324-25.

Praying this prayer, Barth explains, is "not heroic," it is "very unassuming," it is "performed by people in human fashion," it is done in "weakness," yet, "something happens" (pp. 261-2). With this "something that happens" Barth finally makes his crucial but by now characteristic move. Whenever people seriously, bravely, says Barth, pray this prayer — unassuming, in weakness, in human fashion — "then necessarily with their hearts and lips, caught up by what they pray, their whole life and thought and word and deed are set in motion, oriented to the point to which they look with the petition."[15] The whole Christian faith and doctrine developed in the *Church Dogmatics* is called to mind. In the power of Jesus Christ who rose again and lives for them, and through the work of the Holy Spirit, enlightening and impelling them, a radical movement and turning is taking place in their lives. Praying this petition "means having no other choice but to look ahead and also to live and think and speak and act ahead, to run from the beginning, the history of Jesus Christ first revealed in his resurrection, to the goal, its final manifestation, the coming kingdom of God" (p. 262).

In fact, *the heart of the Christian ethos* — Barth's own words — "is that those who are freed and summoned to pray 'Thy kingdom come' are also freed and summoned to use their freedom to obey the command that is given therewith and to live for their part with a view to the coming kingdom" (pp. 262-63).

His point can hardly be any clearer. The heart of the Christian ethos is that people obediently use their freedom to live with a view to the coming kingdom.

But what is this coming kingdom? Barth explains this in terms of God's righteousness, making use of several Biblical references. Central among them is Mal. 4:2 on "Jesus Christ as the sun of righteousness, the sun of grace which lightens all people, Christians and non-Christians, good and bad, which also illumines and enlightens them." Bringing in this day, causing it to dawn, to reveal God's righteousness in its majesty, cannot be the affair of anyone, whether Christian or non-Christian, but is solely of the free mercy of God. However, this could not possibly mean that "those who in the power of the resurrection of Jesus Christ from the dead, enlightened by the Holy Spirit of the Father and the Son, look ahead" could be "idle in the meantime."

Warning against such idleness, he uses strong language and clearly has

15. Joseph L. Mangina, in his *Karl Barth on the Christian Life. The Practical Knowledge of God* (New York: Peter Lang, 2001), offers probably the most instructive attempt available to argue that the formation of the Christian person is in fact very much present in Barth's work, although often overlooked or misunderstood. His final chapter deals with this section from *The Christian Life,* and discusses the role of zeal or passion.

specific people and viewpoints in mind — or perhaps earlier accusations directed against his own theology? It should be unthinkable, impossible for Christians

> to acquiesce for the time being in human unrighteousness and disorder and their consequences, in the mortal imperiling of life, freedom, peace, and joy on earth under the lordship of the lordless powers; so far as possible to adjust themselves during the interim to the status quo; and perhaps even with gloomy skeptical speculation to find comfort in the thought that until God's final and decisive intervention, the course of events will necessarily be not only as bad as previously but increasingly worse.

No, people who zealously pray this prayer will "*wait* and *hasten* toward the dawn of God's day, the appearing of his righteousness" (his italics). "They not only wait but also hasten. They wait by hastening. Their waiting takes place in the hastening" (p. 263). This is the context where Nigel Biggar finds the title of his extremely helpful discussion of Barth's ethics, *The Hastening That Waits.*[16]

How do such people live with a view to this coming kingdom, how do they wait and hasten, wait by hastening? The answer, says Barth, lies in the words *fiat iustitia;* he explains: Christians are claimed for action in the effort and struggle for human righteousness. He is at pains to underline that he is talking about human, not about divine righteousness. He is emphatic about this. Christians should not misunderstand what they are doing and what they are called to do. "Christians can never have anything to do with the arrogant and foolhardy enterprise of trying to bring in and build up by human hands a religious, cultic, moral, or political kingdom of God on earth."

This time in between the beginning and the end, "the time of the presence of Jesus Christ in the Holy Spirit," is a time "for gratitude, hope, prayer, and of responsibility for the occurrence of human righteousness." Christians have to be concerned about this, they have no pretext for escaping responsibility for it. If they want to draw back here, Barth says, there is serious reason to ask whether and how far their gratitude, hope, and prayer are to be taken seriously (p. 264).

This human righteousness, he emphasizes, is always imperfect, fragile, and highly problematical, but this must not tempt Christians to refrain from doing what they have to do in all its relativity. Protestants have always had such an inclination, says Barth, and they should break free from this. They are forbidden all lazy excuses. "Precisely because they are duly forbidden to at-

---

16. Nigel Biggar, *The Hastening That Waits. Karl Barth's Ethics* (New York: Oxford University Press, 1995).

tempt the impossible, they are with great strictness required and with great kindness freed and empowered to do what they can in the sphere of the relative possibilities assigned to them, to do it very imperfectly yet heartily, quietly, and cheerfully."

> They may and can and should, rise up and *accept responsibility* to the utmost of their power *for the doing of the little righteousness.* . . . The only danger arising out of the (ill-founded) anxiety that one might become too righteous and too holy, is the temptation to remain passive where what is required, with a full sense of one's limitations, is to become active (p. 265).

Accepting responsibility for the doing of the little righteousness — this summarizes Barth's understanding of the Christian ethos.

He is fully aware that this is not as self-evident as it may seem to some. To use the expression "righteousness" in the ambivalent, ambiguous, relative sphere of human activity does not speak for itself. In fact, says Barth, this analogy — between God's righteousness and whatever human beings may be doing — is in truth an impossible one (p. 265). He is therefore very careful. "Certainly we should not say too much here, yet we should not say too little either" (p. 266), since there is a certain "correspondence," which makes such human action *"kingdom-like"* and therefore "on a lower level and within its impassable limits (to be called) *righteous* action" (his italics).

What could this mean? asks Barth, and answers that any such action — to be described as kingdom-like, as human righteousness, as in correspondence with the object of the petition — "must in all circumstances take place with a view to people, in address to people, and with the aim of helping people" (p. 266). Why? The answer is again characteristically Barth, namely,

> *Christians can look only where they see God looking* and try to live with no other purpose than that with which God acts in Jesus Christ.[17]

---

17. "Seeing" plays an important role in Barth's understanding of the Christian life, see e.g. my essays "Liturgy and life? On the importance of worship for Christian ethics," *Scriptura* 62 (1997): 259-80; "'Seeing Things Differently' — On Prayer and Politics," in *Theology in Dialogue: The Impact of the Arts, Humanities, and Science on Contemporary Religious Thought,* ed. L. Holness and R. K. Wüstenberg (Grand Rapids: Eerdmans, 2002), pp. 271-84; "On learning to see? A Reformed perspective on the church and the poor," in *Suffering, Poverty, and HIV-AIDS: International Practical Theological Perspectives,* ed. by Pamela Couture and Bonnie J. Miller-McLemore (Cardiff: Cardiff Academic Press, 2003). In short, "the followers of Jesus Christ are given to see the world differently," John Webster, *Barth's Moral Theology* (Grand Rapids: Eerd-

What does this mean, concretely? Once more the answer is typical and to be expected:

> This means that the true and serious and finally important object of their attention, love, and will, and therefore of their thought, speech, and action, in agreement with their prayer and in correspondence with what they pray for, can only be *human beings.*[18]

In support of this, he appeals to the central conviction about the Christian life from Calvin and the Reformed tradition that we are not our own:

> "We are not our own but God's" (Calvin, *Inst.,* III, 7, 1). "We do not belong to ourselves but to the Lord." But because the Lord is the Father, Son, and Holy Spirit who bound and obligated himself to human beings, Christians also belong to humankind and in this concrete sense they belong to themselves (267).[19]

For sure, Christians can never be for human beings or do for human beings what God does, but they can and should be — and again Barth uses a characteristic expression — "witnesses" of what God is and does for human beings.[20] They "may and can and should reflect and practice God's being and

---

mans, 1998), p. 120. It is not surprising that Stanley Hauerwas would make so much of the idea of "seeing correctly," of "looking in the right direction." Talking about Barth, he says: "As Barth uses it, the language of the church is itself already an argument just to the extent that his descriptions and redescriptions cannot help but challenge our normal way of seeing the world. The *Church Dogmatics* is a manual designed to train Christians that the habits of our speech must be disciplined by the God found in Jesus Christ. This training, which requires both intellectual and moral transformation, enables Christians to see the world as it is, and not as it appears," *With the Grain of the Universe* (Grand Rapids: Brazos Press, 2002), pp. 182-3.

18. It is not necessary to repeat how his treatment of all Christian doctrines, creation and covenant; election and reconciliation, everything, points to this fundamental divine Yes to human beings, so clearly narrated in *The Humanity of God* (London: Collins, 1961).

19. For an extremely insightful discussion of Barth's appropriation of this fundamental notion in Reformed theology and piety — that "we do not belong to ourselves" — see William Stacy Johnson, *The Mystery of God. Karl Barth and the Postmodern Foundations of Theology* (Louisville, KY: Westminster John Knox Press, 1997), pp. 176ff.

20. The notion of "witness" plays a crucial role in Barth's thought, whether talking about Jesus Christ, the nature and authority of the Bible, the task of the church, the power of preaching, the calling of believers, or the meaning of his own life. John D. Godsey, in his "Portrait" of Barth, concludes: "Barth desired one thing in life: to be witness. Like John the Baptist in Grünewald's 'Crucifixion,' he has pointed to that One who died on the Cross: *Illum oportet crescere, me minui,*" Karl Barth, *How I Changed My Mind* (Edinburgh: The Saint Andrew Press, 1966), p. 14. The reference is to the Isenheimer Altar, of which a picture hung opposite Barth's

acting for humanity" — and precisely as they do this, they practice the appropriate human righteousness corresponding to the great divine righteousness. In fact, this is the meaning of the *fiat* in *fiat iustitia*:

> That this should be done and occur *(fiat)* in what they think and speak and do, that it should be the orientation and basis of their lives, is the responsibility they are given (p. 267).

Christians are called to this responsibility in the concrete reality of everyday life, the world of unrighteousness and disorder, of evil and corruption, and of shared guilt. They have to swim against the stream — yet another favorite expression[21] — regardless of the cost or consequences. They do this without extravagant gestures or too big a song about what they are doing, as sinners, but righteous sinners, concerned with human beings (p. 267). From the very start they are "humanists" — but not interested in any cause as such, because they always ask, in regard to every cause, whether and how far it will relatively and provisionally serve or hurt the cause of human beings and their right and worth.

> No idea, no principle, no traditional or newly established institution or organization, no old or new form of economy, state, or culture, no so-called patrimony, no prevailing habit, custom, or moral system, no ideal of education and upbringing, no form of the church, can be for them the a priori of what they think and speak and will, nor can any negation or contesting of certain other ideas and the social constructs corresponding to them. Their a priori is not a cause, however great, necessary or splendid it may appear to be or is. It is the righteousness of God in Jesus Christ

---

desk and to which he referred on 51 occasions during his career — for the 50th time in this section on the struggle for human righteousness. For a detailed discussion of all these uses and Barth's understanding of Grünewald's work, see Reiner Marquard, *Karl Barth und der Isenheimer Altar* (Stuttgart: Calwer Verlag, 1995). It is therefore not surprising that Stanley Hauerwas uses the headings "The witness that was Karl Barth" and "The witness of the Church Dogmatics" to describe respectively Barth's life and work in his Gifford Lectures, *With the Grain of the Universe* (Grand Rapids: Brazos Press, 2001).

21. Barth was very fond of the metaphor, "swimming against the stream." Already in Göttingen he described himself in this way, and after the War he entitled a collection of some of his post–World War political writings, *Against the Stream: Shorter post-War writings* (London: SCM, 1964). In *Church Dogmatics* IV/3, p. 528, he still describes the difficulties of Christians who, despite their solidarity with society and the world, often find themselves swimming against the stream, being opposed from all sides. Frank Jehle therefore chose this as the title of his account of Barth's own political involvement, *Ever Against the Stream. The Politics of Karl Barth, 1906-1969* (Grand Rapids: Eerdmans, 2002).

and therefore, in correspondence with this, the person who is loved by God, his or her right and worth — solely and simply human beings (pp. 267-68).

This will certainly call them to say Yes and No and often to do it resolutely, "not afraid of taking sides for or against" — but it will never be an absolute Yes or No, carrying an absolute commitment. They think and speak and act in terms of theses, not of principles. Sooner or later every idea or life-form will prove a threat to human beings. Christians, always looking to the only problem that seriously and finally interests them, will therefore inevitably always experience a certain distance, a certain liberty, saying only a partial Yes or No where a total one was expected, or vice versa. Their total and definitive decision is always for human beings and never for any cause; in fact, exercising this freedom means that they "will never let themselves be addressed as prisoners of their own decisions or slaves of any sacrosanct consistency" (p. 268).

Very specifically this implies that they "must resolutely refuse to swallow some of the strengthenings they are offered in order that they may go through world history with a stiffened backbone." In fact, in this refusal they will show that they have real backbone! They refuse these forms of help and assistance not because "they themselves are possessed by a principial nonconformism," but because they know that the people they are concerned about cannot be helped by such strengthenings, "in the name of absolutes," by "champions of pseudo-deities," by principles claiming to be irrefutable.[22]

Christians see people as human beings, as objects of the eternal covenantal love of the Triune God — and therefore never solely as causes, as members of this or that, not even as Christians or non-Christians, as good or bad. Christians cannot stop here, looking at humankind only in terms of these "garbs," "masks," or "disguises." These are not human beings themselves, even if they should act as if they want to be seen and addressed only in terms of these disguises. No, Christians see deeper, because they have learned to see human beings in the way that the living God — in Christ and through

22. The well-known South African missiologist Nico Smith, who gained position and status in the Dutch Reformed Church as a member of the Broederbond, but later resigned in dramatic fashion, left his teaching post and went back to the ministry in the (then) black Dutch Reformed Church in Africa, often describes a brief conversation with Barth as the turning-point in his own career. Barth simply asked him whether he was free, free to proclaim the gospel — and the challenge of this question changed his life. Being a member of the secret and very powerful Broederbond at the time was a classic form of this kind of ideological "strengthenings" providing influence and power, particularly also to pastors. "Freedom" plays a crucial role in Barth's thought, as many studies have already argued in detail.

the Spirit — sees them. Human beings suffer in many ways, due to the un-righteousness and disorder in life. But they refuse to admit this and act, by way of all these disguises, as if they do not suffer, as if they are in control, pur-poseful, satisfied, and fulfilled. The calling of Christians is to see human be-ings in their suffering — this suffering which they try their best to hide, even from themselves. Such are the people who pray the Lord's Prayer and who serve "the little righteousness" (p. 269).

> The task of little righteousness which Christians are given when they may pray for the coming of God's kingdom is to see and understand human beings in this plight from which they cannot rescue themselves (pp. 269-70).

What do these human beings need? Once again, Barth's answer is char-acteristic of his whole theology. "Being hopeless, they need hope." They need the promise that what they are really longing and looking for is there for them — and "Christians know and have this promise." To bid people hope and to mediate to them this promise, is their task; "concern for this is their conflict." This is the Christian life. This is the Christian calling, witness, proclamation, task, and opportunity. In bringing people this hope,

> they practice the little righteousness which is their affair and portion, in contrast and yet also in correspondence with the great righteousness that God has practiced, practices, and will still practice (p. 270).

In the present, in these times in which we live, this implies that Christians confess their solidarity with all human beings, at every point, as their friends and companions, without regard for the masks and disguises. They cannot separate themselves from others, no matter what names they bear or what kinds of people they are. Christians themselves are also hidden in all kinds of robes and uniforms and rags. They also live solely by hope and therefore by the promises that human right, worth, freedom, peace, and joy have already been actualized by God in Jesus Christ and will ultimately be revealed in their actualization. Of this promise, and for this reason, Christians "have to be wit-nesses, shining lights of hope, to all people" (p. 270).

Here arises the missionary task of the Christian community and of all individual Christians, says Barth.[23] But this again calls for more, namely "a

---

23. In his inaugural lecture as Professor of Missiology at Stellenbosch University, Russel Botman took the theme of hope as central to the task of Christian mission today; see "The end of hope or a new horizon of hope? An outreach to those in Africa who dare hope," *NGTT* 43 (2002):

practical commentary in the acts of those who issue" this promise to all people, a practical commentary in the form of "significatory acts."

Christians also have to be witnesses by "resolutely being there" — and not just as last on the scene, he adds; "on this side of the deliverance that God has begun and will complete, in relative antithesis to human disorder and the lordship of demons, there is wrestling and fighting and suffering for a provisional bit of human right" (p. 270).

Christians have to draw alongside suffering and hopeless people, and "not with good words alone," or "as weary sceptics," but "even in little things," in "taking little steps to relative improvements wherever they attempt them," even in the risk of making mistakes and suffering disappointments with such people. They should not be afraid to say Yes and No in solidarity with such people — even if they may really know better and may be able to do better, and could therefore criticize and correct! — since the most important thing is that they help suffering people by strengthening their courage "not to be content with the corruption and evil of the world but even within this horizon to look ahead and not back" (p. 271).

This experience, says Barth, however difficult it may be, made alongside suffering human beings, "of hoping, seriously, joyfully, and actively in little things, of doing the relatively well relatively better," will be salutary for themselves. It will drive them truly to the great hope, praying the new prayer, Come, Lord Jesus. In bringing this promise to suffering people and in being "credible witnesses" for them that this God like themselves has not abandoned them and will not do so, that the kingdom of the Father, Son, and Holy Spirit has come and will come even for them, they witness to all people that Jesus Christ is their hope too — and these words of course form the very last line of the *Church Dogmatics* (p. 271).

"... In a Special Way"?

Recent years saw the publication of several very helpful new studies, also in the English-speaking world, of Barth's ethics in general and specifically of the ethics of reconciliation. Although not all the controversies have been solved — all the questions of interpretation answered or all the misunderstandings that characterized the reception of his theology and ethics been removed —

22-31. Botman makes use of, amongst others, Bosch's work, who also took the notion of hope very seriously, for example in his *Believing in the Future. Toward a Missiology of Western Culture* (Harrisburg, PA: Trinity Press International, 1995), written after the magnus opus, *Transforming Mission*.

an instructive consensus seems to develop. It is therefore possible simply to call to mind *four* of the now fairly generally accepted rules of such interpretation by way of summary and without detailed argument.

First, Barth was deeply concerned with ethics, including politics, throughout his life and work. John Webster in particular has convincingly demonstrated in several works that any ethical section in the *Church Dogmatics* — and obviously also in any of his other works — should be understood in terms of the purpose and thrust of the whole, and that this whole should be seen as a fundamentally ethical argument. Barth was constructing a new, alternative *moral ontology,* in Webster's terms.[24] Ethics is not a partial or incidental interest of Barth's, but integral to his theological vision and work, from beginning to end, and present everywhere. Doctrine and ethics can never be separated in his oeuvre, and his many readers and commentators, both enthusiastic and critical, who did separate them (amongst them also many in South African theological circles) misunderstood Barth.[25] If we are unable to

---

24. Webster often deals with this theme, for example in *Barth's Ethics of Reconciliation* (Cambridge: Cambridge University Press, 1995); *Barth's Moral Theology. Human Action in Barth's Thought* (Grand Rapids: Eerdmans, 1998); and *Barth* (New York: Continuum, 2000). He uses different expressions to describe this pervasive role of ethics in Barth's whole theology, including "moral ontology" (borrowing from Charles Taylor), "an intrinsically ethical dogmatics," describing "our moral space," "the moral field," "a morally textured reality," "the room of the gospel in which there is room for us" (all from *Ethics,* see, e.g., pp. 1-3, 4, 57-8, 98-9, 214-23); it is "intrinsically an ethical dogmatics, a description of the human covenant partner as agent," "a counter-ontology: a theory of reality unafraid to go against the grain by taking its clues from the Christian confession" (borrowing from John Milbank, see *Barth's Moral Theology,* e.g. pp. 80ff., 95ff., 122ff., 151ff.); it is "a trinitarian moral ontology of the command of God" (*Barth,* p. 150), describing "the moral field," "the situation in which human agents stand," "the moral nature of reality (the space in which we stand, the kinds of creatures we are, the gracious God whom we face)" (*Barth,* e.g., pp. 150, 155).

25. Many in South African Reformed circles were extremely critical of Barth. They were directly influenced by similar ideas in Neocalvinist circles in the Netherlands; see, e.g., the helpful documentation and interpretation of these Dutch debates in Martien E. Brinkman, *De theologie van Karl Barth: dynamiet of dynamo voor christelijk handelen. De politieke en theologische kontroverse tussen nederlandse Bartianen en Neocalvinisten* (Baarn: Uitgeverij Ten Have, 1983). Several South African theologians who did read Barth were more influenced by his theological ideas than by their ethical and political implications. In the volume of South African essays edited by Charles Villa-Vicencio on the occasion of Barth's centenary, *On Reading Karl Barth in South Africa* (Grand Rapids: Eerdmans, 1988), this separation between theology and ethics in the Barth-reception is the underlying theme. It also, however, happened and still happens elsewhere. Webster often complains about such "partial readings . . . as if his writings on ethics do not exist" (*Barth,* p. 141). In his very enlightening interpretation of Barth's theology and ethics, William Stacy Johnson points out that for Barth's project ethics poses "*the* theological problem," *The mystery of God. Karl Barth and the postmodern foundations of theology* (Louisville, KY: Westminster John Knox Press, 1997), p. 173.

appreciate these last paragraphs in the *Fragments,* or his response to evangelical theology and politics in Princeton University Chapel, we fail to understand a deep and fundamental aspect of Barth's own thought.

Second, Barth never turned doctrine into ethics — in spite of a long line
of criticism in this vein, often from the side of Lutheran scholars, like
Ebeling.[26] Barth was in fact extremely serious when he emphasized the importance of *prayer,* of invocation, of calling upon God, and in particular of
petition in this way — and particularly as at the heart of the Christian life and
ethics. Again, anyone who fails to appreciate this misinterprets a central conviction in Barth's vision. The most important act on our part, for him, is to
pray — to call on God, and to wait. God and God alone can and will bring the
kingdom, the divine righteousness. We cannot even cooperate in achieving
this; this can never be our calling.[27] The *radical rejection* of any form of turning the gospel, doctrine, or faith into ethics that characterized his *Romans,* of

26. Eberhard Jüngel has convincingly refuted this criticism from the side of several Lutheran scholars, and particularly by Ebeling (that Barth's approach leads to "the conversion of
dogmatics into ethics," to "an ethicizing of theology"), in careful detail in his essay "Zum
Verhältnis von Kirche und Staat nach Karl Barth," in *Zur Theologie Karl Barths: Beiträge aus
Anlass seines 100 Geburtstags,* Zeitschrift für Theologie und Kirche, Beiheft 6 (Tübingen: J. C. B.
Mohr, 1986), pp. 76-135. Webster is not even in full agreement with Jüngel's position; see, for ex-
ample, "Justification, analogy and action: Barth and Luther in Jüngel's anthropology," in *Barth's
Moral Theology,* pp. 179-214 ("Jüngel draws back from Barth's positive analogy between the
Christian and the civil communities, suggesting that Barth's later writings lack a sufficiently
strong sense of the 'fundamental distinction' between the two. . . . All of this suggests that what
Jüngel rightly sees in Barth is rather uneasily united to a Lutheran insistence on passivity and on
the temporal, political world of human action as, in some sense, not caught up within God's
dealings with his creation," p. 210). Again, for a very positive interpretation of the relation between Barth and Luther, see George Hunsinger, "What Karl Barth learnt from Martin Luther," in
Disruptive Grace. Studies in the Theology of Karl Barth (Grand Rapids: Eerdmans, 2000), pp. 279-
304. Regarding the relationship between law and gospel, which is the issue for Ebeling and
Jüngel, Hunsinger comments: "Often regarded as separating Barth from Luther, the law/gospel
versus gospel/law contrast may actually have more to do with what separated Barth from
Lutheranism," p. 304, n. 41.

27. Prayer occupied a central role in Barth's work from the beginning to the end. Already
in the Münster *Ethics* he discusses prayer. In the *Church Dogmatics* it is often treated at length,
for example in III/3 (God's providence), III/4 (the ethics of creation), in IV/3 (the service of the
congregation), here in IV/4 (the ethics of reconciliation), and Hesselink suggests that it would
have been part of vol. 5 on redemption also ("Karl Barth on prayer," in Karl Barth, *Prayer. 50th
Anniversary Edition,* ed. Don E. Saliers [Louisville: John Knox Press, 2002], p. 77). In *Evangelical
Theology* it is one of the topics under the heading "theological work." Reflecting on the place of
prayer according to the Reformers, Barth concludes that, for them, "prayer is at once word,
thought, and life" (*Prayer,* p. 7). It is precisely this inter-relationship that he took so seriously in
his own work.

moralizing the faith — so typical of the liberal theology of his contemporaries — is still at work here. This is the same radical eschatological critique of all our human efforts.[28] The many voices who have argued that Barth himself is turning the gospel into ethics have clearly either misunderstood or deliberately ignored his clear intentions.[29]

Third, the fact that we can in no way cooperate in establishing divine righteousness does not mean for Barth that we cannot contribute to *human righteousness.* In fact, we are called to do this. Precisely as people who pray, we are called to action. Serious prayer involves commitment. This waiting consists of hastening. This form of moral ontology makes room for human action, human activity, human responsibility. The very nature of the God to whom we pray, on whom we call, to whom we address our petitions, calls for our response. As Father, Son, and Holy Spirit, this Triune God frees us and claims us to be witnesses, to reflect, to live lives of correspondence.[30] Every Christian doctrine therefore has an ethical thrust — revelation, election, cre-

---

28. The relationship between eschatology and ethics in Barth's thought has often been misunderstood. Eschatology certainly "greatly disturbs" *(Romans)* liberal understandings of ethics, but at the same time makes (another form of) ethics possible and indeed necessary. The eschatological 'otherness' of God's action in Christ in fact liberates human action from the dehumanizing effect of having to be the bearer of the kingdom of God, says Webster *(Barth's Moral Theology,* p. 22) — and then he quotes the Tambach lecture from 1919! "We need not therefore be apprehensive of any pessimistic discrediting of our life here and of activity in our life here, if we conclude with Calvin to fix the place of the Christian in society within the *spes futurae vitae,"* "The Christian's place in society," in Karl Barth, *The Word of God and the Word of Man* (London: Hodder and Stoughton, 1928), pp. 324ff. For a very instructive discussion of Barth's views on eschatology and a theology of hope, see Gerhard Sauter, "Why is Karl Barth's *Church Dogmatics* not a 'Theology of hope'? Some observations on Barth's understanding of eschatology," *Scottish Journal of Theology* 52, no. 4 (1999): 407-29. For Webster, who does speak about Barth's "theology of hope" and regards it as "emphatically part of his ethics" (p. 81), see Webster, *Barth's Moral Theology,* pp. 77-97.

29. According to Webster, "Ethical concerns were present from the beginnings of Barth's break with liberal theology. . . . Barth's 'break' with his heritage did not entail an abandonment of its concerns so much as their reformulation through quite different categories" *(Barth's Moral Theology,* p. 4).

30. The notion of "correspondence" is central to Barth's understanding of the relationship between human agency and God's agency. He is often searching for similar expressions, like "parable," "analogy," "testimony," "patterning (not repeating, prolonging or extending)." Our action is "similar, parallel, and analogous to the act of God himself" *(The Christian Life,* p. 175). We are made into God's "covenant partners" and through the Spirit's "formation, direction, indication and limitation" we are made into human agents acting freely and responsibly in correspondence to God's own work. See my essay on "Paradigms of radical grace," in *On reading Karl Barth in South Africa,* pp. 17-43, for a discussion of this theme, focusing on a specific section from Barth's discussion of the miracles of Jesus.

ation, reconciliation, redemption. This God is the One who in loving freedom creates us, saves us, and redeems us, in short, who says Yes to us, to humanity, to concrete human beings. Our lives, in correspondence with this loving freedom, should be lives that also say yes, albeit in our small, human ways, to concrete human beings. The fact that our response is *only* one of witness, *only* striving for human righteousness, is only relative, provisional, historical, does not make it unimportant or less serious. Already in *Romans* — where so many commentators mistakenly saw an absolute negation of human freedom — Barth would ask: "Is 'only' a relevant description of a cloud of dust, if that cloud of dust betrays the whereabouts of a column on the march?"[31]

Fourth, the *church* is liberated and called to this struggle for righteousness.[32] Barth is not interested in abstractions, in theory, or in principles. He sees the real church, the empirical, concrete church in the world, in history, as called to this struggle. This is why his theology was so contextual — during all the phases of his life and work. Again, those who criticized him for not being

---

31. Within context, it reads: "To sum up: there is no human action which is not in itself fashioned according to the form of this world; and yet there are actions which seem almost to bear in themselves the mark of the divine protest against the great error. There is no human action which is in itself fashioned according to the transformation of this world; but there are actions which seem so transparent that the light of the coming Day is almost visible in them. Human conduct is in itself therefore only — but why should we say 'only'? — a parable, a token, of the action of God; and the action of God cannot occur in time; it can occur only — and again, why should we say 'only'? — in eternity. Is 'only' a relevant description of a cloud of dust, if that cloud of dust betrays the whereabouts of a column on the march? Is a shell-hole 'only' a shell-hole, if it marks the place where an explosion has taken place?" Karl Barth, *The Epistle to the Romans* (London: Oxford University Press, 1968), pp. 434-5. The aspect to take note of is, of course, that this argument forms part of the section discussing chapters 12–15 under the heading "The great disturbance. The problem of ethics." Far from doing away with all human ethics, as is often argued, it opens the way for human ethics, responding to the mercies of God in the gospel of Jesus Christ. It does away with the optimistic ethics of liberal theology and religion, yes, but not with the relative and modest, but serious and obedient ethics of those freed, judged, and liberated by the gospel. The similarities between the argument here in 1921 and the argument in *fiat iustitia* in 1962 are indeed remarkable.

32. Some ambiguity has been caused by the fact that Barth sometimes warned against too much attention to the church, even as late as *Evangelical Theology*. On the other hand, he defined theology from the outset as critical reflection on the action of the church, and it was not without very good reason that the dogmatics was called a "Church" dogmatics. For him, the task of theology is to clarify the presuppositions of church praxis, and in particular the proclamation of the church. There is obvious similarity with Wallace Alston's views on the task of Christian theology; see, for example, "The ministry of Christian theology," in *Theology in the service of the church. Essays in honor of Thomas W. Gillespie*, ed. Wallace Alston, Jr. (Grand Rapids: Eerdmans, 2000), pp. 19-35; and *The church of the Living God* (Louisville, KY: Westminster John Knox Press, 2002), pp. 120ff.

contextual and historically interested and politically and socially aware and concerned simply misunderstood him.[33] Here the influence of the Reformed tradition is again particularly clear, and especially his understanding of the nature and role of Reformed confessions. Under normal circumstances, the existing confessions serve as helpful lenses through which Reformed Christians read the signs of their times, the challenges of their day and place. Under abnormal conditions, however, when the truth of the gospel itself is at stake and therefore the credibility of the witness of the church, a state of confession can arise and the need to confess anew, publicly — and precisely about ethical challenges also, in the face of threats to human righteousness, peace, and dignity.[34]

Against such a background one should read his final lectures on the ethics of reconciliation, and against the background of these lectures one should read his response in the Princeton University Chapel. Politics is the human attempt to serve some form of order, peace, and justice — no more, but also no less. Evangelical theology — theology reflecting on the face of the Triune God, trusting the promises of this God, and hearing the claim of this God — inevitably has to do with such politics. Responding to the sanctification given to us and expecting the fulfilment promised to us, we serve this God in this world, as witnesses to this good news of God's free and loving Yes. At the heart of this — human, and therefore thoroughly political — service is our prayer, our petition, our calling for the divine righteousness, for the Son of Righteousness to shine upon us. This happens ultimately by saving us and in the meanwhile by making us reflect something of his justice in our concrete, everyday historical contexts in the face of so many forms of disorder and injustice.

There can be little doubt that most of the South African Reformed theologians already mentioned understood their own work and calling in exactly this way. For them also this was the obvious thrust of their own Reformed tradition and their own understanding of evangelical theology. It is no wonder that they were all inspired, in some way or another, by the theology of Karl

---

33. This makes Timothy J. Gorringes's *Karl Barth against Hegemony* (Oxford: Oxford University Press, 1999) so helpful. While careful not to argue that Barth's theology was ever the predicate of his political views, he does present Barth as a thoroughly contextual theologian, through all his work.

34. See the very instructive study of Barth's relation with Christian confession, both as existing confessional documents and as new challenges to acts of confessions, by Georg Plasger, *Die relative Autorität des Bekenntnisses bei Karl Barth* (Neukirchen: Neukirchener Verlag, 2000); see also my essay "Social transformation and confessing the faith? Karl Barth's views on confession revisited," *Scriptura* 72 (2000): 76-86.

Barth. In fact, his influence in the theological struggle against apartheid and for human righteousness was large. Even when the (then) Dutch Reformed Mission Church confessed its own faith in a new confessional document, the *Confession of Belhar,* Barth's life and work played a direct role. Not only this act of confession, however, but also much of the content of the document can be traced back to Barth's theology, including the third article on the caring justice of God, calling the church to follow Him in this:

> We believe that God has revealed Godself as the One who wishes to bring about justice and true peace among people; that in a world full of injustice and enmity He is in a special way the God of the destitute, the poor and the wronged and that He calls His Church to follow Him in this; that He brings justice to the oppressed and gives bread to the hungry; that He frees the prisoner and restores sight to the blind; that He supports the downtrodden, protects the stranger, helps orphans and widows and blocks the path of the ungodly; that for Him pure and undefiled religion is to visit the orphans and the widows in their suffering; that He wishes to teach His people to do what is good and to seek the right;
>
> That the Church must therefore stand by people in any form of suffering and need, which implies, among other things, that the Church must witness against and strive against any form of injustice, so that justice may roll down like waters, and righteousness like an ever-flowing stream; that the Church as the possession of God must stand where He stands, namely against injustice and with the wronged; that in following Christ the Church must witness against all the powerful and privileged who selfishly seek their own interests and thus control and harm others.
>
> Therefore, we reject any ideology which would legitimate forms of injustice and any doctrine which is unwilling to resist such an ideology in the name of the gospel.[35]

Many of the theological convictions involved here obviously correspond to central motifs of Barth's theology, including God's revelation in Jesus Christ, the Biblical allusions to God's caring justice and concern for human beings,

---

35. The Confessing Church in Germany had a major influence on the developments in apartheid South Africa, and *Barmen* and Barth's theology in particular played an important role. For some account of that, see my essay "Das Bekenntnis von Belhar: Entstehung, Inhalt, Rezeption, Relevanz," *Das Bekenntnis von Belhar und seine Bedeutung für die reformierten Kirchen in Deutschland* (Detmold: Lippische Landeskirche, 1998), pp. 17-33. For the historical circumstances, as well as the text of the *Confession,* see for example G. D. Cloete and D. J. Smit, eds., *A Moment of Truth* (Grand Rapids: Eerdmans, 1984).

the resistance against injustice to which the church is called, and the calling to the church to witness as followers of Jesus Christ.[36]

Sol Iustitiae Illustra Nos?

The motto of our Faculty of Theology in Stellenbosch is *sol iustitiae illustra nos*. It is a prayer, addressed to the Sun of Righteousness, petitioning that he will shine upon us.[37] Perhaps even better than Barth's own *fiat iustitia* this motto expresses the thrust of his theology and work. During the nineteenth century, the then Seminary took the motto from the University of Utrecht in the Netherlands, with which it had strong relations during its founding years.[38] When the Seminary became a Faculty of Stellenbosch University, the motto was retained. After the fall of apartheid, the Faculty underwent a major transformation. It grew into an open, ecumenical Faculty with several denominations officially involved in the training and studies and particularly with a student and staff body leading the way in a new diversity of race, language, and cultural background. As an integral part of this crucially important process of transformation, the new student body had the opportunity to select a new motto for the Faculty, in which to express their newly found identity and the new challenges on their agenda — and chose to retain the prayer *sol iustitiae illustra nos*.

Of course, Princeton and Stellenbosch — and Utrecht, and Basel! — are far removed from one another and in many ways, and as theologians, churches, and Christians we have to find our own way, our own calling, and our own voice, in our respective worlds. Barth knew that very well. In 1935 he was invited to address the theological Faculty in Utrecht. He spoke on the

36. Already in *Romans* he would claim that "Christianity has a certain partisan preference for the oppressed, for those falling short," p. 463. A number of Reformed theologians published a volume of sermon guidelines on justification and justice in which Barth's ideas (particularly on Pontius Pilate as representative of human justice, from *Rechtfertigung und Recht*, translated as "Church and State," in *Community, State, and Church* [Gloucester, MA: Peter Smith, 1960], pp. 101-48) played a crucial role, namely *Riglyne vir prediking oor regverdiging en reg. Woord teen die lig III/3* (Kaapstad: Lux Verbi, 1993).

37. For some of the history as well as informative exegesis of Mal. 4.2, from which the motto is derived, see the essay by the former Dean and Professor of Old Testament of the Stellenbosch Faculty, P. A. Verhoef, "Sol Iustitiae Illustra Nos," in *Sol Iustitiae*, ed. P. A. Verhoef, et al. (Cape Town: N. G. Kerk, n.d.), pp. 1-23.

38. For the history of the motto in Utrecht, see R. Van den Broek, *Hy leeret ende beschuttet. Over het wapen en de zinspreuk van de Universiteit Utrecht* (Utrecht: Universiteit Utrecht, 1995).

Apostles' Creed in lectures that were later translated and published as *Credo* — precisely therefore on what the universal church has in common. In the question and answer sessions afterwards, however, he made it very clear that he was deeply aware of the differences in context between them. "You and I are not standing upon the same ground," he begins. "What separates us relatively is the fact that I have spent the last fourteen years of my life in Germany. But you are living as Dutchmen in Holland. That is not unimportant." All their questions, he explains, seem "specifically Dutch" to him. Why? Because they "betray to some extent that you are still able to pursue theology in *comfort* (his italics), with a certain calmness and detachment in regard to its problems, such as we once knew in Germany, but to-day know no longer." "I come from a Church and I come from a Faculty," says Barth, "whose life outwardly and inwardly is very different from the life of your Church here — and of your faculty. Be clear about what has been happening during these last months in Germany and Bonn. Where such things are possibie a very different wind is blowing."[39]

Although Princeton and Stellenbosch are far removed, several of us who have come to know Wallace Alston have the feeling that in many ways we do have much in common, that we do stand upon similar ground. This suspicion is based not only on his reputation, but also on more solid ground — including three brief but moving scenes in Macky Alston's award-winning film, *Family Name*, which involves Wallace Alston.[40]

In the first scene he narrates a defining moment in his own life when he suddenly became aware that we should see human beings *as* human beings, regardless of who or what they may seem to be on the surface, based on their achievements, status, and actions. This experience evidently played a role in his involvement as a pastor, as narrated by others in the film. References are made to all kinds of social projects aimed at serving and promoting human dignity, including housing, education, employment and combating poverty, and supporting the civil rights movement. There is almost no better way of describing the defining moment in Barth's moral ontology than this: learning to see human beings *as* human beings, objects of the eternal covenantal love of God, Father, Son, and Spirit, and loving them freely because of what we see.

In a second scene Alston speaks about himself, carefully, almost meditatively. Asked whether he would have been a slave owner himself a few centuries ago, he responds that this is an impossible question — is it easy to have a

---

39. Karl Barth, *Credo* (London: Hodder and Stoughton, 1964), pp. 173-4.
40. Macky Alston, *Family Name* (New York: First Run/Icarus Films, 1997).

different view and lifestyle when everyone around you tells you that *this* is the way things are? His words sound like Barth's on the powers, on ideologies, and the pervasive influence of the spirit of the time, even on church and religion. He can only hope, says Alston, that he would have been given "some clues as to the meaning of life" in his faith perspective that would have helped him to see right and wrong, but who knows who we would have been in another time and another place? The better, and more important question, therefore, is the one where we stand *now*, whether we see *now* and whether we are taking a stand *now*.

In a third, final scene he confesses his hope in a time of fulfilment, "when things divided will be reconciled, and when injustice will be overthrown and justice will reign." He has to believe, he says, "in the ultimate outcome of a peaceable kingdom."

To many of us, from afar, from a different time and place, this sounds very familiar indeed. Is it too far-fetched to presume that some of this similar ground between us is due to the influence of the ecumenically minded Reformed tradition we share, read through the eyes of Karl Barth? And is it too far-fetched to hope that after his retirement Wallace Alston will return to visit Stellenbosch and South Africa again, to support many South African Christians through his friendship and experience in their ongoing — albeit small, relative, provisional and ambiguous — struggles to contribute to a little human righteousness, to strengthen a little hope, while praying *sol iustitiae illustra nos,* and waiting?

Guilt, Shame, and the Face of God

Niels Henrik Gregersen

> *The core meaning of "to sin" is the inability to give recognition to anyone or anything. . . . The sinner is not even able to give recognition to himself in this way.*
>
> Christof Gestrich[1]

'Sin' must surely be one of Christianity's most contentious and unpopular concepts. Yet we are nonetheless living at a period of history in which those manifestations of human nature that Christianity has traditionally designated the works of sin are particularly apparent. Acts of cruelty perpetrated in the midst of civilization — from Auschwitz to the Gulag, from Bosnia to Manhattan — pass from the television screen onto the retina and into the soul. Today it thus requires considerable temerity to assert that human beings are fundamentally good. But interiorized forms of sin are also laid bare. The media are more than ready to disclose the moral weaknesses of public figures, whose motives are exposed, whenever possible.

Christianity has been successful in propagating a general awareness of sin in Western culture. By comparison, the church has been considerably less successful in bringing the gospel of forgiveness. And if the reality of sin can be seen in its proper proportions only in the light of redemption, we are still faced with the fundamental task of explaining how sin might be restrained, and how we might learn to live with the persistence of sin that is not easily overcome.

---

1. Christof Gestrich, *The Return of the Splendor in the World: The Christian Doctrine of Sin and Forgiveness* (Grand Rapids: Eerdmans, 1997), p. 202.

In what follows my aim is to counteract the tendency of homogenizing the theological concept of sin. In particular, I want to correlate and put in contrast two distinct forms of sin: *guilt* in relation to some kind of fault or misconduct on our part, and *shame* which rather pertains to our deficiencies and feelings of inferiority. This distinction is by no means new. It can be found already in Dietrich Bonhoeffer's *Ethics,* and over the last decades the phenomenon of shame has again come into the focus of Christian anthropology.[2] And rightly so, for whereas guilt concerns our blameworthiness, shame is related to our feeling of unworthiness. In a phenomenological analysis guided by biblical tradition, I am thus going to elaborate how the well-known triad of guilt concerning self, others, and God does not quite capture the ambivalence of shame. In contrast to guilt, which concerns the relation between the offender and the victim, shame is a self-reflective phenomenon, in which the one who feels ashamed and the object of shame is the same person. Hence according to the biblical traditions, God's response towards guilt and shame is different. Whereas God stands behind justice and forces the perpetrator to acknowledge his or her guilt, God stands up against the powers of social scorn, and rehabilitates the sinner. Thus God's ways of overcoming sin differ markedly. In the present context I shall delimit myself to make clear the difference between God as the Pardoner who forgives sin, and God as the Cleanser who removes the dirt of sin, and the Transformer who enables the self to restore its dignity. In both cases the Face of God is the central biblical symbol for God's capacity to shine forth, overcome sin, and spread the divine blessing in the world of creation.[3]

Escaping the Homogenization of Sin

The broad use of the impersonal singular form 'sin' can cause an indeterminate sense of guilt and powerlessness. This leads to a shift in the doctrine of sin itself. Christian talk of sin, which should always be utterance directed *against* sin, becomes a talk *about* sin, if not indeed a means of playing up its public profile. Vigilance in respect of sin's genera evaporates. Awareness of sin

2. For a helpful discussion of the recent discussion on shame in systematic and pastoral theology, see Stephen Pattison, *Shame: Theory, Therapy, Theology* (Cambridge: Cambridge University Press, 2000), pp. 189-228.

3. This essay accompanies a previous article, "Guilt, Shame, and Rehabilitation: The Pedagogy of Divine Judgment," *Dialog: A Journal of Theology* 39, no. 2 (2000): 105-18. The analysis of guilt and shame, which is presented here, is presupposed there, and the eschatological dimension, which stands in the foreground there, is left out here.

is no longer a matter of purging delusions, so that the world may have its due proportions restored. The doctrine of sin becomes instead a platform for a rhetoric which by dint of its vast arsenal of examples hits home without offering hope. Thus the despondency that the powers of sin had already brought about is reproduced. In theological terms this means that awareness of sin is cut off from forgiveness of sin, sin from atonement. At worst, the doctrine of sin contributes to its own perpetuation. The conception of sin becomes a coil, which both expands so as to be all-inclusive, and at the same time entwines the individual constrictingly.

Certainly, the early movement of dialectical theology, coupled with the Luther Renaissance during the 1920s, made an important contribution towards a more sober understanding of what sin is. Sin should *not* be identified with moral offences of various degrees of gravity. Nor should the acknowledgment of sin be identified with some self-generated feelings of guilt. Rather, the proclamation of human sin establishes a solidarity of sinners, in which one is not less a sinner than others. What has been the unfortunate result of the de-moralization of the theological concept of sin, however, is a homogenization of sins and sinners. It may well be that the cruelty of the perpetrator of evil acts and our own natural fear are one and the same before Divine Judgment. But such latitude in the application of the concept of sin is made from a plane that is not ours. Sin thus conceived is sin viewed *sub specie aeternitatis,* divorced from any mundane context, where distinctions among forms of sin strike us forcibly and make all the difference.

The *dilemma* is here that the concept of 'sin' in its impersonal singular form must be retained to avoid its being moralized. However, when sin is talked about in general terms it either leads to an amorphous feeling of guilt, or to an intellectualization of guilt. Expressed in Reformation terms, the proclamation of the law becomes a force for depravity in the absence of the countervailing power of the gospel. In the twentieth century, it was above all Karl Barth who had to remind the Lutherans in particular that Christians cannot legitimately speak of Law in isolation from the Gospel. Christians should avoid speaking of the faces of sin apart from the face of God in Jesus Christ. I am convinced that Barth here made a theological decision of lasting importance.

In this essay I shall propose one way of evading this dilemma. Instead of applying sin as a homogenous concept, whose substrate is to be sought in one underlying anthropological determination (*concupiscentia, superbia, amor sui* etc.), 'sin' is to be regarded from the outset as part of a *complex semantics* whose extension cannot be finitely codified; its content can only be explained in and through stories and examples of sin, forgiveness, and rehabilitation. As is the case with the idea of *imago dei* or the notion of *Christ and his saints*, sin figures as a compendious symbol which captures a suite of meanings and draws them into a whole (the Greek *sym-ballein* actually means to "throw together" or unite). The semantic field of sin includes the following:

1. Sin comprehends *acts* which — voluntarily or involuntarily — constitute lapses.

2. Sin has to do with *agents*. The agent doesn't just figure in the action but is made manifest by his or her acts in which the actor is involved.

3. The symbol of sin connotes an awareness of a *forum* to which we are answerable. The idea of sin cannot be employed as a neutral concept but presupposes that the individual's missteps are subject to a tribunal of judgment.

4. Sin constitutes a *sphere of power* that extends well beyond the individual and holds him or her captive. It is hardly an accident that biblical language uses spatial concepts to describe spiritual states in this connection. Human persons are "under sin," "constricted" by the power of sin, which narrows their *Lebensraum*. Insofar as this is so, the symbol contains an element of *destiny*, emphasized in the concept of original sin.

5. In the biblical tradition, sin is never just observed but always *counteracted by God's ways of redemption*. As rebellion against God, sin is also destined to be annihilated by God, while the mercy of God protects the sinner and wishes him and her to live. In this sense sin's destiny is always embraced by God's greater will to communion with the creature.

Given the multi-faceted nature of sin's semantic field any attempt at a comprehensive definition would be misplaced. The concept resists encapsulation by never so many examples. 'Sin' figures as an elemental term in the Christian semantic universe and its right application is a primary ecclesiastical and theological duty. Only a discriminating application of the symbol can prevent its fossilization into a homogeneous and inclusive concept blurring all distinctions. The *semantics* of sin is not susceptible of closure. But the *phenomena* which manifest sin in the world can be identified. Only two such phenomena, guilt and shame, will be discussed here.

The Triad of Guilt

Traditionally sin has been defined as *disobedience* in respect of God's commands. The following reflections will evince a different accentuation in which sin is construed first and foremost as a *lack of attentiveness* to God's commands. Talk of disobedience presupposes a clear awareness of an ethico-religious judgment unlikely to be encountered today. Likewise the concept 'disobedience' presupposes a clearly defined hierarchical structure. 'Lack of attentiveness', on the other hand, points to the insidious tendency to evade demanding situations. God's commands are transgressed through not being heeded.

Since we no longer inhabit a hierarchical society but one characterized rather by horizontality, *guilt*, by the same token, has only rarely to do with disobedience in respect of criteria of judgment of which there is not usually much awareness. Far more common is the lack of a sense of what a situation demands of us. Whereas tradition focuses primarily on the guilt incurred in relation to *fathers and mothers,* there may be a need today to stress the forms of guilt that may arise in relation to those with peer status, but who by the same token are in mutual competition with each other: *brothers and sisters,* friends and peers.

Already in Genesis 3 the triadic structure of sin is apparent. 'Guilt' presupposes a responsible *subject,* someone to be responsible *for,* and finally a *forum,* a tribunal or judge, to whom we are responsible. It is God who poses questions to human beings, and humans respond. After the Fall God asks Adam, "Where are you" (Gen. 3:9), and following the fratricide God, by the same token, asks Cain, "Where is your brother Abel?" (Gen. 4:9). And when Cain replies evasively "Am I my brother's keeper?" God emerges as the authority who puts a stop to his evasiveness: "What have you done? Listen, your brother's blood is crying out to me from the ground" (Gen. 4:10). God's insistence on the proper scale of things is not as pronounced in the story of Adam but is implicit in the narrative. Adam seeks to avert the imputation of guilt by placing it on Eve and thus indirectly on God's creation of a helpmate: "The woman whom you gave me to be with me, she gave me fruit from the tree, and I ate"; but also Eve attempts evasion by responding, "The serpent tricked me, and I ate" (Gen. 3:12-13). According to Genesis, God responds to these projections of blame by cursing both Adam and the serpent. In the collective expulsion of the Serpent, Eve and Adam from the Garden of Eden, blame is imputed to all three, and it is made clear that guilt is not something that arises in a stimulus-response manner. Sin emerges between the circumstances of life ("the lurking sin") and the individual's inattentiveness. The cardinal point in the narrative is thus that human failure is never a purely impersonal destiny. Rather, the human contribution plays a crucial part in the battle against sin, as it is also said in the story of Cain: "If you do well, will you not be accepted? And if you do not well, sin is lurking at the door; its desire is for you, but you must master it" (Gen. 4:7; translation unsecure). Thus, the open-endedness of history is preserved also after the expulsion from Eden.

Sin is thus a human action that fails to accord with the demand for attention to the immediately given in a willingness to act that is enjoined on us by the situations we encounter. It is here that the phenomenon of guilt receives its distinctive significance. Since the human creature is in all things a recipient, he or she owes the Creator all. The human person must thus be prepared to give everything away *without making counterclaims*. As human agents we come to an impasse in guilt which — judged by conventional standards — may be calibrated as relatively more or less, but which — seen in the light of God's sheer giving in creation — is absolute, because we owe all to the giver of life. The movement from the sphere of relativity to the sphere of the unconditional shows that the moral standard is God, the "Judge." From here arises the *triad of responsibility and guilt:*

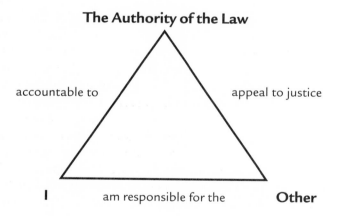

The Authority of the Law

accountable to

appeal to justice

I

am responsible for the

Other

Figure 1. The Triad of Responsibility and Guilt

(1) The concept of 'guilt' presupposes that we *are ourselves involved* — by dint of acts or omissions — in those events which harm ourselves or others. Responsibility is given in virtue of the elementary fact that we are ineluctably drawn into the tissue of interactions. Responsibility and guilt need not presuppose a free power of choice which — in its unconstrained weighing up of the concrete situation — is the "cause" of the error. The person who by accident runs a child over can rightly say, "it wasn't deliberate." But the same

person cannot in the same breath say, "it wasn't my fault." That would constitute an evasion of responsibility. We are thus responsible also for the unintended and unwilled consequences of our acts. Nor does constraint release one from the onus of responsibility. She who finds herself placed in a difficult situation in which — in the circumstances — she has no option but one (e.g. to liquidate an informer) cannot subsequently deny responsibility for the act. She will perhaps be able to justify her action, but any such justification presupposes a prior acceptance of responsibility. The action was her own. The issue of responsibility and guilt is not dependent on the extent to which we perform acts deliberately. Nor is responsibility dependent on the number of alternative options available. What it does depend on is the fact that, given the connection between our present life and our previous acts, we must assume responsibility for our acts, if we wish to retain our personal integrity.[4] Responsibility is given, in other words, with our relation to ourselves, with our ever problematic identity and not with an essential power of free will. Only the absence of the conditions for personal identity (e.g. in serious mental illness, hypnosis, or the influence of drugs) can lead to diminished responsibility.

(2) Second, guilt presupposes a *community* where we need each other and have no choice but to generate expectations one of the other. We are not only dependent on each other; we are also rendered vulnerable to each other in virtue of the expectations that we inescapably raise. As human persons we don't simply react to past and present events, we adopt stances in respect of them. We anticipate the future in both fear and hope. This is what enables us to inflict double harm. We harm each other's lives by withholding something from them. But we inflict harm too by thwarting each other's aspirations and thus the momentum by which those others are carried forward and empowered. When we live in community we do not merely contribute to or fail to contribute to the fulfilment of the other's needs; we are instrumental in expanding or constricting the other's life-options. This future-oriented directionality of our actions constitutes an important reason why we cannot describe human community in a value-neutral way, taking no evaluative stance. Human life has a built-in ethical bias because it is structured on the basis of mutual expectations.[5]

---

4. This point is clearly made by Wolfhart Pannenberg, *Anthropologie in theologischer Perspektive* (Göttingen: Vandenhoeck & Ruprecht, 1983), pp. 107-10: Responsibility is provided by the identity of personhood, not by the availability of alternatives for a disengaged free will.

5. See the now classic analysis of trust by K. E. Løgstrup, *The Ethical Demand* (Philadelphia: Fortress Press, 1971), pp. 8-29. Naturally this does not mean that the good is straightforwardly identifiable with the satisfaction of other people's expectations. Not all expectations can

The ethical sense of guilt enters in with the objective fact that we have the power to harm one another. In assuming responsibility for ourselves, we assume responsibility for the entire situation in which we find ourselves and for the future consequences that flow from whatever stance we take. In addition, those expectations which — for whatever reasons — we cannot meet, involve consequences for which we are responsible. Responsibility attaches not merely to the individual act, considered in isolation. Our responsibility attaches rather to the whole network of expectations that binds us together. This is why it is fully apposite to speak of guilt even when we omit to act. We speak appropriately and tellingly of "sins of omission."

(3) This brings us to the third component, namely the *tribunal of judgment* before which we stand accountable in relation to what we owe our fellows. Tribunals are of varying scope and moment. The Supreme Court stands as the pre-eminent tribunal but only within the judicial system. A case ending in an acquittal in the Supreme Court may still remain highly dubious from a moral point of view. In the spheres of art and theology the classics of the tradition enjoy a similar authoritative status through their establishing a standard against which we measure our own work; but far from preventing us from going beyond tradition, cognizance of this standard is precisely what makes it possible. In the sphere of interpersonal relations there are instances where the criterial judgment is vested in a person. In virtue of their sensitivity to a given situation and their ability to turn it round, certain people are possessed of a kind of natural authority which serves as a mirror for others' self-evaluation. The differentia of judgment in relation to guilt, however, is that its prior character entails its towering above the relative norms of the social context. The criterion of judgment is something other than that of a given community even though it is only in and through community that it becomes manifest. Guilt is not something one can elude just by keeping within the bounds of socially agreed norms or, alternatively, simply by not being discovered. This is particularly clear where children are concerned. Judgment here quite patently does not reside in a simple duplication of the various claims children make on us. On the contrary, it is *our* responsibility to determine whether we should comply with, moderate or refuse children's requests. But it is precisely in relation to children, who carry no authority, that judgment makes itself felt. The very vulnerability of children constitutes an appeal. There is no way in which parents can evade the responsibility of their chil-

---

be fulfilled by us, nor should they be. Expectations may be pitched too high as when, say, the person has fallen in love. Similarly, expectations may be skewed as when agreement or acceptance is taken for granted as a foregone conclusion.

dren's upbringing by gesturing towards the role of social practices generally. This would amount to a dereliction of duty. Guilt is thus established by a standard that extends beyond the relativity of socially agreed norms. This absoluteness of its scope may be one of the reasons why the Christian tradition has favored the phenomena of responsibility and guilt as the gateway to the semantics of sin. However, shame constitutes an equally or more important resource for speaking of sin.

The Triad of Shame

In *Genesis* too the motif of shame plays an important role. With the Fall the sense of being exposed to oneself entered the world. We are told that the eyes of Adam and Eve were opened after eating of the Tree of Knowledge. So it was that the external gaze entered the world: Adam and Eve acknowledged their nakedness and sewed fig leaves together. But with shame's external gaze the fear of God was born. To the Lord's question, "Where are you, Adam?" he replies: "I heard the sound of you in the garden, and I was afraid, because I was naked; and I hid myself" (Gen. 3:10). The feeling of shame seeks to anticipate exposure, but naturally without succeeding in doing so.

Dietrich Bonhoeffer has been particularly attentive to the fact that the experience of shame (Gen. 3:9-10) precedes the awareness of guilt (Gen. 3:11-14). Bonhoeffer thus saw the feeling of shame as related to one's disunion with God and other human beings. "Shame and remorse are not to be conflated. Remorse we feel when we are wrong in something, shame when we are short of something. Shame is more original than remorse."[6] One could of course argue here that even though the awareness of shame was prior to that of guilt, the shame was still caused by the prior disobedience of eating the apples. But the issue is whether the phenomenon of shame as a whole can be derived from guilt. Is shame always guilt-based? It seems not. Bonhoeffer already saw in shame a sign of an estrangement, made visible in the feeling of being exposed and in the consequent urge for self-protection. Since Bonhoeffer confines his analysis of shame to Genesis 3, however, he tends to see shame as a reflex of sin. What I am going to suggest is rather that shame is an unsettling and highly ambiguous experience, which may either lead to a further dissoci-

---

6. Dietrich Bonhoeffer, "Ethik," in *Dietrich Bonhoeffer Werke*, Band 6 (München: Christian Kaiser, 1992), p. 305. "Scham und Reue sind nicht zu verwechslen. Reue empfindet der Mensch, wo er sich verfehlt hat, Scham, weil ihm etwas fehlt. Scham ist ursprünglicher als Reue." This wordplay is untranslatable, cf. Dietrich Bonhoeffer, *Ethics* (London: Fontana, 1964), p. 20.

ation of the self from God and others, *or* be a moment toward a recollection of one's God-given self. The sense of shame is not only awareness of guilt, but also an issue of self-respect.

Accordingly, a Christian theology of shame should distinguish carefully between the *shame of disgrace,* which is rightly located as a phenomenon of shame, and the *shame of self-respect,* which is part of the need for sheltering one's self.[7] In fact, shame may be a necessary mask whereby God protects the human sinner from being merely a victim of the gaze of others. This view in fact corresponds to the "garments of skin" that God made for Adam and Eve according to the Genesis story (3:21), so that they were "clothed."[8] It seems that especially in our time, where pictures of intimacy are culturally disseminated via the media in the form of pornographic bodies and narcissistic self-exposure, a positive sense of shame needs to be recovered.

Much confusion has here been caused by a failing attentiveness to the distinction between the forms of shame. Unfortunately, the English language is not very attentive to a distinction that is more clearly expressed in other Indo-European languages. In German, as well as in Danish, we find the distinction between *Schande/skændsel,* which denotes the disgrace-shame, and *Scham/skam,* which usually (but not exclusively) refers to discretion-shame. Similarly the French have the distinction between *honte,* which refers to the pain one feels after misbehaving, and *pudeur,* which signifies a protective warning in relation to what makes us bashful.[9] In English we have to make a more artificial distinction between a healthy discretion-shame and a potentially dangerous disgrace-shame. However, it is also important to retain a sense of disgrace-shame, if one is not going to be shameless by intruding the zones of intimacy of others. After all, the sense of shame is pivotal to the distinction between oneself and others, without which selfhood and personhood cannot emerge and be developed.

Now the triad of guilt and self differs in characteristic ways from the

7. I owe this distinction to Carl Schneider, *Shame, Exposure, and Privacy* (New York: W. W. Norton, 1987); see also Stephen Pattison, *Shame,* pp. 71-92.

8. Church fathers such as Gregory of Nyssa elaborated on the positive meaning of the "coats of skin" as the sentient parts of the human nature, which are given by God because they are necessary in the state of sin, though they are not destined to last in the life of resurrection (*Oratio Cath.* 7). For a contemporary defense of the notion of *persona* as a mask that liberates us from the terrors of pure intimacy in public life, see Michael Welker, "Is the Autonomous Person of European Modernity a Sustainable Model of Human Personhood?" in *The Human Person in Science and Theology,* ed. Niels Henrik Gregersen, Willem B. Drees, and Ulf Görman (Grand Rapids: Eerdmans, 2000), pp. 95-114.

9. See James B. Twitchell, *For Shame. The Loss of Common Decency in American Culture* (New York: St. Martin's Press, 1997), p. 29.

triad of guilt and responsibility: There is the *person* who is ashamed, there is something he or she is ashamed *of*, and finally there is an authority that he or she who is put to shame stands *before*. The *triad of shame* has the following form:

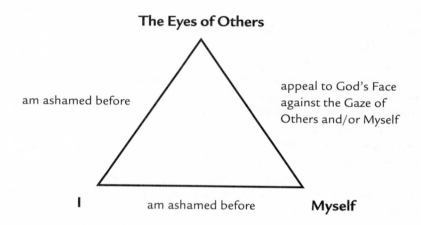

Figure 2. The Triad of Shame

(1) This triadic structure shows that shame — like guilt — ultimately turns on a relation where the individual's fundamental identity hangs in the balance. This distinguishes shame from *embarrassment* which is a more transient phenomenon. One is embarrassed in a particular situation where a remark passes, an attitude or a tone of voice is misplaced. Embarrassment — like shame — requires that we are ourselves present in a social situation, and are affected by it. But we are not always ourselves the cause of embarrassment. We often enough share in another's embarrassment, and we are even more embarrassed if the other person is shameless. However, when it comes to *shame*, we are self-involved in a more principled manner.[10] Shame always concerns oneself, directly or indirectly. Shame relates primarily to our own self-awareness. We experience shame on another's account only if the relation between the

10. See the classic analysis of shame in Hans Lipps, *Die menschliche Natur* (Werke III), ed. Hans-Georg Gadamer (Frankfurt: Vittorio Klostermann, 1977), p. 31: "Verlegenheit ist durch die Situation begründet. . . . Scham *wacht* über etwas. Sie steht am Ursprung des Sich-seiner-selbst-bewusst-seins."

others and ourselves is so close that we can speak of identification as, for instance, is the case with children or parents. Their shame becomes, vicariously, one's own. Their shame or shamelessness falls back upon ourselves.

(2) Shame exactly guards against an *involuntary exposure* to an external gaze which calls our identity into question. Thus it is if we are nakedly exposed to a scrutinizing or dubious look. The sense of shame here anticipates being ashamed, and protects us from involuntary exposure. Since shame is conciliate with the emergence of identity, it has, as it were, a totalizing effect on us. Here the issue is brought into question of who we are when it really comes down to it. We may be ashamed of our own waywardness (in which case shame is related to guilt), but we may also feel shame for who we are, and who we are not. Shame is directed primarily at a state of the self, while guilt is primarily directed towards an action affecting others that springs from this self. Guilt is felt when we have transgressed the inviolable zone of otherness of fellow human beings. Shame is experienced when we have exposed a rift within ourselves, a rift that questions our own identity.

Shame is thus intimately linked to *self-reflection*. To have a sense of shame means wanting to be honest with oneself, and wanting to square up to things. This is the healthy shame. But at the same time, shame impairs the self. Put to shame I am defeated, because I am the person I have no wish to be. Fault lines emerge in my self-image. This shows the Janus face of shame. Without shame we would not become ourselves; and yet shame shows us the fragility of ourselves. At this point, the phenomenon of shame has a similar function to that of anxiety in the awareness of guilt.[11] And it may be that the ambiguous phenomenon of shame may serve as a pivotal intermediary concept that relates the Christian concept of sin to the phenomena of everyday existence. Like anxiety, shame is not sin, but a precondition for self-awareness. Yet it is also the precondition for sin's self-estrangement from oneself, God, and fellows.[12]

---

11. As pointedly observed by Donald Capps, *The Depleted Self: Sin in a Narcissistic Age* (Minneapolis: Fortress Press, 1993), p. 98: "The experience of depletion is to a theology of shame what anxiety was, and continues to be, to a theology of guilt."

12. Compare with the role attached to anxiety in Kierkegaard: it is a pre-theological 'middle term', which is both a precondition for sin and yet the only possible pathway for becoming a full human being, Søren Kierkegaard, *The Concept of Anxiety: A Simple Psychologically Orienting Deliberation on the Dogmatic Issue of Hereditary Sin* [1844], (Princeton: Princeton University Press, 1980), p. 41: "The psychological explanation must not talk around the point but remain in its elastic ambiguity, from which guilt [= sin] breaks forth in the qualitative leap." At the same time, however, anxiety is also the awakening of the spirit, as Kierkegaard points out in the same context.

(3) Shame, however, is also an endemically social phenomenon. With shame, as with guilt, we stand before an *authority*. We are distanced from ourselves in the mirror of the others. Shame involves my measuring myself in terms of how others see me. The evaluative gaze is that of the other people, either present or generalized. But not theirs alone. In feeling shame the individual assimilates to his or her own self-concept the appraisal of others — feeling a fool or useless, as the case may be. But it is far from always the case that social appraisal ends there. There is a look which none can sustain and which the shamed individual will resist. Exposed to *contempt* we may come to regard with contempt some aspect or other of ourselves. But in the case of total self-contempt shame is extruded. The individual who is ashamed continues to hold on to his or her integrity despite the risk of appearing contemptible: "There is more to me than meets their eye," is the tacit presupposition that guards shame from self-contempt.

The judgment of shame thus reaches its nadir when the individual views his or her own shamefulness from the outside. In shame we measure ourselves against our own self-concept. It's not just a case of having exposed our weaknesses to others. We have acted and lived in a way that falls short of what we expect of ourselves. Such self-condemnation poses an intricate question: For where is the self that condemns itself? Beyond that condemnation? Here shame is close to reaching its nadir, but it never does. Put to shame we are exposed to social judgment in the form of the eyes of others upon us. But in shame we relate also to our own self-concept, which is both less *and* more judgmental than the eyes of others. Their gaze rests on our actions; at the worst they go on to make inferences about our person. But the one who is ashamed is aware that there is more to him or her than is revealed in his or her actions. At the same time our own gaze is more penetrating than that of others: the one who feels ashamed takes a hard look at his or her own waywardness and exacts a self-transformation. Ultimately, then, shame can turn to self-contempt. But in the totalization of shame we find, again, that we have moved beyond shame. In shame we take a stance in which we still hold on to our sense of selfhood.

Shame in Cultural Perspectives

One might ask why shame, at first blush, plays such a marginalized role in the Christian symbolics of sin. The primary reason is no doubt the fact that in the Judaeo-Christian tradition the divine Gaze is primarily bound up with the ethically grounded responsibility for our neighbors. When it is a question of guilt, others are in focus. In the case of shame, however, it is oneself. An additional reason might be that in the problematic of shame, absolute Judgment is not immediately manifest. The judgmental aspect of shame is, as we have seen, primarily linked to the eyes of others upon us, and to our assimilation of their regard in our own self-assessment. But exactly the interiorization of shame forces it over and beyond the judgment of the social environment and into a religious dimension. This is precisely what happens in the prophetic and wisdom traditions of the Old Testament, both with roots in the cultic tradition. The religious demand for personal *integrity* unites the judgment of shame with the divine gaze which searches hearts (Psa. 139). The confession of the lips must also be that of the heart (Isa. 29:13); the law is to be inscribed on hearts of flesh and not of stone (Jer. 31:33; Ezek. 11:19).

Much can be said for the hypothesis that *Paul* was the first to bring the problematic of guilt, which has primarily to do with others, under the rubric of shame which has its primary focus in the self. It is because the individual knows that, put to shame, he is exposed to himself that he seeks to secure advance self-protection from the external eyes of the Law, the criterial authority. Through a self-righteous attitude the individual seeks to win the recognition of which the Law deprives him because its demands expose the flaws in his character. Already in the Pauline exegesis from the 1920s onwards one might plausibly speak of a *switch from the theme of guilt to the issue of shame* in the doctrine of sin.[13] It has been the human person's relentless craving for recognition and for being in charge of his and her own life which for the most part of twentieth century theology played the central role in theological anthropology. These analyses were thus mostly guided by the assumption that human beings are triggered by an urge for self-assertion and pride.

Since around 1980, however, theologies of sin have been more concerned about the danger of losing oneself, which is closer associated with the problems of vulnerability and shame. Sin thus springs from the human endeavor to preempt the scandal of shame, but usually in vain. Early feminist theologians in particular contended that pride is not the main form that sin takes for women. Rather it is the feeling of self-loss and diffusiveness which is characteristic for women's experiences.[14] Whether or not this view was empirically warranted or not, more recent feminist proposals have refrained

13. This is typified by Rudolf Bultmann in his highly influential article, "Römer 7 und die Anthropologie des Paulus" (1932), reprinted in *Exegetica* (Tübingen: Mohr-Siebeck, 1967), pp. 198-211. Also Christof Gestrich views sin as a fundamental human strategy aimed at self-justification in the ever-failing fight for recognition, *Return of Splendor*, pp. 197-206.

14. So Judith Plaskow, *Sex, Sin, and Grace: Women's Experience and the Theologies of Reinhold Niebuhr and Paul Tillich* (Lanham: University Press of America, 1980).

from too simple divisions of sins into male and female. In a survey of more recent feminist approaches to the doctrine of sin, Mary Elise Lowe makes the point that "[w]hat we see emerging in these recent proposals is that the line that divided male and female sins has been erased. Regardless of the root of sin — anxiety, insecurity, desire, or violence — these authors acknowledge that all humans experience powerlessness and pride, fear and arrogance, irregardless of gender."[15]

Thus even though both the Biblical traditions and our cultural situation push us to differentiate between guilt and shame, the distinction can also be over-emphasized. This has been the case in several macro-historical hypotheses. Already in 1946 the anthropologist Ruth Benedict claimed that Oriental cultures were primarily shame cultures, while Western cultures were based on the interiorized feelings of guilt. Similarly, Protestants in the northern parts of Europe were supposed to be more guilt-ridden, while Catholics in the south established cultures based on shame.[16] Today it is recognized that also these schematizations do not really work. All cultures presuppose a distinction between "ourselves" and "the others," even though these borderlines differ from culture to culture, and can be more or less flexible. Shame also covers a variety of cases, some of which are related to particular norms of a society, while others are highly self-reflexive and interiorized. If one were to develop a more convincing macro-historical hypothesis, it would rather be that the phenomenon of shame has acquired new forms in late modernity, where personal identities are fluid, reflexive, and re-negotiated in ever new social contexts. Thus shame is no longer so much related to robust social norms, but is more often linked to the failing boundaries of selves. Shame is transported, as it were, from the external authorities of fathers and mothers to the internal networks of fellow brothers and sisters, who have learned to cooperate, but also to compete. Shame is thus a particular problem for achievers in highly competitive cultures. In this light, guilt and shame appear as two interrelated, but distinct phenomena. Shame can emerge as a consequence of guilt and be related to past wrong-doings, but more often disgrace-shame is concerned about the future stability of the uncertain self in a competitive environment. While shame indeed can be related to social codes and mores, as has been the rule in the past, shame is today more often related to the shame of disgrace in face of friends and peers, and in one's own self-image.

15. Mary Elise Lowe, "Women-Oriented Hamartiologies: A Survey of the Shift from Powerlessness to Right Relationship," *Dialog: A Journal of Theology* 39, no. 2 (2000): 136.

16. So Ruth Benedict, *The Chrysanthemum and the Sword: Patterns of Japanese Culture* (Boston: Houghton Mifflin, 1946). The position is rightly criticized by Capps, Twitchell, and Pattison.

Facing God's Liberating Face

Weakness and strength, of course, are in themselves neutral in so far as sin is concerned. Strength is a God-given gift of vital existence, just as the vulnerability of weakness is part of what it means to be a human. And yet Christian teaching on sin is grounded in the experience that the mechanisms of sin are invariably tied up with the phenomena which attach to the strengths and weaknesses that are part of the human condition. Sin is spawned through being nurtured by overweening self-confidence — or by what parades as such, disguising weakness's fear of not matching up or not getting enough.

The Christian message of the forgiveness of sins cannot but receive distinctive content when related to guilt and shame. It is true that the liturgical proclamation of the forgiveness of sins can and must be addressed to all who hear it without discrimination, for the human person's relationship to God is at the center of it. But the reception of the proclamation of forgiveness may well be different. In relation to the problem of guilt it is important to distinguish between the consequences for which a person can and must assume responsibility, and those for which only God can. The old line of demarcation between the temporal and the eternal is here life-essential. From the temporal perspective the blameworthy party must "come to terms quickly with the accuser" (Matt. 5:25). But from the eternal perspective it is God's forgiveness of sins that counts and holds good because God already *has* assumed responsibility for the consequences of our deeds. The forgiveness of sins at one and the same time *presupposes* personal responsibility *(coram hominibus)* and also marks a restriction of that responsibility *(coram deo)*. The forgiveness of sin is morally possible only on condition of the redress that God accords the victims of sin. In this sense, the overcoming of sin by forgiveness implies a reorientation of the sinner from the bondage of the past toward the future life: The future of one's own range of undoing evil, but even more of God's future restoration of the lives that were spoiled by our wrongdoings.

In relation to the problem of shame, however, the overcoming of sin is primarily related to an act of cleansing and reinstatement. The issue of cleansing is essential, since one of the characteristics of shame is exactly its power to spread and contaminate others, just as is the case of embarrassment.[17] While guilt resides and ends in the responsible person (which is why we feel the need to pass on guilt to other persons), shame has immediate social effects on those who are close. Coming close to the ashamed person means sharing in his or her shame, which is probably the reason why the

17. See to this issue Pattison, *Shame*, pp. 87-92.

ashamed person is often shunned by others. Therefore, the ashamed does not only need protection from the judgmental gaze of others (or oneself), but also needs cleansing. But more than that, the ashamed is also in need of a rehabilitation. And this rehabilitation needs to be as public as the humiliation that was suffered under the gaze of others. If this is so, the overcoming of shame needs to take place in a kind of public forum. It is not sufficient to say that we should simply learn to accept ourselves.[18] Rather, what is needed is a social rehabilitation of the self, a rehabilitation that also embraces the self-image.

It is here that the Biblical notion of the *Face of God* becomes central. The face *(panim)* of God marks the presence of God in the midst of human and other earthly presences. So God said to Moses according to Exodus 33:14: "My presence *(panay)* will go with you, and I will give you rest." The face of God does not here signify a mere manifestation of a heavenly God via earthly mediators. The Face of God *is* God: "It was no messenger or angel but his presence *(panayw)* that saved them," as it is said in Isaiah 63:9.[19]

There is here a strong link to the New Testament notion of Jesus as the visible icon of the invisible God (Col. 1:15). Again Jesus is not perceived as a mediator placed at a distance from the real God. Rather, Jesus is the presence of God as revealed to human beings. Placed before the face of Christ we see the glory of God, that *is* the presence of God: "For it is the God who said, 'Let light shine out of darkness' [Gen. 1:3], who has shone in our hearts to give the light of the knowledge of the glory of God in the face of Jesus Christ" (2 Cor. 4:6; cf. 3:7). It is this divine face or presence that liberates the sinner to see the glory of God with an "unveiled face" and thus to be "transformed into the same image from one degree of glory to another" (2 Cor. 3:18).

This transformation of the self does not come from the human person's own resources, including the ability to reflect upon ourselves. The pattern of redemption is here not one of an interior psychological self-scrutiny, but one of being placed in front of the liberating face of Christ, and thus being transformed after his image and likeness. Facing Christ is identical with the facing of God, though much more awaits to be seen on day that we shall God "face

18. The therapy of self-acceptance is proposed by Paul Tillich in his analysis of shame; see Capps, *Depleted Self,* p. 90. However, also Capps's proposal (pp. 92ff.) of a mutual self-mirroring between the idealized self and the grandiose self (in the wake of Kohut's theory of the narcissistic self) stays within the psychological boundaries of the self.

19. See A. S. van der Woude, "panim/face," in *Theological Lexicon of the Old Testament,* vol. 2, ed. Ernst Jenni and Claus Westermann (Peabody, MA: Hendrickson, 1997), pp. 995-1014, who also points out that the Septuagint translation of the divine *panim* of God is usually rendered with *autos,* "God Himself" (pp. 1004-5).

to face" (1 Cor. 13:12).[20] The notions of divine Glory and Face are here intrinsically related to the natural symbol of light that God let shine at the beginning of creation (Gen. 1:3). It belongs to the nature of light to shine forth. But the radiance of God's Face has the particular nature of not stopping short at the human skin. It is the divine Glory that cleanses the one who is the recipient of the divine enlightenment. It is the brightness of the divine Face that radiates and brings back the splendor to the human faces that are now seen by the eyes of God. The Face of God, in short, is both external and embracing, and is transformative exactly by being external to the human psyche. Accordingly, overcoming shame means raising one's head after the experience of 'losing one's face'. The Face of God takes the place of the paralyzing gaze of others as well as of one's own self-estimation.

Nowhere is this more visible than in the liturgical act of divine *blessing*. Especially the Aaronic blessing (Num. 6:22-27) is central here, and it therefore plays a central role in many Christian services despite the fact that it belongs to a part of the Old Testament, which most probably goes back to pre-Israel traditions:

> The LORD bless you and keep you;
> the LORD make his face to shine upon you, and be gracious to you;
> the LORD lift up his countenance upon you, and give you peace

Hereby a new two-way interaction between God and human beings is facilitated: The overflow of the blessing (Hebrew: *barak*, Greek: *eulogeo*) of God liberates the liturgical self to give praise and thanks (Hebrew: *barak*, Greek: *eulogeo*) to God. The inner space of the constrained and burdened self is opened to a divine Face greater than the self. God's Face exhibits the divine glory (Hebrew: *kabod*) that is weightier than the gaze of fellows and foes, and outshines them. In the praise of God the fear of human fellows is overcome.

One can only understand the Aaronic blessing as part of an oral utterance which presupposes the presence of God, who speaks in and through the words and signs of the priest.[21] The sinner's head, which was bowed, is now raised in front of God's face who shines forth and enlightens the self-enclosed mind of the sinner. The liberating face of God overrules the external gaze of other human beings as well as the self-judgment of the sinner.

---

20. This is beautifully elaborated by David Ford, *Self and Salvation: Being Transformed* (Cambridge: Cambridge University Press, 1999), pp. 167-90.

21. See Martin Luther's trinitarian interpretation of the Aaronic blessing in his sermon, "Der Segen, so man nach der Messe spricht ubert das Volck . . ." (1532), in *Weimarer Ausgabe*, III/30, ed. G. von Loeper, Erich Schmidt, et al. (Weimar: H. Böhlau, 1887), pp. 572-82.

Theology and the Human Sciences: Critical Familism and the Law

Don Browning

For several years, I have argued for a more aggressive engagement of theology with the human sciences. I have felt that this is necessary for at least two reasons. First, even though most of the human sciences — psychology, sociology, law, economics, and anthropology — generally aspire to value neutrality, they often unwittingly lapse into both moral and quasi-religious arguments. Second, the power of the human sciences in the modern university and culture has tended to marginalize theology as a discipline that can address common human issues and problems. These two reasons constitute a double bind for Christian theology. In the name of value neutrality, theology is not seen as a science and is therefore discarded as genuinely true, valid, or trustworthy. On the other hand, because the human sciences are almost always implicitly value-laden, they actually begin to function as moral and sometimes religious substitutes for religion and theology, further placing theology as a discipline in a subordinate and ineffective role.

Over most of my career, I have tried to illustrate this situation through analyzing the disciplines of psychology.[1] In recent years, because of my position as director of the Religion, Culture, and Family Project at the University of Chicago, I have been drawn into discussion with the disciplines of law and public policy. This has been a new experience. But it is possible for theology to address law and policy on grounds highly similar to its engagement with more customary dialogue partners such as psychology and sociology. In brief, most disciplines commit themselves to implicit metatheories that control

---

1. See Don Browning, *Religious Thought and the Modern Psychologies* (Minneapolis, MN: Fortress Press, 1987), and the second edition by Don Browning and Terry Cooper (2003).

much of their more focused topics of explicit concentration. Theology can enter into discussion with these disciplines at the level of their metatheories and then go on to analyze and sometimes critique their more specific judgments and pronouncements. This kind of dialogue, among other goals, has been promoted by Wallace Alston during his highly effective period of leadership at the Center of Theological Inquiry. I want to further demonstrate the importance of this enterprise by moving into new areas of inquiry, at least somewhat new for me.

The occasion that calls forth this paper is the new proposals now being promoted in the law to delegalize marriage and make parenthood, whether married or unmarried, the central category of the law. Proposals from the American Law Institute move in this direction. Some legal scholars would go further; they would not only delegalize marriage, i.e., make it a private affair with no status as such before law and the state, but actually make the mother-child dyad the central category of the law, giving legal status to fathers only insofar as they demonstrate the capacity for care and involvement.

In what follows, I set out my position on "critical familism," as I am increasingly being asked to do in various legal and interdisciplinary conferences. I argue that law should not be the center of marriage and family reform, although it does have a role to play. Toward the end of the argument, I demonstrate what critical familism means for the new proposals coming from the law profession that would deemphasize marriage and elevate either parents, married or not, or even mothers alone as the central legal categories for marriage law. In an age when marriage seems to be collapsing yet children still need care, the law profession is toying with these revisions as a way of rendering all parents — married, divorced, or accidental — legally accountable, or even further, making mothers the main beneficiaries of custody and state support. Critical familism addresses these problems, but in a different way.

What Is Critical Familism?

Critical familism is not primarily a legal theory, even though it has implications for the law. It is first of all a normative theory of the family and marriage primarily intended to provide the cultural level of society its ideals and practical strategies for family formation and marriage. It places at the center of religio-cultural aspirations and supports the equal-regard mother-father team with equal privileges and responsibilities in both the public worlds of politics and employment and the more private realms of home, child rearing, and intergenerational care.[2] Critical familism is "critical" in that it attempts to expose, critique, and reform distortions of social, economic, and political power which function to block or undermine the free formation and support of the equal-regard mother-father team. Even though critical familism fully acknowledges that marriage is not always chosen by everyone for the purposes of procreation and child care, as an institution with certain cultural, social, and legal entitlements and responsibilities, marriage should be defined primarily with its child-rearing tasks envisioned as central.

Critical familism has a variety of other names in the current literature. Sociologist Brad Wilcox in a recent review of the family strategies of the mainline churches refers to it as "progressive familism" in contrast to "traditional familism" of the 1950s or "expressive liberationist" approaches.[3] Sociologist William Doherty, partially influenced by critical familism, has developed a perspective on family issues that he calls a "critical pro-marriage" point of view with implications for cultural, social, and legal reform.[4]

Critical familism, as I indicated, is not primarily a legal theory, although it has suggestions for legal practice and public policy. But this is the point: law should not be the center of marriage and family reform although it can contribute to such reform. Critical familism is basically a cultural strategy — indeed a religio-cultural strategy — to be carried principally by the institutions of civil society. It envisions the task of reconstructing family and marriage

2. The basic sources of critical familism are the summary book of the first phase of the Religion, Culture, and Family Project by Don Browning, Bonnie Miller-McLemore, Pam Couture, Bernie Lyon, and Robert Franklin, *From Culture Wars to Common Ground: Religion and the American Family Debate* (Louisville, KY: Westminster John Knox, 1997, 2000). Also see Don Browning and Gloria Rodriguez, *Reweaving the Social Tapestry: Toward a Public Philosophy and Policy for Families* (New York, NY: W. W. Norton, 2001). This book was the background book for the American Assembly's consultation on families held in September, 2000. Critical familism influenced the consensus statement developed by the fifty-three diverse individuals attending that conference and published under the title "Strengthening American Families: Reweaving the Social Tapestry: The 97th American Assembly, September 21-24, 2000." The statement below may take critical familism in directions that some of my co-authors would not share. The following statement must be regarded primarily as my own. The theory of critical familism is also extended into a wider international discussion in my *Marriage and Modernization: How Globalization Threatens Marriage and What Should Be Done about It* (Grand Rapids: Eerdmans, 2003).

3. Brad Wilcox, "For the Sake of the Children? Family-Related Discourse and Practice in the Mainline," in *The Quiet Hand of God: Faith-Based Activism and the Public Role of Mainline Protestantism*, ed. Robert Wuthnow and John H. Evans (Berkeley, CA: University of California Press, 2002).

4. William Doherty and Jason Carroll, "Health and the Ethics of Marital Therapy and Education," in *Marriage, Health, and the Professions*, ed. John Wall, Don Browning, William Doherty, and Stephen Post (Grand Rapids: Eerdmans, 2002), p. 216.

along its theoretical lines as a complex cultural work that requires a delicate set of collaborations between civil society, government, market, and the specialized field of family law.[5]

Religious Thinking and Public Discourse

Critical familism believes that family theory informed by religious traditions has a right to contribute to public policy. It holds this because of the often overlooked symmetry of religious and so-called secular thought. Let me explain. Critical familism holds that all moral, political, and legal thinking — as expressions of practical wisdom *(phronēsis)* — are complex interweavings of several dimensions of thought. These include deep metaphors conveying fundamental views of reality, general principles of moral obligation (e.g., utilitarian, ethical egoism, Kantian, the golden rule, neighbor love), assumed theories of premoral goods that satisfy central human needs, theories of natural and social-systemic patterns and constraints, and finally assumptions about preferred concrete practices, rules, and social roles.[6] These five dimensions of practical wisdom can be uncovered through a process of empirical reconstruction of concrete instances of actual practical thinking in ways similar to how Jürgen Habermas uncovers his three validity claims.[7] This is to say that a careful analysis of concrete instances of practical reason invariably demonstrates assumptions and judgments at these different levels.

Critical familism holds that the deep metaphors of all practical thinking have the status of faith-like assumptions; since such metaphors (e.g., organic, mechanistic, monistic, harmonistic, dualistic, or theistic) can be uncovered in all instances of practical thinking, the distinction between explicitly religious practical thinking and so-called secular moral, political, or legal practical thought is not categorical. Both allegedly secular and religious forms of practical rationality float on a veritable ocean of assumed metaphors about the basic structures of life, their directions, and their trustworthiness or lack of it.[8] This rough commensurability of so-called religious and secular forms of

5. For the idea of marriage reconstruction as a cultural work, see Browning, *Marriage and Modernization*, pp. 24-29.

6. For a fuller discussion of the five dimensions of practical reason, see Don Browning, *A Fundamental Practical Theology* (Minneapolis, MN: Fortress Press, 1991).

7. Jürgen Habermas, *Moral Consciousness and Communicative Action* (Cambridge, MA: The MIT Press, 1990), p. 79.

8. George Lakoff and Mark Johnson, *Metaphors We Live By* (New York: Oxford University Press, 1959).

practical reason means that positions on family theory informed by explicitly religious sources have the right to enter into deliberations aimed to shape public policy. Of course, in contrast to confessional criteria that have their authority within their respective traditions, for explicitly religiously informed family theories to gain a hearing in policy debates, they must advance their arguments in publicly accessible ways.

This can happen when religiously informed perspectives present themselves as mixed discourses in which faith affirmations expressed in metaphor and narrative are interwoven with moral arguments about the right and the good that can be expressed in publicly recognizable forms of philosophy and social theory. Most axial religions contain clear examples of such articulate blends of religious narrative and metaphor with philosophically identifiable forms of argument about the nature of the moral and premoral goods relevant to public policy. Roman Catholicism is informed by Aristotelianism, and liberal Protestantism has been variously informed by Kantianism, American pragmatism, and existentialism. Furthermore, historical research reveals that the family theories of early Christianity contained insights from Aristotelian and Stoic philosophy. Mature forms of axial religions are almost always mixed discourses blending explicitly religious metaphors and narrative with moral-philosophical arguments that sometimes merge into political and economic judgments as well. The problem of linking the deep metaphors of practical thought to their more articulate moral and premoral judgments is a challenge not only for religious thinking; it is a challenge for so-called secular practical thought as well.

Critical familism with its vision of the equal-regard mother-father partnership is grounded on a complex, mixed religio-philosophical discourse of this kind. At its most abstract formulation, the idea of equal-regard is what William Frankena called a "mixed-deontological" concept.[9] It defines the marital contract as a complex social covenant. The covenant between husband and wife is to treat each other as ends and never as objects or means of satisfaction alone. Used as a mixed-deontological concept, it also contains a strong teleological subdimension that entails the obligation to actively work for the good of one's marital partner in all spheres of life, both private and public. The equal-regard covenant or status is a theory of mutuality and is thoroughly reversible; it applies with equal force to both husband and wife. But because of the asymmetrical nature of male and female investments on certain matters such as procreation and child care, the equal-regard covenant does not necessary imply moment-by-moment identical treatment, although it does require equality over the marital life cycle.

9. William Frankena, *Ethics* (Englewood Cliffs, NJ: Prentice-Hall, 1973), p. 43.

The equal-regard covenant is primarily a religio-cultural ideal promoted and implemented by the institutions of civil society. It would be a guide to socialization in family, schools, and religious institutions in their various forms of marriage education, preparation, and support. Government and market should do nothing to undermine the equal-regard covenant and do what they reasonably can to support it. Law in its various forms does not have the primary responsibility for promoting it but should be seen as a source of friendly assistance.

Sources of Critical Familism and the Equal-Regard Covenant

Even though at its core, the equal-regard covenant is a mixed deontological concept, it also has many sources and several levels of additional meaning adhering to it. It takes seriously what Hans-Georg Gadamer would call the "classics" of Western religious and philosophical traditions on marriage and family. For instance, it honors the Ur-myth of Genesis 1 that gives the dignity of the *imago Dei* (Gen. 1:27) to both male and female and that also grants equal responsibility to both in procreation and "dominion" (generally interpreted as economic responsibility) (Gen. 1:28).[10] In addition to these classic texts of Judaism, Christianity, and Islam, the equal-regard doctrine of critical familism takes seriously the Aristotelian theory of friendship between husband and wife as the sharing of utility, pleasure, and virtue[11] — especially the Thomistic enrichment of these concepts with Aquinas's attribution of the *imago Dei* to the wife as well as the husband.[12] This was a significant yet still incomplete step toward balancing Aristotle's theory of proportional justice between husband and wife.[13] Critical familism also values medieval canon law and Thomistic accomplishments that made uncoerced consent on the part of both husband and wife central to the definition of marriage.[14]

Thomas Aquinas provides critical familism with some additional in-

10. Phyllis Trible, *God and the Rhetoric of Sexuality* (Philadelphia, PA: Fortress Press, 1978), p. 19.

11. Aristotle, "Nicomachean Ethics," in *The Basic Works of Aristotle,* ed. Richard McKeon (New York: Random House, 1941), Bk. VIII, ch. 3.

12. Thomas Aquinas, *Summa Contra Gentiles* (London: Burns, Oates, and Washbourne, 1928), 3, ii, p. 118 [hereafter referred to as SCG].

13. Aristotle, *Nicomachean Ethics,* Bk. VIII, ch. 7.

14. John Witte, *From Sacrament to Contract* (Louisville, KY: Westminster John Knox, 1997), pp. 26, 32-33; James Brundage, *Law, Sex, and Christian Society in Medieval Europe* (Chicago, IL: University of Chicago Press, 1987), pp. 361-64.

sights. Aquinas could agree with those contemporary feminists who hold that the primordial family is the mother-infant dyad.[15] The question for Aquinas, as it is for contemporary evolutionary psychologists, was this: What are the conditions which led to the momentously important cultural accomplishment of human males joining the mother-infant dyad and contributing to the provision and care for their offspring and consorts? His answer (also parallel to that given by contemporary evolutionary psychology, but of course without its theory of evolution) contained several elements. The long period of human infant dependency, the father's recognition and certainty that the child was his (what evolutionary theorists call "paternal recognition" and "paternal certainty"), sexual exchange, and mutual assistance between father and mother gradually brought the human male to assist the mother-infant dyad.[16] These are the naturalistic foundations of matrimony which religion and culture sanction and stabilize but do not directly create.

Both Aquinas and much of contemporary evolutionary psychology assume that this was an enormous social and cultural achievement that distinguishes humans from almost all other creatures at the mammalian level. My research suggests that other medieval scholars from different faith traditions such as the Jewish Nachmanides and the Islamic Al-Ghazali also recognized something like this naturalistic archaeology of the marital institution.[17] Marriage as sacrament for Aquinas and marriage as a one-flesh covenant for Nachmanides and Al-Ghazali gave this male connection with the mother-infant dyad the additional stability and reinforcement of sacredness. The sacred character of sacrament and covenant converts the logic of mutual advantage (the logic of costs and benefits) to the logic of mutual obligation and respect; costs and benefits are not ignored but they now become secondary.

---

15. Thomas Aquinas, *Summa Theologica*, III "Supplement" (Boston, MA: Benziger Brothers, 1948), Q. 41, 1 [hereafter referred to as ST]; Martha Fineman, *The Neutered Mother, The Sexual Family and Other Twentieth Century Tragedies* (New York, NY: Routledge, 1995), p. 5.

16. For references to these various moves by Aquinas, see the following texts: ST, III, Q. 41, 1; SCG, 3, ii, pp. 112-8. For analogous points made in evolutionary psychology, see Pierre Van den Berghe, *Human Family Systems* (New York: Elsevier, 1979), pp. 20-21; Donald Symons, *The Evolution of Human Sexuality* (Oxford: Oxford University Press, 1979), pp. 131-6; Barry Hewlett, ed., *Father-Child Relations* (Hawthorne, NY: Aldine de Gruyter, 1992); Robert Trivers, *Social Evolution* (Menlo Park, CA: Benjamin/Cummings Publishing, 1985), pp. 203-38. For a more detailed summary of this comparison between the naturalism of Aquinas and evolutionary psychology, see Browning, et al., *From Culture Wars to Common Ground*, pp. 111-27.

17. Nachmanides, *Commentary on the Torah: Genesis*, vol. 1 (New York: Shilo Publishing House, 1971-1976), p. 8; Al-Ghazali, *Book on the Etiquette of Marriage*, in *Marriage and Sexuality in Islam*, ed. Madelin Farah (Salt Lake City, UT: University of Utah Press, 1984), p. 45. For extensive commentary on these texts, see Browning, *Marriage and Modernization*, pp. 118-25.

Marriage law since the Protestant Reformation, in most Western societies, has in some way recognized for most of this period the priority of the logic of sacred obligation in the marital contract and covenant.

Sacred concepts endow with intrinsic value the human arrangements that they bless. These arrangements are seen to have such intrinsic value that they are regarded as protected and sanctioned as termini for entire ranges of important but less valuable instrumental goods. Until recent decades, Western law has developed certain legal and philosophical concepts that honor understandings of marriage as sacrament (Catholicism, Hinduism), covenant (Judaism, Islam, Protestantism), "one flesh" union (Judaism, Catholicism, Hinduism, and Protestantism) without sanctioning any one model of the sacred. The concepts of "status" and more secularized versions of "covenant" are designed to serve this legal and cultural function of supporting and stabilizing this near unique human accomplishment of joining the father to the mother-infant dyad.[18]

There are additional sources for the ideal of the equal-regard mother-father marital covenant. Of course, Kant and his followers such as John Rawls and Susan Okin are sources of this concept.[19] But critical familism adds additional twists to the Kantian formulation. First, it holds that it is precisely the task of both husband and wife in the equal-regard covenant to promise publicly before the state, friends, extended family, and, if religious, before relevant communities of faith that they will treat one another as ends and never only as means.[20] Hence, the equal-regard marital covenant is also a covenant with other spheres of society beyond the husband-wife dyad. This makes the equal-regard covenant simultaneously both thoroughly private and thoroughly public. It is public in that its promises start with the conjugal couple but also include a variety of spheres beyond it. It is thoroughly private in that neither state nor market should interfere except in emergencies and to support; both state and market must avoid disrupting or replacing the tasks of the conjugal couple as parents and lovers.

Second, in contrast to Kant, the mixed deontological logic of the equal-regard covenant implies that this public pledge also entails equally strong efforts to actualize the welfare of the other (the good of the other) as well as any

18. I say that human males joining the mother-infant dyad is "near unique" at the mammalian level because there are a few other primates where this happens, for instance with Gibbons, but in quite different ways than with humans. See Martin Daly and Margo Wilson, *Sex, Evolution, and Behavior* (Belmont, CA: Wadsworth Publishing, 1983), p. 142.

19. Immanuel Kant, *Foundations of the Metaphysics of Morals* (New York: The Bobbs-Merrill Co., 1959); John Rawls, *A Theory of Justice* (Cambridge, MA: Harvard University Press, 1971); Susan Okin, *Justice, Gender, and the Family* (New York: Basic Books, 1989).

20. Kant, *Metaphysics of Morals*, p. 47.

offspring of their union.[21] But, as Kant himself recognized, his categorical imperative had its predecessors in the golden rule and the Jewish and Christian principle of neighbor love and their various analogues in other religions.

Finally, it should be emphasized that the equal-regard marital covenant is about the conjugal couple and not necessarily the neo–local nuclear family isolated from the rest of society. The equal-regard covenant and critical familism are ecological concepts designed to define families as democracies of work and affection interacting with, contributing to, and supported by wider social and natural networks.

Critical Familism as Antidote to Modernization

The ideal of the equal-regard covenant is also informed by various historical and sociological trends. The development of democratic polities and modernization in Western societies gradually has been interpreted to require something like the equal-regard covenant. The processes of early modernization drew men in the nineteenth century into the wage economy and out of dependence on farm and craft-based economies centered in the extended family.[22] In the twentieth century, modernization and industrialization drew women into the wage economy and away from exclusive economic dependence on husbands. These social processes decreased forced economic dependencies and have had a democratizing influence on marriage and family.

It should be noted, however, that the concept of the equal-regard marital covenant is both compatible with modernization and an antidote to its excesses. Both husband and wife have access to the fruits of the modernizing process. But Habermas argues that the blind processes of modernization also tend to "colonize" the lifeworld of face-to-face social interactions (neighborhoods, families, and marriage) and reduce them to the cost-benefit logics and functional universalism of efficient market productivity.[23] The equal-regard marital covenant places strong limitation on these disruptive excesses of mar-

21. For the neo-Aristotelian Janssens and neo-Thomistic statement of the meaning of equal regard closer to what I subscribe to, see Louis Janssens, "Norms and Priorities in a Love Ethics," in *Louvain Studies* 6 (Spring 1977), pp. 207-88.

22. Gary S. Becker, *Treatise on the Family* (Cambridge, MA: Harvard University Press, 1991), pp. 348-56.

23. For descriptions of both market and bureaucratic forms of rationalization, see Jürgen Habermas, *Theory of Communicative Action* II (Boston, MA: Beacon Press, 1987), pp. 182-96; Alan Wolfe, *Whose Keeper? Social Science and Moral Obligation* (Berkeley, CA: University of California Press, 1989), pp. 52-60, 133-41.

ket forms of modernization. Although critical familism supports appropriate welfare measures, it also places strong limitations on bureaucratic forms of modernization that attempt to remedy the disruptions of families with dependency-inducing forms of assistance that actually encourage further family fragmentation. Critical familism follows the thinking of Roman Catholic subsidiarity teaching; neither government nor market should interfere with or attempt to replace the investments of kin altruism located in the mother-father team.[24] Both spheres of society — but especially government — should be willing to assist families (and indeed all families with children, be they intact yet poor single-parent families, or same-sex families) when the need is clear and beyond remedy by other means.

Practical Strategies

Since critical familism is primarily a theory and strategy for the culture-building and socializing tasks of the institutions of civil society, recommendations for concrete strategies should begin there. The first task is both to recover and reconstruct our inherited marriage and family traditions. Neither the general public nor the specialized professions of law, medicine, education, or therapy understand these traditions. Most people do not comprehend the complex interweaving of Jewish and Christian teachings, Greek philosophy, Roman and German law, and Enlightenment philosophy that have gone into the formation of Western marriage and family traditions. But the retrieval and reconstruction of these traditions also will require a nuanced dialogue between them and more newly visible traditions in Western societies such as Islam, Hinduism, Buddhism, and Confucianism. Critical familism believes that neither our family culture nor our public policies should be developed in such a way as to marginalize either the classics of the Western religions that have shaped our culture or the traditions that were once thought to be exotic but now are part of our daily lives and may have insights to contribute.

The task of the future is both to retrieve and reconstruct all these traditions and find fruitful analogies (not necessarily identities) between them for the purposes of rough cultural consensus.[25] Research by both the Emory

24. Pope Leo XIII, *Rerum Novarum*, in *Proclaiming Justice and Peace: Papal Documents from* Rerum Novarum *through* Centesimus Annus, ed. Michael Walsh and Brian Davies (Mystic, CT: Twenty-Third Publications), para. 12.

25. For a discussion of the distinctions between analogy, identities, and non-identities in correlational thinking, see David Tracy, *Blessed Rage for Order* (Minneapolis, MN: Seabury Press, 1975) and his *The Analogical Imagination* (New York: Crossroad, 1981).

Center for the Interdisciplinary Study of Religion and the Religious Consultation on Population, Reproductive Health, and Ethics suggests that all these classic religions have significant strands that are roughly analogous to the central ideas of critical familism.[26] The goal of this ecumenical retrieval and reconstruction should not be to dictate either public policy or the details of family law. The purpose instead would be to help develop a loose cultural consensus to which public policy and law would be both sensitive and, indeed, respectful.

Critical familism believes that the accomplishment of the Protestant Reformation that made marriage a public institution but one that could be blessed by religious institutions should be retained. This achievement should be preserved now, however, with broad sensitivity to the variety of religious traditions that make up the American social reality.

The development of a powerful culture of critical familism requires more than historical retrieval and reconstruction. It also necessitates effective systems of socialization. Marriage is a complex, intersubjective communicative process that needs advanced levels of "communicative competence."[27] Furthermore, there are analogies between the skills, privileges, and responsibilities of driving an automobile and the skills, privileges, and responsibilities of marriage and child rearing. To take the comparison further, there are similar material and economic costs and benefits to health, safety, pleasure, and utility in both marriage and driving a car. Hence, just as we train people to drive well and safely, society through its various educational and religious institutions should teach people to handle the communicative, cultural, and bio-economic realities of marriage. This is primarily a task for the institutions of civil society rather than law or government, although both can, in limited ways, support this cultural task.

The market is not the primary locus for promoting critical familism.

---

26. For sample publications of the Religious Consultation on Population, Reproductive Health, and Ethics, see Harold Coward and Daniel Maguire, *Visions of a New Earth: Religious Perspectives on Population, Consumption, and Ecology* (Albany, NY: State University of New York Press, 2000); John Raines and Daniel Maguire, *What Men Owe to Women* (Albany, NY: State University of New York Press, 2001); Daniel Maguire, *Sacred Choices: The Right to Contraception and Abortion in Ten World Religions* (Minneapolis, MN: Fortress Press, 2001). For a publication that reviews The Religious Consultation that comes from the Emory Center for the Interdisciplinary Study of Religion, see Browning, *Marriage and Modernization*, pp. 223-44.

27. Although Habermas develops the idea of communicative competence in relation to his discourse ethics and its implications for political procedures, in an era when economic dependence no longer unifies marriage, communicative competence and discourse ethics are relevant to family dialogue as well. See Habermas, *Moral Consciousness and Communicative Action*, pp. 120, 209.

But it can make essential contributions. In addition to a broad array of family-friendly provisions, business and industry should take rapid steps toward implementing what critical familism has called the 60-hour workweek option for married couples with children, to be divided between husband and wife 30-30 or 40-20. It follows that single-parents should be offered 30-hour workweek options and that work requirements for single parents on welfare should not exceed 30 hours per week.[28] These options should be offered with health benefits, and in the case of welfare single parents also should receive child care, medical insurance, and transportation supports. Through the instrument of the 60-hour workweek option, critical familism simultaneously supports the modernizing process but also limits its mindless spread into family life.

This proposal reveals the radical edge to critical familism. Limiting the time and energy that parents dedicate to the wage economy is essential for shaping a society in which the privileges and responsibilities of the public and private spheres of life are equally available to all parents. This recommendation makes critical familism truly progressive in contrast to other contemporary options. The conservative political and religious right wants to contain the spread of the market into private life by retaining the nineteenth-century solution of the divided spheres that placed men in the public realm and women in the domestic realm. Critical familism differs from liberal feminism that would give women full access to the market but has few proposals to radically contain it other than government and business support for child care. Critical familism differs from gynocentric legal feminists who emphasize the elevated status of mothering before law and government but have few proposals to limit the demands of market rationality.

Critical Familism and Family Law

Finally, critical familism has proposals relevant to the law even though law and government are not its primary points of leverage for marriage and family reform. Critical familism is fully aware that the modernizing process has done much to break down old cultural pressures and economic dependencies that functioned to support stable marriage formation. As a consequence,

---

28. For further discussions of the sixty-hour workweek for couples with children and the thirty-hour workweek for single parents, see Browning et al., *From Culture Wars to Common Ground*, pp. 316-8, 327-8; Browning and Rodriguez, *Reweaving the Social Tapestry*, pp. 128-30; and the final consensus statement of the Ninety-Seventh American Assembly attached to *Reweaving the Social Tapestry*, p. 190.

there have been more divorce, non-marital births, and alternative family patterns in modernizing societies. Abundant social-science research has accumulated since the early 1990s indicating that these marriage and family disruptions have not been good for the health and well-being of either children or adults.[29] These negative trends are now showing signs of slowing in the U.S., although not in other parts of the world where they seem to be gaining momentum.[30]

Whether coming or going, these trends are serious enough to require government policies and family law to develop fair and equitable ways for handling family disruption and the strains of divorce, custody, single parenthood, and out-of-wedlock births. But in addressing these issues, law and public policy should not attempt to develop alternative family and marriage cultures that would require heroic redefinitions of inherited cultural patterns. Efforts to de-legalize the marital relation and grant legal status only to parenthood, or perhaps mainly to mothers, would be ineffective and culturally destructive from the perspective of critical familism. They also would arrogate far too much cultural and social power over family matters to law and public policy.[31]

There are, however, steps that law and policy should take both to encourage and support the equal-regard marriage and family and, at the same time, provide a range of universal supports and remedies for all families with children. Policies that would remove the marriage penalty can be recommended. The increase of child tax exemptions and child credits for all families regardless of their form is also clearly in order. Advances in marriage education have been made that are sufficiently researched to justify making it widely available to teens and young people throughout society.[32] Govern-

---

29. Major recent texts that demonstrate the social costs of family disruption are Frank Fuerstenberg and Andrew Cherlin, *Divided Families* (Cambridge, MA: Harvard University Press, 1991); Linda Waite, "Does Marriage Matter?" in *Demography* 32, no. 4 (Nov. 1995), pp. 483-507; Paul Amato and Alan Booth, *A Generation at Risk* (Cambridge, MA: Harvard University Press, 1997).

30. For summaries of the new international trends, see Linda Waite and Maggie Gallagher, eds., *The Ties That Bind: Perspectives on Marriage and Cohabitation* (New York: Aldine de Gruyter, 2000).

31. For an emphasis on parenthood as the center of family law, see "Principles of the Law of Family Dissolution: Analysis and Recommendations" (American Law Institute, 2002); June Carbone, *From Partners to Parents: The Second Revolution in Family Law* (New York: Columbia University Press, 2000). For an emphasis on motherhood as the center of family law, see Martha Fineman, *The Illusion of Equality* (Chicago, IL: The University of Chicago Press, 1991); *The Neutered Mother, The Sexual Family*.

32. John Gottman, *What Predicts Divorce* (Hillsdale, NJ: Lawrence Erlbaum Associates,

ment support of experiments in marriage education, generally offered by various agencies of civil society, is consistent with centuries-old state interests in marriage as a civil institution. From the perspective of critical familism, state-mandated marriage education at the level of secondary schools, as now exists in Florida, is an acceptable idea,[33] just as are experiments in covenant marriage now being conducted in Louisiana, Arizona, and Arkansas.[34] State encouragement of intersector cooperation on marriage education between religion, medicine, welfare agencies, and schools, as is being pursued in Oklahoma, is also worth studying.[35] Children-first legislation that would require the filing of long-term financial plans for children at the time of divorce as proposed by Mary Ann Glendon, Katherine Spaht, and William Galston has considerable merit as well.[36]

Finally, government should pass legislation that encourages business and industry to provide more 20- and 30-hour workweeks with benefits to make more widely attainable the 60-hour workweek for couples with children and the 30-hour week for single parents. Government should take the radical step of curtailing the spread of market demands into the intimate rhythms of families and child care.

As indicated above, the equal-regard covenant recognizes the existence of male-female asymmetries in their respective investments in procreation and child care. In fact, an ethic of equal regard demands additional protections for vulnerable mothers during childbirth and the early years of child care. Similarly, critical familism recognizes the need for additional cultural and social inducements for fathers and husbands to commit to child

1994); *Why Marriages Succeed or Fail* (New York: Simon & Schuster, 1994); Howard Markman, Scott Stanley, and Susan L. Blumberg, *Fighting for Your Marriage* (San Francisco, CA: Jossey-Bass Publishers, 1994).

33. Pam Belluck, "States Declare War on Divorce Rates, Before Any 'I Dos,'" *New York Times*, 4 April, 2000, p. A1.

34. Amitai Etzioni and Peter Rubin, *Opportuning Virtue: Lessons of the Louisiana Covenant Marriage Law* (Washington, DC: The Communitarian Network, 1997).

35. Christina Johnson, Scott Stanley, Norval Glenn, Paul Amato, Steve Nock, Howard Markman, and Robin Dion, *Marriage in Oklahoma: 2001 Baseline Statewide Survey on Marriage and Divorce* (Stillwater, OK: Oklahoma State University, Bureau for Social Research, 2002).

36. See Katherine Spaht's discussion of this proposal in "The Family as Community: Implementing the 'Children-First Principle,'" *Marriage in America: A Communitarian Perspective*, Martin Whyte, ed. (New York: Rowman & Littlefield, 2000), pp. 235-56; see also Mary Ann Glendon, *Abortion and Divorce in Western Law* (Cambridge, MA: Harvard University Press, 1987), pp. 93-5; William Galston, "A Liberal-Democratic Case for the Two-Parent Family," *Responsive Community* (Winter 1990), pp. 23-5; Elaine Kamarck and William Galston, *Putting Children First: A Progressive Family Policy for the 1990s* (Washington, DC: Progressive Policy Institute, 1991).

and spousal support. Because of these asymmetries, it is reasonable for culture and law to give preferential rights and support to mothers in custody matters. But this should not be done at the expense of exempting fathers from their legal responsibilities to assist in guiding and financially supporting their offspring except in clear instances of incapacity or unfitness. Of course, in some instances, these features of incapacity and unfitness may equally apply to the mother, thereby overriding legal and cultural presumptions in her favor.

But it is best for those of us who do not specialize in the law not to become buried in the legal details. It is safer for me to stay at the level of general frameworks, reasserting my belief that marriage and family matters are primarily works of culture to be addressed in civil society and only secondarily matters that can be promoted or remedied by government policy, the market, or the details of family law.

III   Preaching and Teaching

Preaching and Teaching the Old Testament

Patrick D. Miller

The life of the church centers around the word. When Karl Barth began his *Church Dogmatics* with an articulation of the threefold form of the word of God — proclamation, Scripture, and revelation — he rightly identified the beginning point of theology and ethics, of faith and practice.[1] In what it does and what it thinks, the Christian community and specifically its manifestation in the form of the congregation, is inseparable from the word in its threefold form. Of course, this may not be the case in practice. But the principle is so clear that failure to live and think, that is, failure to place at the center of the church's life the word in its three forms, is to skew and distort the very character of the community of faith as the church. For this reason, the church's ministry is by definition a ministry of the word. It is a ministry that constantly points to Christ, places all of life and thought in the light of Scripture, and regularly engages in proclamation of the word.[2]

Indeed one might argue on very practical grounds that the interpretation of the word as a theological enterprise is the peculiar task of ministry in the sense that it is the one activity of the church's life for which the pastor is truly the resident expert. The capacity to bring the light of Scripture and theology to whatever is happening is the one thing that the pastor provides that is not available elsewhere in the life of the congregation, where there are not other and better experts (for example, in financial matters, administration,

---

1. Karl Barth, *Church Dogmatics* (Edinburgh: T&T Clark, 1936), I/1.
2. I realize that in the Reformed tradition, we speak of the ministry of the word and sacraments, but in this instance I am subsuming the sacraments within the word, recognizing that the sacraments are a materialization of faith and practice as given to us in the word and thus not themselves separate from the word.

counseling, education, and the like) often available and a part of the congregation. If the pastor of the congregation is no longer necessarily the most highly educated person and the most knowledgeable in all aspects of the church's life, she or he is still the one who brings understanding of the faith and interpretation of the word to bear on the life of the congregation. The ministry of the word is the primary task of the pastor of the congregation.

This fundamental assumption has obvious implications for theological education. If Scripture is going to shape life and thought for the church *and especially for the ministry,* then a sense of that ought to pervade the theological curriculum. As the center of the curriculum, the Bible is not the focus of the whole of the curriculum. But it is the pivot around which all other matters revolve, and it is the center that helps define what is more marginal and peripheral. That some aspects of theological education are more peripheral, of course, does not make them unimportant.

More Bible courses, per se, are not what is really at stake, although one might well argue that in many seminaries outside evangelical circles, the actual teaching of Scripture has been squeezed to a very minimum. But the minister is a theologian, and once that is seen as the primary characterization of her or his role, then it is clear that the Bible is the source and ground for many dimensions of the work of ministry, and the carefully prepared minister needs to be able to draw upon that source in a variety of ways that require various kinds of knowledge and skill acquisition. The issue is not Bible versus theology, but whether or not the theologian-minister does his or her theology in a sophisticated conversation with Scripture, a conversation that begins to be learned in seminary only as teachers of Scripture assume a theological responsibility for the texts they interpret and the content they teach and as theologians develop an understanding of doctrine and its history that is rooted in Scripture.[3] Gerhard Ebeling has argued that the history of the church is essentially the history of the interpretation of Scripture.[4] Many his-

---

3. I have used the word "sophisticated" intentionally even though some may see that as a weasel word or a cover for license in the handling of Scripture. It is instead a replacement for the customary adjective "critical." I assume the critical aspect of one's sophisticated reading of Scripture, but that is not all that is involved. The best term might be "mature." What is envisioned is the kind of understanding of Scripture and theology that comes from deep study of both, practice in the interpretation of Scripture, familiarity with hermeneutical issues and principles, and a theological framework that informs the understanding of texts and is open to revision in the light of their interpretation. All of that takes time, learning, and practice. It also involves creativity, intuition, and imagination. Some persons are better at such sophisticated interpretation than others, but all may continue to develop in that direction.

4. Gerhard Ebeling, *Kirchengeschichte als Geschichte der Auslegung der Heiligen Schrift* (Tübingen: J. C. B. Mohr [Paul Siebeck], 1947).

torians of the church and of doctrine may find that definition too limiting, but there is a large element of truth to it, and it at least suggests that the teaching of history is not something apart from the preparation of ministers for thinking about how the Bible shapes life and thought — then and now. There is little creedal activity that has not been a wrestling with Scripture, and the most heated controversies of the last half century in the North American church — for example, segregation and racism in American life, the morality of war and the place of the conscience, the nature and value of human life, appropriate understanding and worship of God, and the church's attitude toward same sex relations — have been vigorous debates about what Scripture teaches and how we are to be directed by Scripture.

The issue, then, is the acknowledgment by those who teach in theological education that whatever we do, whether it is interpretation of texts — where the Bible is front and center — or practice in homiletics, or the teaching of doctrine, our subject matter in some ways is constantly engaged with the Bible. Critical to such an acknowledgment, by which I do not mean paying lip service to the importance of Scripture but letting that awareness be an influential and determinative criterion, is the recognition that the Bible is not a specialized area to be left in the hands of Scripture scholars but is the subject matter of all the fields. As the church has always had to live in the tension between affirming the clarity of Scripture and knowing its difficult and dark places and in the tension between receiving Scripture as an ancient, foreign, literary document and as the word of God, so it must also live in the tension between insisting that some of its teachers and doctors devote themselves to a deep and technical knowledge and competence in the Scriptures and holding all other teachers to a responsibility for thinking and teaching in relation to the Word even as they are committed to the development of technical knowledge and skill in other areas of the theological enterprise. This is not an easy task, and the tendency is always to compartmentalize Scripture, that is, for the biblical scholars to claim it, either consciously or unconsciously, as their own domain and for the theologians, historians, and practical theologians to assign it to the biblical scholars in order to get on with their own large tasks. The problem is that those large tasks have too much to do with the Bible for such segmentation to work. The pastor, whose education is the responsibility of the seminary, is not allowed to separate in this fashion. There is no point where she or he does not have to bring the Bible into conversation with all sorts of things in this world and nowhere that the pastor can expect to escape some accountability to biblical revelation. The seminary is in danger of an artificial and thus counter-educational model in its handling of Scripture. At best it is artificial and at worst it is non-professional in that it does not prepare its students for the practice of the profession as it is to be carried out.[5]

There is a piece of this picture, however, that is more fuzzy in conceptuality and less evident in practice. That piece is the Old Testament. We have assumed the inclusion of the Old Testament as a part of the Word that informs faith and life and in the Reformed tradition have done so more vigorously than may be the case in other branches of the Christian church. But in both theory and practice that inclusion is often fragmentary, subordinate, and peripheral. Or we may be unclear about what role the Old Testament is to play and most especially how we are to regard it in relation to the New Testament and the church's preaching. Some of the problems appear to be endemic to Christian theology, which seems always to be clearer about the function of the New Testament than the Old. By necessity, the church has to keep rethinking how the Old Testament is a part of the word and thus at the center of the church's faith and its ministry.

The Old Testament as Scripture

It is as the church reads and interprets the Bible *as a whole* that the Old Testament comes into its place as the word of God. This is a risky business. In our time, we have become highly conscious of the multiple voices of Scripture and careful about not silencing, distorting, or marginalizing any of these voices. The sense of the whole is there, but it is a whole of many and varied parts, sufficiently different in genre, time, perspective, and the like as to dampen serious efforts to think of Scripture primarily as a whole. In the necessary interpretive movement within the hermeneutical circle, we tend to exaggerate the parts and minimalize the whole so that the circle is not really maintained. We are afraid that our sense of the whole will distort the parts, so

5. One of my most vivid and enduring pedagogical memories is of an extended conversation with a class of students at the conclusion of a course on God in the Old Testament. The first time I had taught the course, I had set it up on a history of religion model. That did not work very well. The second time, partly out of my own awareness and partly out of the natural direction that the students wished to move, the course was more theological in character. At the end, I indicated to the class my strong sense that when I taught the course again, I would need to get a theologian colleague to join me and teach the course as a team. With one voice the class resisted and protested that decision on my part, one that had grown out of my own sense of ineptness in dealing with many of the theological questions and issues that arose in looking at what the Bible says about God. They felt strongly that one of the most important features of the course was precisely my being forced to deal, however ineptly, with all the issues and not only the more strictly biblical ones — exactly as they would have to do in their own ministry.

we are careful about articulating the individual voices but resistant to asking how they play their part in and are to be understood in light of the whole. But it is also possible that one may so lack a sufficient sense of the whole that the elements that make it up cannot properly be comprehended *as Scripture.* Interpretation in the light of the rule of faith and the rule of love, even if that is done fairly subconsciously and not overtly, is in order to maintain some sense of the whole and of the character of the Bible as Scripture, the rule of faith and practice.

The danger is already there within the respective Testaments. That is, we are inclined to discern a panoply of theologies within each Testament — the theology of Paul, Johannine theology, and the like. Indeed, Scripture itself encourages us so to view it. After all, the church found four Gospels in its Scripture, and there are clearly significant differences discerned and tensions experienced in their presentations of Jesus Christ. But those four Gospels are a way of saying that the church needs all of this to comprehend who Jesus Christ is and what God was and is doing in him. The neglect of any one of them will skew the Christology of the church even if a harmonization of them is not an easy task and indeed may be impossible.

There is a much larger disjunction, however, between the two parts of the canon, whose formation and character are quite distinct from one another but whose theological wholeness is fundamental to the revelation of God's nature and activity. Because the Old Testament is there, the community of faith knows that God's work in and through Israel is central to what God is doing in the world. Because the New Testament is there, the centrality of Jesus Christ in that divine work in the world is made clear. The church finds the revelation of God's work incomplete without the New Testament. It finds the revelation of God in Jesus Christ both unintelligible and unauthorized without the Old Testament. The interrelation between the two Testaments and the work of God to which they bear testimony may and should be described in different ways, but the centrality of each must be maintained, despite the apparent logical contradiction implied in such a claim.

As the church lives and breathes out of the Scriptures of the Old and New Testaments, it encounters and effects both a *centrifugal* force that tends to push them ever away from one another and a *centripetal* force that tends to draw these Scriptures ever more closely together. The practice of the church is often toward the centrifugal force rather than the centripetal. One reflection of the power of that force is the easy intrusion into theological education and even the practice of ministry of alternative terms for the Old Testament, such as "Hebrew Scriptures," "the Scriptures of Israel," "Tanakh," or the like. The abandonment of the term "Old Testament" has many implications, a few good but others less desirable. The rubrics "Old Testament" and "New Testament" are not to be viewed simply as vestiges of an unenlightened and supersessionist history.[6] They are pointers to the wholeness and indivisibility of Scripture and to a relationship that is not adequately characterized by alternatives — at least so far — and indeed is significantly diminished — sometimes quite intentionally — by their use. The use of the term "Hebrew Bible/Scriptures," or its equivalent, may have some practical uses but such substitutes should not become the defining terms in a theological context.[7] To move in that direction is to place the *language* of the Old Testament as definitive when there is no theological or historical reason for doing so;[8] it focuses on the separation of the Christian Scriptures rather than their unity; and it suggests a wholeness within the Old Testament apart from the other Testament, a position that cannot be maintained in the church, and probably not within Judaism either.[9] Furthermore, it leaves "the New Testament" as an es-

---

6. These standard terms may serve a supersessionist reading of the New Testament and God's work in Jesus Christ, which is one of the reasons some would substitute other terms. But that reading is not intrinsic, nor has there been sufficient attention to the deficiencies in the alternatives. Among the most helpful treatments of the larger theological issues underlying this terminological debate is Kendall Soulen's *The God of Israel and Christian Theology* (Minneapolis: Fortress, 1996). Though he uses the term "Hebrew Scriptures," he is less concerned with terminology and more with supersessionism as a problem for theology and with the possibility of a theological reading of Scripture that is attentive to the wholeness of Scripture as our best clue to what God is doing in the world but is not supersessionist.

7. Here it is important to distinguish between the very different teaching contexts of university and theological school. In the university, there may very well be good reasons for the use of the valid terms Hebrew Bible, Tanakh, and the like, though it should not be assumed that any descriptive phrase is somehow neutral and does not make a decision in one direction or another about how this literature is to be viewed, even if the function of a particular term is to make the theological-faith character of the literature more vague. (On this matter, see now the helpful discussion by Christopher Seitz, "Old Testament or Hebrew Bible? Some Theological Considerations," published originally in *Pro Ecclesia* 5 [1996]: 292-303 and republished in his *Word Without End: The Old Testament as Abiding Theological Witness* [Grand Rapids: Eerdmans, 1997], pp. 61-74). The adoption of an alternative to "Old Testament" in the broader academy has been drawn into theological education much too easily and unreflectively.

8. It is perhaps a minor quibble to note that the term is also inaccurate in that some of the Old Testament was originally written in Aramaic. An alternative term that avoids the focus on language is "Israel's Scriptures." While such a designation is certainly true, it is only half true. Those scriptures are also the church's scriptures, and so the designation serves once again implicitly to separate the two parts of the Christian Bible from one another and relegate the Old Testament to a secondary position in the church's life.

9. Here I am assuming that the Scriptures that arose out of God's story with Israel are always read in relation to some other body of authoritative or normative literature. For Christians, it is the New Testament; for Jews it is the Talmud. The relation of these other bodies of lit-

sentially meaningless term, as is recognized by some who have shifted to "Greek Scriptures," or something similar. The church, in its proclamation and in its preparation for ministry, needs to resist the temptation to solve its supersessionist theological tendencies and problems by the use of non-theological language for speaking about the theological foundation of the church's faith, the Bible.

Even where the church and its teachers hold to a clear conviction about the wholeness of Scripture, there are various ways in which we let them drift apart. One of the more obvious ways is the academic curricular division into Old Testament and New Testament and the corollary division of faculty responsibilities into one or the other Testament. There are good practical reasons for this — division of duties, different languages — but one should not ignore the outcome and the difficulty this division places upon the teachers of Bible — and even more the students — in trying to resist the centrifugal force.

Because the primary subject matter of the Scriptures is the God who is at work in the story they recount and in the world in which we live, the wholeness and coherence of Scripture supersedes its partition. That coherence is real but not self-evident. It may be manifest in various modes. I have already referred to the rule of faith and the rule of love, which are theological and ethical frameworks for perceiving what the Scriptures are about in their entirety.[10] Interpreters have been able also to discern a canon within the canon or a center that holds the whole together in the face of the manifold voices. While the danger of reductionism is always evident in such moves, they are necessary. Further, the Scriptures contain a story that has the Lord God at its center as the chief actor. That story, whose foundations are in the Old Testament, is the framework for the whole and provides a structure that gives coherence even though not everything can be located at some specific moment in the story. All that is there belongs to the story and is not to be understood, interpreted, or proclaimed apart from it.

---

erature to the biblical literature may vary, but in neither instance can one properly comprehend and define the faith that they nurture without attention to their relation to the other literary corpus that also serves to define the community of faith. This does not mean that the shared biblical literature — Old Testament/Hebrew Bible — cannot be genuinely shared, a point that Walter Brueggemann has demonstrated forcefully and explicitly in his recent *Theology of the Old Testament* (Minneapolis: Fortress, 1997), which insists on much common ground between Jewish and Christian reading of the Old Testament but also easily develops ad hoc relationships between the content of the Old Testament and that of the New.

10. See *The Presbyterian Understanding and Use of Holy Scripture* (Louisville: Office of the General Assembly, 1992), a position paper adopted by the 123rd General Assembly (1983) of the former Presbyterian Church in the United States.

The Old Testament and Christ

The sense of the wholeness, the coherence of Scripture, the manifestation of a centripetal force that holds the Testaments together as a single Scripture, leads one into the effort to understand the relation of the Old Testament to Jesus Christ and vice versa.[11] Efforts to uncover modes of coherence that give full place to the Old Testament nevertheless must tend to the meaning of Jesus Christ in relation to the whole of Scripture and not just the New Testament.

In addition to the structuring coherence provided by the story, the wholeness of Scripture as Scripture may be articulated in several ways that are deeply rooted in the Old Testament. From beginning to end the *subject matter* of the Bible is *the Lord,* whose name is revealed in the Old Testament and re-stated in relation to Jesus of Nazareth in the New. The revelation of the name is in the context of the revelation of the words and deeds of the God who created the universe, called Abraham and blessed him and his posterity, and redeemed Israel from its harsh slavery in Egypt. The rest of the story is a further unpacking of that revelation and the meaning of the name. One comes to know who it is that rules this world and has called us into blessing and service, into grace and obedience, only as one begins to read the Old Testament. That one whose name is revealed in the Tetragrammaton "YHWH" has come to be called "the Lord." The use of the Greek term *kurios* as a surrogate for the divine name in the Old Testament as well as an address and title for Jesus Christ in the New Testament — a tradition that has carried over into the translations and so has come to be the practice of the church throughout its life — binds the Testaments inextricably together as it identifies the subject of one Testament with that of the other. The church knows this term — and bows before its reality — only as the name of the God of Israel and the Lord of the church.[12]

---

11. What I am talking about here commonly comes under the rubric "the unity of Scripture." I have no major objection to that term and use it myself. In this context, however, I am appropriating other terms that may, partly in their multiplicity and variety, avoid the dangers of oversimplicity and reductionism that sometimes seem to be carried by the term "unity." The notion of coherence allows for significant complexity and assumes differentiation and variety. In this context, I am not making the case for the complexity because, as indicated above, that case is all too prominent and does not need to be made. It is the question of the coherence of the evident complexity that needs attention. For further discussion of this way of thinking about the whole and its parts, see William Schweiker and Michael Welker, "A New Paradigm of Theological and Biblical Inquiry," in *Power, Powerlessness, and the Divine: New Inquiries in Bible and Theology,* ed. Cynthia L. Rigby (Atlanta: Scholars Press, 1997), pp. 3-20; and Patrick D. Miller, "A Theocentric Theologian of Hope: J. Christiaan Beker as Biblical Theologian," *The Princeton Seminary Bulletin* 16 (1995): 22-35.

12. Technically, the term "Lord" is an epithet and not a proper name, but its substitution

To the extent that the *name of God* is revelatory, the connections between the name of the God of Israel and Jesus Christ are even stronger than in the shared title "Lord." The much-discussed and at least ambiguous form of the divine name of God as it is revealed in Exodus 3 gets its primary meaning *contextually*, that is, from the Lord's word to Moses on the occasion of commissioning him to go into Pharaoh. The term *'ehyeh*, which is the word in the divine name formula *'ehyeh 'ăšer 'ehyeh*, "I will be what I will be" or "I am who I am," occurs twice in the Lord's reassurance to Moses, "I will be with you" (Exod. 3:12 and 4:12).[13] The story in its full form, therefore, identifies the companioning and protecting presence of God with those who serve and worship the Lord as definitive of who this God is. That claim, of course, is carried over into the name "Immanuel," "God is with us," which becomes one of the names of the child born to Mary (Matt. 1:23), thus establishing an explicit continuity between the Lord of Israel and the one for whom Israel had hoped, the one who embodies God's companioning presence with the people. The story itself is structured around this revelation of the character of the God of Scripture, first revealed in the Old Testament and confirmed in the Christ of the New Testament, for the last word we hear about this God is the vision of the new heaven and the new earth and the new Jerusalem and the voice from the throne declaring: "Behold, the dwelling of God is with human beings. . . . God will be with them . . ." (Rev. 21:3). The continuity of name and identity carries forward also in the continuity between the context in which the name of God is revealed, that is, the Lord's hearing of the cries of the Israelites and coming to deliver them, and the other name of the child of Mary, which is "Jesus," that is, "He will save his people" (Matt. 1:21). That the salvation brought by the child is a salvation "from their sins" is an expectation that has arisen explicitly out of the Old Testament (Isa. 52:13–53:12).[14]

What this means is that the church hears afresh in the New Testament what it already knows from the Old Testament about God and God's ways with us. For Jesus is no other than who and what God has always been.[15] The

---

for the proper name of God in the Old Testament puts it in a somewhat different category from other epithets, as indicated by the fact that many translations distinguish between the use of the term "lord" as a surrogate for the divine name and its use as a common name by setting the former in large and small capital letters.

13. This is most obvious in the parallel expressions in Exod. 3:14-15: "*'ehyeh* has sent me to you,"//"*yhwh* . . . has sent me to you."

14. For a more extended presentation of this continuity between the names of God and the names of Jesus, see P. D. Miller, *They Cried to the Lord: The Form and Theology of Biblical Prayer* (Minneapolis: Fortress, 1994), pp. 173-77.

15. The point could be elaborated over and over by placing various texts and contexts

theological way of apprehending this is the *doctrine of the Trinity.* The Trinity is a way of speaking theologically about the richness, wholeness, and coherence of *Scripture* as it identifies these very characteristics within the reality of *God* but not as incidental or developing dimensions or as aspects or persons of the Godhead to be identified with one Testament or the other.[16] It is worthy of note that the representation of the three biblical men or angels who appeared to Abraham at the oak of Mamre for many centuries was "the only iconography of the Holy Trinity; it is still preserved in the Orthodox Church as that which accords best with its teaching." The long tradition of the church has found its most durable representation of the Trinity in the depiction of an Old Testament scene.[17]

The *kingdom of God* is the shared subject matter of both Testaments. That kingdom, whose manifestation is so much the subject matter of the Old Testament but is most often discussed with reference to the New Testament, is most fully in view when seen in the light of both Testaments. The proclamation of the *basilea tou theou* is fundamental to the mission of Jesus and the claims of the New Testament, but the political understanding of the realm of God's sovereignty comes from the Old Testament as does the church's understanding of the shape and character of that rule. The Psalms reach their climax in the Enthronement Psalms (93, 95–99) with the declaration that "the Lord reigns," and the hope of Israel is oriented toward the coming of one who will establish the just and merciful reign of peace that is God's kingdom on earth.[18] The New Testament tells us who this one is while still looking in hope

from both Testaments in conversation with each other, which is what the church has always done. It is important, however, that while notions of promise/prophecy and fulfillment will come to play in such a conversation, that mode of hearing the two Testaments together does not exhaust the way in which the conversation is to be played out. The church has not been helped by confining much of its interpretation of the coherence of Scripture to oppositional motifs (e.g. law and gospel). In this respect, Soulen's book, referred to in note 6 is quite helpful with its focus on blessing and consummation as ways of discerning the wholeness of Scripture in relation to the whole of the story.

16. "The Old Testament fills our understanding about the nature and character of the first person of the Trinity. It is only on this basis that the church can accept the claim that Jesus is one with God. Within the biblical story, there is an identity between the words and deeds of the Lord of Israel and the Lord of the church that presses upon those who live by that story that they are truly one. It is therefore unlikely that the church can hold its scriptures together without a conviction that in the doctrine of the Trinity, we comprehend something of the fullness of God . . ." (Patrick D. Miller, "A Strange Kind of Monotheism," *Theology Today* 54 [1997]: 296). Cf. Robert W. Jenson, "The Bible and the Trinity," *Pro Ecclesia* 21 (2002): 329-39.

17. Leonid Ouspensky and Vladimir Lossky, *The Meaning of Icons* (Crestwood, NY: St. Vladimir's Seminary Press, 1999), p. 201.

18. A classic treatment of the theme of the kingdom of God as an expression of the

for the full realization of that rule both comprehended and expected in both Testaments.

The *Great Commandment*, first set forth in Israel's torah and then authorized as the summary of the whole by Jesus — consistent with the Jewish tradition that grew out of the Old Testament — offers a profound center around which the whole revolves. The role of the elect as following after no other god but the Lord is articulated in the Shema and then reformulated in Jesus' call to discipleship. Christian living listens to both parts of Scripture to discern what that calling involves. Nor is there anywhere in the Scriptures where this center does not hold, where the Great Commandment does not ground what is said either explicitly or implicitly. That is self-evident in the Law and the Prophets. It is just as much the case for the Writings. In the Psalter, the First Commandment is to the fore in all sorts of ways, not least in the significance of trusting in the Lord as the ground of all those human cries inscribed in the psalms of lament.[19] So also for Job, the fundamental question is whether Job fears God for nothing. Will he curse God or love God? Here, as in other matters, the Christian community learns not only from its own ongoing story but also from its Jewish brothers and sisters who know the same command to love the Lord your God as well as your neighbor and the gift and demand that are both present in that injunction.

The Old Testament and Preaching

I will make two claims at this point, knowing there is much more that has been and can be said. The first claim is this: *The preaching of the Old Testament is aimed solely at placing upon the minds and hearts of the congregation the claim of the text as the word of God.* What is intended in this assertion is a resistance to more narrow definitions of the aim of preaching from the Old Testament. While all preaching in some way or another seeks to proclaim the gospel in the sense that the sermon should communicate the grace of God upon the believer in a way that calls forth a response of commitment, it is possible to understand this in an unnecessarily restrictive manner, forgetting that the gospel, the good news of God's salvation from sin and suffering, is not sounded first in the New Testament or only heard via the New Testament.

---

wholeness and coherence of the Old Testament and the New may be found in John Bright, *The Kingdom of God: The Biblical Concept and Its Meaning for the Church* (Nashville: Abingdon-Cokesbury, 1953).

19. For example, Psa. 22:4-5 [Heb. 5-6].

The critical point at which such restriction is usually manifest is in the assumption that Old Testament texts cannot be preached properly except as brought into explicit conjunction with the New Testament or with explicitly christological moves.

Texts are always heard *on their own*, that is, in their particularity as the word of God, and also in *two contexts*. One of those contexts is *the whole of Scripture*, so that wherever the text comes from, its resonance with other voices, its place in the complexity of the whole, is in view and may be a part of its proclamation.[20] There is also, however, the context of *the congregation* that receives the word. It is a community of persons shaped and determined by the whole of Scripture. This means that any preaching of an Old Testament text is to those who live and think, pray and praise, listen and question in the light of the whole of Scripture. God's redemptive work in and through Jesus Christ is a given for the faith and life of those who receive the word preached. Where the particular Old Testament text creates resonances that evoke and draw one also into the New Testament word, that is appropriate and the New Testament word may take its place in the proclamation of the Old Testament text. Often, however, the resonances will be self-evident and so clearly implicit that they may be presumed without being articulated because the congregation always hears the proclamation as a community of *Christian* believers.[21]

The second claim about the proclamation of the Old Testament is this: *The Old Testament gives to the church things that tend to be forgotten or diminished when the Old Testament is neglected in its teaching and preaching.* A number of years ago, the New Testament scholar Nils Dahl wrote an essay titled "The Neglected Factor in New Testament Theology."[22] It appeared in a relatively obscure context, a house organ for Yale Divinity School, but still attracted a lot of attention.[23] The "neglected factor" to which Dahl refers is God. While many have responded positively to Dahl's challenge, the point is still noteworthy precisely because of the danger to which it points us. It is

20. This, of course, is simply an affirmation of the hermeneutical circle as always functioning in the interpretation and proclamation of any specific text.

21. If it is a misunderstanding of the Old Testament as Christian scripture to assume that it cannot be proclaimed apart from explicit reference to the New Testament or to Jesus Christ, it is equally misguided to insist that the Old Testament be heard only "on its own terms" and without reference to the New Testament.

22. Nils Dahl, "The Neglected Factor in New Testament Theology," *Reflections* 73 (1975): 3-8.

23. For a recent extensive effort to pick up Dahl's challenge about the neglect of God, see *The Forgotten God: Perspectives on Biblical Theology,* ed. A. Andrew Das and Frank J. Matera (Louisville: Westminster John Knox Press, 2002).

possible for much careful and important study of the texts of the New Testament to go on without significant reference to the God whose work in Jesus Christ is the subject matter of the Scriptures. That may not be as large a problem as it might seem *if* the Old Testament and its texts are in constant view and play a large role in the church's proclamation. For it is especially there that the community of faith learns about its Lord. There is no way the church can ignore the God of Israel who is also the Lord of the church if it listens constantly to its Old Testament. From the beginning of the Old Testament to the end, its subject matter is the words and deeds of "the Lord our/your God." Proclamation, therefore, that continually sets the texts of the Old Testament before the people will also keep faith's attention focused on the proper subject of the church's worship, its Lord.

The Old Testament also presents the church with its largest picture of the story of God's work. Even more it keeps before us the realm of God's activity. Some of the resistance to the Old Testament is because of its very deep immersion in this world in which we live and suffer and die, in which our personal lives are all wrapped up in larger events of national and international affairs. There is an awful lot of killing and war, family conflict and bad behavior of every kind in the Old Testament. Some of it is quite unpleasant, but it is where the human community lives. The Old Testament touches on every kind of human issue and problem and confronts every kind of theological question. Job's popularity with those for whom the rest of the Scriptures are of little concern is precisely because it confronts the human situation and the question of God so directly. But Job's personal problems and his existential dilemma are only a piece of what the church hears about when it takes up the Old Testament. It also reads about the work of God in a people, defined not only by their allegiance to the Lord but by ethnic and historical factors. Neither the work of God nor human response remains on an individual level. They are part of a much larger picture. Indeed, the story is seen from the beginning to be of universal scope, daring to say that what happens in the affairs of people and nations is precisely what God is about.

Central to constant listening to the Old Testament is also an awareness that the work of God is not something to be understood solely in *salvific* terms. God's redemptive activity is everywhere evident, but it is not all that goes on. The divine way of dealing with the reality of sin and wickedness is in terms of election and blessing, the choosing of a people to be the means by which all the peoples of the earth may find blessing rather than curse and judgment.[24] The Old Testament, therefore, not only confronts us with a real-

24. This assumes that the word and call of the Lord to Abraham are an explicit outgrowth

istic picture of the context of the Lord's activity in the world; it also enlarges our perception of that work. Human *flourishing* as much as human *redemption* is at the heart of God's intention for this world. Indeed, they are not finally separable features of existence, but the former may get lost in our focus on redemption. The Old Testament holds these together in the paradigmatic story of the Exodus from Egypt. At the divine theophany at the burning bush, the Lord begins with these words to Moses:

> I have observed the misery of my people who are in Egypt; I have heard their cry on account of their taskmasters. Indeed, I know their sufferings, and I have come down to deliver them from the Egyptians, and *to bring them up out of that land to a good and broad land, a land flowing with milk and honey,* to the country of the Canaanites, the Hittites, the Amorites, the Perizzites, the Hivites, and the Jebusites (Exod. 3:7-8).

God's salvific work is not only a liberation from the chains that bind us (compare Luke 4:16-21). It is also the gift of new life and blessing. In the profoundest sense possible, the Scriptures of the Old Testament announce that God's offer of life is there for all, that the Lord's intention is that all people shall flourish. Such is the good news we hear in Scripture, and so it belongs always in our proclamation.[25]

---

of what has happened in Genesis 1–11, specifically the way in which sin has led to the judgment of curse, and that all that follows after Genesis 12:1-4a is an outgrowth of the call and promise of God and Abraham's obedient response. The promise of God is so comprehensive and its stake in a faithful and obedient response from Abraham and his seed so large that the rest of the Abraham story focuses significantly on the issue of that response (for example, Genesis 15 and 22). For the significance of God's blessing for the human story, see Claus Westermann, *Elements of Old Testament Theology* (Atlanta: John Knox Press, 1982), Parts One and Two; and Soulen, *The God of Israel and Christian Theology,* Part Two.

25. The argument is not that the New Testament does not know about these things. It knows them and assumes them. But if the New Testament remains the focus of the church's proclamation to the neglect of the Old Testament, it is likely that the complexity and richness of that good news as it has been made known in the fullness of human life and the created order would be diminished and the temptation to reduce the gospel and the Christian message to matters of individual and personal concern alone increased.

Praying with Eyes Open

Jürgen Moltmann

TRANSLATED BY MARGOT KOHL

"Watch and Pray," "Pray and Watch"

What else is Christian spirituality except this watching and praying, watching prayerfully and praying watchfully? Prayer never stands by itself. It is always bound up with watching. Here I want to talk about the watching, which goes with true praying, and to which true prayer is supposed to lead us. Praying is good, but watching is better.

Modern men and women think that people who pray no longer belong properly to this world at all. They already have one foot in the world beyond. Strong men often think that praying is something for old women who have nothing left to them but the rosary or the hymnbook. It has become rather unknown that praying has to do with awakening, watching, attention, and the expectation of life.

It is true enough that our body language, when we pray, doesn't suggest particular watchfulness. We close our eyes, and look into ourselves, so to speak. We fold our hands. We kneel down, lower our eyes — even cast ourselves down with our faces to the ground. No one who sees us would get the impression that this is a collection of especially watchful people. Isn't it rather blind trust in God which is expressed in attitudes of prayer and mediation like this? Why do we shut our eyes? Don't we need much more prayer with open eyes and raised heads? But what are we supposed to watch for? For whom are we supposed to watch? And whom or what shall we expect?

"Could You Not Watch with Me One Hour?"

The most impressive story about watching is also Jesus' hardest hour, the night in Gethsemane. The heading in Luther's Bible is: "The Struggle in Gethsemane"; for this is Jesus' inner struggle with God-forsakenness. His prayer to the God he calls Abba, dear Father, is not answered. The cup of eternal death does not pass him by. The night of what Martin Buber called "the eclipse of God" falls on him and on those who are his, and on this world. To this eclipse of God corresponds what mystics called "the dark night of the soul," where you lose all orientation and all your feelings for life dry up. That is why in this hour Christ began "to be greatly distressed and troubled," says Mark, "to be sorrowful and troubled," writes Matthew. "My soul is very sorrowful, even to death," he tells the disciples. Earlier, he had often withdrawn and prayed all night long by himself in the hills. But in this hour he is afraid of being alone with his God, and he begs his disciples: "Stay here and watch." Jesus prays, and struggles with the dark and theological will of his God, and his disciples are supposed to take over the watching which belongs to prayer. But no; Jesus enters this eclipse of God praying and watching, "not my will, but thy will be done," but his disciples fall into a deep, oblivious sleep. "Simon Peter, are you asleep? Could you not watch with me one hour?" This scene, so saddening for Jesus and so shaming for the disciples, is repeated three times. Jesus wrestles with the dark side of God — and the stifling unconsciousness of sleep descends on the disciples until the night is past and the day of Golgotha begins, into which Jesus goes actively and resolutely: "Get up, let us be going. My betrayer is at hand." We all know what happens after that. But what strange kind of sleep was it, which overcame the truest of the true?

In the monastery of San Marco in Florence, there is a remarkable fresco in one of the cells, painted by Fra Angelico. It is the scene in Gethsemane. Jesus is praying, the disciples are sleeping; but two people are watching at Jesus' side, two women. The one looks wide-eyed in the direction of Jesus as he prays. The other is reading the Bible. It is Martha and Mary. They are watching with Jesus, and over him, in the hour of his God-forsakenness just as the women later watched from afar when Jesus was crucified and died, while the male disciples had fled away.

Why do the disciples fall asleep? If the Master whom they have followed without fear and trembling begins to tremble and fear himself, some cruel and inscrutable danger must surely be lurking. What danger? Through his healings of the sick, Jesus had communicated the nearness of God in ways that could be seen and felt — through the senses. But for the disciples this nearness now evidently turns into God's absence. Their feeling, that God had found them, is turned upside down; it becomes a sense of being lost without anything to which to cling. It is as if they have been felled by some blow. Their reaction is numbness, and the sleep of hopelessness. We know what this is like. Impending danger can stimulate us. But danger with no way out numbs us and we take flight into sleep, a sleep which protects us from what is unendurable. It is not a natural, refreshing sleep. It is the petrifying of all our senses, which makes us sick. Our eyes are open, but we no longer see anything. Our ears are open, but we are deaf and hear nothing. We are apathetic, and feel nothing.

Spiritual Paralyses Today

The paralyzing sleep which fell on Jesus' disciples in the night of God in Gethsemane was not their problem only. It is our problem today too. How do we react to unknown dangers? For millions of years, our consciousness has learned to react to the most widely differing dangers in life-supporting ways. How? Through fear, which keeps us wakeful and all our senses keyed up, so that we can counter whatever threatens us. In our civilizations there are built-in securities for our survival, from lightning conductors to dykes against storm tides.

But today there are dangers which are present without our perceiving them. In 1986, in the catastrophe in the Chernobyl nuclear power station, deadly radioactivity was released, which we can neither smell nor taste nor see. It has contaminated huge stretches of country, and up to now has cost the lives of 150,000 people. In these nuclear dangers our senses let us down. Our highly developed danger-antennae don't react to these perils. "Our nuclear power stations are completely safe," we are told, year after year. But no insurance company is prepared to insure a nuclear power plant against a meltdown, a Super-gau, because human beings are not secure. This is "nuclear numbing."

The way we react to the growing ecological crisis is no different. We don't perceive the destruction of the ozone layer with the help of our senses. It doesn't touch us directly. The connection between the increase in ultraviolet rays and skin cancer has been proved, but only statistically — so no one needs to feel personally concerned. The time that elapses between cause and effect is too long for us to perceive it directly. So the ecological crises also leave us relatively cold. We suppress our knowledge of them because "we don't want to know"; we don't want to know about the damage we are inflicting today on the already damaged world in which our children and grandchildren are going to live. This is "ecological numbing."

197

The growing climatic changes are much more threatening than we have assumed up to now. According to the Third Report of the International Panel of Climate Change 2001, global warming must definitely be put down to human activity. In the next forty years temperatures are going to rise by 2-5 degrees Celsius. Ocean levels will rise, the river estuaries will be flooded, many islands in the Pacific will disappear, there will continually be "natural" catastrophes which are in fact man-made. In the year 2050 there will be about 150 million climate refugees. But our "Modern way of life" must be preserved, and, as we know, this way of life is characterized by its extensive use of energy and by even more extensive atmospheric pollution. Our eyes are open but we don't see; our ears are open but we don't hear — until catastrophe overtakes us. And then we will swear: "this is all new to us."

We are no longer aware of true reality. We live only in our own dreams, and think that our illusions of reality are reality itself. And that, again, means that we are not wide awake to reality. We are asleep in the agreeable dreams of our fantasy worlds.

What is especially seductive and fascinating in these wishful-worlds of ours is our own image of ourselves. We see ourselves as we should like to be. As in the fairytale, "Mirror, mirror on the wall" is always supposed to tell us that we are "the fairest one of all" — or the strongest, or the cleverest, or whatever we like best. Learn to see yourselves in the mirror of other people's eyes, and especially the eyes of the victims. That is painful, and hurts the image of ourselves we cherish so much, but it helps us to wake up out of our dreams and to come face to face with reality.

Watch and Pray

My old Bible lexicon tells me that "watching discerns the danger — praying brings help from God." That is true; but what is coming first? First watching — then praying, or first prayer — then waking up and watching?

What are we seeking when we pray? When we pray, we are seeking the reality of God, and are breaking out of the Hall of Mirrors of our own wishes and illusions, in which we are imprisoned. That means that we wake up out of the petrifications and numbness of our feelings. If in prayer we seek the reality of God's world — remember the first line of the "Our Father" prayer: "hallowed be thy name, thy Kingdom . . ." — then that is the exact opposite of "the opium of the people." Prayer is more like the beginning of a cure for the numbing addictions of the secular world.

In prayer we wake up to the world, as it is spread out before God in all its heights and depths. We perceive the sighing of our fellow creatures, and hear the cries of the created beings that have fallen dumb. We hear the song of praise of the blossoming spring, and chime in with it. We feel the divine love for life which allows pain to cut us to the quick, and kindles joys. So real prayer to God awakens all our senses and alerts our minds and spirits. The person who prays, lives more attentively.

Pray watchfully — that is possible only if we don't pray mystically with closed eyes, but pray messianically, with eyes open for God's future in the world. Christian faith is not blind faith. It is the wakeful expectation of God, which touches all our senses. The early Christians prayed standing, looking up, with outstretched arms and wide-open eyes, ready to walk or to leap forward. We can see this from the pictures in the catacombs in Rome. Their posture reflects tense expectation, not quiet heart-searching. We don't watch just because of the dangers that threaten us. We are expecting the salvation of the world. We are watching for God's Advent. With tense attention, we open all our senses for the coming of God into our lives, into our society, to this earth.

Watch prayerfully — It is the ancient wisdom of the masters of prayer and mediation that it is good to pray in the morning, at the dawn of the day, in the hour between sleeping and waking, and to rejoice in the reality of God and his world.

Concentrating — praying — waking up — watching and praying: all this reveals to our lives the daybreak colors of the future, and it leads to the call of Jesus who, having watched and prayed in Gethsemane, calls to his sleeping disciples, "Get up, let us be going." Let us wake up and see what God will bring on this new day.

"Watch and Be Sober" (1 Thess. 5:6, 8). That is the next thing we hear. If what we want is to be full of enthusiasm, this brings us down to earth. The people who are sober are the ones who are not drunk and so don't suffer from hallucinations, and who don't let themselves be deluded by illusions, either pious or secular. When sobriety is added to the wakefulness that comes from praying, we shall not fool ourselves, and shall not let ourselves be fooled either. We shall see reality as it is, and expose ourselves to it in its workaday guise as well as in its surprises. Then we shall discover that reality is far more fantastic than our best fantasies. But we shall perceive too that the pain which reality imposes on us is better than the self-immunizations with which we try to protect ourselves, but through which we in fact wall ourselves in.

In German the word for "sober" can also mean "empty" — an empty stomach. People who are "sober" in this sense have not yet eaten anything, and begin the day fasting. They are hungry. In a transferred sense we call realists sober. They see reality as it is. If we are sober in this sense, we are hungry for reality, for God is in the reality; and then we forget the thousand possibilities upon which we dream. One single experienced reality is richer than a thousand conceived possibilities. That is why contact with reality is so important.

Watch and Expect — When we wake up in the morning we expect the new day; and in the same way, the waking which springs from prayer to God also leads to the expectation of God in the life we experience. I wake up, and open all my senses for life, and for death too — for the fulfillments and also for the disappointments — for what is painful as well as for what gives joy. I expect the presence of God in everything I meet and everything I do. His history with me, and with us, goes on. There is nothing more exhilarating, than to experience one's life-history with God in full awareness: What has God in mind for me? What does God expect of me? What is he saying to me through the things that are happening in the world?

Watch and See — Remarkably enough, watching and praying have not so much to do with faith, but have everything to do with seeing. "The Lord opens the eyes of the blind" (Psa. 146:8); and Israel's Wisdom tells us even that "the hearing ear and the seeing eye are both made by the Lord" (Prov. 20:12). For it is by no means a matter of course that people who have eyes can also see, and that people with ears can hear. "Seeing, they do not see," complains Jesus, according to Matt. 13:13, and "hearing they hear not. They understand nothing." He means the presence of the kingdom of God among us. But he means his presence among us today too: "'I was hungry and you gave me no food, I was thirsty and you gave me no drink, I was a stranger and you did not welcome me.' . . . Then they will answer, 'Lord, when did we see you hungry or thirsty or a stranger or sick?' Then he will answer them, 'What you did to one of the least of these, you did (or did not do) to me.'" And that is the great Judgment pronounced on us.

How do we learn to have seeing eyes for Christ's presence among us? Where are our eyes opened? Archbishop Oscar Arnulfo Romero was a faithful, conservative churchman. When he was 59 years old he had a conversion experience. "He discovered in the poor the way of faith in God," writes Jon Sobrino; "in all the crucified men and women of history, the crucified God became present to him. . . . In the faces of the poor he saw the distorted face of God." Romero put himself on their side, and a short time afterwards was shot in front of the altar in the church in San Salvador, at the orders of the rich.

Where was God when the mass murders took place in the World Trade Center on September 11? Ought we to ask why God permitted this catastrophe, and answer like some well-known fundamentalist preachers: it was because he wanted to punish secular, liberal, or homosexual America? But wouldn't that mean that our God is the God of terrorists, and that the terrorists were the servants who carried out his orders? Ought we not rather to ask: where was God in those mass murders, and look for his presence among the victims? Doesn't God weep over the death of so many of his beloved children? Jesus wept over the coming destruction of Jerusalem (Luke 19:41). So tears will have run down the face of the suffering God at Ground Zero, and people who believe in God for Christ's sake are called to "stand beside God in his suffering," as Dietrich Bonhoeffer wrote, during the resistance to the Nazi murderers.

Watch and Perceive. To go through life with eyes open for God, to see Christ in oppressed and unimportant people; that is what praying and watching is all about. We believe, so that we can see, not so that we can shut our eyes to the world. We believe so that we can see — and can endure what we see.

If we want to sum up what watching and praying is about, we have to say: it is about an attentive life. Goodwill and helpfulness are fine, but they are not enough. Attentiveness is necessary, so that we do the right thing at the right time in the right place.

"Watchman, What of the Night?"

Darkness — night — is always a symbol for the God-forsakenness of the world and for the lostness of men and women. In the darkness and in the night we see nothing, and the best thing is to sleep until day. There is an apt passage in Isaiah. In exile and far from home, strangers among strangers, the Israelite prisoners come to the prophet and ask, "Watchman, what of the night?" He answers, "The morning is coming but it is still night. If you will inquire, come back again" (Isa. 21:12). But Paul, Christ's witness, proclaims, "The night is far gone, the day is at hand. Let us then cast off the works of darkness and put on the armor of light" (Rom. 13:12). So it is "time to get up from sleep" and to live life in the light of God's new day.

In these daybreak colors of Christ's day we will pray and watch, watch and be sober, watch and expect God, see and perceive Christ in our minds, and learn to live attentively in God's Spirit, wholly present with all our senses and all our powers.

In our dreams, each of us is alone. But when we wake up we are in a world we share with others, for as Heraclitus said, "The wakeful share a world, whereas every sleeper turns to the world that is his alone." The wakeful perceive and know each other in the world they share.

"Get up," says Christ to his benumbed disciples, "and let us be going."

In Pursuit of Good Theological Judgment: Newman and the Preacher as Theologian

John S. McClure

> ". . . the church should not be wise of itself, should not devise any-
> thing of itself but should set the limit of its own wisdom where Christ
> has made an end of speaking."
>
> Calvin, Institutes of the
Christian Religion, 4.8.13[1]

One significant but unspoken undercurrent among homileticians and preachers is the idea that preaching requires a well-tuned sense of theological judgment. Among other things, preachers who have this faculty are able to discover the strongest and most timely elements in any theological subject and communicate them in the fullest and most satisfying way. There are certainly many voices encouraging preachers to develop good judgment. Here, however, we will focus on good theological judgment. Where does it come from, what does it entail, how does a preacher obtain it, how does it influence preaching, and is it an adequate guide for preachers who desire to become preacher-theologians today?

I will pursue answers to these questions by examining a distinctive theological epistemology that has been around for many years. This epistemology is inherited in part from Aristotle, for whom good judgment was the key to *phronēsis*, or "practical wisdom." When it comes to theological thinking, however, one of the clearest expositions of good judgment occurs

---

1. Ed. by John T. McNeill, trans. and indexed by Ford Lewis Battles (Louisville: Westminster John Knox Press, 1960).

in the writings of John Henry Newman, especially in his magnum opus, *An Essay in Aid of a Grammar of Assent*. In this essay, Newman argues in favor of a distinctive human faculty of judgment called "the illative sense." He situates this faculty at the heart of a theological epistemology of dogmatic assent. I will argue that, for a variety of reasons, many preachers still aspire to a form of theological judgment similar to Newman's illative sense, a quality of mind that can be extremely helpful in a skeptical and relativist culture. Yet, as we will see, this quality is not without serious theological and ethical problems.

John Henry Newman and the Illative Sense

In 1852, John Henry Newman published the *Idea of a University*, comprised of a set of lectures on education delivered in Dublin. One of the most telling sentences in these lectures is this: "Judgment does not stand . . . for a certain homely, useful quality of intellect, that guards a person from committing mistakes to the injury of his fortunes or common reputation; but for that *master-principle* of business, literature, and talent, which gives him strength in any subject he chooses to grapple with, and enables him to seize the strong point in it."[2] In short, Newman was asserting that a certain form of human judgment is important not only as a guide to personal decision-making or as an arbiter of moral value and aesthetic taste. According to Newman, this form of judgment is one of the keys, if not the key, to *reasoning and knowledge*. Personal judgment is a "master-principle" at the heart of human knowing through which one is able to "seize the strong point" in an idea.

This master principle of personal judgment makes possible what Newman calls a "real apprehension" of truth and reality. By real apprehension Newman does not mean a scientific measuring of objects. He has in mind the kind of apprehension that emerges through a sustained personal relationship with a subject matter or field of knowledge such as theology. This relationship is largely rhetorical for Newman; it is sustained through a process of conversational give-and-take, argument, persuasion, and an incremental learning and adjustment of language and categories that yields a series of qualitative judgments about the subject matter itself. As Walter Jost points out, "Newman in fact is the first modern thinker to articulate what rhetoricians these days call "epistemic" rhetoric — the view that rhetoric has an

---

2. John H. Newman, *The Idea of a University*, ed. I. T. Ker (Oxford: Clarendon Press, 1976), pp. 151-52.

epistemological or truth function. . . ."[3] Through persuasive interaction, a person apprehends, not a thing, but a *proposition* (especially a predicate), and by the action of personal judgment, gives unconditional assent to this proposition as real and true.[4]

For Newman the epistemological goal of real apprehension is "real assent." Real assent lies just beyond "notional," or intellectual assent (inference). According to Newman, the problem with intellectual assent is that it is forever restless and gains its pleasure "not in finding the truth, but in seeking it."[5] For this reason, it does not necessarily affect our conduct or lifestyle. Intellectual assent "requires no apprehension of the things inferred; . . . it begins with itself, and ends with itself; . . . does not reach as far as facts; . . . is employed upon formulas . . . (and) . . . takes real objects . . . not as they are, but simply . . . as materials of argument or inquiry."[6] Real assent, on the other hand, "presupposes some apprehension" of the things assented to. For this reason, real assent can "kindle devotion, rouse the passions, and attach the affections; and thus it leads the way to actions of every kind, to the establishment of principles, and the formation of character, and is thus again intimately connected with what is individual and personal."[7] In other words, real assent does not simply think about the truth, it *lives into* the truth. According to Newman, "life is not long enough for a religion of inferences; we shall never have done beginning, if we determine to begin with proof."[8] The mind is below truth, not above it, and is bound, not to descant upon it, but to venerate it."[9]

In his masterpiece on religious epistemology, *An Essay in Aid of a Grammar of Assent*, first published in 1870, Newman named the human faculty of judgment that makes real apprehension and real assent possible "the illative sense."[10] The illative sense, like Aristotle's practical wisdom, acts as "the directing, controlling, and determining principle in . . . matters (of conduct)

---

3. Walter Jost, *Rhetorical Thought in John Henry Newman* (Columbia, SC: University of South Carolina Press, 1989), p. xiii.

4. John H. Newman, *An Essay in Aid of a Grammar of Assent* (New York: Doubleday and Company, Inc., 1955), pp. 29-31, 36.

5. Newman, *Grammar of Assent*, p. 171.

6. Newman, *Grammar of Assent*, p. 87.

7. Newman, *Grammar of Assent*, p. 87.

8. Newman, *Grammar of Assent*, p. 91.

9. Quoted in John F. Crosby, "Newman on the Personal," *First Things* 125 (Aug./Sept. 2002): 48.

10. Illation refers to the act of reasoning from premises or principles. By linking the word to "sense," Newman implies that the ability to reason in this way is a natural or acquired aspect of human sensibility.

personal and social."[11] Although originating in "nature itself," the illative sense is "an acquired habit" and "is formed and matured by practice and experience." It is "a capacity sufficient for the occasion, deciding what ought to be done here and now, by this given person, under these given circumstances."[12] John F. Crosby attributes this idea to Newman's "Athenian spirit," which he opposes to the "Spartan spirit" that was invading the universities in Newman's day. The Spartan spirit is found "in those who slavishly follow and apply rules that remain external to them." The Athenian spirit, on the other hand, is found "in those who have so internalized rules and laws as to be eminently free in living by them and imaginative and resourceful in connecting them to concrete situations."[13]

For Newman, we are always already caught up in a rhetorical (suasive) conversation about the nature of reality, truth, morals, beauty, and God. This conversation is richly textured by our experiences, chosen instruments of experimentation or knowledge, relationships, duties, personal histories, and habits of mind and action. The illative sense guides each individual in this conversation and "has its function in the beginning, middle, and end of all verbal discussion and inquiry, and in every step of the process."[14] Newman did not believe that there was any way to determine truth or reality apart from this deeply personal, judgment-centered form of rhetorical reasoning. Neither rigorous syllogistic logic nor experimental scientific methods can avoid or circumvent human judgment in ascertaining truth and reality. According to Newman, "in no class of concrete reasonings, whether in experimental science, historical research, or theology, is there any ultimate test of truth and error in our inferences besides the trustworthiness of the illative sense that gives them its sanction. . . ."[15] In short, we are thrown into the midst of a set of conversations about religious truth and reality, with only our illative sense, or good judgment, to guide us to the ultimate truth of things.[16]

It is crucial that the illative sense is not seen reductively, as a form of enlightened religious common sense. In fact, according to Newman, the illative sense involves a distinctive form of imagination. A child of the Romantic era,

---

11. Newman, *Grammar of Assent*, p. 277.

12. Newman, *Grammar of Assent*, p. 278.

13. Crosby, "Newman," p. 45.

14. Newman, *Grammar of Assent*, p. 283.

15. Newman, *Grammar of Assent*, p. 281.

16. Illation may resemble perception, in the way that Merleau-Ponty describes it. That is, it is a faculty able to discover not only what is visible, but, simultaneously, that which is "the invisible *of* this world." See Phillip Blond, "Introduction," in *Post-Secular Philosophy: Between Philosophy and Theology*, ed. Phillip Blond (London and New York: Routledge, 1998), p. 26.

Newman was committed to the role of the religious imagination in the real apprehension of religious truths. Because of this, religious *conversion* stands at the center of Newman's theological epistemology. Conversion is not to be understood emotionally or experientially. It is, rather, an imaginative and transformative quality that exists at the very heart of the illative sense itself — a sustained ability to "think outside the box," that carries one past an infinity of inferences onto the solid ground of living dogma. As Stephen Toulmin points out, this conversion is not "a leap across a logical gulf, but rather . . . a 'change of posture' in the order of viewing" reality.[17] This conversional act of judgment is in many respects a fitting response to the aesthetic, theological, and moral impressions made by dogma itself. When Newman spoke of his earliest faith conversion he emphasized an imaginative and intellectual reception of dogma that had lasting effect on his life: "When I was fifteen [in the autumn of 1816] I fell under the influences of a definite Creed, and received into my intellect impressions of dogma, which, through God's mercy, have never been effaced or obscured."[18] The illative sense, therefore, is that act of personal judgment which responds to and receives "impressions of dogma" in such a way as to imaginatively transform and reshape human life accordingly.

The dogma that is received becomes the progenitor of further knowledge and a deepening of faith. According to Newman: ". . . dogma has been the fundamental principle of my religion: I know no other religion; I cannot enter into the idea of any other sort of religion: religion, as a mere sentiment, is to me a dream and a mockery."[19] In the *Apologia,* he called this the "dogmatical principle." As Etienne Gilson points out, for Newman, "the only way to restore Christianity in the hearts and minds of men [and women] is to teach them how to assent to dogmas as to so many real and particular objects . . . the revival of real assent to dogmas. . . ."[20] Religion based on sentiment, private (non-rhetorical) judgment, and the endless drawing out of inferential conclusions receives Newman's strenuous condemnation.

For Newman, then, knowing the truth of the Christian faith can only be a result of a set of personal judgments whereby one knows what is true and right by virtue of an extensive, converted, and committed relationship with church dogma, in the context of the church itself. It is this relationship and

17. Walter Jost, *Rhetorical Thought*, p. 232. See Stephen Toulmin, *The Uses of Argument* (Cambridge: Cambridge University Press, 1958), p. 254.

18. Quoted from the *Apologia* with dating by Etienne Gilson in the introduction to *Grammar of Assent*, p. 17.

19. *Apologia pro vita sua*, ed. Martin J. Svaglic (Oxford: Clarendon Press, 1967), p. 54.

20. Newman, *Grammar of Assent*, pp. 19-20.

this context of persuasion that gives someone the ability to judge about the true nature of religious truths. Wise theological *judgment* is possible at all stages of life, but is best exemplified as the highest pinnacle of a lifetime of faith-based learning. It is, in the last analysis, a distinctive and controlling aspect of practical theological wisdom that is earned through years of disciplined reflection and rhetorical suasion.

Preaching Dogmatic Convictions, Not Theological Conclusions

As the illative sense is developed and does its work in the life of the preacher, the preacher as theologian is able to move with ever increasing surety and clarity of mind across the abyss that separates his or her critical reason, inclined to the mundane tasks of assessing and weighing the best exegesis, theology, and experiential evidence, onto the far ground of dogmatic finality. In other words, a preacher's good theological judgment makes it possible to quit preaching *conclusions* and to begin preaching *convictions* or what Newman called "certitudes."[21] For Newman, "certitude" is not the same as "certainty." "Certitude is a mental state; certainty is a quality of propositions."[22] Certitude is arrived at through "the *personal* estimate of a convergence of myriad probabilities. . . ."[23] According to Newman: "We are considered to feel, rather than to see, its cogency; and we decide, not that the conclusion must be, but that it cannot be otherwise."[24] As the preacher gains a deeper personal, decisive sense of what "cannot be otherwise," the wishy-washiness of clamoring inductively (or deductively) after ever-receding conclusions gives way to the "firmness of assent" or "certitude" as the ground from which preaching takes flight.

This has a significant impact on *what* is preached (rhetorical invention). The preacher with a developed illative sense has the confidence to decide what thoughts or ideas are relevant to a particular subject matter. This, it goes without saying, is no small feat for most preachers who spend hours embroiled in "finding something to preach." Facility in theological invention for preaching can only arrive with the personal confidence in one's powers of judgment and a clear sense of the boundaries and internal dimensions of the idea at hand.

21. Newman, *Grammar of Assent*, pp. 173-208.
22. Newman, *Grammar of Assent*, p. 293.
23. Jost, *Rhetorical Thought*, p. 227.
24. Newman, *Grammar of Assent*, p. 321.

The illative sense also helps a preacher put the elements of an argument or thought into an appropriate order (rhetorical division). This is largely due to the fact that powers of judgment are required in order for a preacher to decide which rhetorical considerations come first, which are corollaries, which should constitute the foreground, and which the background and so on. Within the larger theological corpus, the illative sense helps the preacher-theologian assess the positive and negative weight of all kinds of ideas, so that they can be appropriately correlated with the weight of sin and the hope of redemption.

All of this is due ultimately to the fact that good judgment enables the preacher to see the *whole* of a subject matter, and not just the parts. The illative sense is a form of informal, convictional reasoning that sees an imaginative theological whole in all of its depth where formal reasoning and probabilistic exploration get bogged down with the parts. This is why great preachers seem to have an "epic" rhetorical sensibility — the gift of catching hold of the larger theological idea in such a way as to illumine and suggest all of its parts, *even those unspoken.* The illative sense insures that the theological forest is not lost for the trees.

Self-Reflexive Authority and the Illative Sense

Marxist and critical theorist Louis Althusser, in a well-known essay on ideology, argues that human subjectivity is constituted in large part as a product of "self-reflexive" ideology.[25] As social and cultural beings, we are positioned in relation to a variety of ideologies and confirmed by self-recognition within a certain set of ideological influences. Althusser's work parallels that of psychoanalyst Jacques Lacan, who argues that a specular or mirroring process occurs whereby a dominant ideology "hails" or "interpellates" individuals as subjects. Individuals, hearing themselves "hailed" by a dominant ideology, begin to recognize themselves in the image of the dominant ideological subject.[26] Valerie Pitt argues that something like this ideological "hailing" occurred in Newman's relation to Catholic dogma. Indeed, to a significant extent, in his

25. Louis Althusser, "Ideology and Ideological State Apparatuses (Notes Towards an Investigation)" in *Essays on Ideology* (London: Verso, 1984). Althusser probably overstates the relative passivity of the human subject in this process, but in Newman's case, because he himself argues for the overwhelming power of dogma as defining his own subjectivity, Althusser's ideas seem very appropriate.

26. Althusser, "Ideology," p. 41. See also Jacques Lacan, *Écrits: A Selection*, trans. Alan Sheridan (London: Tavistock/Routledge, 1977).

argument for the illative sense, Newman was demonstrating how this was the case. According to Pitt, Newman's elaboration of the illative sense was, at one level, an extensive apologetic for an almost self-hypnotic process of lining himself up under the dominion of dogmatic authority.[27] The idea of the illative sense provided Newman with an organ for the reception of, and assent to, dogmatic truth; an organ which, at the same time, could establish the veracity of those truths for one's life. Just as in his early years he "fell under the influences of a definite Creed," and received into his intellect "impressions of dogma," so he continued to hear himself hailed by this dominant authority, becoming, with increasing clarity of purpose and remarkable creativity, its self-reflexive *product*. The more Newman brought himself under the influence of this single authority, the more all other authorities were ruled out as arbiters of meaning or truth. This narrowing of authorities, of course, served an important purpose: to help Newman locate, accept, and communicate the absolute authority of Christian dogma in the midst of an increasingly liberal, skeptical, and complex culture.

Another authority was also "hailing" Newman. This, of course, was the authority of his Oxford mentors, friends, and colleagues, especially members of the older High Church traditions in the Church of England, and, of course, his fellow Tractarians, Keble, Froude, and Pusey. The measured style of practical rhetorical reason and personal judgment that permeated this culture, modeled as it was on Aristotelian and Ciceronian rhetoric, deeply influenced Newman's idea of the illative sense. Because of this, when confronted with the infinite regress of inferential reasoning that permeated German higher criticism, it seemed altogether adequate to Newman to appeal to a proper, practical, and personal *condition of mind* (good personal judgment), as it was practiced within the academic and ecclesiastical culture that surrounded him, to carry him, and others, onto the solid ground of indisputable dogmatic authority.

Newman's self-assured sense of dogmatic and communal-ecclesiastical authority is paradigmatic of much of what has been, and is still considered helpful by many preachers faced with a culture of skepticism, faltering authorities, and overwhelming complexity. In this case, we observe two things. First, similar to Newman's absolute commitment to the authority of dogma, many preachers as theologians find it comforting to enter into some kind of increasingly self-reflexive relationship with Christian dogma, doctrines, or

27. Valerie Pitt, "Demythologizing Newman," in *John Henry Newman: Reason, Rhetoric and Romanticism,* ed. David Nicholls and Fergus Kerr (Carbondale and Edwardsville, IL: Southern Illinois University Press, 1991), pp. 23-25.

confessions. Without jettisoning entirely the critical process whereby they have arrived at the gates of the house of dogma, they use those critical skills primarily to align themselves under these theological truths. This helps them achieve a sure and certain authority above and beyond religion tainted and diluted by the excesses of critical reason. Instead of preaching from the seams and edges of dogmatic formulations, or from those places where dogma becomes inadequate to express the truth of faith, preachers search for a solid place of theological authority as believers and communicators, and give full assent to a dominant theological model in order to become an extension of its authority, to become its "subjects" in the pulpit. In the last analysis, critical forms of subjectivity will not do for these preacher-theologians, only a subjectivity that is founded on a conversional "giving in" to dogma, on answering to its "hailing" or "impressions."

The second thing that these preacher-theologians do is to submit to the "hailing" by various academic and ecclesiastical authorities. By answering to these authorities, they hope to learn those things that constitute right thinking and thus good personal judgment in the pulpit. This, in any generation, is the practical wisdom, or what we might call today the "practices" or "best practices," of those who constitute a select group of experts (exegetes, preachers and theologians) to whose *condition of mind* preachers aspire within a particular ecclesiastical culture. This group of experts will vary, of course, inasmuch as the preacher's ecclesiastical culture is conservative evangelical, mainstream Protestant, Roman Catholic, Pentecostal, etc. It is here that good judgment asserts itself as a deeply personal "acquired habit" of mind,[28] one that is in large measure learned through entering into an imitative or mentoring relationship with a particular set of pastoral, homiletical and theological authorities. The renewed interest amid today's generation of preachers in celebrating and cultivating distinctive forms of "practice," "pastoral imagination," or "pastoral excellence" in retreat settings or in structured programs of peer-learning testifies to this interest. Preachers attend these events so that they can engage in extended conversation with those who have cultivated what they consider to be the best theological and homiletical judgment.

Rhetorical *topoi* and the Illative Sense

In his book *Rhetorical Thought in John Henry Newman,* Walter Jost accentuates the sophistication of Newman's masterful use of rhetorical *topoi* or topics

28. Newman, *Grammar of Assent,* p. 278.

as the key to his form of rhetorical knowing. According to Jost, brilliant rhetoric is a direct function of "inventional and discriminative excellence."[29] Rhetorical invention is the search for the most "comprehensive view,"[30] or what Newman, accentuating the role of judgment, called the "juster view" of a subject.[31] It is the choice of the best possible rhetorical *topoi* or topics that will make this superior view of a subject possible. As Jost puts it, a topic "comprises an angle or perspective, a 'view' we take of the concrete; hence it is a wedge or opening into reality."[32] Jost points out that Newman's idea of the educated person was not unlike the Ciceronian orator "who had mastered, not all things, but the arts of discovery and invention of intellectual principles and methods necessary to address and eventually take up any calling. . . ."[33] In his writings on educational philosophy, Newman desired that the product of university education become a responsible public person who was able, above all else, to garner the multiple perspectives on a particular subject and then to adjust and correct the *topoi* involved in approaching that subject so as to persuade others to a still more excellent view.

This process of getting a more excellent view through the sophisticated adjustment of rhetorical *topoi* is informed, according to Jost, "by an orientation to reality *as a totality.*"[34] Again, anticipating his idea of the illative sense, Newman, in *The Idea of the University,* called this "the power of viewing many things at once as a whole, of referring them severally to their true place in the universal system, of understanding their respective values, and determining their mutual dependence."[35] In order to create this "universal system," rhetorical *topoi* are typically organized into dyads through the use of contrast or difference. This view of reality as a totality that can be topically/dyadically organized pervades Newman's own writing and preaching. It is evident in his own brilliant topical invention and careful division of thought.

Again, the kind of knowledge that comes from this epistemology is not factual or metaphysical knowledge, but rhetorical knowledge, based almost entirely upon the "views" provided by the selection of topics or first principles on the part of the truth-seeker. In this sense, Newman's epistemology mirrors non-foundational, postmodern epistemologies, in which the key to

29. Jost, *Rhetorical Thought,* p. 183.

30. Jost, *Rhetorical Thought,* pp. 170-208.

31. Jost, *Rhetorical Thought,* p. 173. See John H. Newman, *Autobiographical Writings,* ed. Henry Tristam (New York: Sheed and Ward, 1957), p. 259.

32. Jost, *Rhetorical Thought,* p. 185.

33. Jost, *Rhetorical Thought,* p. 192.

34. Jost, *Rhetorical Thought,* p. 193.

35. Newman, *University,* pp. 122-23.

knowing reality shifts from establishing correspondences between words and things to the rhetorical task of determining the best *use* or adjustment of existing language, speech acts, or practices in relation to a subject under continuing examination. This crucial adjustment of topics is ruled and guided, for Newman, by the illative sense, or good judgment, which leads the truth-seeker toward those topics and divisions that will provide a more comprehensive or "juster" view of the subject matter at hand. As Jost comments, "Newman's primary concern has always been more to locate principles, to open up views, to create new places (topics) for perception and discrimination, than to work out the details."[36] As Newman himself put it in *A Grammar of Assent,* "[T]he great discoverers of principles do not reason. . . . It is the second-rate men, though most useful in their place, who prove, reconcile, finish, explain."[37]

As for the actual circle of thought or conversation within which the illative sense generates good judgments regarding rhetorical (homiletical) *topoi,* Jost points out that Newman assumes (as do Berger, Novak, and Polanyi) a "fiduciary framework," the "more or less implicit and unarticulated set of 'encased knowns' that provide relatively stable sets of assumptions, beliefs, and so on to interpret the world."[38] Instead of considering traditional theological assumptions about a subject to be in any way wanting, Newman accepts them as a positive context in which to engage in the task of making good judgments. According to Jost, "Given the framework (or horizon, paradigm, view) we inhabit, we use what is at hand until we have reason to doubt."[39] In this way, Newman is decidedly anti-Cartesian. As he states in the *Grammar:* "Of the two, I would rather have to maintain that we ought to begin with believing everything that is offered to our acceptance, than that it is our duty to doubt of everything. The former, indeed, seems the true way of learning. In that case we soon discover and discard what is contradictory to itself. . . ."[40] As is reflected by his eventual self-reflexivity within the framework of Catholic dogma, Newman feels comfortable to reason out the faith from within the entire fiduciary framework of Western Christianity and especially within the Anglo-Catholic segment in which he himself lived and worked.

Newman's commitment to good judgment as the key to the selection of excellent theological topics indicates several practices that continue to be pursued by preacher-theologians. First, preachers as theologians seek good

36. Jost, *Rhetorical Thought,* p. 203.
37. Quoted in Jost, *Rhetorical Thought,* p. 203. Newman, *Grammar of Assent,* p. 245.
38. Jost, *Rhetorical Thought,* p. 233.
39. Jost, *Rhetorical Thought,* p. 233.
40. Newman, *Grammar of Assent,* p. 243. Quoted in Jost, *Rhetorical Thought,* p. 234.

judgment, not only to give them the confidence to decide what to preach, but also in order to learn inventional and discriminative *excellence*. They learn, often tacitly, that the key to good theological preaching is the ability to choose the best possible theological *topoi* or topics so that a "juster view" of a theological subject becomes possible. Part of what preachers are searching for when they read biblical commentaries, attend conferences, watch video tapes, listen to audio tapes or CDs, and read the sermons of "great preachers" are new angles of vision, new and better *topoi*. They are learning by imitation, aspiring to "inventional excellence" themselves.

Second, most of these preachers are decidedly anti-Cartesian. Rather than beginning by questioning the adequacy of their tradition, they accept, by and large, the theological *topoi* that have been handed down in the appropriate tradition, entering directly into an ongoing theological conversation regarding traditional theological subjects. Within that conversation, the preacher, exercising an ever-refining sense of theological judgment (the illative sense), works hard to learn how to choose the best possible *topoi* for this Sunday's sermon, adjusting them to contemporary circumstances, so as to provide a more comprehensive angle or "wedge" into reality. The range of contributors to this conversation regarding potential or possible *topoi* for preaching varies, of course, according to the preacher-theologian's understanding of the fiduciary framework that is permissible for reasoning about theological matters such as sin, evil, atonement, eschatology, and so on.

Third, the preacher-theologian works to achieve good judgment in order to discover a "view" that is comprehensive enough to provide an orientation to God's work in the world *as a totality*. The focus is not on working out the details. Inconsistency between the parts is less important than discovering and communicating the whole. The focus is on principles, or, as Jost puts it, "to open up views, to create new places (topics) for perception and discrimination. . . ."[41] It does not matter whether topics are managed inductively or

---

41. Jost, *Rhetorical Thought*, p. 203. This way of thinking is very similar to what Nancey Murphy calls "post-modern non-relativism." She attributes this way of thinking in the current generation to Imre Lakatos, Theo Meyering, and Alasdair MacIntyre. Murphy calls this a "fractal philosophy." Reminiscent of Newman's attempt to find a "comprehensive view," fractal philosophy, according to Murphy, is "an attempt (similar to that of chaos theorists) to find order on a higher level of analysis, and — this is the crucial factor — the higher level findings exhibit coherence rather than self-stultification." She goes on to assume that "whatever circularity there is in the reasoning appears virtuous rather than vicious." Nancey Murphy, *Anglo-American Postmodernity: Philosophical Perspectives on Science, Religion, and Ethics* (Boulder, CO: Westview Press, 1997), pp. 60, 233. Elsewhere, Murphy calls this quality of reasoning "supervenience." "Supervenience is a relation between properties of different types or levels

deductively. The vision must be large or "epic" enough so that many things can be seen at once as a whole, as a part of a universal framework.

Finally, preachers as theologians in our postmodern day and age freely admit the theory-laden or "confessional" quality of their own perspectives. They are not afraid to entertain other theological paradigms or perspectives, inasmuch as those paradigms demonstrate some "grounds for commensurability" with their own.[42] Other theological perspectives are welcomed into conversation inasmuch as those paradigms "work" in relation to the preacher's own view or larger model, as long as they help provide a "juster view" when taken altogether. In other words, theology can be pluralistic within a range, if the variety of views ultimately supports, either negatively (by contrast) or positively (by correlation), a more comprehensive view. The preacher's judgment always discovers *topoi* at a higher level either where the *coherence* of a plurality of theological perspectives begins to become clear, or where the distinctions between them point to irreconcilable contradictions, calling for opposition or further examination.[43]

Questions for Consideration

> "'Let (the one) who speaks . . . speak only the words of God' [I Pet. 4:11]. . . . What is this but to reject all inventions of the human mind (from whatever brain they have issued) in order that God's pure Word may be taught and learned in the believers' church?" (Calvin, *Institutes of the Christian Religion*, 4.8.9)

I have argued that something similar to Newman's epistemology is still with us, especially among a significant group of preachers who aspire to theological excellence in the pulpit. Because of the continuing importance of the illative sense and the epistemology it presupposes, it is important to pose a series of questions for further consideration. I do so on behalf of preachers in our historical epoch, many of whose questions, in all fairness, Newman never con-

---

such that if something instantiates a property of the higher level, it does so in virtue of (as a noncausal consequence of) its instantiating some lower-level property. In such a case, the higher-level property is said to supervene on the other" (pp. 22-23).

42. Jost, *Rhetorical Thought*, p. 205.

43. For an excellent model for placing confessional theology into a model of critical conversation across and among commensurate and conflicting paradigms, see David J. Lose's idea of "critical fideism" in his book, *Confessing Jesus Christ: Preaching in a Postmodern World* (Grand Rapids: Eerdmans, 2003).

fronted. These questions emerge from our current situation in which the suffering caused by holocaust, genocide, globalization, civil and human rights abuses, and terrorism looms large. I also ask these questions on behalf of those for whom something like Paul Tillich's "protestant principle," or "the expression of doubt in the act of faith," encourages some caution when it comes to the role of rhetorical reason in theological thinking and in preaching.[44]

I begin by asking the most comprehensive question of all: Is this kind of rhetorical reason, or something like it, the best pathway to theological truth in the pulpit? Becoming masters in the manipulation of theological *topoi* in service to a more comprehensive sense of theological totality in the pulpit may strike some, especially those outside the fiduciary framework in which these *topoi* are being invented and arranged, as a troubling, or even domineering, vision for the production of theological speech in the world today. We live in a world in which we are ever more aware of woeful gaps of resources, power, and privilege when it comes to the pursuit of knowledge. We are also aware that theology cannot be blind to the many resources brought by history, the sciences, and the arts. The assumption that most of what is needed for the adjudication of theological truth claims in the pulpit can be provided by a set of dogmatic *topoi*, adjusted toward a more comprehensive view in relation to a range of commensurate and conflicting ideas, could make theological production a mostly intramural enterprise. Theological knowledge within such an epistemology can close itself off from the testimonies of neighbors near and far as well as from the critical reflections of the larger community of scholars and artists. Is it wise within a complex global village to encourage preachers to become reflexive products of comprehensive dogmatic formulations in order to better convert persons into an existing core of theological meaning within a defined range of interpreters? Perhaps it would be better to encourage preachers to abandon hard and fast identities and to wander into the desert places between theological paradigms and religions. Would at least some element of epistemological and theological dislocation be an appropriate corrective to the potential insularity of illative reasoning? Would it be helpful, for instance, to check and counter-check good theological judgments with persons who suffer in large part because they fall into the gaps between, or beyond, the dominant models of theological meaning that currently exist?

44. According to Tillich, the "protestant principle" is "the critical element in the expression of the community of faith and consequently the element of doubt in the act of faith. Neither the doubt nor the critical element is always actual, but both must always be possible within the circle of faith. From the Christian point of view, one would say that the Church with all its doctrines and institutions and authorities stands under the prophetic judgment and not above it," *Dynamics of Faith* (New York: Harper and Row, 1957), p. 29.

Another, related question concerns the ability of good judgment to access that which is beyond its own inventive excellence. Is the truth discovered by the illative sense really open to the ongoing activity of God *in the world?* Or as we have already suggested, does it produce a proclivity toward an imaginative truth whose grounding is mostly semantic and tropic in nature? At this point, it is the dyadic nature of rhetorical *topoi* that presents us with a problem. If we believe that God is at work beyond the boundaries of our rhetorical constructs in, through, and upon real human bodies and minds in history and in the cosmos, how can our epistemologies break free from the construction of totalities and systems built around the binary relationships and imaginative juxtapositions of theological topics (same/other, self/world, church/culture, salvation/sin, good/evil, exile/establishment, God/humanity, etc.)? How can theological knowing come into the presence of those aspects of faith that cannot be known by means of our theological constructs as they currently exist, namely the "God beyond the gods"? Should preacher-theologians be invited to learn a more iconoclastic, parabolic, or even ironic rhetoric that accentuates the limits of dogma and opens up new spaces for language, thought, and speech about God? Would face-to-face exegetical and interpretative study of Scripture with lay believers, non-believers, and believers from other faiths engender soft-heretical speech that might accomplish a similar goal?[45]

This raises a still more radical question, one that is well beyond the scope of this essay to pursue: If God's activity in the world can be discerned and communicated through the careful management of theological *topoi*, what is the exact nature of this God? We might wonder what this God has to do with the wild and alien God who could be recognized only by the demons in Mark's gospel — i.e., recognized by someone/thing entirely outside the spiritual community and its theological constructs. How are we to reconcile these visions of God — one hitched reflexively to a traditional, dogmatic framework, and the other hitched up to that which is completely outside all usual frameworks for discerning the truth of Christian faith?[46]

This being said, what are we to make of the kind of truth that emerges through practices of illation or rhetorical judgment? In the first place, can we

45. By "iconoclastic, parabolic, and ironic" speech and "soft heresy," I have in mind the kind of thinking, writing, and preaching represented by the Reformers and their followers who gathered to the Scriptures in search of a way beyond the tyranny of well-reasoned dogma. Calvin believed that even the testimony of idolaters might have some value, since there is "a sense of the deity inscribed in the hearts of all," Calvin, *Institutes of the Christian Religion*, 1.3.1.

46. For a very provocative study of this problem, see David Jaspers, *Rhetoric, Power and Community* (Louisville: Westminster John Knox Press, 1993).

trust it? And more disconcertingly, do we have a choice but to trust it? Is illation what indeed happens in all human knowing, even mechanical engineering or scientific experimentation, as Newman suggests?[47] If it is, then just how *far* are we to trust this kind of reasoning, especially when it is being done on our behalf, albeit benevolently? Are we dealing with theological truth, or simply the truth of what is believed to be the truth? Is the *virtue* of the theological thinker, the fact that he or she is making theological judgments in good faith and in all sincerity, enough to make us abandon our own hesitations and enter into his or her fiduciary framework? Is the authoritative "hailing" of dogma and the company of preachers enough to engender trust among those in the pews on Sunday morning? What about the possibility of perjury or false testimony within the ranks? And what about good faith testimonials that are in fact not worthy of fiduciary commitment on our behalf? None of these questions can be adequately answered here (or, perhaps, elsewhere), but they do not simply *go away,* once one has decided that there is an inescapable element of personal judgment (illation) in all rational processes. At the least, they require a constant critical vigilance to insure that theological judgment is as informed and critically rendered as possible. At the most, they require us to pursue an alternative, or seriously attenuated, form of reason, one that takes with utmost seriousness the real empirical effects of theological judgments on the lives of persons and communities, especially inasmuch as they may yield needless violence or human suffering.

This leads us squarely to the question of authority. Is it adequate in the twenty-first century to opt for a form of homiletical and theological authority that is in large part lodged in the preacher's reflexivity with dogma and with selected cultural and ecclesiastical authorities? Is this the best way for theological rhetoric to have authority in today's world? Are the communal authority of rhetorical comprehensiveness and the formal, aesthetic beauty of best arguments and best practices adequate to persuade people in the public arena of the authority of Christian theology? Is this form of authority going to establish what Rebecca Chopp calls the "public feasibility and credibility" of theology in the world today?[48]

Several correctives suggest themselves at this point. First, the conversa-

---

47. Again, according to Newman, "in no class of concrete reasonings, whether in experimental science, historical research, or theology, is there any ultimate test of truth and error in our inferences besides the trustworthiness of the illative sense that gives them its sanction . . . ," *Grammar of Assent,* p. 281.

48. Rebecca Chopp, "Theological Persuasion: Rhetoric, Warrants and Suffering," in *Worldviews and Warrants: Plurality and Authority in Theology,* ed. William Schweiker and Per M. Anderson (New York and London: Lanham, 1987), p. 17.

tional, suasive, or perspectival aspect of making good theological judgments might be turned away from the task of shoring up dogmatic, ecclesial, and personal identity and toward larger public concerns of historical and theological praxis. This means that preachers will need to seek new perspectives from which to preach, to leave their peer groups, conferences, lectionary helps, video and audio tapes of great preachers behind and seek out a multitude of other social locations, thinkers, artists, and face-to-face relationships as the locus for thinking about the reality of God in the world.

Second, the role of "notional assent" and "inference" in rendering good theological judgments can be increased and given over, in part, to critical theory which would provide a stronger consideration of privilege, interest, power, and what Chopp calls "systematic distortions or false ideologies within the normative and legitimized sanctions and beliefs of society."[49] Preachers will want to consider ways in which the self-reflexivity that they enjoy in relation to Christian dogma and their chosen set of ecclesiastical authorities can be monitored for capitulations to interests designed to protect and hoard social (or economic or career ladder) power or influence.

Third, theological judgment could be modified to incorporate an orientation away from dogmatic iteration toward the transformation of traditional theological premises. This would require a broader anamnestic and eschatological impulse, in which reason's commitment to adjusting the *topoi* stored within the house of its tradition is interrupted by the "dangerous memory" of those whose lives and testimonies have seldom or never been heard or incorporated within the broader fiduciary framework for the development of dogma. This, of course, means introducing into one's practice of homiletical-theological judgment conversations with the poor, and all of those who, as Gutierrez puts it, are "outside" of history.[50] As Chopp points out, the "non-persons" should be privileged in this conversation "not because of their own moral superiority but because they break through an anthropology of domination" and expose "the epistemic, functional, and genetic properties of modernity which has universalized the 'rich' to be the universal human subject . . . i.e. the person thematized in terms of common human experience."[51] It is here that illative judgment encounters, and is potentially transformed by *ethical counter-judgment*.

In conclusion, the formalism and totalism of the illative sense and its al-

49. Chopp, "Theological Persuasion," p. 17.

50. See Gustavo Gutiérrez, *The Power of the Poor in History: Selected Writings*, trans. Robert R. Barr (Maryknoll: Orbis Books, 1983).

51. Gutiérrez, *Power of the Poor*, pp. 26-27.

legiance to the authority of a dominant tradition should be broken across a theology of God's ultimacy and across a firm solidarity with those who suffer as strangers within and beyond the tradition. Preachers committed to discovering principles or *topoi*, who are committed to the "whole," can be invited to go in search of both the "God beyond the gods," and of lost or yet unconsidered human "parts," incorporating Newman's "second-rate" men and women, those who worry about "reconciling" the whole and the parts, into deeper and more substantial conversations regarding the viability of all comprehensive principles discovered by masterfully adjusting theological *topoi*. In order for preached theology to have authority in today's world, it will have to rise above (or move beneath) its obsession with the majesty of its own good judgment and tether itself to a sustainable and workable vision and practice of human, historical, social, political, and theological transformation. To accomplish this, preacher-theologians should be ever mindful of their allegiance to a God who resists comprehensive topical views and to neighbors whose particularity contests every rhetorical totality.

The Preacher of the Word and a
Southern Recipe for Creeds and Politics

Milner S. Ball

The schismatic "Southern" Presbyterian Church (Presbyterian Church in the United States) was born in the nineteenth century in the sin of slavery, and it never recovered. But by the 1970s when it finally began to move toward re-union, and the larger, national Presbyterian body (United Presbyterian Church) began to consent to the reunion that would take place in the early 1980s, the old "Southern" Church, in spite of itself and its origins, had produced a generation of ministers who were adept both in theology and social change. Wallace Alston belonged to that generation, and he is both marked by and exemplary of it.

The Academy and the Pulpit, Theology and Belief

When the Presbyterian Church first made its way into the deep South, it came bearing both the Calvinist tradition and a contagious dedication to learning and scholarship. By the middle of the twentieth century, its members had long assumed that the clergy would be in fact the well-educated Teaching Elders they were officially described to be. They were expected to be theologically accomplished, and theology was expected to serve the preaching of the Word. In consequence there was considerable commerce between ministers and academic theologians and often no distinction between them.

In this regard, John Leith was typical. A Calvinist devotee and one of Wallace's influential teachers at Union Theological Seminary (Richmond, Virginia), Leith long insisted on the theological centrality of the local congregation and had himself served as minister of the First Presbyterian Church in

Auburn, Alabama, from 1948 until he joined the Seminary's faculty in 1959. Wallace would subsequently be called to the pulpit of the Auburn Church and there begin a career-long investment of his life as a scholar in pastoral service. It is of a piece with his heritage and his own service that he would, most recently, give new life in the twenty-first century to the received interdependence of preaching and theology through the pastor-theologian program at The Center of Theological Inquiry.

Leith's publication of an important collection of creeds[1] was not coincidental, for he was typical, too, in his expectation that the Church's theologians and pastors would share not only a joint enterprise, but also a common confession. They would be believers, real believers, as well as scholars. They would be creedally committed and creedally tested. It was in this sense that "Southern" Presbyterians thought of themselves as church rather than as denomination, a distinction noted by Dietrich Bonhoeffer.

Bonhoeffer has been accurately described as "something like our theological de Tocqueville."[2] His keen observation of American Christianity began with his first visit to the United States in 1930-31 at Union Theological Seminary (New York). Following his abbreviated second and last visit in 1939, he wrote a telling assessment titled "Protestantism Without Reformation"[3] in which he noted that American Protestant communities characteristically think of themselves as denominations rather than as churches; as denominations constituted by culture, liturgy, community life, and organization rather than as Church whose identity is determined by creed and therefore by urgent concern for theological truth. But he also observed that "The Episcopalians, the Lutherans, and the Presbyterians are consciously churches, even if in the eyes of the others they are only denominations along with the rest."[4] The "Southern" Presbyterian Church certainly thought of itself as church.

Creeds and Racism

In Germany, the Confessing Church that Bonhoeffer served was bound to creeds, and creeds and truth fueled its resistance to Nazism. The "Southern"

1. John Leith, ed., *Creeds of the Churches* (New York: Anchor Books, 1963).
2. George Hunsinger, "Barth, Barmen and the Confessing Church Today," *Katallagete* 9, no. 2 (Summer 1985): 14-27.
3. Dietrich Bonhoeffer, "Protestantism Without Reformation," in *No Rusty Swords: Letters, Lectures and Notes, 1928-1936, from the Collected Works of Dietrich Bonhoeffer*, ed. and trans. Edwin H. Robertson, trans. John Bowden (London: Collins, 1965), p. 92.
4. Bonhoeffer, "Protestantism," p. 94.

Presbyterian Church, too, was creedally oriented and concerned with theological truth, and such commitments could not forever coexist with capitulation to racism. Theologically determined opposition to racism in the predominately white Church was, however, painfully slow to take shape.

But it eventually did make a start. A southern institution that lacked an aristocracy would scarcely be southern, and the "Southern" Presbyterian Church was no exception. Some of the Church's influential aristocratic fathers and mothers — especially the mothers — of Wallace's generation signaled their understanding that the creeds and truth would eventually prevail, or prevail at least over the direct expression of racism in the Church, and they began to prepare the way for action to be taken by their sons and daughters. Nonetheless, it took the civil rights movement outside the white Church to make the tension between creedal truth and racist practice obvious and its resolution unavoidable.

A young minister in Mississippi in the 1960s reported that, after one of his sermons, a leader of the congregation departing the service confessed that he had come to understand that the point of the sermon was correct, that Jesus would surely have opposed segregation in the Church, but that this congregation would stay segregated notwithstanding. A defining issue was in the open, and decision and action could no longer be avoided by resort to silence, euphemism, metaphor, coded language, or indirection.

Pastor-theologians now had to be not only scholars and believers but also politicians, ecclesiastical politicians in the first instance. One 1960s minister in Alabama reported that, whenever newly-elected Ruling Elders from his congregation attended Presbytery for the first time, he always made sure to drive them to the meeting so that he could explain on the way that there were two sides and which side to vote with.

Theology and Politics

Pastor-theologians could not limit themselves to politics in the Church only. They needed also to learn and to practice the secular politics that creedal commitment required as a response to God's active presence in the world in the midst of life. They needed a theology of politics, and one was available.

Wallace spent his second year of seminary at the Harvard Divinity School. The late fifties and much of the sixties were exhilarating years on Divinity Avenue in Cambridge, Massachusetts. They were rivaled in twentieth-century America only by the theological electricity generated a couple of decades earlier at the Union Theological Seminary (New York) that Bonhoeffer knew. The two schools in those moments had some things in common.

For one, no little of the substantive excitement at both schools in both times originated in Europe, predominately in the German-speaking world: Reinhold Niebuhr's Union was the central point of entry into the United States for Karl Barth's theology. And when Harvard's turn arrived, it imported some suitably lustrous representatives of continental schools of biblical studies and Church history. (In both periods, the Presbyterian Church required candidates for ordination to the ministry to have a working knowledge of the Hebrew and Greek languages. The Church did not require competence in German, but rudimentary theological literacy made it necessary.)

Another common factor was Paul Lehmann. Bonhoeffer had met Lehmann at Union, and the two became fast personal and theological friends.[5] Years later, Lehmann was necessary to the theologically critical mass that Harvard assembled at its Divinity School. From Niebuhr, Lehmann had learned the importance of theological attention to the world, and from Barth he had learned the central priority of Christ for thinking about and acting in the world. He then developed his own distinctive political theology. It is a theology of the biblical God who practices politics, bringing pressure on people and events to the end of making human life human in the world.[6]

Lehmann was a deeply affecting teacher, and his theology provided a creative medium for thinking about the role of the Church in the South and about the clergy's responsibility for faithful preaching and action. Wallace was drawn to Lehmann's theology, and he would become an adroit participant in the politics of God in the South through his preaching, his theology, and his example.[7] He would also prove to be an essential friend to Lehmann.

Those "Southern" Presbyterian clergy who confronted racism gained from the conflict experience and training that equipped them for other continuing struggles, including war, misogyny, homophobia, and extreme poverty in the midst of extreme wealth.

5. An interesting photograph of 1930-31 Union faculty and students, including Niebuhr, Bonhoeffer, and Lehmann, may be found facing p. 33 in Dietrich Bonhoeffer, *Gesammelte Schriften*, Band I, ed. Eberhard Bethge (Munich: Chr. Kaiser Verlag, 1965).

6. See Paul Lehmann, *Ethics in a Christian Context* (New York: Harper & Row, 1975); *The Transfiguration of Politics* (New York: Harper & Row, 1975); *The Decalogue and a Human Future* (Grand Rapids: Eerdmans, 1995).

7. It was not only the situation of the Church that gave personal moment to political theology for Wallace. He was already predisposed to politics, a politics that, in its mature development, has tended more to the Lyndon Johnson than the Jimmy Carter style of persuasion. And then, too, he was already a professionally accomplished, willing performer of the country music that has long accompanied successful political campaigns in the South. Wallace's guitar picking and high, lonesome voice were unaffected by the Lehmann connection.

Politics and Action

The southern struggles were personal but also institutional, with institutional lessons to teach, and much of Wallace's life in the Church in the meantime has been devoted to a politics of institutional care and maintenance. The Center of Theological Inquiry of the later years has been a crowning achievement of institutional politics.

There is risk involved in entanglement in institutions and what William Stringfellow warned about as their fallenness.[8] But purity of heart is not what the politics of God would have us seek. "There is no glory," Bonhoeffer observed, "in standing amid the ruins of one's native town in the consciousness that at least one has not oneself incurred guilt."[9] What we seek is not self-justification but forgiveness. We depend "on a God who demands responsible action in a bold venture of faith, and who promises forgiveness and consolation to the person who becomes a sinner in that venture."[10]

Yet to Come

Wallace and his generation have acted. Ancient struggles continue. Some, like overcoming antisemitism in the Church, are under way but are in their early stages. Others are just beginning.

Fascination with the day's developments in the German-speaking theological world was well-justified in Wallace's time, but it cannot now restrict a more generous, fruitful curiosity about God's presence in the thinking and living of other peoples. The South Korean theologian Chung Hyun Kyung reports that she "stopped reading dead white European men's theologies and memoirs" after completing her Ph.D. in order to turn her atten-

8. See William Stringfellow, *A Private and Public Faith* (Grand Rapids: Eerdmans, 1962); *My People Is the Enemy* (New York: Holt, Rinehart and Winston, 1964); *An Ethic for Christians and Other Aliens in a Strange Land* (Waco, TX: Word Books, 1977); *Conscience and Obedience* (Waco, TX: Word Books, 1977).

9. Dietrich Bonhoeffer, *Ethics,* trans. Neville Horton Smith (New York: Simon & Schuster, 1995), p. 335.

10. Dietrich Bonhoeffer, *Letters and Papers from Prison,* ed. Eberhard Bethge, trans. Reginald Fuller (New York: Simon & Schuster, 1997), p. 6. In a comment on Bonhoeffer, Jean Bethke Elshstain noted, "One . . . acts in full knowledge of guilt. One knows one cannot expiate the wrongs one has committed. But one embraces forgiveness — what Hannah Arendt calls Christianity's greatest contribution to politics. . . ." Jean Bethke Elshstain, "Freedom and Responsibility in a World Come of Age," in *Theology and the Practice of Responsibility,* ed. Wayne Whitson Floyd and Charles Marsh (Valley Forge: Trinity Press, 1994), p. 277.

tion to what was taking place in her own world, especially the world of Asian women.[11]

The Church need not abandon the good in the European and American fathers, dead or alive, in order to accept the challenging gift offered by the mothers and sisters of the world. Perhaps Wallace's 2002 trip to China is a sign of possibilities for larger exchanges of gifts.

*　　　*　　　*

Paul Lehmann once said that dogmatics is that which one generation chooses to pass on to another about what it has found to be essential. Wallace has discharged an essential theological and institutional responsibility in helping to insure that dogmatics is done for tomorrow's pastor-theologian-politicians.

11. Chung Hyun Kyung, "Dear Dietrich Bonhoeffer: A Letter," in *Bonhoeffer for a New Day: Theology in a Time of Transition* (Grand Rapids: Eerdmans, 1997), p. 11.

"Not That We've Done Anything All That Bad . . .": Pastoral-Theological Reflections on Sin

Allen C. McSween, Jr.

An uncle of mine, who was an Elder in the church I serve, was fond of telling people that he "taught me all I know . . . about sin." Some might say the same thing about Wallace Alston. But in these reflections on sin we will be more "broadly ecumenical."

A good friend of Wallace Alston, Sandy McKelway, tells of reading a prayer of confession in the bulletin of a Presbyterian church which began, "O God, our sins are ever before us — not that we have done anything all that bad, but. . . ." Then followed a tiresome litany of the "politically correct" failings for which the congregation was expected to feel mildly guilty.

It is easy to laugh at such theological naivete. But in so doing I am laughing at myself. I must confess that too often it is with a good bit of self-consciousness that I use the classical language of sin in my preaching and teaching and rarely in pastoral care. Anselm's reply to Boso could equally well be directed to me: "You have not yet considered the great weight *(ponderis)* of sin."[1] This paper is an attempt by one involved in pastoral ministry to reflect theologically on the loss of the language of sin in the church and offer resources for its recovery.

Once sin was a strong, foreboding word, with great power and drama. No other word in the English language articulated so powerfully the depths of the human dilemma. The concept of sin gave voice to the radical brokenness of life without falling into utter despair. It served to name the madness that keeps being played out in the headlines of every day's news without cynicism or utopian fantasies.

---

1. Anselm, *Cur Deus Homo?* (Douglas John Halls calls this the "most penetrating insight ever stated in the area of harmatiology.")

But for a host of reasons the stern old language of sin has fallen into disuse and disfavor. To many in "progressive" mainline churches the word itself has a quaintness that smells of musty sanctuaries and renders its recovery problematic. Mention the word sin at a cocktail party and listen to the embarrassed silence. Sin has become the ultimate conversation-stopper, even in the church. Talk too much about sin in mainline Protestant pulpits, and, one way or another, the congregation will let you know that they do not come to worship to be told "how bad they are." They come for enough uplift and encouragement to get them through another week. The last thing many of our members want from their religion is to make them or their children "feel guilty." Fearing to offend those who pay our salaries, we pastors, says Kathleen Norris, "can be so reluctant to use the word 'sin' that in church we end up confessing nothing except our highly developed capacity for denial."[2]

But however uncomfortable we in the church may be with the word sin, our bluff has been called by events throughout the world. On September 11, 2001 "history caught up with us," and we experienced in an emotionally powerful way what people in many parts of the world face almost daily. The "irrational exuberance" of our tremendous prosperity over the past decade had enabled us to forget or repress for a while the fact that we live in a world of vast brutalities — "ethnic cleansing" in Bosnia, suicide bombers in Jerusalem and Baghdad, an HIV/AIDS pandemic in Africa, the daily death toll from the war in Iraq. We live in a brutal and brutalized world where the human wreckage cries out to heaven. In such a world there can be nothing "innocent" in our loss of a theology of sin. It is a manifestation of sin itself.

It matters greatly that the concept of sin has fallen into disuse. The words that have been proffered to take the place of sin — estrangement, alienation, social dysfunction — cannot carry anything like the full gravity of sin. None has the weight of centuries of profound reflection and tradition behind it. Sin is the given language of scripture and Christian faith. It cannot be psychologized without loss of its most salient feature — its direct and inescapable reference to God. Even Paul Tillich, who developed in a helpful way the concept of "estrangement," agreed that "the word sin can and must be saved, not only because classical literature and liturgy continuously employ it but more particularly because the word has a sharpness which accusingly points to the element of personal responsibility in one's estrangement."[3]

2. Kathleen Norris, *Amazing Grace: A Vocabulary of Faith* (New York: Riverhead Books, 1998), p. 165.

3. Paul Tillich, *Systematic Theology*, vol. 2 (Chicago: University of Chicago Press, 1957), p. 46.

227

To lose a profound concept of sin is to lose the ability to speak honestly and deeply about the human predicament. In a homiletical idiom Tom Long warns that "An anthropology that lacks a vigorous doctrine of sin is headed for constant disillusionment, chronic and bitter disappointment, and ever deepening spirals of rage over the inability or unwillingness of human beings to act responsibly."[4] That may be rhetorical over-kill, but as any pastor or novelist knows, "to the hard of hearing you shout, and for the almost-blind you draw large and startling figures."[5]

Even those who are uncomfortable with the language of sin are nevertheless keenly aware that things are not as they ought to be, and we are not as we ought to be. The question must be faced: from whence comes this turning away from a deeply felt, if not clearly articulated, norm? Why do so many of our best intentions produce disastrous consequences? Why does there seem to be an ineradicable perversity to human life? And why do we have such a phenomenal capacity to deny it? Yes, "Our sins are ever before us . . . ," whether they are named as such or not.

Whether we use the word sin or not, there is still the haunting sense that life as we know it ought to be significantly different and better than it is. The Christian doctrine of sin seeks to articulate what lies behind that deep disorder — the profound disruption, the rampant alienation, the brutality and banality — that in one form or another we all encounter every day of our lives.

In seeking a deeper understanding of sin for pastoral ministry, one of the best resources comes not from a theologian but a professor of the Humanities at Columbia University, Andrew Delbanco. His book *The Death of Satan: How Americans Have Lost the Sense of Evil* is one of the most provocative recent treatments of sin and evil. It ought to be required reading for anyone concerned with our rapidly accelerating cultural slide into banality and depravity. In the midst of an ongoing "war on terrorism" the book has a sharp prophetic edge. Delbanco portrays graphically how Americans have lost the powerful symbolism of sin and evil at the very time when a huge "gulf has opened in our culture between the visibility of evil and the intellectual resources available for coping with it." Delbanco writes:

4. Thomas G. Long, "God, Be Merciful to Me, a Miscalculator," *Theology Today* 50, no. 2 (July 1993).

5. Flannery O'Connor, *Mystery and Manners* (New York: The Noonday Press, 1992), p. 34. Tragically enough it often seems to take some form of violence to open our eyes to reality. O'Connor goes on to say, ". . . in my own stories I have found that violence is strangely capable of returning my characters to reality and preparing them to accept their moment of grace. Their heads are so hard that almost nothing else will do the work" (p. 112).

The repertoire of evil has never been richer. Yet never have our responses been so weak. We have no language connecting our inner lives with the horrors that pass before our lives in the outer world. . . . when some new shocking cruelty does seize our attention, it is likely to be met with consternation or annoyance. We shudder or wince; then we switch the channel.[6]

Delbanco says that the impetus for his book on evil came "out of the belief that despite the shriveling of the old words and concepts, we cannot do without some conceptual means for thinking about the sort of experiences that used to go under the name of evil."[7] He argues that even if we no longer operate with the concept of a malignant force with an ontological essence of its own (Satan), we still experience something like such a force at work in our lives and "we still discover in ourselves the capacity to inflict (evil) on others. Since this is true, we have an inescapable problem: we feel something that our culture no longer gives us the vocabulary to express."[8]

Without the weight of the classical language of sin and evil, we find ourselves dumb in the face of unspeakable atrocities. Delbanco warns,

No one should underestimate the destructive effects of the theological beliefs that have fallen away. . . . I believe that our culture is now in crisis because evil remains an inescapable experience for all of us, while we no longer have a symbolic language for describing it.[9]

In similar fashion the political philosopher, Jean Bethke Elshtain, warns of the serious social and political consequences of the woefully inadequate anthropology of the "thinned-out sentimental humanism" so prevalent in mainline churches. Pastor-theologians would do well to heed her warning and take seriously her invitation.

It is vital for theologians, in the name of a decent present and a hopeful future, in the name of faithfulness to that complex tradition of which they are heirs, to take seriously the account of the fall and the interpretations of its continuing effects. The human race is a fallen race. If we forget that, we fall into anthropocentric arrogance.[10]

6. Andrew Delbanco, *The Death of Satan: How Americans Have Lost the Sense of Evil* (New York: Farrar, Straus, and Giroux, 1995), p. 3.

7. Delbanco, *Death of Satan*, p. 9.

8. Delbanco, *Death of Satan*, p. 9.

9. Delbanco, *Death of Satan*, p. 224.

10. Jean Bethke Elshtain, "Beyond Traditionalism and Progressivism, or Against Hardening of the Categories," *Theology Today* 58 (April 2001), p. 9.

Yes, "our sins are ever before us. . . ." Yet still we persist in excusing or justifying them, most often by blaming other people or structures for them. That is true across the theological and political spectrum. No one I know of has dealt more profoundly with the "double dynamic" of pretended innocence and external blame than Miroslav Volf in his stunning work *Exclusion and Embrace,* a book that becomes more painfully relevant to our situation in the United States by the day. Volf writes,

> In a world so manifestly drenched with evil everybody is innocent in their own eyes. . . . Perpetrators tirelessly generate their own innocence, and do so by the double strategy of denying the wrongdoing and re-interpreting the moral significance of their own actions. This double strategy is fertile ground for ideologies by which systems and nations seek to mask a violence and oppression they perpetrate. And this same double denial is the stuff out of which the peculiar blend of fraud and self-deception is concocted, by which individuals seek to evade being held responsible for evildoing.[11]

Across the political and theological divides, sin is largely viewed as external, societal, and structural. The suggestion that *we* bear significant responsibility for the evils around us is often rejected out of hand either as a matter of "blaming the victim" or as a threat to our self-esteem, our most prized possession or most sought after virtue. On the conservative side it is disturbing to see the extent to which a significant number of evangelicals (who clearly ought to know better) have bought into the ideology of "self-esteem" at the cost of any serious doctrine of sin.[12] On the liberal side the "valorization of the victim" has nearly silenced any serious reflection on the "noninnocence of victims." Once again it is Volf who has the theological courage to speak a profound word about the "solidarity in sin" of perpetrator and victim without losing the capacity to render moral judgments and pursue the rightful demands of justice.

> Violence ensnares the psyche of the victim, propels its action in the form of defensive reaction, and — robs it of innocence. . . . She (Marjorie Suchocki) writes, "To break the world cleanly into victims and violators

---

11. Milroslav Volf, *Exclusion and Embrace* (Nashville: Abingdon Press, 1996), pp. 79-80.

12. The most egregious example is Robert Schuller, *Self-Esteem: The New Reformation* (Waco, TX: Word Books, 1982). But a host of other examples could be given. See Paul Vitz, *Psychology as Religion: The Cult of Self-Worship* (Grand Rapids: Eerdmans, 1977), or for a sociological critique, see James D. Hunter, *The Death of Character* (New York: Basic Books, 2000).

ignores the depths of each person's participation in cultural sin. There are simply no innocents." . . . In addition to inflicting harm, the practice of evil keeps re-creating a world without innocence. . . . Intertwined through the wrongdoing committed and suffered, the victim and violator are bound in the tragic and self-perpetuating solidarity of sin.[13]

Volf hastens to insist that "solidarity in sin" is not a matter of seeing all sins as equal and thus undercutting rightful demands for justice. To say that "all of us are equally sinners" does not mean that "all sins are equal." The fact that victim and violator are neither innocent does not place them morally on an equal footing. But it does join them in a powerful, yet rarely explored, solidarity. Volf insists,

> There is no escape from noninnocence, either for perpetrators or the victims or for a "third party." . . . Every person's heart is blemished with sin; every ideal and project is infected with corruption; and every ascription of guilt and innocence is saddled with noninnocence. This, I think, is what the doctrine of original sin teaches.[14]

Has the concept of sin been too corrupted, too trivialized, to be useful in the church today? Absolutely not! Even if at times we must use other terms — alienation, self-centeredness, brokenness — to interpret sin, none can take its place. None carry the gravity of the stern, foreboding word sin. We have no choice but to recover and reclaim the Christian understanding of sin, not for the sake of clinging to our tradition, but for the sake of a world that quite literally cries out for the truth of the human condition to be spoken and embodied.

In seeking to recover a more profound sense of sin for pastoral ministry, we must continually insist that sin is a uniquely religious/theological concept. Understood biblically, sin is not merely an ethical concept — something we *do* that is wrong. Sin is a *theological* concept — naming that which betrays or breaks our relationship with God. Fleming Rutledge puts it simply, "Sin is only understood to be sin when God is understood to be God."[15]

Sin is not defined abstractly in scripture. It is narrated concretely. We know sin only in the light of the unfolding drama of God's will for our life together. Sin is not merely the violation of a moral code, however serious may be its consequences. Sin is the disruption of the network of covenant relation-

---

13. Volf, *Exclusion*, pp. 81, 92.
14. Volf, *Exclusion*, p. 84.
15. Fleming Rutledge, *The Bible and the New York Times* (Grand Rapids: Eerdmans, 1998), p. 89.

ships for which we were created by God. Its inevitable result is the disruption of all our relationships with nature, others, and self. Daniel Migliori sums up well the implications of such a view.

> If being human . . . means life in free response to God who freely and graciously addresses us, then sin can be described as the denial of our relatedness to God and our need for God's grace. From this vantage point sin is fundamentally opposition to grace, saying No to the invitation to be human in grateful service to God and in fellowship with our fellow creatures. Sin is the great refusal to live thankfully and gladly by the grace of God that makes personal life in community with diverse others possible. Thus we misunderstand the depth of sin if we see it only as a violation of a moral code; it is, instead, primarily the disruption of our relationship to God.[16]

Even when sin is properly understood in relational terms, it always defies definition. "Sin" that could be understood or explained would not be sin in the full Christian understanding of it. We have no vantage point outside of sin by which to define sin except in light of God's revelation of our true humanity in Jesus Christ. To define sin too precisely is inevitably to trivialize it. Our definitions turn sin into specific acts (sins) which can be described and proscribed, and thus inevitably lead to various forms of legalism or moralism.

But while the origin of sin cannot be specified without trivializing sin's universality, we must nevertheless insist that its origin is not in bodily human life. Sin is not rooted in finitude, temporality, sexuality, ignorance, or unjust social structures. "Sin posits itself" (Reinhold Niebuhr). Christian faith insists that sin is not a part of our created nature. It is a corruption of that nature. Whatever may be the origin of sin, the fact is that we are all born into a "fallen" situation in which sin is already an encompassing reality. In the words of Alexander Solzhenitsyn, "the line separating good and evil passes not through states, nor between classes, nor between political parties — but right through every human heart."[17]

Sin is not just a wrongful act. It is a state of being "curved in on oneself" (Luther). Sin is a radical, persistent self-centeredness that can never be "cured" by acts of the self-centered self, regardless of how sincerely they are intended or how nobly they are performed. The self-centered self is not free to will or to work its own liberation from its self-centeredness.

---

16. Daniel L. Migliori, *Faith Seeking Understanding* (Grand Rapids: Eerdmans, 1991), p. 130.

17. Quoted in Paul Vitz, *Psychology as Religion: The Cult of Self-Worship* (1977; reprint, Grand Rapids: Eerdmans, 1998), p. 127.

The crux of the matter has to do with how two of the more "offensive" aspects of the doctrine of sin are construed — namely, the "bondage of the will" and "total depravity." The "bondage of the will" no doubt strikes many American churchgoers as being even more "absurd" than "original sin" (and down-right unAmerican!). Yet if our wills are as free as many claim, why is what we freely will often so trivial, so self-centered, so vain and empty? The ideology of "freedom of choice" fails to take sufficient account of the tragic dimension in both the choices we "freely" make and those we are forced to make.

As for our "total depravity," that "peculiar gift" of the Reformed tradition, it would seem that such an idea would undercut the whole modern enterprise with its emphasis on progress and self-liberation. Exactly! That's the point of it! "Total depravity" does not mean that we are as evil as we could possibly be (what Albert Outler called "teetotal depravity"). It means that every human being and every aspect of human life is tainted by the radical self-centeredness of sin. Thus every program, every technique, of self-salvation, self-liberation, self-conferred self-esteem, will eventually prove empty and lead to disillusionment. Such disillusionment is not bad. The "dis-ing" of illusions can be the first and necessary step toward a rightly ordered confidence in the ultimate Giver and Redeemer of life, the triune God.

A large part of the immense subtlety of sin is seen in its ability to "morph" into a countless variety of forms. All attempts to specify a single root of sin are futile. At times sin finds expression in active self-centeredness — pride, defiance, willful disobedience. Other times, perhaps more often, it is expressed in passive self-abnegation — in weakness, passivity, banality, and triviality. At times sin is expressed in the prideful centering of life around one's inflated self; other times in the despairing centering of life around one's broken self. In one of his most profound insights Augustine noted that "Many sins are committed through pride, but not all happen proudly . . . they happen so often by ignorance, by human weakness; many are committed by men weeping and groaning in their distress."[18]

In articulating sin we cannot avoid using the language of paradox. In order to do justice to the realities of life under God as revealed in scripture and experienced in our own lives and history, we must affirm at the same time that sin is both a universal human condition and a self-chosen human act. We bear a measure of personal responsibility for that which enslaves the whole human race. (In Niebuhr's phrase sin is "inevitable, but not necessary.") Sin involves the corruption of the individual will, but is powerfully

18. From *Nature and Grace*, xxix, quoted by John Leith in a sermon given at the 165th annual session of the Synod of NC, Charlotte, NC, June 6, 1978.

present in social and corporate structures. Sin is made manifest in acts which are readily condemned as evil or wicked, but it is subtly at work in what is applauded as virtue, warping our self-perception and deceiving us into thinking that our virtue is greater than it really is. As Reinhold Niebuhr pointed out so often, the worst evil is often done not by obviously evil people, but by "righteous" people who do not know the limits of their righteousness. (Listen well, America!) Under the universality of sin, our righteousness is never as pure or disinterested as we may suppose. Surely one of sin's most insidious powers is its ability to turn the good we intend into the evil we despise. We of the Vietnam generation know painfully well how easily our self-righteous use of power can turn us into the very enemy we oppose — a lesson we best not forget in these days when we so willingly sacrifice large measures of freedom for small measures of security. Again Volf puts it powerfully,

> We are ensnared by evil not only with full consent, but without a thought of dissent and without a sigh for deliverance. With the inner workings of our will in its hold, evil can dispense with force and rule by lure. And so, paradoxically, we feel free only in the prison house of unrecognized evil.[19]

All the paradoxes of sin flow from the central paradox at the heart of the Christian view of humanity, that we are exalted and fallen at the same time. The two must be kept in appropriate tension. In a particularly insightful development of this essential paradox, the political scientist Glenn Tinder writes:

> The fallen individual is not someone other than the exalted individual. Every human being is fallen and exalted both. This paradox is familiar to every informed Christian. Yet it is continually forgotten. . . . Sin is ironic. Its intention is self-exaltation; its result is self-debasement. In trying to ascend, we fall. The reason for this is not hard to understand. We are exalted by God; in declaring our independence from God, we cast ourselves down.[20]

---

19. Volf, *Exclusion,* p. 90.

20. Glenn Tinder, *The Political Meaning of Christianity* (San Francisco: Harper Collins, 1991), pp. 35-44. Tinder goes on to say, "Our exaltation depends on the mercy of God, who is not a being in the world, and is reflected in destinies that lead us beyond our world. Exponents of worldly philosophies, denying God and unconscious of destiny, move back and forth between two contrasting misunderstandings. Trying to maintain the dignity of human beings, they affirm their goodness; that is the only possible source, for them, of their dignity. When they discover that most human beings display little goodness, they are forced to question their dignity. Thus, they fluctuate between complacency and cynicism. Only those conscious that the world is transcended, and that our lives in the world lead beyond the world, can say that a human being is morally perverse yet of measureless value, fallen yet sacred."

For all the tragic depths of sin, in the final analysis the doctrine of sin is good news. There is reason for the brokenness of life and hope for its ultimate redemption. We seek to render a realistic account of the pervasiveness and perniciousness of sin in order to move toward repentance and the redemption promised in the gospel. Sin must never be taken more seriously than the grace of God. As Paul insisted, "Where sin increased, grace abounded all the more." Scripture narrates graphically the reality and deadly power of sin, but always in the wider context of the "extravagance of grace." "God has consigned all to disobedience that he may have mercy on all" (Rom. 11:32). Because sin is a breach of a relationship with the One whose love will not let us go, it can never be the first or final word! Sin is unnatural, a perversion, that which God does not will and wills to destroy. Sin is parasitic on the good, and thus is inevitably self-destructive. Sin "feeds on itself." The honest acknowledgement of sin can save both from arrogance and despair, from cynicism and utopian illusions. It can free one from the terrible burden of being responsible for everything that happens without destroying a sense of human responsibility for the good that is within our power. It saves us from being surprised when expected good has unintended consequences for evil, and from the romantic idealism that leads to despair and violence when its utopian dreams are not readily achieved.

A more profound understanding of sin can make us more modest in our claims for ourselves and our own accomplishments so as to be more expectant of what God can and will accomplish in and through us or in spite of us. In a time of media-inflated egotism, any gain in modesty would come as a breath of fresh air.

No pastoral reflection on sin can close without a call to a more profound self-examination. If, as Delbanco says, "Evil has returned as the blamable other — who can always be counted on to spare us the exigencies of examining ourselves,"[21] we as Christians have a counter-witness to offer: *Mea culpa,* said neither in despair nor resignation, but in profound trust in the Christ who "while we were yet sinners . . . died for us." Serious, sustained pastoral efforts to recover a more profound understanding of sin could go a long way toward helping the church move out of its triviality and denial, so as to become virtually the only place in a society trapped in the violent lies of its own self-righteous myths, where the truth is told and reality is faced. A more important ministry for the Church of the Risen Crucified Christ in our time and place can hardly be imagined.

21. Delbanco, *Death of Satan,* p. 234.

The Missing Spirit of -Uality

Virgil Thompson

Interest in spirituality continues to ride atop the rising tide of the cultural seas. Bookstores — religious and secular — appear adequately supplied to meet the demand of interest. My local Barnes and Noble, for example, is well stocked in spiritual self-help books, bearing titles that require little annotation to suggest their gist: *Best Spiritual Writings; How to Know God; Spiritual Genius; The Hidden Gospel: Decoding the Spiritual Message of the Aramaic Jesus; One River, Many Wells;* and rounding off the sample, the best-selling *Prayer of Jabez.* The Internet hosts thousands of sites for whatever brand of spirituality seekers might be searching — Buddhist, Christian, Feminist, Islamic, Jewish, Liberationist, New Age, or Pagan. Seminars and retreats are offered all over the map. Parish pastors eager to occupy a respectable position in the cultural imagination train to offer "spiritual direction" for seekers. That spirituality has set sail in popular imagination, there can be no question. There is question, however, what spirit, or spirits, informs the spirituality that is everywhere about us.

On the one hand, chroniclers of spirituality, Louis Dupré and Don E. Saliers, celebrate the new spiritual situation of faith:

> The twentieth century has witnessed a remarkable convergence and mutual interanimation of diverse traditions of spiritual life. Not only have the ecumenical and liturgical movements created an unprecedented sharing among Roman Catholic, Orthodox, and Protestant communions, but the increased social contact of ordinary believers, especially in North America and where pentecostalism and charismatic movements in Africa and Latin America have cut across denominational lines, has made shar-

ing of mutual approaches to spirituality more natural, less proscribed by historical traditions as well as within traditions which have historically at times been polarized. The growing awareness and appreciation of ways of spirituality across traditions have created an entirely new climate. At the same time, the most essential and most venerable of the strands of Christian spirituality, in practice and in theology, have emerged with more force precisely because of the new situation.[1]

Alister McGrath, on the other hand, is not so entirely sanguine about the spirit of contemporary spirituality. In his study of the subject, he has charged that much of contemporary spirituality is informed by a "sectarian mentality . . . dominated by the impulse to withdraw from the world."[2] It would no doubt qualify as hyperbole to say that McGrath's sentiment is echoed by millions. Still, McGrath is not entirely alone in his criticism of contemporary spirituality. As James Kittelson has pointed out, critics of popular spirituality can be found across the ecumenical waterfront.[3] He notes for example that Philip J. Lee's book, *Against the Protestant Gnostics,* which condemns the gnostic spirit of the new spirituality for its syncretistic and narcissistic tendencies, has received approving reviews in publications as diverse as *The Christian Science Monitor* and *The Thomist.*[4]

The new spirituality in many of its manifestations does make itself a big target for the criticism leveled at it by critics such as McGrath and Lee. The spiritual program prescribed by the *Prayer of Jabez,* for example, does seem to be driven by an unvarnished spirit of self-indulgence and narcissism. Spirituality is reduced to a formula for successful living measured in terms of personal material gain. Pray this prayer word for word over the course of thirty days and you will be blessed beyond your wildest imagination, the book promises. With nine million copies of the book sold and thirteen some odd million in print, one does not need to speculate about it. Across the land there's a hunger and thirst for the spiritual life.

While crassly self-indulgent spirituality of this sort has its critics coming out of the evangelical woodwork, more subtle variations on the theme tend to go unrecognized, even embraced by the same critics. That is to say,

---

1. Louis Dupré and Don E. Saliers, eds., *Christian Spirituality: Post-Reformation and Modern* (New York: Crossroad, 1989), p. xxiii.
2. Quoted in James M. Kittelson, "Contemporary Spirituality's Challenge to Sola Gratia," *Lutheran Quarterly* 9, no. 4 (Winter 1995): 367, from Alister McGrath, *Spirituality in an Age of Change. Rediscovering the Spirit of the Reformers* (Grand Rapids: Zondervan, 1994), pp. 194-5.
3. Kittelson, "Contemporary Spirituality's Challenge," p. 367.
4. Kittelson, "Contemporary Spirituality's Challenge," p. 368.

what is the difference between spiritual practices bent toward material enrichment and spiritual practices bent toward spiritual enrichment? Particularly from the point of view of the sixteenth-century Reformation the question presses itself into theological reflection about the spiritual life. In both instances, it appears from the Reformation vantage point, the self, with all its utopian dreams and schemes, occupies the center of the picture. And there's the real rub of contemporary spirituality. The insight of the Reformers, set forth five hundred years ago, continues to be crucial to theological reflection about spirituality. Luther appreciated that the human heart left to its own designs is a fabricating heart, constantly producing and projecting its own visions of the kingdom come. Nothing is sacred to the fabricating heart. It will even turn God into an idol. As Calvin saw, the human heart is in this respect a perpetual factory of idols. We attach our prospects to the heart's fancy because the heart itself has fabricated them.[5] Just so, both variations betray and play to original sin, as articulated by Augustine, *homo curvatus in se!* Both offer a program of spirituality for the old sinful self. Instead of signaling the end of human existence curved in upon itself, giving way to the new self, liberated to live for the other, the new spirituality merely plays to the old *homo curvatus in se*. In that sense the new spirituality proves not to be so new, but as old as those old Pelagian sermons on the Parable of the Sower, which encourage anxious contemplation of the condition of the self's spiritual soil. Finding it rocky, shallow, hard, and thorny, seekers are exhorted to get busy and make improvements. And preachers turned spiritual directors are, of course, prepared to offer a program designed to cultivate a deeper spiritual life.

To invoke Pelagius in connection with spiritual programs designed to elevate sinners to a higher existence or designed to renew and refresh the righteous, weary-worn from the battle, but which only serve to exacerbate sin by sanctifying life curved in upon itself, is not arbitrary. Pelagius was the first to coin the term spirituality. According to James Kittelson, "The first use in Latin of what became the modern word, although without its contemporary meaning, probably came from the pen of none other than Pelagius, who was congratulating a novice on his decision to live *spirituale* or 'spiritually' by rejecting the world in favor of concentrating on his interior life."[6]

Of course, modern spirituality is not necessarily born from a spirit of rejection or escape from mundane, broken, unsatisfying worldly existence,

5. The essay is indebted to Oswald Bayer for the insight. The monograph, translated by Geoffrey Bromiley, is forthcoming from Eerdmans. In the typescript the discussion occurs on pages 32ff.
6. Kittelson, "Contemporary Spirituality's Challenge," p. 376.

though sometimes it is. But even where it is born of a spirit of retreat for the sake of renewal for and restoration to the battle against sin, death, and the power of the devil, is the spirit or instinct salutary? From the standpoint of the Reformation the answer is a quick and unequivocal no. No matter who is giving the advice, a fifth-century heretic or a twenty-first-century spiritual director, it leads directly into the "slough of despond." As Bunyan describes it:

> Here therefore [Christian and Pliable] wallowed for a time, being griev-ously bedaubed with the dirt . . . therefore is it called the Slough of De-spond; for still as the sinner is awakened about his lost condition, there ariseth in his soul many fears, and doubts, and discouraging apprehen-sions, which all of them get together, and settle in this place. And this is the reason of the badness of this ground . . . here hath been swallowed up at least twenty thousand cart-loads, yea millions of wholesome instruc-tions that have at all seasons been brought from all places of the King's dominions, and they that can tell say they are the best materials to make good ground of the place. If so be it might have been mended, but it's the Slough of Despond still and so will be when they have done what they can.[7]

Bunyan is not mistaken about it. Whenever the sinner turned seeker is driven into retreat by anxiety and exhaustion over the lost condition of the self or society, there is no escaping the mire of "fear, doubt, and discouraging appre-hensions."

The problem at root is that the modern conceptuality of spirituality as retreat into the self or the contemplative wilderness misconceives spiritual ex-istence. It looks for renewal one hundred and eighty degrees in the wrong di-rection. It should be clear enough from the story of Jesus. If the story of his life tells anything about the direction of the spiritual life then you have to be-lieve that spiritual existence does not lie in retreat and disengagement but in the opposite direction. His whole life was lived from beginning to end toward the conflict and death that awaited him in Jerusalem. This is what his life shows. "If possible," he prayed in the garden, "remove this cup from me." The answer came quickly, "Arise, my betrayer is at hand." Events move rapidly for-ward to the cross and resurrection. The story reveals that the spiritual bless-ing of political conflict lies precisely in the death we die to our utopian aspira-tions to save ourselves and our neighbors. It is not so much that we are not up to the project, not merely that it wears us out, defeats us, drives us into fears, doubts, and discouraging apprehensions. The real problem is with the uto-

7. John Bunyan, *The Pilgrim's Progress* (New York: Signet Classic, 1964), pp. 22, 23.

pian dreams themselves. Utopia, literally, no place, imaginary, it does not exist. We will not admit that utopia, as we conceive it, does not exist. The only cure for utopian dreams is death, that we might be born again to the world as it is with promises yet to be by God's saving grace. As Luther once put it, "The thirst for glory is not ended by satisfying it but rather by extinguishing it."[8] Just so such cruciform existence prepares us for the word of God's promise in Christ. And if that word does not give us life then there is no life to be had. It is the word of God's forgiveness.

No one since Paul and Augustine has understood this better than the Reformers of the sixteenth century. Therefore they took an altogether radical approach to the question of spirituality. Lutheran and Reformed, each in their own particular way, conceive spirituality not as withdrawal from the world into a regimen of exercises designed to elevate, renew, sanctify, or otherwise improve the self. Such ministrations, they appreciate, given the nature of the human predicament, ultimately end in the opposite of their intended result. Instead of renewing the self to re-enter the political fray of daily existence, they lead either to despair or to deadly self-righteousness. For the Reformers spirituality was conceived as the existence granted by the promise of God. The emphasis here is on promise. It is God's way of saving the human being from despair and/or self-righteous fanaticism in the same breath. As Oswald Bayer explains, "In order that those who are renewed and regenerated do not in arrogant or despairing introspection refer again to themselves, we need not only the law that punishes and slays self-will, but especially also the gospel that prevents this from happening. The spontaneity of the new obedience is protected against the wrong kind of fanaticism, lest in blinded self-conceit we individualistically and egotistically claim that it is our own possession. The gospel shows us that we must take it as the gift of another, and that in its power we can live our lives by faith."[9]

Retreat into silence is from the point of view of Reformation theology even more deadly. The Reformers held out no prospect of escaping — religiously, spiritually, or otherwise — the rough and tumble of political existence. They held out no prospect of escape because there is no escape, not even momentary escape. The human being is stuck on this earth for good or ill. The human being is stuck in its habitation. The Word of the Lord does not offer escape, but promises that there is reason for hope and justification

8. Jaroslav Pelikan and Helmut T. Lehman, eds., *Luther's Works,* 55 vols. (St. Louis and Philadelphia: Concordia and Fortress, 1955ff.), vol. 31, p. 54 [hereafter cited as LW]; quoted in Gerhard Forde, *On Being a Theologian of the Cross* (Grand Rapids: Eerdmans, 1997), p. 94.

9. Bayer, p. 78.

for living out that hope in the midst of the rough and tumble realities of the present.

The Reformers understood that vacation is one thing; spiritual renewal is another. They begin with an understanding of spirituality anchored deeply in Christ, who has come down, entered in, intent upon redeeming this life, the only life that the human being has for the moment. Let Luther speak for the Reformers, drawing out the implication for a Christian understanding of spiritual existence. "Spiritual," he argues, "is nothing else than what is done in and by us through the Spirit and faith, whether the object with which we are dealing is physical or spiritual."[10]

Regin Prenter sets forth the Reformers' understanding of the Holy Spirit as the driving spirit of spirituality in terms of fleshly and spiritual existence. According to his explanation, fleshly and spiritual existence is not understood as it seems universally to be understood across the board of contemporary spirituality in classical Greek categories. Accordingly, flesh is equated with material, corporal existence, which holds the human spirit captive to a low-down existence, keeping it from soaring upward to the heavenly habitation of peace, righteousness, and contentment. Rather, as Prenter points out, for the Reformers as for Paul:

> Flesh is the whole of man when his conscience is under dominion of the law, by which it is forced to seek its own righteousness. This is the situation we know from its culmination in inner conflict, by which man is driven to wish that God did not exist. Spirit is the whole man, when he is driven by the Spirit of God so that he does not seek his own, but lives by the mercy of God and thereby is in conformity to his will. . . . But how does man become spirit? The answer is, by the Spirit of God. The spirit is man when the Spirit of God dwells in him. Man is flesh when the Spirit of God is absent. The struggle between flesh and Spirit is therefore a struggle between the flesh of man and the Spirit of God. Therefore the gospel about Christ's work and alien righteousness to be accepted by faith is lined up in this struggle against the conceit of the flesh with its faith in works stimulated by the law.[11]

Two points are worthy of emphasis in the interest of shaping an understanding of Christian spirituality in the tradition of the Reformation. In the

10. LW, vol. 37, p. 92. The quotation is cited in Kittelson's article, and it is that article which has alerted me to the import of Luther's treatise for the contemporary imagination with respect to spirituality.

11. Regin Prenter, *Spiritus Creator* (Philadelphia: Fortress, 1953), p. 78.

first place, spiritual existence does not take the human out of its political habitat, but rather it is political existence undertaken by faith in God's gracious promise and by love for the neighbor. The promise of such a life is not peace and tranquility. As Oswald Bayer has put it, "Those who have faith do not close their eyes to injustice and suffering, yet they do not give them the last word, but rather lament and live against them — by faith."[12] It may be an existence of strife fraught with dilemmas that would cross Solomon's eyes. The promise of such an existence is that the self is lost by faith in God and love for the neighbor. It is in the midst of such a rough and tumble existence, and this is the second point, that the Holy Spirit comes to possess the believer — through the means of sermon and sacrament — with the word of forgiveness for despair, self-righteousness, and doubt and in the same breath with word of the promise renewed. As Paul puts it, "When we cry, 'Abba! Father!' it is that very Spirit bearing witness with our spirit that we are children of God, and if children, then heirs, heirs of God and joint heirs with Christ — if, in fact, we suffer with him so that we may also be glorified with him" (Rom. 8:15-17). For the Reformation tradition spirituality is not a movement or preparation of the believer toward God. Spirituality is the movement of God's Holy Spirit, employing the regular means of the church's ministry of Word and sacrament, toward the believer caught up in the rough and tumble world of everyday existence.

Spiritual seekers will of course find the news less than inspiring. "Is that all? Just the preacher's word for it? Just a sip of wine and a bit of bread? That's all you've got? That doesn't seem very spiritual." Precisely just such dissatisfaction has launched the contemporary spiritual quest. To which dissatisfaction the Spirit answers, "That's it. Just these low-down material means of getting at you with the saving word of your Lord. Saving you, for starters, from embarking on a spiritual quest that takes you away from the 'low-down' life of everyday earthly existence, which is the only life for you." The point is that here, as Gerhard Forde says,

> God is doing to us the kind of thing he intends to do. He is working his forgiveness in us by destroying the kind of spiritual pride that will not see or receive God in creation, in earthen vessels. . . . By this action, God puts to death the old Adam, that is, he demolishes the man who seeks God in a spiritual heaven and raises up a new man content to live as God's creature with his feet on the ground. . . . God's spirituality is his becoming flesh, his giving of himself in bread and wine, his invasion of our isolation. . . .

12. Bayer, p. 81.

'This is my body broken for you,' 'This is my blood shed for you.' It is as if to say, come down out of the clouds; come down to earth, to the stuff of earth! Come have communion with men, real men![13]

In the Large Catechism Luther drives the point home to faith:

If you are asked, What do you mean by the words, "I believe in the Holy Spirit"? you can answer, "I believe that the Holy Spirit makes me holy [or spiritual], as his name implies." How does he do this? By what means? Answer: "Through the Christian church, the forgiveness of sins, the resurrection of the body, and the life everlasting. . . . The Holy Spirit reveals and preaches that Word, and by it he illumines and kindles hearts so that they grasp and accept it, cling to it and persevere in it."[14]

The "it," which the Spirit "reveals and preaches" and which faith "grasps and accepts," to which faith "clings and perseveres," is Christ himself. The preaching of the Spirit moves or inspires believers to promise that they will live in Christ, which is to say, as we have been saying, toward God in faith and hope and toward the neighbor in love. The Spirit, as we have been saying as well, does not preach directly, but through the means of ordinary believers, and just so restores us to our neighbors in faith. Where two or three are gathered together in his name, Christ lives for faith. Faith cannot bear to go it alone. As Luther put it, "For this purpose, he has appointed a community on earth, through which he speaks and does all his work."[15] That community is of course the church, which may not necessarily inspire high hopes. To locate the promise of spiritual renewal in the community of the church as it is known in the local congregation will certainly sound unpromising to the contemporary seeker. The contemporary spiritual sensibility, as already acknowledged, has been born in part of profound disenchantment with the church. And there is no question but the membership provides plenty of foundation to substantiate the charge of disillusionment. The *simul* of Reformation anthropology is everywhere in evidence among the church membership — one in the same *(simul)* sinner and saint. But just there is the promise of our life together. Again, Luther: "Although we have sin, the Holy Spirit sees to it that it does not harm us because we are in the Christian church, where there is full forgiveness of sin. God forgives us, and we forgive, bear with, and aid one another."[16] To

---

13. Gerhard Forde, *Where God Meets Man* (Minneapolis: Augsburg, 1972), p. 84-5.
14. Theodore G. Tappert, ed., *Book of Concord* (Philadelphia: Fortress, 1959), p. 416.
15. Tappert, *Concord*, p. 419.
16. Tappert, *Concord*, p. 418.

locate the promise there is, according to the creed, a matter of faith — *Credo!* I believe! — in the promise of God, not a matter of empirical possession. It is precisely by such faith that one has eyes to see the community of faith for what it is. Consider for example the community of faith as it took up the protest for civil rights in the 1960s.

In a powerful theological retrospect of the civil rights movement, J. Louis Martyn argues this is exactly the Spirit that possessed the community of protesters, led by the American Moses, Martin Luther King, Jr. At the invitation of Martyn, "Transport yourself for a moment to the Sixteenth Street Baptist Church in Birmingham, Alabama, on an evening in the month of May, 1963."[17] From that evening Martyn recalls a speech in which a prominent sports figure several times congratulates the congregation, "You people are doing a great thing here in Birmingham." Finally, an old deacon of the church arises from the shuffling embarrassment of the congregation to correct the misapprehension of the visitor, "We're not doing this! God is doing this!" The deacon asserts what the whole congregation knows to be the truth of the matter. In case one is inclined to hear the deacon's confession as a pious platitude, it may be recalled that the deacon has been marching all day. It is his own body that has been put on the line, that has risked police clubs, police dogs and fire hoses, marching to secure the recognition of constitutional rights denied to his neighbors. The deacon's assertion can only be understood in Reformation logic. Accordingly, "We must do all that we have to do as if there were no God." Faith does not lead to quietism but to taking up what of necessity lies at hand. Faith is not in opposition to works. Rather faith saves the believer from relying salvifically on works, getting arrogant when things go well and worried when things go wrong. Faith sees its life as "God's mask, under which he conceals himself and so marvelously exercises dominion and introduces disorder in the world."[18] The remark of the deacon bears witness to the truth held by faith "that God has begun the apocalyptic war [against evil] by striking the decisive blow in Jesus Christ, thus making certain that the ultimate future of the world is the future of Christ, the corporate One of the New Age."[19]

But if not a pious platitude, the promise in which faith is invested seems nonetheless weak in comparison to the political power that governs the everyday affairs of the human community. This power, which Martyn calls "Old-Age power," is built solidly on the old principle of *quid pro quo*, this for

17. J. Louis Martyn, *Theological Issues in the Letters of Paul* (Nashville: Abingdon, 1997), p. 284.

18. Bayer, p. 48.

19. Martyn, *Theological Issues*, p. 285.

that. If the civil rights movement had undertaken its cause in the terms of this power it would quickly have suffered defeat. It had little to none of such power. But the movement was animated by the power of a different order, not visible to "Old-Age" eyes. The animating power or spirit of the movement was, as Martyn describes it,

> the unconditional grace in the cross of Christ . . . the uncontingent love of God . . . that is powerful enough to keep the black community walking on sore feet every day. . . . It is the grace known by Rosa Parks and her sisters and brothers, as they sing into the face of the unredeemed world, "I once was lost, but now am found, was blind, but now I see!" See that in the literal crucifixion of Jesus of Nazareth God invades without a single if. Not *if* you repent. Not *if* you learn. Not even *if* you believe. The absence of the little word if, the uncontingent, prevenient, invading nature of God's grace shows God to be the powerful and victorious Advocate who is intent on the liberation of the entire race of human beings.[20]

Once this Spirit possesses a person, heart and mind, the "Old-Age" power will not prevail against it. As Martin Luther King, Jr. explained to his fellow clergy in the Letter from the Birmingham jail, "as the Apostle Paul left his village of Tarsus and carried the gospel of Jesus Christ to the far corners of the Greco-Roman world, so am I compelled to carry the gospel of freedom beyond my own home town."[21] It is this Spirit's utterance that found voice in the preaching of King with remarkable eloquence, as for example in the "I Have a Dream" sermon delivered on the steps of the Lincoln Memorial in Washington D.C. on August 28, 1963. In that sermon King declared,

> I have a dream today. I have a dream that one day every valley shall be exalted, every hill and mountain shall be made low, the rough places will be made plain, and the crooked places will be made straight, and the glory of the Lord shall be revealed, and all flesh shall see it together. This is our hope. This is the faith with which I return to the South. With this faith we will be able to hew out of the mountain of despair a stone of hope. With this faith we will be able to transform the jangling discords of our nation into a beautiful symphony of brotherhood. With this faith we will be able to work together, to pray together, to struggle together, to go to jail together, to stand up for freedom together, knowing that we will be free one day.[22]

20. Martyn, *Theological Issues*, p. 289.
21. Martin Luther King, Jr., *Why We Can't Wait* (New York: Signet Books, 1963), p. 77.
22. Martin Luther King, Jr., *The Peaceful Warrior* (New York: Pocket Books, 1968).

Even if the "Old-Age" power slays the voice that bears testimony to the decisive truth of God's apocalyptic act in Christ, the Spirit will not fall silent. It will possess others as it possessed King. Those possessed may not always rise to such heights of rhetorical eloquence or heroic endeavor. But wherever believers are moved by faith to undertake service of the neighbor's well-being, no matter how mundane and trivial, there the Spirit is at work to bring about God's new day. In that new day we are restored to our true humanity, restored to the life — with all its challenges, ambiguities, and demands — for which we were created in the first place. Disappointment or disenchantment with this life merely betrays our alienation from creation, self, and God. One can hear the difference between false and true spirituality in the way that the believer regards mundane earthly work. Consider for example the father's attitude toward diaper duty, as Luther does in a treatise on marriage:

> Now observe that when that clever harlot, our natural reason (which the pagans followed in trying to be most clever), takes a look at married life, she turns up her nose and says, "Alas, must I rock the baby, wash its diapers, make its bed, smell its stench, stay up nights with it, take care of it when it cries, heal its rashes and sores, and on top of that care for my wife, provide for her, labor at my trade, take care of this and take care of that, do this and do that, endure this and endure that, and whatever else of bitterness and drudgery married life involves? What, should I make such a prisoner of myself? O you poor, wretched fellow, have you taken a wife? Fie, fie upon such wretchedness and bitterness! It is better to remain free and lead a peaceful, carefree life; I will become a priest or a nun and compel my children to do likewise."
>
> What then does Christian faith say to this? It opens its eyes, looks upon all these insignificant, distasteful, and despised duties in the Spirit, and is aware that they are all adorned with divine approval as with the costliest gold and jewels. It says, "O God, because I am certain that thou hast created me as a man and hast from my body begotten this child, I also know for a certainty that it meets with thy perfect pleasure. I confess to thee that I am not worthy to rock the little babe or wash its diapers, or to be entrusted with the care of the child and its mother. How is it that I, without any merit, have come to this distinction of being certain that I am serving thy creature and thy most precious will? O how gladly will I do so, though the duties should be even more insignificant and despised. Neither frost nor heat, neither drudgery nor labor, will distress or dissuade me, for I am certain that it is thus pleasing in thy sight."[23]

23. LW, vol. 45, p. 39.

In the final analysis, from the theological point of view of the sixteenth-century Reformers it appears that the contemporary understanding of good and evil, material and spiritual, requires a complete overhaul. Accordingly, spiritual existence is not to be understood as a level of existence above the material or apart from the political. The distinction between material and ethereal, between fleshly and spiritual, has to do in the imagination of Reformation theology with how things are used. Fleshly existence uses things to justify, serve, and elevate the self. Spiritual existence uses things to serve the well-being of the neighbor. As Luther put it in that treatise from 1527:

> The glory of our God is precisely that for our sakes he comes down to the very depths, into human flesh, into bread, into our mouths, our heart, our bosom: moreover, for our sakes he allows himself to be treated ingloriously both on the cross and on the altar, as St. Paul says in I Corinthians 11 that some eat the bread in an unworthy manner. . . . The spiritual is nothing other than what is done in us and by us through the Spirit and faith, and it makes no difference whether the object with which we are dealing is physical or spiritual.[24]

The spiritual life, that is to say, does not move away from material, political existence but into material, political existence for the purpose of giving the self there freely in service of the neighbor's well-being, just as God in Christ has come and comes in the same way for us; so we believe and live.

In Reformation perspective spiritual life is a down-to-earth life. As Luther sums up the spiritual life, according to God's friendly admonition, "Go, eat your bread with enjoyment, and drink your wine with a merry heart. . . . Enjoy life. . . . Whatever your hand finds to do, do with your might (Eccl. 9:9-10)."[25]

24. LW, vol. 37, pp. 92, 72.
25. Quoted in Bayer, p. 48.

A New Liberalism of the Word

Fleming Rutledge

You know neither the Scriptures nor the power of God.

Matt. 22:29; Mark 12:24

For God has consigned all men to disobedience, that he may have mercy upon all.

Rom. 11:32

What ails the mainline churches? The question has become almost commonplace. As this collection of essays is being assembled, the American denominations in direct descent from the Reformation are being challenged as never before in our history. Weekly if not daily, it seems, a new article declares that the mainlines are "losing ground" or are "in decline," if not "collapsing" or "imploding" or "in free fall." At the same time, the denominations are splitting along lines described as "liberals" vs. "conservatives," "revisionists" vs. "traditionalists," with acrimony to spare. Perceptive observers of the American scene emphasize the chasm between the intellectual and media elite, on the one hand, and the huge, politically influential "Christian Right" on the other. The mainlines are barely holding their traditional center. Although many individual congregations are actually thriving, the overall statistics and projections for the traditional Protestant churches are dire.

The purpose of this essay is to state the case for a resurgence of Protestant vigor, confidence, and theological strength in the midst of widespread predictions of mainline demise. Never before in American history have the denominations descended from the Reformation had such an opportunity for renewal, yet we find ourselves beset with weakness as others set the agenda for us.

I am writing not as an academic, but as a pastor-theologian who spends a good deal of time visiting and interacting with congregations throughout the United States. My argument for describing our era as uniquely suited to Protestant renewal arises out of several observations. To begin with, a great deal of political and sociological commentary during the past few years indicates that most of "red" America has enthusiastically embraced the common description of itself as the most religious country in the Western world. The intellectual, urban "blue-state" elite is dismayed by this designation, but at the same time, even in those circles there remains a residual respect for educated, liberal Protestantism (the role of Catholicism, while vital, lies outside the scope of these reflections). Signals coming from the op-ed pages of *The New York Times* suggest that even militant secularists might welcome a stronger, reasoned voice coming from the mainline churches as a counterweight to the politically conservative Christian Right.

In twenty-first-century America, there will be a continuing threat to our national values as anxiety about terrorism results in increased bellicosity and violation of civil rights. Some of the most penetrating commentary since September 11 has come from writers who are worried about the way that Americans are being encouraged to think in terms of neat divisions between Good and Evil. This breezy, unexamined confidence about American motives cannot withstand the critique of Scripture, but the witness of the mainline Protestant denominations has been muted because these churches have become focused on internal issues and lack the confidence to speak truth to power. The mass media are interested in us only if we are fighting about sexuality; we seem to be losing our public voice.

Another defining factor since September 11 is the tremendously heightened attention being given to the polarity between religious faith that has adapted to modernity, on the one hand and, on the other, what is increasingly being called "fundamentalism." This is the way the conflict is being framed by many of our leading journalists and commentators. We should, I think, resist this way of describing the situation. For one thing, there is a strong case to be made (though it is often repressed for political reasons, as in the current debate about the European Constitution) that Christianity was a leading factor in making modernity possible in the first place.[1] A second problem is the

---

1. "Modernity" is to be distinguished from "modernism." This essay does not address the question of modernism and post-modernism.

term "fundamentalism." It is no longer being used in its strict sense to denote a specific movement within twentieth-century American Christianity. As with the term "liberal," it may be too late to reclaim this word; it is now being used to mean "fanaticism." The trouble is that anyone who holds strongly to a biblical view and argues for it with energy and passion is in danger of being called a fanatic. This is doubly true in circles where theology and Christology have been weakened by the inroads of enormously popular and influential books questioning the New Testament canon and the creedal affirmations about Jesus. A strong offensive from clergy and lay leaders can offset this trend, but this offensive must be undertaken in a spirit suited to the times, with a high degree of tolerance for ambiguity, nuance, and irony. When this happens, the culture pays attention.

There are other aspects to my argument about the demonstrable need for a renascence of Protestantism in our time. People of genuine community spirit recognize the need for thriving churches, because healthy congregations mean increased social services. Such people of good will acknowledge that they want to see the churches succeed in their traditional role of helping and rescuing. They want to see programs for lonely seniors, advocacy for the homeless, adult guidance for young people. None of this is possible if the mainlines are not strong. Moreover and quite plainly, a healthy society needs well-managed institutions. The spectacle of mainline decline is not encouraging to anyone except, perhaps, those in the nondenominational mega-churches who note that attrition in the traditional denominations feeds their own mission. In addition, though on an admittedly lower level of importance, the sight of a thriving, well-maintained landmark church building on Fifth Avenue, Nassau Street, or Copley Square is encouraging even to those who never go into them, whereas a dilapidated or abandoned church building creates a sense of unease and civic malaise.

Excellence in leadership will always be recognized in local communities. It is true that the respect which automatically used to be extended to the white ministers of America[2] has eroded dramatically since the sixties, but in my extensive travels around the mainlines I have noted that this need not be so. Clergymen and women of stature who have genuine gifts of leadership still command respect in their towns and small cities, and not only in the South, either — in some cases even the great cities of America. Yet these are exceptions. In most cases, the role of the clergyman or woman as a commu-

---

2. Many black ministers still command respect in the wider community, partly because many of them have retained their biblical voice, seamlessly weaving their way in and out of public issues.

nity force is not what it might be. Many pastors see themselves chiefly as therapeutic figures, seeking validation from their ministrations to their own flock person by person, so that their effectiveness is evaluated by their congregations on the basis of their kindness to parishioners in time of need, rather than the power of their witness to the gospel. This trend is not new; it has been under way since the middle of the nineteenth century.[3]

Hand in hand with this trend is the degree to which the academic and intellectual elite have succeeded in cowing the mainline clergy. I have often reflected upon an occasion when I was having lunch with a person in this category and he asked me conspiratorially, "Do you believe in God?" Obviously he had known many pastors and priests who were evasive about such questions; he half-expected me to say, "Well, no, not really." Many clergy, finding themselves in this atmosphere, have capitulated; my files are full of clippings about clergy who seem to take pride in their skepticism about God — the God of the Bible in particular. However, two decades of interacting with writers, academics, and pundits in New York City has convinced me that, in spite of all appearances, the secular ruling classes do not entirely intend to intimidate us. I am convinced that we *lose* respect when we capitulate to the imagined expectations of the supposedly enlightened, and that such people actually react more favorably to us when we remain faithful to our authentic calling than they do when we temporize. Granted, it often does not seem that way; one must be prepared for dismissive remarks, theologically ignorant pronouncements, and withering assessments of the Church for its many sins. In my view, however, we have allowed ourselves to be intimidated by this for too long. In Leander Keck's formulation, the church may repent, but it must not whimper.

This description of the situation in the mainline churches is necessarily sketchy. I do not mean to suggest that pastors should abandon hands-on works of mercy and return to their studies. Still less do I mean that the church should be content to become one community organization among many simply because the country needs "faith-based institutions." I am only arguing that the churches need to be strong in order to mount the critique of the body politic that the biblical faith requires. When theological confidence wanes, such critiques are impossible. Church members lose their sense that, as Paul Lehmann used to say, "God is up to something in the world." They therefore fall back on ministries that are indistinguishable from those of secular social

---

3. This shift from power in the pulpit and community to ministry in the private and domestic sphere is described by Ann Douglas in her classic study, *The Feminization of American Culture* (New York: Knopf, 1977).

agencies, and God is not praised through their work. Nor is the worshipping community upbuilt in such cases, for a rationale built on works alone cannot sustain the radical conviction that God justifies the ungodly, the uncooperative, and the illiberal (Rom. 5:6-8). Without an undergirding commitment to God's justification of the ungodly, there can be no true fellowship with those members who cannot or do not work the works at the same level as the congregation's leaders.

Speaking as one who has traveled extensively through the mainline churches and listened to hundreds of sermons over a number of years, I believe that the essential problem can be precisely identified in the words of Jesus to the Sadducees: "Is not this why you are wrong, that you know neither the scriptures nor the power of God?" Jesus' point against the Sadducees is that the power of God is able to create an entirely new reality that transcends all human categories.

The link between the two — the Scriptures and the power of God — is the key. The power of God is manifest through his Word. This is the power that called the creation into being, it is the force that created the Church in the first place, it is the engine that drove the Reformation — yet this power today is increasingly less heard from mainline pulpits, either as thunder or as a still small voice, for we have largely ceased to believe that God speaks. All the symptoms arise from that cause. That is the underlying ailment that is producing the morbid effects.

Flannery O'Connor, patron saint of those who care about language and Christian doctrine, wrote to a friend:

> One of the effects of modern liberal Protestantism has been gradually to turn religion into . . . therapy, to make truth vaguer and vaguer and more and more relative, to banish intellectual distinctions, to depend on feeling instead of thought, and gradually to come to believe that God has no power, that he cannot communicate with us, cannot reveal himself to us, indeed has not done so and that religion is our own sweet invention.[4]

We have gradually come to believe that God has no power and has not revealed himself to us. That, I think, is exactly what has happened. Over and over again, for years upon years, I have listened to sermons which begin well but drift off before the end. The staying power is just not there. The mighty climax never takes place. Preachers begin promisingly and then the conviction and the narrative force just dribble away. In the final analysis the prob-

---

4. Flannery O'Connor, "Letter to Alfred Corn," in *The Habits of Being* (New York: Farrar, Straus, Giroux, 1979), p. 479.

lem is not rhetorical; it is *theological*. The subject of these sermons is not God. The current emphasis on "spirituality" puts the focus on us and our religious activities, rather than on God. The "spirituality" so much in vogue today is *anthropo*logical rather than *theo*logical.

Underlying all of this is the question of power, of *dunamis*. The idea that the Word of God is powerful *in and of itself* has been fading in the mainlines for a long time. I am reminded of a characteristic locution in the African-American churches. A church member will say, "Who is going to bring the message today?" or "Thank you, Reverend, for bringing the message." We don't say that in the mainlines. We say, "Who's preaching today?" or "Thank you for the sermon." The idea of a message coming *with its own power* seems to lie outside our set of convictions; yet the entire biblical story is founded on that reality, and without it, the essential meaning of biblical revelation is lost. Take for example the characteristic self-introduction of Elijah the prophet:

> Now Elijah the Tishbite, of Tishbe in Gilead, said to Ahab, "*As the Lord the God of Israel lives, before whom I stand,* there shall be neither dew nor rain these years, except by my word." *And the word of the Lord came to him.* (1 Kings 17:1-2)

This resounding declaration sets forth some fundamental presuppositions of biblical faith:

- Our God is a living God.
- Those chosen to be his servants stand before him to receive their commissions.
- His word comes to us with power to execute what it demands.

How do we go about reclaiming this confidence in *the God who speaks?* How can seminary professors and academic theologians contribute to the revitalization of the churches? How are the preachers to make this God known to our people, especially if we are not certain ourselves? How are we to shake off our timidity before the culture and its apparent imperatives? *If the trumpet gives an uncertain sound, who shall prepare herself for the battle?* (1 Cor. 14:8).

The vitality of Protestantism will come in the present as it came in the past, through the power of the Word itself — the reinvigorating, re-creating and revolutionary *dunamis* of the Holy Spirit, enlivening and interpreting the message. Let us therefore take a look at the message itself, and the way that it can easily be misread and weakened as a description of our religious selves, rather than a proclamation *(kerygma)* that is itself the power of God. Here for example is Romans 10:14-17, with some words emphasized in Greek for reasons that will become clear:

> But how are they to call upon him in whom they have not believed? And how are they to believe in him of whom they have never heard? And how are they to hear without a preacher [better translated as "one heralding" or "one announcing" — the root is the same as *kerygma*]? And how can people preach unless they are sent? As it is written, "How beautiful are the feet of the ones who announce [the root is *euangelion*] good things!" But not all obeyed the gospel [*euangelion*]. As Isaiah says, "*Kurie*, who has believed our *akoē* [*šĕmûʿâ*]? So then faith is from *akoē*, and the *akoē* is through [by means of — *dia* seems to denote efficient cause here] the word of Christ *(rhēmatos Christou)*.

First we should note that the word meaning "preach," or "announce," is also the word for the gospel itself. As is so often the case with our Scriptures, nouns have the force of verbs. The principal point I wish to make, however, has to do with the Hebrew word *šĕmûʿâ*. which, in the book of Isaiah, denotes the revelatory and performative Word of God. In the LXX, the word is translated in Greek as *akoē*. This linguistic link is crucial. In the passage just cited, Paul is quoting Isaiah; he uses the word *akoē* in place of *šĕmûʿâ* ("Who has believed our *akoē*?" "Faith comes from *akoē*"). How is this word to be translated into English? Let us investigate.

The passage seems to be about preaching, a human activity with God as its object. "How are they to believe [in God] . . . without a preacher?" The preacher's job, in this view, is to speak about God in order that people will believe; the sermon directs the attention of the hearer toward the sermon's object, which is God. This is the way that the Romans passage would ordinarily be read by anyone who was not sufficiently instructed in the way that Paul's Greek works. But this is not at all what Paul intends. Verse 17 gives us the clue:

> *ara hē pistis ex akoēs, hē de akoē dia rhēmatos Christou* — "So faith comes from what is heard, and what is heard comes by the preaching [or word] of Christ" (RSV and NRSV).

Everything depends on the crucial phrase *ex akoēs*, how it is understood and how it is translated. If we read it without Luther and Calvin breathing down our necks, we are likely to put the emphasis on human reception of the proclamation. The tradition of the Reformation, however, has taught us to look again. Even a lover of the King James Version such as myself must admit that many improvements were needed, and this is such a case. The KJV says "Faith cometh *by hearing*." The NIV also has "faith comes by hearing." Most people will understand this to mean that *hearing* is a human response to the preaching of the gospel. That's not what the KJV translators meant to convey, since they go on in the next clause to translate that *hearing comes by the Word of God*. Most people who have not been instructed in the theological language of the Bible, however, will miss the point, having already misunderstood Paul to be saying that *our receptive listening* results in faith. Naturally this leads us to place the emphasis on the human act of hearing, thus making human beings the central agents both in the speaking and in the receiving of the evangel. This in turn will lead to preacherly exhortations to have more faith, or to work harder at having faith, and consequently to much worry about not having a sufficient amount of faith, or an acceptable quality of faith, and this leads to more and more emphasis on human activity and less and less emphasis on the creative activity of God. Thus the *kerygma* is lost.

In Isaiah, however, the word translated "hearing" in English clearly does not mean that in Hebrew or in Greek. It means *the message itself*. That is the chief insight. If we translate the word *akoē* as "hearing," with the human being as the acting subject doing both the speaking and the hearing, we will be so far off Paul's track that we will have great difficulty getting on again. Careful scrutiny (*pace* the KJV and NIV teams) will reveal that there really is no way to translate *akoē* as "hearing." It makes no sense to say, "Lord, who has believed our hearing?" For once, the New English Bible, of all things, has it right: "Isaiah says, 'Lord, who has believed *our message?*'" and Paul goes on, "We conclude that *faith is awakened by the message*, and the message that awakens it [faith] comes through the word of Christ" (The RSV and NRSV are also not far off the mark, rendering *akoē* as "what is heard").

So, to sum up this analysis of Romans 10:17, Paul is relying on the LXX translation of Isaiah's *šĕmûʿâ* as *akoē*, to convey his meaning. The power in Christian proclamation is *God's message itself*. Therefore if *akoē* is wrongly translated as "hearing," the emphasis is on the human choice. But if it is translated "message," meaning *God's revelatory and performative word*, then all the emphasis is transferred to God's action, not ours. This is the message, the *evangel*, understood as victorious power, the power that removes human "spiritual" capacity to the margins altogether, so that God says (again from Isaiah):

> I have been found by those who did not seek me;
> I have shown myself to those who did not ask for me (Isa. 65:1).

As if to underline his meaning, Paul quotes from this paradoxical Isaianic passage in order to show that the Word of God penetrates even the will that is set against God. The emphasis is on the message *(akoē, kerygma, euangelion)* as invading, victorious power. As Paul reminded the Thessalonians, "Our gospel came to you not only in word, but also in power and in the Holy Spirit and with full conviction" (1 Thess. 1:5). When Paul speaks of full conviction, he does not mean what we would mean by such a phrase; he does not mean that he himself was fully convinced, but that the Spirit was the agent of fully convincing the Thessalonians through the *akoē* itself. Thus the agency remains with God throughout. This is a crucial distinction, because a major theme of the Scriptures is the purposeful action of God's Word, not the distorted reception of that Word by flawed human beings.

Reflecting then on the difference between what is *kerygmatic* and what is not, we may say that the *kerygma* is unconditional because it does not stand back and wait to see how the human being will respond. It is an announcement that creates its own conditions. The *kerygma* makes something happen. It does not *ask for* something to happen, it does not *suggest that* something happen, it does not *question whether* something *might* happen *if* the congregation cooperates. Rather, *in the very words themselves,* it is *already happening.* Belief in this power of the Word of God is a gift; its nature is to grant confidence that the Word will accomplish that which it promises. "Grant what you command," prayed Augustine, "and then command what you will" *(Da quod jubes, et jube quod vis).* "My word shall not return to me empty, but it shall accomplish that which I purpose, and prosper in the thing for which I sent it," says the Lord (Isa. 55:11).

How is all of this related to the future of the mainline Protestant churches? I am arguing two things:

First, we need a renewed confidence in the Scriptures and the power of God. Another way of saying this is that we need to recover the theology of the Word of God. I am not speaking here only of preaching, since we can all think of congregations that have gathered around great preaching only to drift away because insufficient attention was given to the equipping of the saints. The really powerful congregations today are those whose members are not only inspired, converted, convicted, and empowered by the Sunday sermon but also nurtured and stretched during the week by the call to discipleship. The balance here is quite delicate; just as we can think of examples of congregations that have a shallow commitment to a showy preacher, so also we can name congregations that are involved in countless programs of social outreach but have no theological understanding of why they are doing these things. Either way, the gospel suffers. A renascence of confidence in the gospel will give us a context in which to engage the controversies in which we find ourselves embroiled. This leads to my next point.

Second, we need a stronger theological basis for inclusivity than we have at present. The underlying reason that the mainline denominations are in danger of splitting is not that people disagree about homosexuality. The reason is that a strong minority of the members of these denominations are beginning to recognize — however inchoate their understanding may be — that the theological foundation of the new teaching about sexuality is insufficient, and that the Scriptures are not being interpreted with the sort of reverent searching that believers would like to see from their leaders.

Many of these distressed church members are beginning to fall back on the labels "liberal" and "conservative." This is unfortunate. Perhaps it is too late to reclaim the word "liberal," but its connotations surely belong to the spirit of the Christian gospel: generous, open-handed, free, spacious, abundant, bountiful. How can "conservative" compete with that? It sounds narrow, pinched, fearful, retrograde — and for that very reason many Christians who stand on the Scriptures and the Creeds refuse the term. Theological liberalism in the mainlines today, however, is open to serious criticism because of its sentimental insufficiency.[5] To give just one of many possible examples, the slogan of the Episcopal Church during the nineties was, "No outcasts." This sounded wonderful; who could object to it? Surely this is in the spirit of Jesus who made a special point of befriending outcasts. But because the slogan lacked theological grounding and was never connected to the full biblical story — which does after all have something to say about the universal reign of sin and judgment for all parties — it was by default associated with the specific administration of one Presiding Bishop. The "conservatives" in the denomination soon began to feel, with some justification, that they were the new outcasts. The slogan, in other words, lost its connection to the story of God and became an identifying tag for a particular kind of human project with all the prejudices that necessarily accrue to such ventures. The foundation for inclusivity was not strong enough or broad enough to include those who were, rightly or wrongly, labeled as evangelicals, conservatives, or (worst) fundamentalists.

By the same token, of course, the litmus tests administered by the conservatives for full status within their assemblies have left various people feeling marginalized as well. No matter how "Christ-centered" and "Bible-

---

5. Perhaps the terms "post-liberal" and "post-conservative" may prove to be more helpful.

believing" (to use some of the code words) those persons might be, there was no room for them if they did not toe the line on such matters as abortion, stem-cell research, and homosexuality. Many sincere evangelically-minded clergy have known the pain of being declared "not sound." Speaking generally of church life today, neither on the right nor on the left have we seen a truly radical understanding of what the gospel declares to be true about our status before God and one another. The doctrine of justification by grace through faith alone is given much lip service, but the reality on the ground seems to be justification by right doctrine, whether it be a narrowly conceived biblicism on the right or a set of politically correct dogmas on the left. These polarizations have become so predominant in mainline church life that it is difficult to point to exceptions. Many congregations claim to be largely free of conflict, but that is usually for one or two reasons: (1) those who disagree have gone elsewhere; or (2) the difficult issues — homosexuality in particular — are being studiously ignored.

Our urgent need, I would therefore argue, is a serious and intentional theological examination of the question, "On what basis can we be truly liberal?" I was much struck by the recent testimony of Andrew Young, whose liberal political credentials are beyond question. In a wide-ranging interview he spoke of his concerns for the world we are bequeathing to his grandchildren, "the confusion we're creating in the global order." He is described as the most popular Democrat in the state of Georgia, black or white, but even so, he is intensely disliked by Georgia Republicans, and remains the butt of hateful racist jokes. Yet he said this about his days in Congress: "Almost everything I tried to do in Congress I was able to do because I worked both sides of the aisle. Conservatives were always in the prayer groups, and I attended. Every Wednesday morning, we had Bible study. Almost everybody there was an extreme conservative. But they saw me as sincere, and I could also share their religious conviction — but give it a little different twist."[6]

We should not romanticize or idealize African-American Christians, but as the spirit of the black church has led the way for us before, it might do so again. Andrew Young's model is one that the liberal mainlines might ponder. In the black church there is a tradition of forgiveness and tolerance, a faith in the power of redemption for every person, which perseveres in spite of endless slights and hurts. Might we not see a hint of a new type of genuine liberalism here? The model is based in a sincere love of Scripture and a trust in its power to create a new reality, the power of the God who "makes a way

6. David M. Halbfinger, "Young May Try to Add 'Senator' to Résumé," *The New York Times,* 18 August 2003.

out of no way" in a formulation made famous by Rev. Young and his colleagues. This is the God who "raises the dead and calls into existence the things that do not exist" (Rom. 4:17).

There are times when Christians' varying stances on such subjects as (for instance) homosexuality, war, abortion, and capital punishment seem to render fellowship across the left-right divide impossible. Each of us has our flash points; there are issues which we care about so fundamentally that we cannot imagine achieving any sort of rapprochement with those who disagree. There is such a thing as a *status confessionis* and there are times when Christians must divide. It is instructive to note, however, that there have been only a few such times in our history. The Confessing Church of the Nazi era was the paradigm. In America, the failure of many of the white churches to support the civil rights movement made another such witness necessary. Perhaps it trivializes the apocalyptic (revelatory) nature of those apocalyptic times to call this or that movement in the churches today by the name of Confessing Church. Dietrich Bonhoeffer looks more important today than he ever has, not so much as a systematic theologian but as a model for what a radical Christian looks like. How would he fit into the Church today? He can be (and is) claimed by evangelicals and liberals alike, but this is owing more to his status as a martyr than to the challenging nature of his late writings which, when read without hagiographic backlighting, have the capacity to unnerve everyone. The exact meaning of his call for a "religionless Christianity" will always be open to debate, since he did not live to put it into context, but the depth of his trust in the Scriptures and the power of God cannot be doubted, and his radical questioning arises out of a faith grounded in just that way, while at the same time proving itself utterly fearless about anything that modernity might throw in its direction.

The lay Episcopal theologian William Stringfellow was another figure who does not easily fit into either camp. The body of work that he left us suffers from sloppy editing and unchecked polemical ire, but its value consists in its radical challenge to the principalities and powers *precisely on Biblical grounds*. He knew both the Scriptures and the power of God. That is what continues to make him unusual as a figure who is cherished by the liberal wing in the church. His vision of what a Christian should look like was (and is) enthusiastically embraced by the left, but his theological stance was actually more encompassing than many realize. Stringfellow's theological project was able to accommodate the likelihood that God was working not only through the *bien-pensant* Left but also through the disreputable Right. This was even more true of another radical figure who is still with us, Will Campbell. It was Campbell who, from his post on the frontier of the darkest hours of the civil rights movement, shockingly reminded us that under certain circumstances, blacks would be perfectly capable of marching whites into death camps. Like many other theologians who have drawn deeply from the well of the Reformation, Stringfellow and Campbell both refuse to declare anyone innocent, either on the Right or on the Left. By the standards of Romans 9–11, these two are as thoroughly Pauline as anyone in the Church today in their conviction that the power of God's Word will overturn all our conventional assumptions and cause something completely new to come into being — something that will bring surprise and shock to absolutely everyone across the spectrum, as in Matthew 25 where both "sheep" and "goats" are confronted with a message that they clearly did not expect. A key text here is Romans 11:32: "For God has consigned all men to disobedience, that he may have mercy upon all."

Therefore the difference that really counts between liberals and conservatives in the Church is not specific issues such as homosexuality or even peace and justice, because individual Christians may disagree in good faith about exactly how peace and justice are to be achieved. Nor, I think, is it even the problem of "fundamentalism." My sense is that the question that really counts is whether or not there is a living God. I do not say "loving" God, because the mainlines are not failing to preach a loving God. The issue that divides us is not the centrality of *agapē* in the proclamation of the gospel; it would be difficult to disagree about that. The question, rather, is whether God and his Word are "living and active." The issue is whether God is "up to something in the world."

To repeat, Flannery O'Connor's assessment is correct. We have "come to believe that God has no power, that he cannot communicate with us, cannot reveal himself to us, indeed has not done so and that religion is our own sweet invention." If this is true, the question now arises, what is the antidote for this condition we find ourselves in? The antidote will begin with a recognition that we are suffering from a famine of the Word of God (Amos 8:11), which *speaks into existence that which does not exist.* This is the creation *ex nihilo.* Where there is no faith in the power of God, the power of God creates faith. Where there is acrimony and dissension, exposure to the living Word means a new vision where even our most important religious distinctions are abolished — circumcision is nothing, and uncircumcision is nothing, as Paul says three different times (1 Cor. 7:19; Gal. 5:6; 6:15). Therefore the human activity of reading and expounding the power-filled Word of God is the antidote.

In saying this, I am in no sense proposing a retreat from active involvement in social problems. On the contrary. Doing real Christian *theology* puts us in the forefront of all the struggles of our time, because that is where our

God *(theos)* is at work. He is up to something. Our task is to discern, through study of the scriptures in the context of the worshipping community, what God is doing in the world so that we can move where he is moving. The events of the twentieth century in America — the civil rights movement, the anti–Vietnam War protests, the nuclear disarmament, and environmental movements — were catalysts for the mainline churches, who were significantly represented on the front lines in spite of our inner divisions. This background should have equipped us for engagement with the issues of our present time, but instead, we seem to be in retreat. My proposal is that the single most powerful factor in overcoming the liberal-conservative theological divide is a renewal of confident preaching and teaching of historic, Nicene, Biblical faith.

My experience is that when Christians of varying perspectives are willing to study Scripture together in a seriously committed way, remarkable things happen. This is difficult to accomplish in the present atmosphere of the mainlines. William Stringfellow tells a story both amusing and alarming:

> I recall, a few years ago, serving on a commission of the Episcopal Church charged with articulating the scope of the total ministry of the Church in modern society. The commission [included] a few laity and the rest [were] professional theologians, ecclesiastical authorities and clergy. . . . Toward the end of [the first] meeting, some of those present proposed that it might be an edifying discipline for the group, in its future sessions, to undertake some concentrated study of the Bible. It was suggested that constant recourse to the Bible is as characteristic and significant a practice in the Christian life as the regular . . . celebration of the Eucharist, which was a daily observance of this commission. Perhaps, it was suggested, Bible study would enlighten the deliberations of the commission. . . .
>
> The proposal was rejected on the grounds, as one Bishop put it, that "most of us have been to seminary and know what the Bible says; the problem now is to apply it to today's world." The bishop's view was seconded (with undue enthusiasm, I thought at the time) by the Dean of one of the Episcopal seminaries as well as by the clergy from national headquarters who had, they explained, a program to design and administer.
>
> The point in mentioning the incident . . . is that the notion implied in the decision not to engage in Bible study is that the Gospel, in its Biblical embodiment, is . . . a static body of knowledge which, once systematically organized, taught, and learned, [is thereafter used] ceremonially, sentimentally, nostalgically.[7]

7. William Stringfellow, *Count It All Joy* (Grand Rapids: Eerdmans, 1967).

261

I quote this passage at some length because it so precisely identifies the various components of the problem: the busy commission with its agenda, the learned scholars who disdain the layman, the bureaucrats who are wedded to their programs (today we are more likely to hear of "process"), the bishops who have no sense of themselves as theologians, the seminary dean who is accustomed to thinking of the Bible merely as one of several academic subjects taught by specialists in his institution. Stringfellow's diagnosis is right on target: the life-giving power of the Word of God is unknown to the group's leaders. The decision-making bodies in the churches have an exaggerated sense of their own importance and very little understanding of the way that the *kerygma* creates new realities wherever it is heard — and particularly when it is at work in groups of people who would not otherwise be capable of coming together around a genuinely *theo*logical message. As Douglas Harink puts it in his important new book, "The Scriptures have the power not only to direct and guide the community *but also to constitute the world for it*."[8] This is where we have been lacking confidence. We have lost hold of the conviction that the message is not only powerful in itself but also is able to bring into being a new reality that is part of God's eternal order, already planted in the world.

The Christian community has no independent existence. It must be perpetually renewed and refashioned by the power of God. "Constant recourse to the Bible" is indeed the "characteristic and significant practice" of the Church when it is receiving its life *theo*logically and not *anthropo*logically. Anthropology as an academic discipline is a noble field of study, but it does not get us very far along in the Christian life because it is solipsistic; it goes round and round on itself. Thus, when visiting museums of anthropology, one reads label after label saying, "The Inuit believe that . . . ," "the Old Norse religion was . . . ," "this amulet was thought to. . . ." There is no sense whatsoever that any of this is founded in any sort of reality beyond anthropological practice. The museum-goer is implicitly invited to respect all these different beliefs while at the same time subtly distancing herself from them. In contrast, the Scripture states with a shocking lack of tact, "I am the Lord, there is no other." When the community receives this Word in faith, the transforming power of God shapes our consequent actions *theo*logically, according to the *theos* who speaks. For this reason the Church's true witness can never be simply imitations of trends in the culture and indistinguishable from them. The radical message of the justification of the ungodly cuts across race, class, ethnicity, political views, and degrees of moral worthiness as such things are or-

8. Douglas Harink, *Paul Among the Postliberals* (Grand Rapids: Brazos Press, 2003), p. 19.

dinarily measured. It reaches far beyond the currently fashionable mantra of "inclusion." The insufficiency of this buzz-word becomes apparent when it proves too small to "include" those who are out of fashion with the current keepers of the ideological gates.

One way to illustrate the problem might be to ask what would happen if the "conservatives" capitulated on the issue of, say, homosexuality. Would they be welcomed back into the fold? What then? What would the next issue be? And what would the criterion for discernment be then? Sooner or later the cut must be made; we cannot be "inclusive" to the world's end unless we are willing to turn it over to God and live in the meanwhile "as though not" *(hōs mē)*. Surely this is something like what Paul meant when he wrote to the Corinthians, "The appointed time has grown very short; from now on let . . . those who mourn [live] as though they were not mourning, and those who rejoice as though they were not rejoicing, and those who buy as though they had no goods, and those who deal with the world as though they had no dealings with it. For the form of this world is passing away" (1 Cor. 7:29-31). Andrew Young's Congressional Bible study was an example of disagreeing "as though not" disagreeing, for the form of this world in which Christians are at odds with one another is passing away — and in its place there comes a world where there is neither agreeing nor disagreeing, but a new creation. In the verse immediately following the text for this essay, Jesus says something remarkably similar to the Sadducees: "In the resurrection they neither marry nor are given in marriage, but are like angels in heaven." Thus our sights are lifted so that we can catch a glimpse of the world of the Kingdom of God where every human category is swept away so that God can be all in all.

These convictions underlie my proposal for a new type of liberalism even more "inclusive" than the old type. It will arise out of the story of God's movement to us in Jesus Christ, not our movement toward him; it will be celebrated in the praise of God without reference to our own deeds except in thanksgiving because we have been given the power of the Spirit to participate in God's work. A new alliance of academy and pulpit will be required for the task of reviving the voice of the mainline churches without flagging in our longstanding commitments to social action. We need to find more and better ways to bring the very best biblical and theological scholarship to bear not only on creating new members of the academic guilds but also on the formation of men and women who will go out to be ministers of the Word. The artificial split between biblical studies and theology in the academy needs now more than ever to be bridged, as does the division between the Testaments. Congregations and clergy alike need equipping for the battle against the new gnosticism and the new skepticism about Jesus Christ. We need leadership for making the turn away from anthropology to theology. The antidote to mainline malaise in the present moment is a revivifying dose of Scripture and the power of God.

> Let all the earth fear the Lord,
> let all the inhabitants of the world stand in awe of him!
> For he spoke, and it came to be;
> > *he commanded, and it stood forth.* (Psalm 33:8-9)

Praise the Lord!

The Story That Shaped Paul's Way with Women

L. Ann Jervis

Myths play in the background of many of our statements and actions.[1] This commonsense observation is critical to effective communication. Understanding what story informs a person's or community's actions or words influences the meaning we make of them.[2] Perhaps one of the most valuable re-

---

1. I will use the terms 'story' and 'myth' interchangeably. As is commonly known, the basic meaning of the Greek word *muthos* is story or narrative. Of course, while a myth is always a story, a story is not always a myth. The difference between a story and a myth is that the story of a myth involves superhuman or extraordinary characters and events, whereas a non-mythic story need not. When I exchange the word 'story' for 'myth' it should be understood to signify a mythic rather than an ordinary story.

G. S. Kirk makes the valid point that there is not one definition of myth and that myths differ in terms of their social function (*Myth. Its Meaning and Functions in Ancient and Other Cultures* [Cambridge: University Press, 1970], p. 7). Nevertheless, it is possible, and for our purposes useful, to adopt the following definition of myth offered by D. Davies: "from the perspective of religious studies . . . myths [are] stories which enshrine religious and social ideals expressed through the activities of divine, human or animal figures within an environment where astonishing things may happen" ("Introduction: Raising the Issues," in *Myth and History*, ed. J. Holm and J. Bowker [London, New York: Pinter Publishers, 1994], p. 2).

It should be noted that whether or not myths also speak of history is not germane for my purposes. An ahistorical myth can have as profound an influence on individuals or a culture as can a historical event.

2. I venture to say that in this regard I share the view of Wallace M. Alston, Jr. In an important chapter titled "The Story of the Church" in his work on ecclesiology, *The Church of the Living God. A Reformed Perspective* (Louisville, KY: Westminster John Knox, 2002), Alston recognizes that to understand the church aright we must understand the story that undergirds it. Understanding this story means, in Alston's words, that to be part of the church is "to be joined with our Creator and Redeemer in the task of renovating the world" (p. 29). I have been privi-

sources for interpreting the statements and deeds of others (and of ourselves) is an awareness of the myth that influences them.

Among other things, myths tell stories in ways which convey judgments about what is right and what is wrong, about what is good and what is bad, about what is normal and what is not. Myths are not prescriptive but they are productive. They do not lay out rules for life, but they do produce explanations either of what is, or of what was, or of what could be, which may affect the choices we make. That is, myths convey values, but they do not prescribe them. For instance, the myth of the Superman, which, through Nietzsche, influenced and informed Nazism in the early part of the twentieth century,[3] did not prescribe the 'Final Solution', but its explanation of what could be — a race of superior people who conquered weaknesses of various sorts — affected the actions and words of the Nazi party. The myth of Odysseus, which influenced Greco-Roman civilization and has influenced our own, did not prescribe a life of journey towards home — of keeping one's eyes focused on a goal — but it has almost certainly influenced western culture to think and act in ways that value endurance, discipline, and individual courage.

Nevertheless, as already implied, the values that myths produce are not always logical outcomes of the myths themselves. For instance, the myth of Aeneas, as told by Virgil, in which Aeneas, after much torment, decides to leave Dido for the sake of his mission, influenced an antique worldview in which romantic love was seen as secondary to fulfilling a call. The struggle Aeneas faces in this regard might also have produced a worldview which recognized the empowering nature of romantic love and its essential role in helping people meet their goals.[4] Even though myths present values, they do not dictate values. And the values that may be endorsed by a myth are neither the only values the myth can be used to undergird, nor necessarily entirely consistent with it.

The question explored in what follows has to do with Paul and women. This, of course, is a question that has been asked many times. It is a question that comes not only because some of what Paul says about women clashes with modern western sensibilities, but also because Paul seems to clash with himself over this matter. This question will be explored in a new way, seeking

---

leged to see firsthand Dr. Alston's own commitment to this understanding of the story into which the church fits, and also to have benefited greatly from his friendship and encouragement, both of which reflect his participation in this story.

3. Crane Brinton wrote: "*Mein Kampf* . . . could hardly have been written without the aid of two of the great names in the cultural heritage of the West — Richard Wagner and Friedrich Nietzsche" (*Nietzsche* [Cambridge, MA: Harvard University Press, 1941], p. xv).

4. Perhaps this myth was an influence on the ideals of Medieval chivalry.

to hear Paul on this matter by uncovering the myth that may have informed his actions in regard to women, and his words about them.

Many have noticed the tension evident in Paul's letters between, on the one hand, his comfort with women as co-workers (see Rom. 16, Phil. 4:2-3), along with his statement in Gal. 3:28 that "in Christ there is not male and female," and, on the other hand, his patriarchal directives: "the head of a woman is her husband" (1 Cor. 11:3); or "women should keep silence in the churches; for they are not permitted to speak, but should be subordinate, as even the law says . . . it is shameful for a woman to speak in church" (1 Cor. 14:34-35).[5] This tension has produced a puzzle to which many scholars have turned their attention. The puzzle is usually arranged like this: on the one side we have evidence shaped by Paul's egalitarian views and practice, and on the other side we have evidence shaped by Paul's patriarchal views. The goal of the puzzle is to put the opposing shapes together into one whole.

One solution to the puzzle is that Paul had a vision for a *spiritual reality* which was gender-neutral. This vision forms the basis for his statement that "in Christ there is not male and female" (Gal. 3:28). However, Paul recognized that this spiritual reality could be only partially realized in the present. In the present moment the 'new order of creation' co-exists with the 'old order' of creation. And so, on the one hand, Paul felt comfortable with women praying and prophesying in public, working alongside women in his missionary work, and having women leaders in the churches. And yet, given that Paul understood that God had not completed God's work of healing the world, at times Paul endorses gender hierarchy. For Paul, the 'old order' remains until the Lord returns. Consequently, Paul can say (perhaps reluctantly) that the head of a wife is her husband and that women should be silent in church.[6]

Another solution to the puzzle is that Paul thought that Christ's work does not change the 'order of creation' — man is the lord of the woman, since woman was created out of man (Gen. 2). Christ's death and resurrection redeems, but does not change, the order of creation. In Christ the headship of man over woman is established in a new context. Gal. 3:28 simply means that both men and women are redeemed in Christ to take their proper (hierarchical) roles.[7]

---

5. I do not consider 1 Timothy to have been written by Paul. Consequently, 1 Tim. 2:9-15 does not factor into my considerations in this paper. I am agnostic about the authenticity of Colossians and Ephesians, and so neither do they figure in this investigation.

6. See, for example, R. B. Hays, *The Moral Vision of the New Testament. Community, Cross, New Creation* (New York: Harper San Francisco, 1996), p. 55.

7. For example, J. B. Hurley, *Men and Women in Biblical Perspective* (Grand Rapids: Zondervan, 1981), esp. pp. 138-61.

In what follows I attempt another solution to the puzzle. My investigation will explore the possibility that correctly identifying the myth that informed Paul's way with women can allow us to see the way the conflicting pieces of his words and actions may, in fact, rest comfortably together. The attempt to determine what myth may have influenced Paul's way with women has rarely been made, because the question has rarely been asked.[8] Some have indeed recognized the importance of hearing the myth that informed initial *misunderstandings* of Paul's words by, for example, the Corinthians.[9] Following in this line of inquiry we ask the question: What story lies behind Paul's *own* understandings about women and actions in regard to them?

In my view, two main contenders for the story or myth that influenced Paul on women have played in the background of interpretations of Paul on this matter. That is, interpretations of Paul's views of women have assumed, usually without argument, and in most cases seemingly unconsciously, that one of two myths influenced Paul.[10] One option for the underlying myth is that of the androgyne, and the other the myth of a divinely ordained two-gender humanity. It is to be noted that both stories are about the beginnings of humankind; both the story of androgyne and the myth of humanity created in two genders describe the origins of humanity. Consequently, they also imply something of its goal. As noted earlier, the issue of historicity is of no importance to the present discussion. Whether or not these myths speak of an actual event, they may significantly affect the cultures and individuals who know and use them.

The Myth of Androgyne and Paul's Way with Women

The story of androgyne, as it is found in the Jewish-Christian tradition,[11] reads the words of the first chapter of Genesis — "God created human kind

8. Daniel Boyarin stands out as one who has inquired along this line: "Following in the wake of Philo and thinkers like him, much of early Christianity beginning with Paul seemed to be dedicated to seeking a transcendence of gender . . . putting on Christ, baptism, meant for Paul . . . an eradication of gender, becoming like Philo's Therapeutae an avatar of the first Adam for whom there was no male or female" ("Gender," in *Critical Terms for Religious Studies,* ed. M. C. Taylor [Chicago: University of Chicago Press, 1998], p. 122).

9. W. Meeks, "The Image of the Androgyne: Some Uses of a Symbol in Earliest Christianity," *HR* 13 (1973): 165-208; L. A. Jervis, "'But I Want You to Know . . .': Paul's Midrashic Intertextual Response to the Corinthian Worshipers (1 Cor. 11:2-16)," *JBL* 112, no. 2 (1993): 231-46.

10. Perhaps, in fact, the influence of a certain myth has been greatest on the Pauline interpreter, who, often unwittingly, reads it into Paul.

11. See W. D. O'Flaherty for a survey of the myth of the androgyne in native North Amer-

in his image, in the image of God he created them; male and female *(arsen kai thēlu)*[12] he created them" (Gen. 1:27) — to mean that the original being created by God, and who is in the divine image, is androgynous. In the story of the androgyne the second creation account (Gen. 2), in which God creates a man out of the dust of the ground and a woman out of the man's rib, is regarded as the unfortunate second chapter; the man created out of the dust of the ground is not in the image of God and is cursed with being only male, and the woman who is formed out of this man is cursed with being only female. Genesis 2, then, tells the story of the beginnings of the human dilemma — the problem of humanity in two genders.

Here the myth of androgyne conveys the idea that the image of God is both male and female and that the ideal image for humanity is also androgynous. Wholeness for humanity comes when the unfortunate differentiation into two genders is overcome. When there is not male and female, then humanity is as it should be.

It is easy to understand how some have heard echoes of this myth in Paul's words in Gal. 3:28.[13] For one thing, the Greek words for male and female in Gal. 3:28 are exactly what they are in the Greek of Genesis 1:27. Paul's words to the Galatians may then be understood to be consciously echoing the first creation story; baptism into Christ means that believers are restored to the original androgynous image. Through baptism believers recapture the wholeness that was lost when the genders were divided. The goal of the story of androgyne — reunification of the genders — is achieved through Christ.

Before thinking more about whether the story of androgyne is in fact the best plot line into which to fit Paul's way with women, it is important to ponder what this myth came to signify in Paul's culture.

Myths create a certain order for people.[14] As noted above, myths create an understanding of what is right and natural, and of what is wrong and what is unnatural. Myths produce worldviews, although the worldview created by a myth is not always a logical outcome of it. Most often we are simply able to

---

ican, Australian, African, and South Asian societies (*Women, Androgynes, and Other Mythical Beasts* [Chicago, London: University of Chicago Press, 1980], pp. 283-334). Of course, it is also part of Greco-Roman culture (see, for instance, Plato, *Symposium,* 189c-191d).

12. This, of course, is the LXX translation.

13. H. D. Betz, for instance, proposes the hypothesis that behind Gal. 3:28 lies an understanding that Christ is androgynous and so are those baptized into him (*Galatians,* in Hermeneia [Philadelphia: Fortress, 1977], p. 199).

14. D. Davies notes that myths have "explanatory power" and make the world "less strange" (*Myth and History,* p. 1).

observe (without being able to give reasons for) the worldview connected to a myth. As was remarked earlier, the myth itself does not determine the values and social expectation which it is used to authenticate or nurture. At different points in history, in different contexts, a myth may be used for different purposes and to support different agendas. Consequently, while a myth creates order and an understanding of what is right and natural, this order and these values are not intrinsic to the myth but arise from the conversation between the myth and the culture in which it speaks. We may then *observe* what values and norms are regarded as consistent with a myth at a particular moment in time, although this observation is not at the same time an explanation of *why* these values or norms are attached to a myth.

At the time of Paul the worldview connected to the story of the androgyne appears to have included the idea that the male is normative and good, and that sexual abstinence was a way to achieve human perfection. This is evident when Philo and the *Gospel of Thomas* use the story of the androgyne. We see this also when Jerome alludes to the myth of androgyne.

Behind Philo's commentary on Genesis lies the story of the androgyne. Philo thought that the second creation account told the story of what he called the "man from the earth," which, in Philo's view, was a description of the human dilemma; human beings are stuck in the earth, whereas what we truly desire is to attain a vision of God. Proximity to divinity requires that we be reborn into the human being Genesis describes — the human being made after the divine image, the one who is neither male nor female (*Op. Mundi,* 133ff.). The way to achieve this goal is to use our minds and to subdue our senses. If we are to be transformed from the man formed of the earth we must, through the use of our minds, rid ourselves of our senses, which bind us to the earth. Philo, along with others such as Plato and Aristotle, identified as female the things that bind us to the earth. On the other hand, Philo identified the mind as male. Consequently, Philo writes: "perfect progress . . . is changing into the male, since the female gender is material, passive, corporeal and sense perceptible, while the male is active, rational, incorporeal and more akin to mind and thought."[15]

The *Gospel of Thomas* attributes to Jesus a saying in which Jesus tells his disciples that they will enter the Kingdom of heaven "when you make the two one . . . when you make the male and the female one and the same, so that the male is not male and the female is not female" (Log. 22). And yet, seemingly paradoxically, when Simon Peter says to Jesus that Mary should leave the group of disciples because she is a woman, Jesus' response is: "I myself shall

15. Philo, *Quaestiones et Solutiones in Exodum,* I.8.

lead her in order to make her male, so that she too may become a living spirit resembling you males. For every woman who will make herself male will enter the Kingdom of Heaven" (Log. 114).

These two examples demonstrate that contemporaries of Paul who were informed by the myth of androgyne saw that myth as consonant with a worldview in which the male was normative and what was female was deficient.

The story of androgyne was also regarded as consistent with an exaltation of celibacy. In Greco-Roman thinking abstinence from sexual activity was thought to allow a person more readily to attain the image of God.[16] As exaltation of celibacy finds its way into the Christian church, it does so at times through allusions to the story of the androgyne. For instance, Jerome, writing at the end of the fourth century, says: "*when difference of gender is taken away* and we put off the 'old man' and put on the 'new' (referring to Col. 3:9-10), then we shall be reborn in Christ, a virgin."[17] Jerome considers that to live in celibacy is to live like angels: "virgins begin on earth what others will be afterwards in Heaven."[18]

The myth of androgyne, then, bears the weight of the conviction that what is male is normative and what is female is to be discarded. Furthermore, it can serve to endorse the view that, in pursuit of perfection, sexuality is to be shunned.

We now ask whether this story can provide a context for understanding Paul's way with women. As mentioned, some have proposed that it does. This, however, is a proposal that is contradicted by some of the Pauline evidence. Indeed it is the case that, on the one hand, the myth of androgyne sits easily with Paul's words in Gal. 3:28 that there is not male and female. And, furthermore, if Paul is operating with this myth, the worldview attached to the myth of androgyne in his time could be seen to be reflected in those words which assume that the male is normative ('ask your husbands at home', 'the man is the head of the woman'); and in Paul's statement that he wishes everyone were unmarried, as he is (1 Cor. 7:7).

16. Philo, for instance, recounts with enthusiasm the activities of a group of celibate men and women — the Therapeutae. These men and women spent most of their time in private prayer cells. When they came together for the Sabbath, or for special feast days, they behaved with decorum, always returning to their private cells. Philo calls the Therapeutae citizens of heaven and friends of God, because they lived celibate lives totally devoted to God (*De Vita Contemplativa*, 90).

17. Jerome, *Against Jovinian*, quoted from E. A. Clark, *Women in the Early Church* (Collegeville, MN: The Liturgical Press, 1983), p. 128; italics mine.

18. Clark, *Women*, p. 131.

Nevertheless, if the story of the androgyne were behind Paul's words, it is curious that he should speak of women as his fellow-workers, without suggesting that they become male, or male-like.[19] One of the more telling challenges to the idea that the myth of androgyne informed Paul comes when we compare his attitude to men and women praying and prophesying together with Philo's. In the Corinthian church men and women prophesied and prayed together, experiencing the Spirit of God in such a dramatic way that Paul was convinced that if others came in they would recognize that God was in their presence (1 Cor. 14:25). Philo also describes a group of men and women who pray and prophesy and have God's presence with them (the Therapeutae). For our purposes, one of the features distinguishing the community Philo describes from that which Paul addresses is that Philo is convinced that their celibate lifestyle was the condition for God's presence with the Therapeutae.[20] After their gathering each of the Therapeutae goes alone to his or her private prayer cell to spend the rest of the week seeking the vision of God. This is not the case with the Corinthian Christians. The men and women who pray and prophesy together at Corinth are married; when they leave the assembly they return to the intimacy of married life.

It appears, then, that the story of the androgyne does not satisfactorily account for the full weight of the Pauline evidence. We turn now to investigating whether the other myth that has been heard behind Paul's words has more explanatory potential.

The Myth of Humanity in Two Genders and Paul's Way with Women

The other candidate for the underlying myth is, as mentioned earlier, based on the second creation account. The story, as the rabbis allude to it, goes like this: when God first created humanity, God created a two-faced being, that is, an androgynous being. But the creation of humanity was not finished until God cut this two-faced being in half and turned the resulting halves around.[21] In other words, humanity is supposed to be in two genders. The

19. We noted above that Philo and the *Gospel of Thomas* used the story of androgyne in a seemingly paradoxical way — to require females to become as males.

20. Philo, *De Vita Contemplativa*, 88-90.

21. E.g., "And God said let us make a human. . . . R. Samuel the son of Nahman said: 'When the Holiness [Be it blessed] created the first human, He made it two-faced, then He sawed it and made a back for this one and a back for that one.' [The Rabbis] objected to [R. Samuel]: but it says, 'He took one of his ribs.' He answered it means, 'one of his sides', simi-

Genesis 2 creation account is, then, not the second unfortunate chapter of the story of creation. The human goal is not to transcend the problem of the genders. Humanity is *meant* to be in two genders.

We find this story also in earlier commentaries on scripture. For instance, the Book of Jubilees, a Jewish commentary on Genesis from the second century B.C.E., considers that God designed humanity to be in two genders. Jubilees adds to the Genesis account that, as soon as the man saw the woman who had been created from his ribs, "he knew her."[22] In Jewish meditations on Genesis 2, then, sexuality is part of the goodness of creation. The man has sexual relations with the woman before the fall. The story of humanity in two genders does not consider that the goal of human life is to transcend the genders. Rather, humans are supposed to be in two genders and to find a mate and procreate.

There are similarities and differences between the worldview associated with the story of a divinely ordained two-gender humanity and the story of the androgyne. The *difference* is obvious. Whereas the story of the androgyne is associated in our period with an exaltation of celibacy,[23] the story of humanity in two genders lends itself to a celebration of sexuality and procreation. On the basis of the story of a two-gender humanity we find a rabbinic statement like: "a man who has no wife [will be banned from heaven]" (b. Pes. 113b).[24]

The *similarity* in worldview between the two stories is that, in both, the male takes priority. We have seen this in the worldview associated with the story of the androgyne — it is as a person becomes male that that person gets closer to God. The story of humanity in two genders also prioritizes the male, although in a different way. The worldview associated with this story creates rigid roles for men and women.[25] The male's role is that of leadership, of headship, because he is the one out of whom the woman was created. The woman is created as a helpmate, the one who is to help the male achieve his religious and social duties.

It would seem that the story of humanity in two genders influences readers of Paul (which is different from saying that it influenced Paul him-

---

larly to that which is written 'and the side of the tabernacle'" [*Genesis Rabba* 54-5; Theodor and Albeck].

22. *Jubilees* 3.6, trans. O. S. Wintermute, in *The Old Testament Pseudepigrapha*, vol. 2, ed. J. H. Charlesworth (New York: Doubleday, 1985).

23. The views of Philo and Jerome were mentioned above.

24. Quoted from T. Ilan, *Jewish Women in Greco-Roman Palestine* (Peabody, MA: Hendrickson, 1996), p. 57.

25. Noted by Boyarin, "Gender," p. 131.

self) to interpret his words in 1 Cor. 11:2-16 and 14:34-36 as meaning that women should never, in any circumstance, take leadership, for that would go against the divinely ordained hierarchy of the genders.[26] That is, the myth of a divinely ordained two-gender humanity appears to underlie the second solution to the puzzle set out above — that the order of creation is redeemed but is not changed in Christ.

The question is whether this myth informed Paul himself. In answer to that question, we note that it might explain his direction that women should not speak in church, and make sense of his statement that "the head of every woman is her husband." However, if this story *did* shape Paul's views, it is curious that Paul should himself be unmarried and even encourage others to remain unmarried. It is also curious that he should say that in Christ there is neither male and female, and that he should treat women as equal partners in working for the gospel.

Another Story about Beginnings and Paul's Way with Women

In light of the problems with regarding either the story of androgyne or the story of humanity in two genders as shaping Paul's way with women, it is here proposed that another story about beginnings informed the way Paul thought about and acted with women. The proposal made here is that the story which shaped Paul's way with women (as it did just about everything else in his life) was the story of Jesus Christ.

The idea that the story of Jesus is foundational to Paul's thought and action is now commonplace in Pauline studies.[27] However, the idea that this story also informed and influenced Paul's way with women has not been explored to any significant extent. We will begin this exploration by assuming

26. The following comment on 1 Cor. 11:2-16 is representative of this type of interpretation: "Paul reprobates this behaviour as unbecoming to a woman, because God has established a hierarchy in both the natural and the religious spheres, in which the female is subordinated to the male sex. This hierarchical subordination of the woman should be recognized in her behaviour and dress. The veil is a symbol of this subordination" (R. Kugelman, "The First Letter to the Corinthians," in *The Jerome Biblical Commentary*, ed. R. E. Brown, J. A. Fitzmyer, and R. E. Murphy [Englewood Cliffs, NJ: Prentice-Hall, 1968], p. 270).

27. R. B. Hays's influential monograph, *The Faith of Jesus Christ. An Investigation of the Narrative Substructure of Galatians 3:1–4:11*, SBLDS 56 (Chico, CA: Scholars Press, 1983), which presents the idea that Paul's theology (at least in Galatians) is rooted in the story of Jesus Christ, is representative of the dominant view on the entire Pauline corpus.

without argument that the story of Jesus Christ did undergird Paul's views on and actions towards women in the church, and then proceed to note the aspects of Christ's story which Paul emphasizes that are most interesting in this regard. Finally, we will test whether this story, as we are able to glimpse Paul's use of it, might indeed be the one that informs and influences his way with women.

Our first observation is that Paul emphasizes aspects of the story of Jesus Christ that would have been considered un-masculine in his culture. Paul's story of Jesus focuses on Jesus' shameful execution. Paul characterizes his message as a 'word of the cross' (1 Cor. 1:18). In fact, Paul is at pains to remind his converts that Jesus' crucifixion does not disappear in the resurrection light.[28]

As is well known, in Paul's time crucifixion was reserved as punishment for those society had shunned and discarded. It was the most shameful way to die. For a man to be crucified was for a man to be shamed; to be declared worthless, of no account. In Greco-Roman Mediterranean culture the most important thing a man had was his honor, and the worst thing that could happen to a man was to be shamed. To be shamed was, in effect, to lose one's masculinity, to take the female role.[29]

Paul lived in this culture. And, in response to interpretations of the Christian gospel that wanted to stress, almost exclusively, Jesus' victorious resurrection — interpretations such as the one some of the Corinthians were adopting; or that Paul's opponents in Galatia were preaching[30] — Paul stresses the cross. Paul stresses, in other words, the least masculine feature of the story of Jesus.

We might notice also that Paul does not take advantage of Jesus' willingness to die in order to draw attention to Jesus' courage — a virtue associated in the Greco-Roman world primarily with males.[31] Paul, however, does not say that Jesus faced his ignoble death with courage but rather that Jesus

---

28. We see this particularly in his correspondence with the Corinthians.

29. B. Malina makes the point that while there is female honor in Mediterranean cultures, a female is honorable as she acts out of sensitivity to shame. Honor works in reaction to its opposite — shame. The male aspect of honor is honor and the female aspect is shame (*The New Testament World. Insights from Cultural Anthropology*, 3rd and rev. ed. [Louisville, KY: Westminster John Knox, 2001], p. 53).

30. See my *Galatians*, NIBC (Peabody, MA: Hendrickson, 1999), p. 6.

31. The assumption in the Greco-Roman world was that, while women could be brave (see Musonius Rufus, *Fragment* 3 [*That Women Too Should Study Philosophy*]), courage, like the other cardinal virtues, was the province of the male, the one who had the freedom to make choices and who was blessed by nature with the capacity to reason. See Aristotle, *NE*, iii.6-9.

was obedient, like a servant: "taking the form of a servant, being born in the likeness of humanity, and being found in human form, Jesus humbled himself and became obedient unto death, death on a cross" (Phil. 2:8). Unlike the author of Revelation, Paul does not describe Jesus as a conqueror. The features of Jesus' story that Paul emphasizes (obedience, slavery, crucifixion) would not have commended Jesus as a man's man in the first-century world. Paul clearly decided to fight against a trend in the early Christian movement that sought to diminish the crucifixion chapter of Jesus' story. He chose not to shape his gospel solely around Jesus' mighty resurrection and glorious ascension. Instead, Paul never lets hearers of his letters forget that Jesus was like a humble slave, an obedient person who died an outcast's shameful death.

We might notice also what Paul does *not* say when he refers to the story of Jesus. Paul does not say that Jesus was male as opposed to female. Paul, of course, refers to Jesus as a man. However, Paul never uses that fact. That Jesus was a male and not a female was a historical fact; that Jesus, the Son of God, Messiah, would be anything other than male was unthinkable. Paul, however, does not accord Jesus' maleness a significance that some in later generations did. In fact, that Paul does not endorse a male-only leadership for his churches is clear evidence that he is thinking very differently on this matter from those who came later. To paraphrase Mary Daly's famous line, we do not find support in Paul for the idea that "if Christ is a male, then only males are as Christ."[32] In addition to the fact that Paul worked with women leaders (e.g., Phoebe), it is to be noted that Paul affirmed that in Christ there is not male and female. And, furthermore, that Paul does not make the paradoxical leap from that idea to the one that the female must become male, such as we find in the *Gospel of Thomas.* Furthermore, Paul can say that the head of a woman is her husband, but he does not say that this is so because the head of every man (Christ) *is male* (1 Cor. 11:3). Clearly, Paul is not inclined to take advantage of the masculine gender of the hero of his foundational story.

Jesus' male gender appears to be of so little consequence to Paul that, even when he does direct his churches to behave in ways that accord with his patriarchal society, Paul does not use Jesus Christ's male gender to validate his prescriptions. This fact is even more striking when we realize how much more logical it would have been for Paul to assume or argue for the priority of the male on the basis of the story of Jesus than it was for those affected by the story of the androgyne or the story of humanity in two genders.

The other absence worth noticing in Paul's reference to the story of Je-

---

32. Daly wrote: "If God is male, then the male is God" (*Beyond God the Father. Toward a Philosophy of Women's Liberation* [Boston: Beacon Press, 1973], p. 19).

sus is to Jesus' unmarried state. Paul makes nothing of Jesus being unmarried. Not once does Paul use Jesus' singleness either to validate his own or to endorse Jesus himself. Unlike Philo and other Hellenistic thinkers who associate celibacy with having special access to divine truth, Paul never refers to Jesus' sexual abstinence as an indication of Jesus' integrity and self-control, or as one of the reasons to trust him. This absence suggests that Paul is not operating with the myth of androgyne which, as we noted, was associated with an exaltation of celibacy. It suggests instead that Paul is working with a new story.

We might draw our attention also to the fact that when Paul encourages believers to imitate him and Christ,[33] he makes no mention of Jesus' gender or of his sexual life. Believers are to imitate Jesus by participating in Jesus' faith,[34] Jesus' death, and hoping to participate in Jesus' resurrection (e.g., Phil. 3:8-11). Paul tells believers that they have been incorporated into Christ and describes Christ as the one who loves, who gives himself, who is obedient unto death. In all of this there is mention neither of Jesus' masculinity nor of his celibacy.

It was noted above that stories are associated with worldviews. The worldview that might be produced by those aspects of Paul's story of Jesus we have touched on is very different from that associated either with the myth of androgyne or of humanity in two genders. The worldview which may be produced by the story of Jesus Christ values humility and service, and devalues honor and striving. In other words, if we were to 'genderize' the story of Jesus, in the way the genders have traditionally been viewed, it is a very feminine story. In my view, the worldview consonant with this story is one in which the traditional female virtues are prized and the traditional male virtues are challenged. Maleness as normative, which was a feature of the worldviews associated with both the other two myths, is absent from this one. What needs immediately to be noted, however, is that Paul does *not* 'genderize' the story of Jesus; he does not use the story to prioritize either gender. The values which shape Paul's story of Jesus Christ encourage viewing men and women as valuable not for their gender or their marital status, but as they, like Jesus, live lives of self-sacrificial love.

At the outset we noted that while myths convey values, they do not prescribe values. This fact is demonstrated by noting that, of course, the story of Jesus has been used to endorse precisely the opposite worldview from the one I have just described.

---

33. 1 Cor. 11:1, 1 Thess. 1:6, and implied in 1 Cor. 4:16.
34. I take the subjective genitive reading of *pistis christou.*

We now test whether, when we hear Paul speaking about and relating to women, we hear echoes of Paul's story of Jesus. The immediate answer is yes. We might hear echoes of it when Paul says that believers put on Christ and so there is no male and female; the identity of believers is now Christ, not their Jewishness or Gentileness, not their slavery or freedom, and not their maleness or femaleness. The statement in Gal. 3:28 indicates that for Paul the important thing about Christ is not that he was a freeborn Jewish male, but that he is the crucified and risen one.

The story of Jesus may be seen to be shaping Paul's worldview also when Paul works alongside women and receives help from women for his missionary work. The story of Jesus is reflected in Paul's comfort with women taking active roles in the church. Their gender, just as Jesus' gender, is not at issue. Echoes of this story may be heard also when Paul describes the body of Christ as being composed of different members with different gifts — none of which are gender-specific. The story of Jesus may also have influenced Paul's willingness to use female imagery when he speaks of his love for his congregations. For instance, Paul describes his tender care for the Thessalonians as like a nurse caring for her children (1 Thess. 2:7). Paul's use of the imagery of giving birth to his congregations (Gal. 4:19) also indicates his comfort with using illustrations from the world of women. Paul's relative freedom to connect himself to women and even to describe his experience using female examples may be because male honor is not featured in Paul's story of Jesus.

The story of Jesus Christ may also be seen when, perhaps even without his knowing it, Paul's inherited worldview is shaped into one more consistent with this story. When Paul affirms the convictions of his patriarchal culture — "the head of a woman is her husband"; or when he uses prescriptions from his patriarchal culture to address situations in his churches — "women should keep silence in the churches . . . if there is anything they desire to know, let them ask their husbands at home" (1 Cor. 14:34-35), he qualifies these affirmations of patriarchy with words like: "the head of every man is Christ . . . and the head of Christ is God," or, "make love your aim" (1 Cor. 14:1). With God as the head of Christ, and Christ as the head of every husband, whatever else being head of a wife meant for Paul, it must have meant reflecting the self-sacrificial character of God and Christ.[35] Likewise, Paul's words to the women to be silent in church and his direction that they should ask their husbands at home, occur in a context where he is teaching the Co-

35. See my, "'But I Want You to Know . . .': Paul's Midrashic Intertextual Response to the Corinthian Worshipers (1 Cor. 11:2-16)."

rinthians that the greatest spiritual gift is love, and that even in the moment of greatest spiritual ecstasy, considerate love should reign. Paul's patriarchal instructions are not intended to serve gender hierarchy but rather to encourage the creation of a considerate spiritual community.[36] It seems that the story of Jesus Christ worked in Paul's life to reshape the values he had inherited.

After Damascus, the story of Jesus set the trajectory for Paul's life and for Paul's way, including his way with women. Paul, of course, did not perfectly integrate the story of Jesus either into his own life, or into his decisions about his churches. Paul knows, as he himself says in Philippians, that he is not perfect (Phil. 3:12). Though at times the story of Jesus shines more brightly on Paul's way than others, it is here suggested that he strove to have it enlighten his responses to women, as to everything else in his life. Interpreters of Paul might choose to do the same.

36. See my "1 Cor. 14:34-35: A Reconsideration of Paul's Limitation of the Free Speech of Some Corinthian Women," *Journal for the Study of the New Testament* 58 (1995): 51-74.

IV Reformed and Ecumenical Theology

The Scope of Biblical Interpretation in the Reformed Tradition

Thomas W. Gillespie

Definitions of interpretation are like fingerprints. No two are the same. One reason for this diversity is the lack of agreement on the scope of the operation denoted by the term. By *scope* is meant both the *goal* of the task which interpretation is expected to achieve and the *range* of the process which achieving the goal requires. What determines the scope of the operation in this sense is not some pre-given, normative concept of interpretation, but the decision of the interpreter regarding the aim, goal, or purpose of a particular interpretation. As one literary critic puts it, "The object of interpretation is no automatic given, but a task that the interpreter sets himself. *He* decides what he wants to actualize and what purpose his actualization should achieve."[1] This choice determines the extent, range, and compass of the interpretative process.

The point may be illustrated by a discussion I once had with a prominent Old Testament scholar who claimed that the primary, indeed the *sole* goal of biblical interpretation is to provide an accurate translation of the most reliable text. Most professional exegetes would consider this position extreme, the guild opinion being that the goal of historical-critical interpretation is to explain what a text *meant* within the original context of its composition and circulation — in distinction from what it possibly *means* for us today in our different time and place (Stendahl). At the time of that conversation, however, I was serving as a pastor whose interpretation of biblical texts

---

1. E. D. Hirsch, Jr., *Validity in Interpretation* (New Haven and London: Yale University Press, 1967), p. 25. The date of publication may account for what is now heard as gender-exclusive language.

focused upon "the specific *minister's* problem, the *sermon*" (Barth). Thus, the *primary* interpretative goals of this Old Testament scholar and the guild were for me as a preacher merely *preliminary* and *intermediary* steps, respectively, in the task of interpreting biblical texts for today. The point is not that one goal is privileged over the others, but simply that the difference between them determines the *scope* of the interpretative process and thus what is entailed in *understanding* the *meaning* of the scriptures.[2]

I

My question then is whether there is a scope of biblical interpretation characteristic of, even if not unique to, the Reformed tradition in which I stand. Traces of such appear in Karl Barth's treatment of the subject in reliance upon the early Reformed theologian Amandus Polanus (1561-1610),[3] who defined biblical interpretation as *"explicatio veri sensus et usus illius."*[4] The goal of making clear the "true sense" of scripture and its "true use" is pursued, Polanus argues, by a process that moves from *explicatio* to *meditatio* to *applicatio.* This delineation of the scope of interpretation Barth cites with approval and develops his own position according to its rubrics.

The first phase of this hermeneutical operation *(explicatio),* according to Barth, "is entirely concerned with the *sensus* of the word of Scripture as such" (p. 722). This is the task of exegesis in which the interpreter of a text seeks to explain "what it has to say to us." Although the divine Word in the form of the human scriptural word exposes itself to the ambiguity inherent in all discourse, and thus to misunderstanding, Barth contends that the scriptural text retains the power "to present itself," i.e., to explain itself. The task of the interpreter is "to follow this self-presentation, to repeat it and as it were to copy it" (p. 722). Thus, interpretation as explanation is "an introductory attempt to follow the sense of the words of Scripture."

Because scripture is an instance of historical literature, such following presupposes the need for "literary-historical investigation." Barth assumes the use of literary methods such as "source criticism, lexicography, grammar, syntax and appreciation of style," as well as the need to read the words of the prophets and apostles "as documents of their concrete historical situation."

2. Wallace M. Alston, Jr., my friend and colleague, is fully aware of this hermeneutical issue, having come to the directorship of the Center of Theological Inquiry from a distinguished twenty-three-year pastorate of the Nassau Presbyterian Church in Princeton, New Jersey.

3. Karl Barth, *Church Dogmatics* I/2, pp. 710-40. [Further references given in parentheses]

4. Amandus Polanus, *Syntagma theologia Christianae* (1609), pp. 635f.

But the goal of following the *sense* of scripture is engagement with its *reference,* which Barth identifies as the *subject-matter* of the text. This distinction between *what* a text says (its sense) and what it says something *about* (its reference) is important in that it creates the possibility of a theological interpretation of the Bible. "The image which their words conjure up reflects a certain object," Barth writes of the biblical authors, and it is the task of the interpreter "to reproduce and copy the theme whose image is reflected in the words — for they are related to it" (p. 723). What is thus "mirrored" in scripture varies from text to text, of course, but the primary and unifying reference of scripture for Barth "is quite simply the name Jesus Christ, and these texts can be understood only when understood as determined by this object" (p. 724).[5]

The second phase of the process of biblical interpretation "is the act of reflection on what scripture declares to us" (p. 727). This is *meditatio,* "the middle point between *sensus* and *usus, explicatio* and *application.*" The task here is to "apprehend" by means of our own understanding *what* is said in scripture *about* its object. The interpreter now seeks "to assimilate" the testimony of scripture into his or her own thinking. With this, Barth acknowledges the reality and the inescapability of our *preunderstanding* of scripture's subject-matter (and thus the impossibility of interpretation without *presuppositions*).[6] *Meditatio,* as Barth sees it, is the arena where the struggle occurs between what the text says about its subject-matter and what the interpreter already thinks about God from the theological tradition in which he or she stands. Sometimes the text reaffirms convictions long held, while on other occasions it challenges cherished views. Assimilation of the witness of scripture, as Barth understands it, entails everything from simple affirmation to radical reorientation. The task of meditation is not a sublime contemplation of reality already known, therefore, but is often a spiritual and intellectual struggle of considerable magnitude.

At this point the interpreter has already entered the third phase of inter-

---

5. Two points in Barth's discussion of the referential character of biblical texts merit careful attention. One is his claim that the object attested by the prophets and the apostles *controls* the words used by the authors in their witness to it, thus identifying himself as more of a linguistic realist than a nominalist. The second is his indebtedness more to Aristotle than to Plato for his philosophy of language. Whereas Plato viewed words as simply *signs* that point away from themselves to the realities they designate, Aristotle understood them as *images* that reflect or mirror the realities they attest.

6. It is this point which legitimizes the important issue of the relationship between biblical interpretation and a particular theological tradition, in view of the fact that practitioners of the historical-critical method have devoted three hundred years to trying to liberate themselves from the "prejudices" of such traditions.

pretation, namely, *applicatio.* Barth calls this "the act of appropriation" or "assimilation" (p. 736). By this he means "that what is declared to us must become our very own, and indeed in such a way that now we really do become *conscientes,* those who in virtue of what is said to them know themselves, and can, therefore, say to themselves and to others what is said to them, those who not only reflect on it but think it themselves" (p. 736). Thus, appropriation is not a third act which may or may not be added to the already complete interpretation of scripture. "Exposition has not properly taken place so long as it stops short of assimilation, so long as assimilation has the appearance of a work of supererogation by means of which we have to make exposition fruitful by making something for ourselves of the Word of God as already expounded" (p. 736).

From this brief treatment of Barth's hermeneutical theory, it is clear that the scope of interpretation — its goal and compass — determines what is entailed in *understanding* the *meaning* of biblical texts. If the goal of interpretation is limited to *explicatio,* for example, then understanding the text is a matter of recognizing its sense. If the goal includes *meditatio,* then the meaning of the text is constituted by both its sense and reference, and understanding includes recognition of what it says as well as apprehension of its subject matter. If the goal entails *applicatio,* then the meaning of the text includes a claim upon the interpreter that must be appropriated or assimilated in order to be understood. Put simply, the scope of understanding the meaning of a text contracts or expands in relation to the chosen goal of the interpretative process.

II

That the scope of interpretation envisioned by Polanus and Barth is not merely arbitrary is evident from the discussion of interpretation theory outside the domain of theological reflection. The hermeneutical reflections of the French philosopher Paul Ricoeur and the American literary critic E. D. Hirsch, Jr., with particular reference to their respective treatments of the distinction between textual "sense" and "reference," will now be sketched in order both to support and to modify Barth's proposal.

Citing Frege's famous essay "Über Sinn und Bedeutung,"[7] Ricoeur also

---

7. Gottlob Frege, "On Sense and Reference," in *Translations from the Philosophical Writings of Gottlob Frege,* ed. Peter Geach and Max Black (Oxford: Basil Blackwell, 1970), pp. 56-78.

differentiates between the *sense* and the *reference* of the text.[8] Contending that the basic form of discourse is the sentence, and that the predominant form of the sentence is the proposition in which someone says something about something to someone else, Ricoeur identifies this basic unit of discourse as "the 'said as such.'"[9] What is said in the event of discourse, whether in speaking or writing, originates in the mind as a *noetic* (mental) act. As expressed in language, however, discourse assumes a *noematic* (rational) content. Even in oral speech, what we say can be remembered and repeated by ourselves or by others who have heard us say it. It is this *noematic* content of discourse which Ricoeur designates as the *sense* of discourse or, when committed to writing, the *sense* of the text. It comes to expression in accordance with the grammar and syntax which govern the formation of sentences in a particular language and, with regard to literary works, in accordance with such controlling principles as genre, composition, and style. For Ricoeur, then, the sense of the text is the "what" of the text, the "what is said," or the "said as such."[10]

The meaning of discourse is not limited to its sense, however. Meaning is constituted by the sense of discourse in interaction with its reference, the extra-linguistic reality about which it speaks. Thus, Ricoeur writes:

> The "objective" side of discourse itself may be taken in two different ways. We may mean the "what" of discourse or the "about what" of discourse. The "what" of discourse is its "sense," the "about what" is its "reference."[11]

He is well aware that not all discourse is referential. It may also be commissive, in the sense of performative, as in a command, or expressive, as in a shout of joy. Yet he wonders, "If language were not fundamentally referential, would or could it be meaningful?"[12] For it is only by the power of reference that discourse escapes the limitations of ideal meanings and puts us in contact with what is. Thus, for Ricoeur, the scope of interpretation is determined by the nature of discourse itself (oral or textual), constituted as it is by

8. Paul Ricoeur, *Interpretation Theory: Discourse and the Surplus of Meaning* (Fort Worth, TX: The Texas Christian University Press, 1976), p. 19.

9. Ricoeur, *Interpretation Theory*, p. 25.

10. This is as close to the *intention* of the author as the interpreter can come. The *noematic* content of the text represents the *noetic* act of the author. What the text actually says is the only clue to what its author *intended* to say. The attempt to relive authorial experience through the text and thus grasp authorial intention (Schleiermacher and Dilthey) is as impossible as it is unnecessary. Interpreters assume that authors write what they intend, and thus the *sense* of the text represents that intention.

11. Ricoeur, *Interpretation Theory*, p. 26.

12. Ricoeur, *Interpretation Theory*, p. 27.

the interplay between "what" it says and "about what" it speaks. Understanding the meaning of discourse, therefore, requires something like comprehending its sense as well as appropriating what it says about its reference.

Accordingly, Ricoeur and Barth agree with Polanus that the goal of interpretation begins with the *explicatio* of the *verus sensus* of the text. Ricoeur's "what" of discourse or the "said as such" is the equivalent of Barth's "what [the text] has to say to us." Both Ricoeur and Barth distinguish between the sense and reference of the text, between the *noematic* content of speech and its subject matter (ideal or real). Barth, with some justification, subsumes this interplay between the "what" and "about what" of discourse under *explicatio,* the first of the three hermeneutical moves advocated by Polanus. One wonders, however, if it would not be conceptually clearer if the interplay between the sense and reference of the text were made the object of *meditatio,* particularly when the subject matter is theological. For here the interpreter is required to ponder how, if at all, what the text says about God or, as Barth would put it, Jesus Christ can be "appropriated" by or "assimilated" into the pre-understanding of this subject matter, however informed, which the reader inevitably brings to the text. At this point in the process important theological decisions are required.

III

E. D. Hirsch, Jr., also relies on Frege's essay for his distinction between the "meaning" *(Sinn)* and the "significance" *(Bedeutung)* of a text, but with a difference from Ricoeur that is more than translational. As he explains in an appendix to *Validity in Interpretation:*

> The distinction between the meaning and the significance of a text was first clearly made by Frege in his article "Über Sinn und Bedeutung," where he demonstrated that although the meanings of two texts may be different, their referent or truth-value may be identical. . . . Frege considered only cases where different *Sinne* have an identical *Bedeutung,* but it is also true that the same *Sinn* may, in the course of time, have different *Bedeutungen.*[13]

While Ricoeur would agree that the *Sinn* of differently articulated statements may have the same *Bedeutung,* he could not concur with the inference Hirsch

---

13. Hirsch, *Validity,* p. 211.

draws from Frege's work that the *Sinn* of a text may change its *Bedeutung* over time. The reference of a text remains constant. Clearly Frege's terms are being used differently by Ricoeur and Hirsch.

The problem is not with the word *Sinn*. Hirsch is as adamant as Ricoeur on the stability of the "what" of the text. It is *Bedeutung* that they understand differently. According to Hirsch:

> *Meaning* is that which is represented by a text; it is what the author meant by his use of a particular sign sequence; it is what the signs represent. *Significance*, on the other hand, names a relationship between that meaning and a person, or a conception, or a situation, or indeed anything imaginable. . . . Significance always implies a relationship, and one constant, unchanging pole of that relationship is what the text means. Failure to consider this simple and essential distinction has been the source of enormous confusion in hermeneutic theory.[14]

Hirsch's textual *meaning* clearly parallels Ricoeur's "said as such" (and Barth's "what it has to say to us"). The *meaning* of the text is for Hirsch determinate and thus determinable (or, as Barth would say, able "to present itself" in such a fashion that the interpreter can "follow this self-presentation," even "repeat it and as it were . . . copy it").

In point of fact the burden of Hirsch's theory is to refute the popular notion in literary circles that the meaning of a text changes when read at a time and place different from that of its composition. The basic idea of this "semantic autonomy of the text" is that whenever meaning is committed to writing and published, it soon slips the chain which tethers it to the intention of the author and takes on a life of its own. The meaning of the text now depends not upon the understanding of the author expressed in the text, but upon the understanding of the interpreter. Since the author is no longer present to defend the intended meaning, the text means whatever the interpreter construes it to mean. In opposition to this view, Hirsch writes in defense of "the sensible belief that a text means what the author meant."[15] Conceding that the advocates of semantic autonomy have their finger on an important point (something does change as a text is interpreted at later times and in different circumstances), Hirsch argues that what changes is not the meaning of the text but its significance.

This notion of textual *significance* — the relationship between what the text says and "a person, or a conception, or a situation, or indeed anything

14. Hirsch, *Validity,* p. 8.
15. Hirsch, *Validity,* p. 23.

imaginable" — seems closer, however, to that of *relevance* than to subject matter, to Barth's *applicatio* than to Ricoeur's *Bedeutung*. What Barth has in mind by the application of the text is that personal appropriation of the testimony of the scriptures to God by which what is declared to us becomes our very own. Hirsch's *significance* accommodates this by allowing for the relationship between what the text says and "a person, or a conception." But it also provides for a more expansive application of what is said to "a situation," thus improving the notion. While Barth insists that *applicatio* necessarily completes the interpretative process, Hirsch merely affirms the legitimacy, if not the necessity, of discerning the significance of a text — provided that the distinction between *meaning* and *significance* is observed.

IV

The differences between Ricoeur and Hirsch in their respective treatments of Frege's distinction between the *Sinn* and *Bedeutung* of a text illustrate the importance of determining the scope of interpretation. For Hirsch, textual meaning is limited to what Ricoeur designates as the sense of the text. For Ricoeur, the meaning of a text is constituted by the interplay between its sense and reference. For Barth (and Polanus), the meaning of a text includes its sense, its reference, and what Hirsch would call its significance. Conversely, Hirsch claims that a text has been understood when its *Sinn* has been comprehended. Ricoeur would add that understanding includes dealing with what the text says about its subject matter. And Barth contends that understanding is completed when what the text says about its subject matter is personally appropriated. What the discussion with Ricoeur and Hirsch demonstrates is that there is nothing arbitrary about the scope of the task as envisioned by Polanus and Barth. Barth, Ricoeur, and Hirsch agree that explaining the *Sinn* of the text is basic (exegesis). Barth and Ricoeur agree that the reference of the text is constitutive of its meaning. And Hirsch grants legitimacy to the idea of applying what the text says to something outside the text by his notion of textual significance.

In summary, the scope of interpretation in the Reformed tradition includes comprehending the sense of the text, appropriating what is said about the reference of the text, and discerning the significance of the text through application of what it says about its subject matter to some aspect of human life. Such indeed is the task of the preacher of biblical texts.

The Not-So-Plain Meaning of Scripture

J. Harold McKeithen, Jr.

Introduction

From our very beginnings we Christians have gone through times when we found ourselves painfully giving up one well-established belief or practice to embrace one which we felt to be more in line with God's will for us. In the Bible, we see the Apostle Peter moving painfully from a belief that the new church was only for converted Jews to an acceptance of the inclusion of gentiles. In our own more recent history, we found ourselves moving from acceptance of slavery to rejection of slavery, from racial segregation to racial integration, from an exclusion of women from ordination to an inclusion of women, from a refusal to accept divorce under any circumstances to a willingness to accept it in certain circumstances. Are we now being called by God to move from a rejection of homosexual persons as candidates for ordination to an acceptance of them? Consider some of the changes we have found ourselves making in times past and, in that light, examine the issue which we find ourselves dealing with today.

I

Most of us with a southern American heritage had great-grandparents who were earnest Christians and who believed that the institution of slavery was ordained by God and was a part of the natural order of things. They believed that the Bible plainly supported this belief. They cited Genesis 9:24-27 which says of Noah's son, Canaan, who was believed to have been the progenitor of dark-skinned people, "Cursed be Canaan; a slave of slaves shall he be to his brothers." Moreover, they pointed to numerous passages in Exodus and Leviticus where God gives specific instructions regarding the treatment of male and female slaves and nowhere questions the validity of slavery. Moreover, they cited, from the New Testament, the example of the Apostle Paul who sends the runaway slave, Onesimus, back to serve his owner and master, Philemon.

With such plain evidence of Scripture's support of the institution of slavery, how in the world did the church ever come to the conclusion that slavery was not of God? Well, it began with Christians up north in places like New England and New York and Pennsylvania who discerned, with the leading of the Holy Spirit, that our spiritual ancestors were products of the culture of their times and that their beliefs and practices simply were not consistent with the character and purposes of God as we see them in the Bible as a whole and in the life and teachings of Jesus. They began to become aware that even Paul seemed to be getting an inkling of this when he wrote in Galatians 3:27 and 28, "As many of you as were baptized into Christ have put on Christ. There is neither Jew nor Greek, there is neither slave nor free, there is neither male nor female; for you are all one in Christ Jesus."

Those of us down south disagreed with this interpretation. We believed that Paul was not condemning slavery but simply saying that both slaves and free people were important to God. We opposed the abolitionists, and there was a north-south schism in our Presbyterian Church over the issue. We finally fought a war over whether our states were going to have the right to have slaves or whether the federal government was going to be able to tell us what to do. We lost the war; but, more to the point, we all believe now that the abolitionists among us were right. We know that slavery is an abomination, no matter what the plain meaning of Scripture seemed to be. Ironically, even southerners have come to revere what was virtually the national anthem of the abolitionist movement, "The Battle Hymn of the Republic."

II

However, if slavery was not God's will, it was certainly clear to our grandparents and to many of us that segregation was. We believed that, even though God may have made all of us human beings equally in his image, he did not intend for us to intermingle. Leviticus 19:19 plainly prohibits the mixing of different kinds. In that text God says, "You shall not let your cattle breed with a different kind; you shall not sow your field with two kinds of seed; nor shall there come upon you a garment of cloth made of two kinds of stuff." More-over, Israelites are clearly commanded to keep themselves separate from gentiles. Birds of a feather are supposed to flock together, and we believed that what was true of birds was certainly true of people. When I was growing up in Winston-Salem, North Carolina, friends and I would sometimes take the bus downtown to go to the movie. When black people got on the bus and went to the back, even though there were seats in the front or middle, that seemed to me to be the way things were supposed to be in the plan of God.

How did we ever come to the point where the General Assembly of our Southern Presbyterian Church could shock us all by declaring that segregation was contrary to the will of God, when Scripture and our tradition so plainly said otherwise? Well, again the Holy Spirit led us to a new discernment. We looked again at Acts 10, where the Apostle Peter has a vision which simply contradicts the Leviticus passage. He sees this sheet let down with all kinds of animals and reptiles and birds mixed up in it. He is then told to go down and bring into the church, Cornelius, a gentile, a person with whom Peter would previously have had no association. The movement for racial integration in the church began to grow.

The new interpretation was rejected by many. A prominent business-man in Miami began organizing a conservative group called "Concerned Presbyterians" to oppose the direction the church was going. Two ministers in the Alabama presbytery where I was serving in the early sixties helped begin the Reformed Theological Seminary in Jackson, Mississippi, which aimed at training ministers who would stick to spiritual matters and not get involved in controversial issues like race. The groundwork was laid for another schism, which came in the seventies when a small minority of churches pulled out of our denomination to form the Presbyterian Church in America. It all began with racial integration.

How did we come to the point of believing, as most of us seem to do now, that racial integration was and is God's will for us? We came to that point because the Holy Spirit brought us to see that that is more consistent with the character and purpose of God as revealed in the Bible as a whole and in the example and teaching of Jesus as a whole, even though Jesus says nothing specifically about it.

III

But, if the plain meaning of Scripture was not as plain as we thought on matters of race, it certainly seemed to be on the matter of gender. If there is anything clear in the Bible as a whole, it is the primacy of men over women. Authority and leadership in both Israel and the church is reserved for men. In connection with marriage, the Apostle Paul says plainly in Ephesians 5:22 and 23, "Wives, be subject to your husbands, as to the Lord. For the husband is the head of the wife as Christ is the head of the church." In connection with her place in the church, Paul says plainly in 1 Timothy 2:11 and 12, "Let a woman learn in silence with all submissiveness. I permit no woman to teach or to have authority over men; she is to keep silent."

All of that is so plain that it governs policy and practice in the Roman Catholic Church and in the fundamentalist Southern Baptist Convention. It was also plain to many of those who withdrew from the Presbyterian Church, U.S. to form the Presbyterian Church in America. In the fastest growing churches in America today, the ordination of women as ministers and church officers is seen as a departure from the plain meaning of Scripture.

How did we come to depart from that view? How did we come to the decision that the place of women in the home and in the church should be a place of equality rather than a place of subjugation? It was not because of anything that the Bible says specifically. It was primarily because of what, with the leading of the Holy Spirit, we began to see and to hear in Jesus. His affirmation of women, his friendship with women, his talk with women, all of which scandalized the patriarchal traditions and attitudes of his contemporaries, began to be seen by us as a revelation of the mind and will of God. What about Paul? Was he just wrong? In a word, "Yes." Paul was as much a man of his times as we are of ours. He was formed and guided by the customs of his time as we are by the prevailing beliefs and customs of our times. On matters of gender, many of us believe that the Holy Spirit has led us into a broader and deeper discernment of the will of God.

IV

Well, maybe we have had to rethink the plain meaning of the Bible with respect to the place of women, but surely we cannot disregard its plain meaning on the matter of divorce and remarriage. In Mark 10:10-12, Jesus himself says, "Whoever divorces his wife and marries another, commits adultery against her; and if she divorces her husband and marries another, she commits adultery." There are other texts which are just as clear in their prohibition of divorce. And these texts, again, govern policy and practice in the Roman Catholic Church and in many conservative Protestant churches. A few years back, a woman came to me, said that she was a thirty-year member of a certain church in Newport News, said that she had been divorced and now wanted to marry again and asked if I would be willing to counsel with her and her fiance and to marry them at Hidenwood Presbyterian Church where I was the pastor. I said that I would be willing to do that and asked why she was not getting married in her own church. She broke into tears and said that the pastor there would not even discuss it with her since she would be living in sin if she re-married.

How in the world did the Presbyterian Church (USA) get away from the plain meaning of the Bible on this matter? We did it because we decided, with what we believe was the leading of the Holy Spirit, that what seemed to be the plain meaning was not as plain as it seemed. We concluded that Jesus was describing the painful realities of divorce, realities which most, if not all, divorced people experience. They realize that you cannot undo the physical intimacy shared with a marriage partner, that it remains as a fact even after divorce. But Jesus does not say that remarriage is prohibited. Jesus was consistently helping us fallible human beings pick up the pieces of our lives and move on, after any and all of our failures. We have determined that we will be governed by the example and spirit of Christ rather than by an interpretation of texts that runs counter to that spirit.

V

That brings us to the issue with which the Presbyterian Church (USA) and other denominations are now struggling and, over which, folks are threatening, as they have in the past, to leave if the plain meaning of the Bible is rejected. That issue is homosexuality. Emotions actually seem not to be running as high as they were over the issue of slavery, and they are not running any higher than they were over the issues of integration and women's rights and divorce. We have tended, with the passage of time, to forget just how intense our feelings were over those issues; and, in fact, we do not like to be reminded. It is a little embarrassing. But, at the present, the plain meaning of Scripture seems, for some Christians, to be that homosexuality is contrary to the will of God.

There are only five passages in the Bible that touch on the issue at all. They are Genesis 19:1-38 (the story of Sodom), Leviticus 18:22 and 20:13 (verses in what has come to be known as "The Holiness Code"), and Paul's words in 1 Corinthians 6:9-10, 1 Timothy 1:9-10, and Romans 1:18–2:16. The problem is that the meaning of these passages is by no means plain with respect to committed, consensual, exclusive, and permanent homosexual relationships. Marion Soards is a conservative Biblical scholar who does believe that the Romans text gives us clear moral guidance prohibiting homosexuality, but he does not believe the other texts provide that.

He points out that in the story of Sodom and Gomorrah the crime was rape. It would have been a crime whether the victims were male or female. If they had been female, we could not argue that heterosexual relations are a crime. In the same way, we cannot argue that since the victims were male, homosexual relations are the crime. In fact, according to Ezekiel 16:49, the crime for which Sodom was punished had nothing to do with sex. Ezekiel writes, "Behold, this was the guilt of your sister Sodom: she and her daughters had pride, surfeit of food, and prosperous ease, but did not aid the poor and needy."

The Leviticus texts read, "You shall not lie with a male as with a woman; it is an abomination." That seems plain enough. It is, however, one prohibition in what is known as "The Holiness Code," Leviticus 17:1–26:46, which contains these equally plain statements: "You shall not eat any flesh with the blood in it" (19:26); "Everyone who curses his father or his mother shall be put to death" (20:9); no priest with "a blemish . . . one who has a mutilated face or a limb too long . . . or an injured foot . . . or a hunchback . . . or a man with a defect in his sight . . . shall approach the altar . . . that he may not profane my sanctuaries" (21:16-23). There are many other very clear requirements in the Code, and the text makes very clear that every one of them is as binding as the others. You cannot legitimately pick one as binding and ignore the others. The consensus in the church over the years has been that the Code was applicable to Israel at a particular time in its history and is no longer applicable to the church.

What about Paul's words in 1 Corinthians 6:9 and 10 that "fornicators, idolaters, adulterers, male prostitutes, sodomites, thieves, the greedy, drunkards, revilers, robbers — none of these will inherit the kingdom of God"? What about 1 Timothy 1:9 and 10 where he describes as "the godless and sinful" those "who kill their father or mother . . . murderers, fornicators, sodomites, slave traders, liars, perjurers"? Those texts would be plain enough if there was any agreement among interpreters about what "sodomites" are. Many are of the opinion that Paul is referring to males who violate others sexually, as the men had done in Sodom. They do not think he is talking about same-sex relationships which are consensual, committed, exclusive, and permanent.

Marion Soards believes, however, that the case is different with Romans 1:26-27. There Paul expresses the view that homosexuality is a result of idolatry, of a failure to honor God. He writes, "For this reason God gave them up to dishonorable passions. Their women exchanged natural relations for unnatural, and the men likewise gave up natural relations with women and were consumed with passion for one another." Soards believes that passage settles the issue, that it provides definitive and permanent guidance for the church.

I think that it does not settle the issue. Paul's complicity with slavery did not settle that issue for us. Paul's clear assertion that wives are to be subject to and submissive to their husbands did not settle that issue for us. Many of us ministers are no longer comfortable with asking women, at their weddings, to promise to "love, honor and *obey*" their husbands. Paul's equally clear assertion that women are not to exercise authority in the church did not settle that issue for us, although it did and has for many others. The passages which seem to convey the plain meaning of the Bible on divorce do not, in the Presbyterian Church, convey what we believe to be the will and ways of God.

Conclusion

Whether God will lead us Presbyterians to continue our long-standing condemnation of homosexuality, or whether God will lead us to beyond that condemnation remains to be seen. In the Presbyterian Church (USA) we are in the very middle of our struggle with the issue, and we are very divided in our views. One thing I know for sure. Unlike some Presbyterians, I will continue to be a part of this denomination no matter which way it goes. There were people who left the Presbyterian Church when it took a stand against slavery. There were those who left when it became inclusive of blacks and elevated the status of women. There will very likely be persons who will leave if and when the church drops its ban on the ordination of homosexuals. I believe, however, that the vast majority of us will realize what a precious heritage we have in this church and will remain a part of it, believing that Christ, the Head of the Church, is leading us in the way we need to go.

Midrash and the Recovery of Biblical Authority

Cynthia A. Jarvis

Preface

My first memories of loving the study of biblical texts coincide with my first memories of listening intently to sermons Sunday after Sunday. The preacher was a nervously serious man whose habit of wringing his wrists throughout morning worship only heightened my interest in his three points. He kept nothing from us: questioning Paul's authorship of certain letters, noting the later additions tacked onto various parables, laying out the distinctive editorial styles of J, E, P, and D. Suddenly I had been given a book to which I could set my *mind!* Unlike my more literal and religious friends, I had nothing to fear when gospel accounts were found to be contradictory. Neither did I shy away from heated ethical debates whose conclusion could not be decided with a proof-texted verse. This was an interesting book, even a primary book with which to wrestle as I wrestled with the issues of growing up in America in the sixties. The story and its truth, however, eluded me.

My second memory of loving biblical studies coincides with my later memory of listening for the stories and for the truth I could know in no other way than *through* the words and stories of Scripture. Studying parables under a Jesuit whose questions of the text were surely rabbinic in character, writing parables and fables as an exercise in listening to a text's silences as well as its phrases, eavesdropping on cross-cultural conversations centering in a text whose meaning became multi-layered in the process: suddenly I had been given a book — the same book, a second time — to which I could set my heart and life!

Now I have been given a congregation whose minds and hearts are elsewhere. Intellectual engagement with Scripture and theology is presumed to be irrelevant by all but the whiter heads. Even more troubling, the stories of Scripture have been so lost to parents and their children, the images so overpowered by the culture's pace, that the task of getting the next generation's attention long enough to listen for God's address in Scripture is the task which has seduced many a preacher into eschewing exegesis for entertainment. Serious study of Scripture or ongoing conversation concerning biblical texts gathers a precious few. Much as I would like to believe these few are the leaven in a community not given to rising on a Sunday morning for a class on the Bible, the evidence is not convincing.

In addition, I am ordained into a part of Christ's church divided against itself over what have been presented as social issues argued on biblical grounds. We are divided, in truth, over the nature of Scripture and over the way in which Scripture's authority and truth are operative within human community. We seldom speak across the divides and, when we do, it is over matters of institutional organization and power. Scripture is studied within the camp — often in order that we might be readied for battle — each camp believing the other to be entirely mistaken about a text's meaning and incapable of reasoned conversation.

Given this state of affairs, my hunch throughout this paper is that our foot in the door, our means of post-modern popular engagement with Scripture, will require a communal study of Scripture centered as much in Scripture's silence as in its speech, centered as seriously in a divided and dwindling community's questions as in the answers asserted by various faithful remnants. This hunch sent me to another community's engagement with Scripture as a model Christians only unconsciously embrace. Midrash or *aggadah* is, to put it negatively, the non-legal literature of rabbinic Judaism. Positively, *aggadah* includes narratives, parables, homilies, pithy ethical and theological statements, all of which are the response of a rabbinic community to a "close" reading of Torah.

I began with a particular text: the binding of Isaac. Given that the silences in this story were deafening, I was certain the midrash written in response to this story would be rich with pastoral insight. However the more I read, the more I began to see larger implications for a recovery or discovery of midrash within the Christian community. How many of our New Testament texts are just that! They are stories a teacher, whom we confess to be the Christ of God, told on the stories already given. Through these stories and sayings, Jesus addressed the silences or responded to the inconsistencies or engaged the current confusion concerning the law and the prophets. He thus engaged the Scripture of his own community with stories told to tease out of his listeners a faithful response. Might we, therefore, do well not only to consider the midrashic character of various New Testament writings, but also to investigate midrash as a means of reengaging our congregations and our colleagues in conversation, trusting anew Scripture's community-creating authority?

One last word needs to be said as preface to the paper before you. This study will require the suspension of a long-standing Protestant suspicion which has relegated the gift of human imagination vis-à-vis Scripture to the bowels of an anti-intellectual conspiracy. One may venture clear into the mind of God with theological systems, but God forbid one should venture theological response to Scripture in the form of a story. Mariology looms darkly on the horizon! Yet midrash presents itself as a very different and distinct enterprise which is worthy of more than uninformed disdain. Therefore this is the beginning of an attempt to recover, for the Protestant mind (and, perhaps practice), an ancient and honorable response to scripture by scholars who likely loved Torah more than we love our paper pope! The *love* of Torah: therein lies the key to midrash and to the recovery of biblical authority in our day.

The Rediscovery of *Aggadah*

At the beginning of the twentieth century two Russian Jews, Hayim Nahman Bialik and Yehoshua Hana Ravnitzky, set before themselves a monumental task. One a poet, the other a journalist, both were intent upon reviving the Hebrew ethos in their country through the compilation of Rabbinic legend and lore. The result, *Sefer Ha-Aggadah (The Book of Legends),* is overwhelming in its scope. Over eight hundred pages of the non-legal teachings of Rabbinic Judaism's early sages offer a window into the life, imagination, and faith of a people. Here I ventured in search of midrashim, of stories told upon the story of the Akedah. Instead, I stumbled upon another community's crisis of faith and a response to that crisis which shed an unexpected light on the path ahead.

The crisis, according to David Stern, was a crisis Bialik had "suffered through most terribly" himself through "the loss of faith, the collapse of the traditional structures and tenets of Jewish belief, the erosion of the security of existence that those religious structures and tenets had previously ensured."[1]

---

1. David Stern, "Introduction," in *The Book of Legends. Sefer Ha-Aggadah: Legends from the Talmud and Midrash,* ed. Hayim Nahman Bialik and Yehoshua Hana Ravnitzky (New York: Schocken Books, 1992), p. xxi.

To be sure, the description of Bialik's situation at the beginning of the twentieth century in Russia echoed the emptiness of our own. The collapse of traditional structures and tenets of Christian belief, the erosion of the security of existence that the Church and its faith had previously ensured — this strangely matched our situation.

But the similarity does not end with the statement of the problem. What Bialik and Ravnitzky believed themselves to be doing through the compilation of Rabbinic legend and lore had little to do with the reclaiming of faith. Rather, faith had been replaced by ideology and institution in the form of Zionism. From the intrinsically religious enterprise practiced by the ancient rabbis in the writing of *aggadah* ("If you wish to know Him by whose word the world came into being, study *Aggadah;* you will thereby come to know the Holy One, blessed be He, and hold fast to His ways"), Bialik counselled, "whoever wishes to know the nation of Israel . . . let him 'go to *Aggadah.*"[2] Therefore, for Bialik and Ravnitzky, the enterprise of assembling and ordering *aggadah* eschewed the recovery of faith in the living God and headed toward the recovery of the cultural, social, and political structures which, if strengthened, could offer a security of existence previously known through religious belief.

Granting the significant divide between cultural Judaism's understanding of religion's role in human community and the church's increasingly feeble but continued insistence that faith in God has something to do with the "practice" of Christianity in our culture, there is still a strong ring of similarity between Bialik's purpose and our own. In this day, our response to the crisis of biblical authority, the crisis of the loss of faith, the crisis of the collapse of religious structures, has been a response riddled with ideology and institutionally driven tactics for survival. We look to Europe's empty cathedrals, to England's emptying churches, to the statistics signaling the slow death of mainline Protestant communities, to our own community's ignorance of or indifference toward tradition, and we devise techniques, we adopt strategies, we flock to organizational experts, on the one hand, capable of reviving our religious institutions.

On the other hand, when we are not tinkering with institutional structures and styles, the more substantively inclined among us speak of reclaiming or reasserting the authority of Scripture and tradition in our churches, not to mention our hope of reasserting its influence over our culture's rampant secularism. Yet in so doing, we have majored in politicized theology and an ideologically based reading of the Bible, both of which have served only to

2. Stern, "Introduction," p. xxi.

deep the crisis. Sadly, even when we are trying to be substantive, we appropriate Scripture and tradition in order to secure the borders of the camp to which we belong.

Fortunately for Bialik and Ravnitzky, the method they chose to address the crisis of faith at the beginning of the twentieth century, the compilation of *aggadah*, was a literary form that, by definition, resisted the purpose they had in mind. Therefore, at the beginning of the twenty-first century, we would do well to explore how the imaginative engagement of the scriptures, practiced by the ancient sages in the writing of *aggadah*, may offer itself as a way of listening closely to Scripture and tradition, of taking Scripture seriously through the hitherto threatening gift of human imagination, and of allowing disparate "hearings" of Scripture to exist side-by-side for the sake of the building up of the body.

The Practice of *Aggadah*

Knowing nothing of *aggadah* before this study, save for the reading of midrash as it strayed into Christian theology, I begin with a grateful attribution. The writings of David Stern (professor of post-biblical and medieval Hebrew literature at the University of Pennsylvania), both in his introduction to Sefer Ha-Aggadah and in his *Midrash and Theory,* have served as a spark to my own imagination. In addition, the clear writing of editor Barry Holtz and his fellow contributors, in an appropriately titled anthology *Back to the Sources: Reading the Classic Jewish Texts,* helped place midrash in a larger context of Jewish scholarship. What follows is an attempt to summarize what I have learned of midrash and what has been suggestive for the question of biblical authority before us today. Before we consider midrash directly, however, some general comments seem in order for an audience whose ignorance on the matter may match that of this writer.

First, a word should be said about the place of midrash in the more general rabbinic interpretation of Scripture. According to rabbinic tradition, Torah may be interpreted on four levels. The first is *pashoot* which is the simple, literal meaning of a text. The second, *ramaz*, is the allegorical reading of Scripture. *Drash*, from which midrash comes, is the moral interpretation. Finally there is *sod*, the mystical reading, which in these days enjoys popularity through the renewed study of the *Kabbalah.*

In the nineteenth century, traditional Jewish biblical scholarship underwent a redefinition similar to historical-criticism as "'Wissenschaft des Judentums' — a movement advocating 'scientific' study of and critical research into the classic texts"[3] — rose to prominence. According to Barry Holtz, "Wissenschaft was, to a certain degree, tied to the Haskalah (Enlightenment) movement within European Jewry and represented for some a way to identify with Judaism and still retain connection to the allure of Western European secular culture."[4] He goes on to note the apologetic aspect of this movement whose intent was to "demonstrate to the non-Jewish world that classic Jewish literature had a legitimacy of its own, and Jewish scholarship could be as rigorous and critical as anything being done in the world of non-Jewish research."[5]

Yet the paucity of this singular approach to Scripture for the community of faith, not to mention for the human spirit, sent Jewish scholars back to classic texts in search of an interpretation which would not be limited to scientific study or critical research. This, in part, accounts for the renewed interest among Jewish congregations and scholars in the literature of *aggadah* as well as the more popular interest in the *Kabbalah*. This also offers the possibility of illuminating our own situation from the perspective of another community's history of textual interpretation and current attempts to recover Scripture's authority.

Second, a word should be said about the way in which texts are studied. Unlike our current model of scholarship which lauds the individual "hold-up" in a study, intent on publishing the newest angle on a particular text for personal advancement, all study of Torah occurs in the context of community. Says Robert Goldenberg of the traditional *yeshiva*, "students study in pairs, reading every word of the text out loud, never going on to the next phrase until they have exhausted the meaning of the one under discussion. . . . This mode of study, called in Aramaic *havruta* ("fellowship"), turns text study into dialogue and makes books into tools for overcoming, not strengthening, isolation. It makes the tradition of rabbinic learning a powerful source of community cohesion, a source of speech rather than silence. . . . The life of the mind and the life of society were thus made one."[6] Surely there is for Christian interpretation a lesson to be learned in this understanding of how the text is studied. Having done part of the research for this paper in a Reconstructionist seminary library, I can attest to the unending "conversation" which marks the study of Torah. Rabbinic students were constantly lob-

3. Barry Holtz, "Introduction: On Reading Jewish Texts," in *Back to the Sources: Reading the Classic Jewish Texts*, ed. Barry Holtz (New York: Summit Books, 1984), p. 25.
4. Holtz, "Introduction," p. 25.
5. Holtz, "Introduction," p. 25.
6. Robert Goldenberg, "Talmud," in *Back to the Sources: Reading the Classic Jewish Texts*, ed. Barry Holtz (New York: Summit Books, 1984), pp. 168-9.

bing questions across the room concerning a text's inconsistency. Their "close" readings clearly fueled a repartee, which made the library into a place for communal and intellectual arm-wrestling rather than into a place for lone and silent scholarly research.

Third, something must be said about the rabbinic love of Torah. Holtz asks our question for us: "How could the rabbis do it? How could they have allowed themselves the freedom and flexibility to make such startlingly new interpretations, to change the laws of the Bible itself?"[7] His answer is the most important clue we may be given as we struggle toward a recovery of biblical authority within the Christian community. Torah "was an eternally relevant book because it was written by a perfect Author, an Author who intended it to be eternal."[8]

This is no doctrine of inerrancy, nor will it allow the rabbis to remain on the first level of interpretation, *pashoot,* that of the simple and literal meaning. Rather, the belief that the Creator intended Torah to be eternally relevant led the rabbis to conclude that the Author could foresee the need for new interpretations. Torah is filled with gaps and inconsistencies so that those who loved it would be eternally engaged with its mystery. Yet because the listening of the rabbis to the text was so close, because they believed Torah was God's revelation in its entirety, all interpretations were already *in the text* and waiting for each generation to uncover them. That the Bible says little about motivation or feelings or thoughts of its characters is, according to the rabbis, the Author's way of calling forth midrash. Midrash fills in the gaps "to tell the details that the Bible teasingly (intentionally) leaves out."[9]

"To appreciate Midrash," writes Stern, "it is crucial to understand that, for the rabbis, the Bible was not only Torah, the divine source for Israel's Law and its history. The words of Torah, its text, were also the lens, the prism, through which the sages viewed their own world. The Torah gave them the terms of reference in which they experienced their daily lives, the vocabulary through which they articulated their every feeling and thought."[10]

In other words, the question brought by the rabbis to Scripture was not a question of history, nor did they come in search of a literal and singular interpretation. Scripture was, for them, realistic in relation to human existence (and therefore, presumably, realistic within itself). That their response to the

---

7. Barry Holtz, "Midrash," in *Back to the Sources: Reading the Classic Jewish Texts,* ed. Barry Holtz (New York: Summit Books, 1984), p. 185.

8. Holtz, "Midrash," p. 185.

9. Holtz, "Midrash," p. 180.

10. Stern, "Introduction," p. xx.

narrative character of Scripture was a story told within or beyond the given story, whose impetus was their own situation, implies that the authority of Scripture was the truth it told eternally about human existence in the presence of the living God.

Again, writes Stern, "When [the rabbis] sought . . . the meaning*fulness* of that verse or phrase [in Torah], they would search after it, first, in themselves, in their own experiences and in what they knew to be true. If Scripture could not lie, neither could it be false or contradictory to the rabbis' own selves and to their knowledge, their sense of the world and of their place in it."[11]

We must be clear: the rabbis' search into themselves is not to be equated with our current propensity to grant primary authority for truth to personal experience, using that as the screen through which to critique Scripture and tradition. Rather, the rabbis began with Scripture read as though through a fine tooth comb, pausing on word or phrase, on silence or inconsistency, and seeking after the truth lurking in that verse or phrase in relation to the life they had experienced. The presumption was Scripture's truth. The engagement with Scripture turned on reading Scripture, its vocabulary and terms of reference, back into their lives.

Though the scale is grander than that of a singular life or the life of a particular community in time:

> The collapsing of time and history that is so characteristic of Midrash — as when the rabbis unselfconsciously portray figures from the distant past like the patriarchs in their own image [here we begin to anticipate the midrashim on Abraham and, to a lesser degree, on Isaac] — should not be viewed as a matter of naive anachronizing on the rabbis' part or as self-serving exploitation of Scripture for their own ends. Rather . . . by bringing their own experiences to the interpretation of the word of Torah, and taking back from Torah the language that allowed them to articulate their own experiences, the rabbis created a kind of mythical, timeless realm removed from the travails and injustices of contemporary history. In this realm, the beliefs they valued, the lives they wished to live, their hopes, their dreams, even their moments of anguish, could take shape, unimpeded by hostile forces, and be realized, however complexly so.[12]

---

11. Stern, "Introduction," p. xx.
12. Stern, "Introduction," p. xx.

The Particularity of *Aggadah* on the *Aqedah*

When we look to the extended midrash compiled on the *Aqedah,* we can hear the interplay of Scripture and the experience of rabbis: tested by God, tried by the sacrifices required, caught in domestic realities, tempted to waver in devotion. Consider the midrash on, "And it came to pass after these things that God tried Abraham," which depicts a feast given in Isaac's honor. Satan asks God here (much as Satan asks God at the beginning of Job), "Master of the universe, out of the entire feast that this old man, upon whom You bestowed fruit of the womb at the age of one hundred — out of the entire feast he prepared, could he not have spared, say, one turtledove, one fledgling, as an offering to You?" God replies that the feast was for his son, but if God required the sacrifice even of his son, Abraham would obey. "Try him," says Satan. At once "God tried Abraham."[13]

We can only speculate about the feasts held in honor of first sons, the community celebrations forgetful of the Holy One, the sons taken in times of religious persecution, and thus the story told in response to the story given, which was told to lend meaning to their moments of anguish. Careful as we are, in our pristine exegesis, to view Abraham as a singular biblical character tested by God, to stay precisely within the story, the rabbis needed more from Abraham's trial. They paid attention to the story, verse by verse, but paid attention from out of their lives. Thus, in the next midrash, the mythic dimension of Abraham appears:

> And he said: "Take, I beg thee *(na),* thy son." R. Simon bar Abba said: "The word *na* can imply only entreaty. The matter may be illustrated by the parable of a king of flesh and blood who had to face many wars, in all of which he had one mighty warrior who invariably achieved victory. In the course of time, he faced a war particularly severe. The king said to the mighty warrior, 'I beg you, stand with me in this war, that mortals should not say, "The earlier wars were of no substance."' Likewise, the Holy One said to Abraham, 'I have tried you with many tests, and you have stood up to them all. Now, I beg you, stand with Me in this test, that it not be said, "The earlier ones were of no substance."'"[14]

Abraham is like a mighty warrior who has gone before the rabbis. The Holy One is a God who has respect for Abraham, reasons with Abraham, and almost takes Abraham as his partner in revelation. This is a God who enlists

13. Bialik and Ravnitzky, *Book of Legends,* p. 39.
14. Bialik and Ravnitzky, *Book of Legends,* pp. 39-40.

the help of human beings, like a King enlisting the help of his greatest free-dom fighter. For the sake of the King's honor, the loyal warrior stands with him in this test. We can hear the "mythical, timeless realm" represented in this midrash, even as we hear the skirmishes of the rabbis' lives in the foreground. The rabbis' hearing of the *na* in Scripture gave them the inch they needed to portray the Holy One as One with whom they could reason and as a God who begged for their help, rather than acted as merely another tyrant over their lives. This transformed their position from victim of their historical circum-stances to brave warrior in league with God's purposes: "Precisely because the rabbis' beloved ancestors, the patriarchs, had faced the same dilemmas and challenges as the rabbis themselves," continues Stern, "and overcome them, or so the aggadic retelling of biblical narrative asserted, they could serve as such perfect examples for their descendents."[15]

But the battles were not always epic. The domestic lives of the rabbis, "the beliefs they valued, the lives they wished to live, their hopes and their dreams,"[16] and their ordinary relationships are also the subject of midrash. This is especially so in the midrashim which are told to include Sarah in the story:

> Abraham meditated in his heart, saying, "What am I to do? Shall I tell Sa-rah? *Women tend to think lightly of God's commands.* If I do not tell her and simply take off with him — afterward, when she does not see him, she will strangle herself." What did he do? He said to Sarah, "Prepare food and drink for us, and we will rejoice today." She asked, "Why today more than other days? Besides, what is the rejoicing about?" Abraham: "Old people like ourselves, to whom a son was born in our old age — have we not cause to rejoice?" So she went and prepared the food. During the meal, Abraham said to Sarah, "You know, when I was only three years old, I became aware of my Maker, but this lad, growing up, has not yet been taught [about his Creator]. Now, there is a place far away where young-sters are taught [about Him]. Let me take him there." Sarah: "Take him in peace."
>
> "And Abraham rose up early in the morning." Why early in the morn-ing? Because he said: "It may be that Sarah will reconsider what she said yesterday and refuse to let Isaac go. So I'll get up early and go while she is still asleep. Moreover, it is best that no one see us."[17]

15. Stern, "Introduction," pp. xx-xxi.
16. Stern, "Introduction," p. xx.
17. Bialik and Ravnitzky, *Book of Legends*, p. 40.

Surely when the rabbis read the story out of their own experience, they knew that no self-respecting Jewish mother would stand for the sacrifice of her son. In this midrash, the theological reason given is marvelous: women tend to think lightly of God's commands. Abraham therefore keeps the real reason of his journey from Sarah, even as he prepares her for the child's encounter with the living God. Staying for a moment with the theological logic in asking after Sarah's hidden character in this story, Phyllis Trible's reflections on the story during the *Genesis* conversations with Bill Moyers, would give the midrash a similar but slightly nuanced twist. Her contention is that the attachment of Abraham to Isaac was not to be compared with Sarah's devotion to her son. Nowhere does Abraham refer to Isaac as *my* son, *my beloved,* says Trible, whereas Sarah is depicted, before Genesis 22, as a mother singularly devoted to "my son." Therefore Trible takes this story as a story that, by its silence, tests Sarah.

Beyond the theological, there is the recognizable interplay between husband and wife. Abraham is well aware of Sarah's response to the deed he is about to do. What can he tell her to elicit her consent? He cannot lie to her. He begins by calling forth her gratitude. They must continue to rejoice at the gift of Isaac to their old age. But Sarah persists. So he tells her as much of the truth as she can bear: it is time that her son be taught about his Creator. She agrees and this explains why Abraham rises early, lest she change her mind. The details clearly have their origin in the domestic affairs of the rabbis and their wives. Mixed with the theological assertion of women less taken with God's commands, this is a tale told for those whose responsibility is that of religious head of the household. Abraham, again, is a model for dealing with the faith of one's spouse.

There is yet another layer here, however. If it is so that Bialik compiled this *Aggadah* on the binding of Isaac during a time of "the loss of faith, the collapse of traditional structures and tenets of Jewish belief," then the discovery of this particular midrash surely spoke anew to the experience of Russian Jews at the beginning of the twentieth century. Here were families with sons who had not been taught about their Creator. A far journey was required (Bialik and Ravnitzky eventually emigrated to the land of Israel where this collection was reprinted numerous times). Abraham had faced the dilemma they faced and took his son, early in the morning, to a mountain where (according to the previous midrash) God's glory awaited him.

From these examples, we can see the imaginative conversation between the rabbis and the Scripture, as well as the narrative extended toward the reality of the world in which they lived. Because Scripture and *aggadah* dealt with the truth of human existence, this truth continued to confer meaningfulness on the human situation in Russia at the turn of the century. The question at the beginning of the next century for Christian readers of Scripture, readers who also face crises in biblical authority and the collapse of traditional structures and tenets, is first of all a question concerning the legitimacy of midrash in relation to our understanding of Scripture. Clearly midrash would not have the status of serious biblical criticism and scholarship. But could the imaginative engagement with Scripture embodied in *aggadah* be reclaimed — or tried out by Christians for the first time — as a strategy for listening to Scripture in community, for hearing the reality of Scripture as it lends meaningfulness to the reality of our lives, and for allowing multiple readings to exist side-by-side in this time of polarized and politicized readings of biblical texts?

The Theory of Midrash

David Stern begins his conversation on *Midrash and Theory* with a question: "Is there a logic to interpretation in midrash, a set of rules or exegetical conventions governing the free play of its commentators?"[18] The logic, in the end, would seem to be precisely the lack of singular logic! What characterizes the habit of midrash and what undergirds the practice of midrash is the belief that Scripture contains, within itself, multiple meanings. This is marvelously illustrated by two sayings from the Talmud cited by Stern:

> Abbaye [a fourth-century Babylonian sage] said: "The verse says, 'Once God has spoken, but twice I have heard' (Psa. 62:12). A single verse has several senses, but no two verses ever hold the same meaning."
> It was taught in the School of Rabbi Ishmael [a second-century Palestinian sage]: "Behold, My Word is like fire — declares the Lord — and like a hammer that shatters rock" (Jer. 23:29). Just as this hammer produces many sparks [when it strikes the rock], so a single verse has several meanings.[19]

"The idea of Scriptural polysemy presented in these two sayings," according to Stern, "represents a virtual ideological cornerstone of midrashic exegesis."[20] From this cornerstone, Stern goes on to note, "The notion of

18. David Stern, *Midrash and Theory: Ancient Jewish Exegesis and Contemporary Literary Studies* (Evanston, IL: Northwestern University Press, 1996), p. 15.
19. Stern, *Midrash and Theory*, p. 17.
20. Stern, *Midrash and Theory*, p. 18.

Scriptural polysemy raises several questions. If every verse has several meanings, what did the Rabbis believe was the meaning of Scripture? Did the Bible even have a determinate sense for the Rabbis, or did they consider it essentially an open text, an unbounded field for the unlimited play of interpretation? If so, was any interpretation of Scripture valid? Or did there exist exegetical criteria, constraints upon the free activity of Scriptural interpretation, and if so, what were they? In the case of contradictory, mutually exclusive, or opposed exegeses, what criteria existed for resolving conflicts of interpretation?"[21]

Stern's questions are our questions. On the surface, they are questions characteristic of an approach to Scripture that would major more in certitude than in an ongoing engagement with the reality of the narrative as it lends meaningfulness to the reality of human existence. Yet they are questions asked out of a time and a culture gone mad over subjective truth and the indeterminacy of texts: it means what you want it to mean and, finally, it means nothing. This is precisely where midrash does not go! Rather midrash presupposes that all contradictory interpretations come from the speech of God himself. Different houses of interpretation hear the legitimate voice of God in contrary ways such that "even if they contradict each other, [differing interpretations] are considered equally true; identically alive to Torah's meaning, to the words of the living God."[22]

This approach to Scripture is seemingly without parallel. At Qumran, the term for exegesis of Scripture was *pesher,* which means "to release, to resolve, and solve." Now we are in more familiar territory! Stern connects this approach to the ancient practice of dream interpretation wherein the purpose was "to unravel the one and only meaning of the dream, pesher interpretation [viewing] Scripture as an enigma to be solved and decoded."[23] [An aside: this begins to come close to much of what offers itself to the unsuspecting parishioner from the shelves of Borders Bookstore on the code of scripture.] Curiously, the political and social situation at Qumran almost dictated the absoluteness of its claim to right and singular interpretation. Siege and survival shaped the reading of Scripture such that no room could be left for doubt or contrary belief. The parallel to our time's mentality must be vouchsafed!

This is precisely why the form of midrash — like the form of parable — has resisted any ideological or political agenda, including the agenda of our

21. Stern, *Midrash and Theory,* p. 18.
22. Stern, *Midrash and Theory,* p. 22.
23. Stern, *Midrash and Theory,* pp. 22-23.

Russian poet and journalist. By adopting the practice of interpreting Scripture with stories, of hearing Scripture's various voices, the rabbis turned from the absolutist claims to a "hermeneutic of multiplicity," leaving us with "a virtually ideological policy of polysemy."[24]

If we venture into Christian exegesis, the closest we come to the polysemy of midrash in the Church Fathers is Augustine. "In one of the most inspired exegeses in the entire history of Scriptural interpretation," says Stern, "Augustine reads God's blessing to mankind 'to be fruitful and multiply' (Gen. 1:22, 28) as an injunction to multiply interpretations of Scripture, to express in manifold ways what we understand in but one, and to understand in manifold ways what we read as obscurely uttered in but one way."[25] Augustine attributes this to the biblical author more than to God's intention. Thus we who are left to interpret Scripture will find it impossible to capture the original intention of a verse and are left to invent our own! What we invent, however, must have about it the "truth" and be "congruous with the truth taught in other passages of the Holy Scriptures."[26] Thus we come to the question of the rule of faith which, for Augustine, was *caritas*.

Is there a rule of faith for the expanse of biblical interpretation called midrash? Are there any theological or dogmatic or institutional constraints placed upon the writing of midrash? To be sure, there were schools of exegesis with distinct approaches and lists of hermeneutical rules. One also must note that the close attention of midrash to every *word* of Scripture leads to a conclusion that midrashic interpretation, even in its wildest imaginative leaps, stays closer to the text than many a historical-critical monograph. But when midrash is collected, there remains no hierarchy of interpretation. About as close as we could get, according to Stern, is Frank Kermode's "tacit knowledge of the permitted range of sense."[27] Holtz ventures not much closer, noting that if there is any one dogma in rabbinic Judaism, it is that in Torah, "everything is contained therein."[28] In other words and in our framework, isogesis is exegesis for those who are lovers of Torah.

Another element of midrashic theory worth noting, especially in a time like our own, is the sense of humor ingredient in the enterprise. We who are searching for the one, true, ecclesially sanctioned interpretation tend to be a bit serious and mean over the conclusions we reach through exegesis. "As an interpretive activity, midrash is a form of study that is also an avenue of en-

---

24. Stern, *Midrash and Theory*, p. 23.
25. Stern, *Midrash and Theory*, p. 24.
26. Stern, *Midrash and Theory*, p. 25.
27. Stern, *Midrash and Theory*, p. 25.
28. Holtz, "Midrash," p. 185.

tertainment, playful and serious at once."[29] To return to the midrashim on the binding of Isaac, there is found a hint: "'And he [himself] saddled his ass.' Love disregards dignity! How many menservants, how many maidservants did that righteous man have, yet he himself saddled his ass in his eagerness [to do God's will]."[30]

Midrash also offers us a helpful understanding of Scripture's relationship to God. According to Stern, Torah is God's blueprint, God's set of directions, God's ongoing plan for the creation and existence of the world.[31] Thus there is an identification, on one hand: every word and letter and verse is meaningful because it is God's, and the "essential unity of Scripture [is] the expression of the single divine will."[32] Torah is studied by those who seek the mind of "the divine architect," so that God may be followed and imitated within the confines of human existence. But, as we have seen, this divine will is discerned through the multiple voices contained within the whole of Scripture: there is not just *one way*. In fact, the wit of midrash is sometimes most delightfully expressed in the unexpected and stretched ways the rabbis used Scripture to interpret Scripture, leading them to know a God of surprises on top of surprises.

On the other hand, the identification of Torah with God is anything but literal, and stands over against the mystical, kabbalistic readings now so popular in this age of "spirituality," as well as standing at a distance from the prophetic pretensions of any given interpreter. This identification and non-identification stems from the realistic situation of the rabbis in relation to God:

> Following the destruction of the Temple, the text of the Torah became for the Rabbis the primary sign of the continued existence of the convenantal relationship between God and Israel, and the activity of Torah study — midrash — thus became the foremost medium for preserving and pursuing that relationship. Understood this way, the object of midrash was not so much to find the meaning of Scripture as it was literally to engage its text. Midrash became a kind of conversation that Rabbis invented in order to enable God to speak to them from between the lines of Scripture, in the textual fissures and discontinuities that exegesis discovers. The multiplication of interpretations in midrash was one way, as it were, to prolong that conversation.[33]

29. Stern, *Midrash and Theory*, p. 28.
30. Bialik and Ravnitzky, *Book of Legends*, p. 40.
31. Stern, *Midrash and Theory*, p. 28.
32. Stern, *Midrash and Theory*, p. 29.
33. Stern, *Midrash and Theory*, p. 31.

The Recovery of Midrash for the Church

At the heart of this current crisis of biblical authority, there is the crisis of a meaningful, helpful, challenging, and life-giving conversation atrophied by a multitude of factors. Many have already been mentioned. The political and ideological agendas which have emerged out of a society's profound dislocation from its religious and moral underpinnings, the growth of para-church camps within denominations which vie for influence and power more profoundly than they seek the purposes of the living God, the secular world bettering the church as the church defines herself in competition with the same, the explosion of communications which, paradoxically, has threatened the gathered community and privileged the virtual community, the fascination with a free-floating phenomenon referred to as *spirituality* which, for the most part, is self-referential, the pluralism wherein truth is subjective, no text is common and every text is read through the lens of one's own "accident" of birth.

We could go on. Suffice it to say, the concept of authority, itself, has fallen on hard times. The more authority is asserted, the less authoritative the church becomes in the real lives of people. In many ways, I do not weep for the effect this has had on the moribund institutional church of our day, but I do mourn the loss of the biblical narrative authoritatively heard at the center of our common life. This is the most tragic loss of all to people whose lives are desperate for the very meaning awaiting them through its narrative. Nevertheless, there is a sense in which our temple has been destroyed by the Romans (or was it by our own fears?), and we are left to ask after the purposes of God surely operating within the circumstances of our postmodern lives.

The coincidence of two crises — both the crisis of the Temple's destruction which gave rise to midrash as the means of prolonging the conversation with God, and the crisis faced by Bialik and Ravnitzky at the turn to the twentieth-century in Russia — put alongside our own has led me to investigate midrash as a means for our reengagement of Scripture's reality with the reality of human experience, by conceding the significance of the latter more magnanimously and carefully than much current scholarship will allow.

At this point, I will simply list some of what I think could be helpful from midrashic theory and practice for our current ecclesial morass vis-à-vis biblical authority:

- The understanding of Scripture as a prism, a lens through which we may view our own world;
- The way midrash listens to the reality of Scripture from out of the reality of human experience, gleaning the terms of reference from Scripture

wherein our lives are given new meaning, reclaiming the vocabulary of Scripture as a vocabulary through which to articulate feelings and thoughts;
- The resistance of midrash to ideology and politics, granting that this unfortunately arose from a distrust of history as any longer revelatory of God's purposes;
- The playfulness with which midrash engages Scripture, reminding us not to take ourselves as interpreters too seriously;
- The conversation prolonged through the stories told from out of the stories of Scripture which claim only to be conversations with the God whom we meet in the biblical narrative;
- The polysemy of Scripture and scriptural interpretation which could lead us out of the hierarchy necessary to orthodoxy's claims and the indeterminacy of postmodern pluralism.

Luke Timothy Johnson, in his revised *Scripture and Discernment: Decision Making in the Church,* offers for consideration "A Midrashic Model for an Ecclesial Hermeneutic." He suggests that the church today should seek to imitate the process by which the New Testament writings came into being, namely the process of midrash. He merely skims the surface, but his points underline the potential fruitfulness of such an exploration.

Johnson contends, "as midrash is a category that enables us to understand the process of the text's creation, so is it a category that enables us to move in the direction of a properly ecclesial hermeneutic."[34] He likens the prism through which the Talmud throws light upon Torah to the New Testament as the prism through which "the light of the experience of Jesus the crucified Messiah and risen Lord"[35] is thrown upon Torah.

Further, he underlines the significance for our times of the rabbis' insistence on listening to multiple voices, "in all their conflicts and disagreements, for it is precisely in those elements of plurality and even disharmony that the texts open themselves to new meaning, so that they are allowed to speak to the disharmonies and disjunctions of contemporary life."[36] Precisely!

A significant problem awaits us, however. First, we have no common understanding of Scripture that would coincide with the earliest rabbis' absolute clarity concerning Scripture's perfect Author and perfect authority. The

34. Luke Timothy Johnson, *Scripture and Discernment: Decision Making in the Church* (Nashville, TN: Abingdon Press, 1983), p. 39.
35. Johnson, *Scripture and Discernment,* p. 39.
36. Johnson, *Scripture and Discernment,* p. 39.

confident playfulness of *aggadah* could be allowed because Torah was also the subject of *halakhah,* a set of rules known as Jewish law that govern Jewish life. According to Robert Goldenberg, *halakhah* "embraces far more than the term 'law' usually suggests in English. . . . *Halakhah* naturally became [the rabbis'] chief concern, a concern that fit their theological conviction that Judaism essentially amounts to learning precisely what the Torah commands and then *doing* it."[37]

The earliest rabbis aimed at "the extension of holiness from the limits of the Jerusalem Temple to a wider range of everyday life . . . [turning] life into an inexhaustible supply of opportunities to fulfill divine law, and thus to sanctify life."[38] So too did the scribes devote "their entire lives to the study and teaching of Holy Writ" because they "considered the Scriptures a source of infinite wisdom."[39] This coupled with the "dogma" that "everything is contained therein" makes midrash the playful extension of Scripture's authority rather than an imaginative threat to Scripture's serious theological content.

We as Christians have no comparable communal claim to make about Scripture's perfect Author short of the claim that leads us toward inerrancy's orthodox straitjacket. Those Christians who "love" the Bible tend toward a latter-day biblicism while those who may thrill to its "stories" are wary of making communal claims concerning the truth contained therein. We have no schools of rabbis reading between the lines in such a way that our lives are taken seriously. There are only scholars interpreting texts whose primary referent tends to be the academy rather than the congregation.

The only Word we have been given as both limit and license in our response to Scripture's truth is Jesus Christ. He is enough! In a sense, the story we are told of his life, death, and resurrection is God's eternal midrash made flesh on the law and the prophets. In addition, we may look at Jesus' take on the Scripture of his community and learn from him the questions to ask, the silences to hear, the contradictions to notice which will call forth our own midrash. He will be our teacher for the stories we may truthfully and playfully tell out of the story we have been told in him.

Further, a model of *how* Jesus Christ is limit and license, in relationship to some recovery of midrash as interpretive genre, is given us in the synoptic gospels, the Gospel of John, and the Pauline letters. There is surely some degree of polysemy in the New Testament itself. In fact, the gospels within the canon could be said positively to glorify polysemy. Still, there are limits and

---

37. Goldenberg, "Talmud," p. 138.
38. Goldenberg, "Talmud," p. 130.
39. Goldenberg, "Talmud," p. 130.

there is a limit set by the canon that must not be lightly overstepped. The model of New Testament writers coupled with the stories and sayings of Jesus also may act as limit and license, even as Jesus acts as our teacher who alone can guide us through his midrash to the midrash of our time and community.

Then there is his church. As it is given to be a living hermeneutic of the gospel, the church ought to incarnate a midrashic gathering of motivations, feelings and thoughts unexpressed in Scripture but acted out in the ongoing story which is our human response to Scripture. If the church could be guided by pastor-theologians studying Scripture across denominational lines or within denominations across theological camps, and led by scholars studying Scripture among diverse theological faculties as well as across academic disciplines, then perhaps the resulting midrashim could be used in congregations as a mean of reengaging the reality of people's lives with the reality, power, and authority of Scripture. Because midrash was written only in community and by those who loved Torah, so would the Christian community look to those whose love of Jesus Christ would be limit and license as together they listened to Scripture in faith, telling those stories in response to Scripture's silence and inconsistencies which bear witness to the same Christ therein revealed.

We *could be* in the perfect situation, because of Jesus Christ, to play in the fields of midrash with some degree of discipline and abandon. How this would affect the study of Scripture among seminarians, or the centrality of Scripture within the life of congregations, or the authority of Scripture as it reorders the common life is not in our hands but God's. First, however, we must return to Scripture *together, to* the primary place where Christ meets us, as God's eternally relevant Word. Then whatever by grace we may venture in his name, we can be sure that God is able to do exceedingly more than we can ask or imagine!

Christ Outside the Walls

A. J. McKelway

Among American Protestants a debate is under way regarding the presence of revelation and salvation among non-Christians — whether the work of Christ takes place outside the walls of the church, which is to say, apart from its scriptures, confessions, and preaching. The question is not new, but has been given new impetus by the concerns of pluralism and multiculturalism, whose concerns are all the more relevant in a world savaged by religious fundamentalism. Thus it happens that an old issue has given rise to a fierce and divisive debate regarding what Christians can and should believe about the relation of Jesus Christ to other faiths. The level of animosity generated by the debate is due to the fact that some commentators within the mainline denominations have come to the conclusion that an equitable God would necessarily provide both revelation and salvation to those outside the circle of Christian belief, and that, consequently, a correction of Christian dogma is required. On this view, confessional claims regarding Jesus' divinity must be diminished in order to make room for other expressions of the divine elsewhere.[1]

---

1. For instance, among Presbyterians, the philosopher and theologian John Hick has argued in his various books, but nowhere more so than in his *The Myth of God Incarnate,* that the dogma of the divinity of Christ rules out other faiths and makes inevitable the spiritual imperialism of Christianity. Of similar views, inspired by the concerns of feminism as well as pluralism, an example is the key-note address of the Rev. Dirk Ficca at the 2000 Presbyterian Peace Making Conference. To serve the cause of interfaith peace, Ficca proposed that the Gospel is not about Jesus, but about his teaching concerning love and justice. His office is simply that of a prophet. The "Ficca Affair" caused much controversy, and the degree to which his views are not considered extraordinary may be seen in the fact that, when asked to do so, the Presbyterian's

Against this position many hold to the traditional belief that there is neither knowledge of God nor hope beyond the grave apart from faith in the Triune God of the Bible. According to this view, the Second Person of the Divine Triad is the Son, fully and *exclusively* known in the image of Jesus portrayed in scripture and interpreted in the Confessions. Against both sides in this dispute there are those who insist upon the full divinity of Jesus Christ, as expressed, for instance, in the Nicean formula, but who are unwilling to deny the possibility of the promises of God in Christ outside of Christian belief. While this view achieves some expression in recent Protestant Confessions,[2] it finds only occasional support in the Church's confessional tradition. For this reason it is a position more often asserted than argued, with the result that it has had little influence in the current debate.

The problem is that those who would abandon Nicea, and many who hold to it, view the Christian faith as necessarily and absolutely exclusive, because in both cases the identity of Jesus Christ is restricted to the historical circumstances of his Incarnation — and his present work to the mediation of the church. If the Word made flesh can be apprehended *only* through the witness of the Apostles and the preaching of the church, then other possibilities of revelation are, indeed, denied. That, however, is not the case, for the Bible clearly testifies to an identity of Jesus Christ which is not limited by his flesh, and to a gracious activity of Word and Son of God outside the community of faith.

The Biblical Witness

Here we can only note briefly what a more extended analysis might provide. In the Old Testament, the divine Word creates all that is, speaks to the patriarchs, and addresses the world through the prophets. If we believe with John that this Word was "In the beginning," was "with," and "was God," and that "*he* was in the beginning," that "without *him* was not anything made that was

---

General Assembly Council could find no grounds for rebuke. Cf. Leslie Scanlon, "GAC affirms earlier statement of Ficca; critic says council 'not fit to lead'," *The Presbyterian Outlook* 183, no. 10 (March 12, 2001): p. 3; and my article, "Reflections on Dirk Ficca's Speech," *Presbyterian Outlook* 183, no. 15 (April 16, 2001): pp. 6-7.

2. Cf. the Presbyterian *Confession of 1967*, especially 9.08, 9.10, 9.18, 9.20, 9.41, and 9.42. This confession distinguishes the "Christian religion" from "God's revelation," and frequently alludes to the fact that "The gift of God in Christ is for all men." Strangely, the more recent *Brief Statement of Faith* (1991) contains no such references, *The Book of Confessions* (Louisville, KY: The Office of the General Assembly, 1991).

made," and that this "he" of whom John speaks became flesh in Jesus Christ, then we must recognize both his Person and his work in the original and universal act of creation. The Fathers understood John 1:1-5 to refer to Jesus Christ before his infleshment, and this conception requires us to see the Person and work of Christ as the Word which reveals the will of God throughout the Old Testament. In those texts he who was the Word did not confine himself to the Covenant Community as such, for before its establishment with Abram, he spoke to primordial figures like Adam, Eve, Cain, and Noah. Afterward, he spoke also to people outside the boundaries of Israel's faith like the royal Melchizedek, the soothsayer Balaam, and the Persian king Cyrus. In the Old Testament the Word we know as Jesus Christ was never confined by or to a particular religious community or belief.

In the New Testament we find an extension of this underlying theme in the presence of the Magi in Matthew's account of the Nativity — and we might also include the Ethiopian Eunuch and even Paul, who did not encounter Christ in the flesh, and whose conversion took place outside the ministry of the church.

The Gospels

In so far as the issue before us involves the question whether a reception of Christ and his benefits is dependent upon some sort of confessional faith, then we find in the Gospels a strange anomaly. On the one hand, we have the general requirement of belief — and the self-identity of Jesus which supports it. He is the "Son of the Father," who on that account is the "way, the truth, and the life" which his disciples must follow. They must "believe in him whom [God] has sent," for "no one comes to the Father, but by me" (John 14:6). Thus, belief or faith is often presented in the Synoptics as a precondition to the forgiveness of sin and its correlate in the healing of bodies and the promise of divine favor.[3] Given the development of the Church's mission, it is not strange that we find in John an even greater emphasis in this regard.[4]

On the other hand, there are many texts where, rather than a condition, confession of faith appears as a *consequence* of Jesus' ministry and gracious activity. To take John as an example, in the story of the man born blind in chapter 9, the healing itself was followed by uncertainty. ". . . whether he is a sinner,

---

3. Among many such passages we need only mention Matt. 8:13; 9:28-29; Mark 11:23; and Luke 8:12 and 50.

4. Again, among many, cf. John 1:12; 3:16; 4:46ff.; and 11:40.

I do not know; . . . [but] now I see." The healing and saving power of the Word made flesh was revealed to him prior to his subsequent recognition of Jesus as the Christ. In respect to our particular concerns, it is worth noting that, in other texts, the miraculous activity of Jesus appears neither to require or produce faith in those benefitted by it. This is clear enough in John's account of the wedding at Cana in 2:1-11. It is also evident in the various accounts of the man who "took up his bed and walked." Neither in Matthew 9, Mark 2, or John 5 is there any indication that the man or his helpers believed before or after his healing. Similarly, in both the Synoptics and John, the account of Jesus delivering his disciples from a storm-tossed sea (whether he is walking upon it, in the boat, or on the shore) expressly mentions their "fear" and their "little," or absent "faith," and only in Matthew's description of Peter's venture upon the water is there a subsequent confession by the others that, "Truly, you are the Son of God." Otherwise, Jesus' calming of the sea produces only the question: "What sort of man is this?" and Mark goes so far as to report that "they did not understand" and that "their hearts were hardened."[5]

The claim that the healing, redemptive, and salvific work of Jesus Christ depends upon his being recognized and confessed in faith cannot without reservation be confirmed by an appeal to the Gospels. And if it be objected that in the above or other cases *some* faith was evident prior to the event, it is not at all clear what sort of faith that was. This was certainly true of Jesus' transforming encounter with the Samaritan woman, which produced in her as well the question: "Can this be the Christ?" (John 4:7-30), and a similar ambiguity arises in the story of the man born blind and also for the father who cried out: "I believe, help my unbelief!" (Mark 9:24). In neither case do we have a clear recognition of Jesus' identity. The same might be said for the woman (and nameless others, according to Matthew) who was healed by touching Jesus' garment. In these instances some sense of Jesus' healing power was no doubt present, but there is conspicuously absent the "belief" which Jesus elsewhere required — and there is certainly no confession of his identity which accompanies many other displays of his saving power.

If Jesus' work was not conditioned by what people believed about his identity, neither was a recognition of his identity determined only by what they saw him do. There are, of course, many declarations of faith expressed by those Jesus healed, and we have no reason to doubt their authenticity, but given the unpredictability of the responses to those events, we may wonder whether another factor was not present, whether it was not Jesus' action in concert with the Father and the Spirit which opened the eyes of faith. The

5. Luke 8:22-25; Matt. 8:23-27; 14:22ff.; Mark 4:35-41; 6:47-52; John 6:16-21.

most authoritative declaration of faith was pronounced by Peter: "You are the Christ, the Son of the living God." Peter was a witness to Jesus' mighty acts — and to other aspects of his ministry as well, but it was not, according to Jesus, those "flesh and blood" events which revealed his identity to Peter, "but my Father who is in heaven" (Matt. 16:16-17). Since Jesus elsewhere and in various ways states that he and the Father "are one," a unity spelled out more fully by John and Paul, we have to conclude that Jesus Christ known in the flesh was also active outside of it.

The recognition and then confession of Jesus Christ as Lord must always have included this other factor — the presence of a power not constrained by the form in which it was seen. The same point can be made for what many regard as the classic statement of Christian exclusivity in Acts 4:12: "And there is salvation in no one else, for there is no other name under heaven given among men by which we must be saved." But what is meant here by the name "Jesus"? It is often noted that proper names functioned somewhat differently in the ancient world; the modern concept of "personality" was as yet unknown, and among Jews names were apt to be either functional or family-relational and typically bore a meaning which extended beyond their object. These reflections, however, do not much ameliorate the fact that it is still Jesus, the Galilean Rabbi, who is meant. The point must rather be that, when Peter in Acts insisted upon the "name" of Jesus he had in mind not only his master and friend according to the flesh, but also the strange reality of the resurrected "Son of God," who, even before the events of Good Friday and Easter, could not be known by "flesh and blood" alone.

Paul

Regarding the present controversy over the relation of Jesus Christ to those outside the Church, the witness of the Apostle Paul is claimed by both sides. On the one hand, we have Paul's marvelous vision of the universal reach of Christ's grace in Romans 11: "For God has consigned all men to disobedience, that he may have mercy upon all." This aspect of Paul has caused some to think of God as a sort of saving machine, so that there is no need for the atoning work of Christ, no need for an Incarnation — and, thus, no need for a Trinity. Overlooked, however, is the fact that, for Paul, this God is known only through Jesus Christ, who, alone, made possible that mercy for "all."[6]

6. Here we may think of all those New England Congregationalists who became Universalists on their way to Unitarianism.

On the other hand, we have Paul's urgent mission to the Gentiles, his preaching of a Gospel which had the power to save men and women from the power of sin and death — to inspire in them a "faith," which, according to Luther, "alone" saves. This aspect of Paul encourages those who insist that salvation depends upon a conscious conversion to Christian faith. On this understanding of Paul, however, several comments are in order. The whole of Paul's thought is governed by the idea of faith rather than works, and so the question arises: what sort of willing and thinking is a "faith," which at the same time is not a "work"? It could hardly have been Paul's intention to set the human act of believing as either the efficient or secondary cause of our salvation. When Paul wrote to the Galatians that they "have come to know God," but then immediately corrects himself and writes: "or rather [that you have come] to be known *by* God," we are reminded of his constant insistence that a person's salvation does not ultimately depend upon any human action (whether the church's proclamation, or a believing response to it) but upon the prior action of God in Christ.

Because of this overriding theme in Paul, a number of exegetes have argued that in many places Paul's insistence upon "faith in Jesus Christ" should be better rendered as "the faithfulness of Jesus Christ." This re-translation of familiar texts is based upon what is called the "subjective genitive" in Greek grammar, which comes into play when the noun of the genitive phrase produces the action.[7] Among exegetes, attention to this aspect of Greek arose in the nineteenth century and was used throughout Barth's *Romans*, where "faith in Jesus" is retranslated as "the faithfulness of Jesus," or in other contexts, "the faithfulness of God."[8] This employment of the subjective genitive has recently been taken up by a number of New Testament scholars, including Lloyd Gaston, Louis Martyn, and Richard Hays,[9] and while their occasional replacement of *our* "faith" with God's or Christ's "faithfulness" does not remove from many other texts Paul's insistence upon our believing, it does better reconcile what otherwise seems to be Paul's contradictory placement of the human work of faith over against his Gospel of pure grace. Our conclu-

7. The subjective genitive occurs ". . . when the noun in the genitive [phrase] produces the action, being therefore related as *subject* to the verbal idea of the noun modified." H. F. Dana and Julius R. Mantey, *A Manual Grammar of the Greek NT* (New York: Macmillan, 1953), p. 78.

8. Cf. his rendering of Romans 1:17, ". . . the righteous shall live by my faithfulness," or 3:28, ". . . a man is justified by the faithfulness of God," etc.

9. See Richard B. Hays, *The Faith of Jesus Christ: An Investigation of the Narrative Substructure of Galatians 3:1–4:11* (Chicago: Scholars Press, 1983); Lloyd Gaston, *Paul and the Torah* (Vancouver: University of British Columbia Press, 1987); and J. Louis Martyn, *Theological Issues in the Letters of Paul* (Edinburgh: T&T Clark, 1997).

sion, then, is that Paul cannot be used to place confessional faith alongside Christ's faithfulness as a requirement for the reception of his benefits.

The faithfulness of God that inspires and enables human faith and authentic confession was for Paul the work of the man Jesus — a man, however, who, because of his unity with God, met him in another, resurrected, form on the road to Damascus. For Paul, therefore, Jesus was the "Lord," and we recall that the Jews used the term "Lord" *(adonai)* as the correct way to speak God's otherwise unspeakable and mysterious name. It is significant that the same term was used by the disciples when addressing Jesus.[10] Paul employed this usage and at the beginning of his letters often used it in the couplet: "God our Father and our Lord Jesus Christ." Paul had to speak of Jesus as God, since he viewed him as "the image of the invisible God . . . in whom all things were created . . . [who] was before all things . . . [and] in whom was the fullness of God" (Coi. 1:15-19). Elsewhere, Paul asserts that Jesus was "the Son of God," who "was in the form of God," and equal to God (Phil. 2:6), and that "God was in Christ, reconciling the world . . ." (2 Cor. 5:19).

Thus in Paul we find the beginning of a Christology hinted at in the Synoptic Gospels and echoed in John. For Paul, Jesus Christ, the eternal Son and revealer of the Father, did not hold his "equality with God" a thing "to be held as his own, but emptied himself" *(heauton ekenōsen)* of that exclusivity and took "the form of a servant . . . in the likeness of men" (Phil. 2:6-7). In this *kenosis* he did not abandon what God cannot abandon — his own divinity — nor did he transform it into creatureliness, which amounts to the same thing. Rather, he moved from the status or "form" of pure invisibility and hiddenness to become known among his creatures without forfeiting those qualities.[11] When the Word became flesh in Jesus it did not become less than it was.

If the Person of Jesus Christ is constrained by his human form, or his work limited to it, then any knowledge or reception of his grace is inexorably restricted to the Bible and to the witness of the church. We have found, however, that both the Gospels and Paul recognize another factor in the Person and work of Christ — that he lives outside the circumscription of his particular history. This other factor achieved further exposition and clarification in the dogmatic tradition of the church — and to it we must now turn.

10. Refer to Kendall Soulen, "The Name of the Holy Trinity: A Triune Name," *Theology Today* 59, no. 2 (July 2002): pp. 244-261.

11. That the Nicean Fathers interpreted Paul in this way is illustrated by the judgment of Leo the Great who spoke of this "self-emptying, whereby the invisible made himself visible," so that it was "a condescension of compassion, not a failure of power," *Epistola dogmatica ad Flavian,* Letter 28.3; see Gerald O'Collins, *Christology* (New York: Oxford University Press, 1995), p. 158.

Dogmatic Developments

The Christology of the Fathers before and after Nicea was not, as Harnack claimed, an unfortunate misrepresentation of the Bible's straightforward portrayal of Jesus as a teacher of the Fatherhood of God and the brotherhood of man. Nor, as sometimes argued by champions of a "Christology from below," did it obscure the Gospel's portrayal of Jesus as the Revealer of a just and loving God. Put in the simplest way, the Nicean Fathers were only trying to state the meaning of the prologue to the Gospel of John. Just as John tried to express the divinity of Jesus taught by Paul, exhibited in the Synoptics and believed by the church, so, too, centuries later Athanasius and others tried to sort out the implications of John's claim that the "Word became flesh." We noted above John's identification of the Word with Jesus by assigning the personal pronoun "he" to the Word who "was in the beginning with God." Unless we can imagine that John was somehow already in possession of a developed doctrine of Trinitarian Persons named as Father, Word, and Spirit, we have to accept the fact that, when he assigned the personal pronoun "he" to the Word, he was identifying that divine being with Jesus. When, therefore, he says that the "Word became flesh," he does not mean that he became another than who he was, but rather that Jesus, the Son and Word, took on another form.[12]

We cannot here review the slow progress of theological reflection that resulted in the Nicean Creed and its final clarification at Chalcedon in 451. The results of that development are best reflected in the quadrilateral formula of Chalcedon, namely, that Jesus Christ in his divinity was of the same substance or being as the Father; that in his humanity he shared the creatureliness of other human beings; that these divine and human natures were perfectly united in one Person; but that in that unity both natures retained their own recognizable and different qualities. While the controversies that surrounded this development all bear upon the issue at hand, our particular interest is in the way the Fathers conceived of the "other factor" involved in the Person of Jesus Christ, namely, the way his identity and activity were not limited by his existence in the flesh, but in some sense operated independently of it both before and after its occurrence.

---

12. While Luther and the translators of the King James Bible were syntactically correct in translating the *houtos* in John 1:2 as "the same" (Luther, "*Dasselbige*"), that term could refer just as well to an impersonal eternal Word as to Jesus. Modern translators are surely right in rendering *autos* as "he" to better maintain John's identification of the Eternal Word with Jesus.

When the early Fathers spoke of the *Word* who became flesh, they, like John, employed a term with a rich philosophical heritage, but gave it quite a different meaning, for it was not, as with Stoicism, immune from materiality. For Justin Martyr, the Word was "a certain rational power," which "God begat before all creatures," but it was also the *dābār Yahweh*, the "Word of the Lord" spoken through the prophets, a *Person* who was "Holy Spirit," an "Angel," the "Son," "Wisdom," and finally "Lord and Logos," and "can be called by all those names."[13] It must be admitted, however, that, although Justin speaks of these forms of the Word as a Person, that characteristic is obscured in his conception of the Word as "rational power," particularly when he speaks of the Logos as bearing "seeds" which enlighten all rational minds.[14]

Things become clearer with Tertullian, whose doctrine of the one (divine) nature of the three Persons of the Godhead — and the two (divine and human) natures of the one Person Jesus Christ, set the stage for Nicea a century later. Following the Gospel of John, Tertullian insisted upon the absolute identity of Jesus Christ with the eternal Logos, and rejected any division of the Word into "Son," "Christ," and "Jesus," because they were "One Person."[15] For Tertullian, and all the Fathers following him, the problem was how to express and explain the New Testament's witness to the divinity of Christ without implying polytheism — or diminishing the divine presence in, and empowerment of, the salvation found in the real man Jesus. Thus, the church early on rejected the Jewish heresy of the Ebionites, which denied the divinity of Jesus, and Irenaeus condemned Gnosticism, which denied his real humanity. Later, the Fathers rejected the subordinationism of Arius, which understood the Logos to be a second order divinity created by God and, as well, the modalistic "monarchianism" of Sabellius, which denied the distinctive personhood of the Son.

If the true divinity and true humanity of Jesus Christ was established by the final statement of the Nicean Creed at Constantinople in 381, the more vexing problem of the relation of those natures in Jesus remained. It was

13. Justin Martyr, *Dialogue With Trypho*, LXI, in *The Ante-Nicene Fathers*, vol. 1, ed. A. Roberts and J. Donaldson (Grand Rapids: Eerdmans, 1967), p. 227.

14. Justin Martyr, *Second Apology*, VIII, XIII, in *Nicean Fathers*, pp. 191, 192.

15. Tertullian, *Adversus Praxean*, 27, and also 2, 10, 11 in O'Collins, *Christology*, p. 167. Because "person" *(prosōpon)* could mean "nature," one sometimes finds in the Greek Fathers "two persons" ascribed to Christ, but they meant "two natures." Clement of Alexandria represents another early identification of Jesus Christ with the eternal Word: "Christ was, indeed, the ancient Logos and [the cause] of our being . . . but now the same Logos has appeared to men . . . ," Reinhold Seeberg, *Text-Book of the History of Doctrines* (Grand Rapids: Baker Book House, 1964), p. 143.

agreed that, in becoming flesh, the Word entered into and fully participated in our humanity, but the fleshly humanity of Jesus must necessarily be different and distinct from his divinity. At the same time, however, the union of the divine and human natures in Jesus Christ was understood in such a way that there was an interpenetration *(perichoresis)*[16] in which the attributes proper to divinity and humanity could be communicated to, or shared in, the person of Jesus — a *communicatio idiomatum*. Such a conception was necessary if the eternal Son of God suffered on the Cross — and if the man Jesus exhibited the miraculous power of God, but how can such a view maintain his real humanity in its distinctive, creaturely limitation? How can we maintain Irenaeus's dictum: "He became what we are so that we might become what he is," if we can no longer see that he became "what we are"?

This question was raised with particular force by Nestorius, the (ultimately deposed) Patriarch of Constantinople, who objected to the notion of a fusion of natures, or an exchange of divine and human properties in the person of Jesus. For him, the title "bearer of God" *(theotokos)* assigned to Mary was unacceptable, because, while "the Word became flesh," the honor of God demanded that a distinction be maintained between the Word and that flesh. The purely human activity of Jesus' life and the activity of the divinity to which his humanity was joined must not be confused. While Nestorius's views shifted somewhat in his long and intricate controversy with Cyril of Alexandria, and while the degree to which his views were unorthodox is much debated, it is enough to say that he was *understood* by his contemporaries to so distinguish between Christ's two natures that there existed in him two persons: the eternal Son/Word — and the man Jesus.[17]

---

16. *Perichōreuō* "to dance around or about" illustrated the exchanging of places and functions of the Trinity. It may be understood as a "passing into one another of the divine persons [so that] the divine modes of being mutually condition and permeate one another so completely that one is always in the other two and the other two in the one. . . . [The term] implies both a confirmation of the distinction in the modes of being, for none would be what it is (not even the Father) without its co-existence with the others, and also a relativization of this distinction, for none exists as a special individual, but all three 'in exist' or exist only in concert as modes of being of the one God and Lord who posits Himself from all eternity," Karl Barth, *Church Dogmatics* I/1, p. 370.

17. Although it was not so intended, the idea of a "double birth" of the Son of God (eternally from the Father — in time and flesh from Mary) encouraged some to think of two persons co-existing in the man Jesus. The formula of a double generation seems to have arisen from Paul's reference to God's Son who was also a descendant of David in Romans 1:3. It was adopted by Ignatius of Antioch, Irenaeus and many others, including Cyril of Jerusalem and Cyril of Alexandria. The latter was sometimes charged with a two-person theory, but clearly did not teach it. See O'Collins, *Christology*, pp. 166ff.

The church's faith in the giving of God's Self in the Incarnation, the forgiveness and acceptance gained on the Cross, and the eternal hope provided by the Resurrection of Jesus — all of that required that it was really God who did those things in a real and single human life. To the extent that God was not understood as joined to that Person — just to that extent was the faith of the church rendered uncertain, because, as Gregory of Nazianzus put it: "That which is unassumed is not healed."

To think with Tertullian of Jesus Christ as one person with two natures requires a dialectical imagination which Nestorius did not possess, but which Athanasius insisted upon. While he is best known for supplying the central teaching of Nicea — that Jesus Christ, the Son, was of the "same substance" *(homoousios)* as the Father, Athanasius was just as important in showing how we must think of the way humanity and divinity were joined in the one person Jesus. In the following quotation from his treatise on the Incarnation we can therefore properly substitute the proper name, "Jesus," for all pronominal references to the bodily form of the Word:

> The Savior of us all, the Word of God, in His great love took to Himself a body and moved as a man among men. . . . He banished death from us and made us new; and invisible and imperceptible as in Himself He is, He became visible through His works and revealed Himself as the Word of the Father, the Ruler and King of the whole creation. There is a paradox in this last statement which we must now examine. The Word was not hedged in by His body, nor did His presence in the body prevent His being present elsewhere as well. When He moved His body He did not cease also to direct the universe by His mind and might. No. The marvelous truth is that . . . existing in a human body, to which He himself gives life, He is still the source of life to all the universe, present in every part of it. . . . His body was not for Him a limitation, but an instrument, so that He was both in it and in all things, and outside all things, resting in the Father alone. At one and the same time — this is the wonder — as Man He was living a human life, and as Word He was sustaining the life of the universe, and as Son He was in constant union with the Father.[18]

In his long controversy with Nestorius, Cyril of Alexandria echoed the sentiments of Athanasius: ". . . the flesh [of Jesus] was neither changed into the nature of the divinity, nor, indeed [was] the ineffable nature of the Word of God altered into the nature of the flesh . . . when he was visible and still re-

---

18. St. Athanasius, *St. Athanasius on the Incarnation,* trans. Religious of C.S.M.V. (London: A. R. Mowbray & Co. Ltd., 1953), pp. 43-45.

mained an infant in swaddling clothes . . . he filled the whole creation as God, and a co-ruler with the One who begot him."[19] On the eve of Chalcedon, Leo the Great confirmed the insistence of Athanasius and Cyril upon the unity of divine and human nature in the one person of Jesus Christ. According to Grillmeier, this unity was the "point on which the pendulum" of Leo's dialectical view of Christ swung. "This 'person' in Christ is not a third element which only results from the union of the two natures . . . [because] he who becomes man is the Son of the Father who has already existed from eternity and is thus *pre-existent as a person*."[20] Thus the creed of Chalcedon confesses, "One and the same Christ, Son, Lord, Only Begotten, made known in two natures [which exist] without confusion, without change, without division, without separation; the difference of the natures having been in no way taken away by reason of the union, but rather the properties of each being preserved, and [both] concurring in one Person *(prosōpon)* and one *hypostasis* — not parted or divided into two persons *(prosōpa)*, but one and the same Son and Only begotten, the divine Logos, the Lord Jesus Christ. . . ."[21]

*   *   *

We began with the question whether the presence and power of Jesus Christ is available to those outside the Christian Faith — whether the Person and work of Jesus Christ is confined to a knowledge and acceptance of his portrayal in scripture as it is interpreted and mediated by the Church. That question is forced upon us both by those who, for the sake of inter-religious harmony, would demote Jesus to the office of a prophet, and, equally, by those who would restrict the presence and work of the Son of God to a faith informed by scripture and Christian preaching. We have found, however, that the requirement of confessional faith cannot be sustained by appeal to scrip-

19. Cyril of Alexandria, *Letters*, 1-50, trans. John I. McEnerey (Washington, D.C.: The Catholic University of America Press, 1985), p. 83. Calvin no doubt had this passage in mind when he wrote in his *Institutes*, II.13.iv: "They thrust upon us as something absurd the fact that if the Word of God became flesh, then he was confined within the narrow prison of an earthly body. This is mere impudence! For even if the Word in his immeasurable essence united with the nature of man into one person, we do not imagine that he was confined therein. Here is something marvelous: the Son of God descended from heaven in such a way that, without leaving heaven, he willed to be borne in the virgin's womb, to go about the earth, and to hang upon a cross; yet he continuously filled the world even as had done from the beginning!"

20. Aloys Grillmeier, *Christ in Christian Tradition*, trans. J. S. Bowden (London: A. R. Mowbray & Co. Ltd., 1965), pp. 467-8.

21. The translation of V. Sellers in Grillmeier, *Christian Tradition*, p. 481. For a full discussion of Nestorianism, see pp. 363-452.

ture, since the benefits of Christ often appear in the Gospels without it. We
have also found that, where faith in Jesus as the Son of God does occur, it occurs, not by what according to the Gospel narratives is visible, not as Jesus
said, by "flesh and blood," but by a secret working of God in Christ himself.
We have found, in other words, that, when considering the person of Jesus, we
have to do with "another factor," namely, his identity as the eternal Son and
Word of God, who, according to Paul, John, and the Nicean Fathers was and is
God. It was this factor which preoccupied the debates which led to the
Church's final articulation of Christology at the synod of Chalcedon — and it
is this factor which denies the restriction of the Person and work of Jesus
Christ to his fleshly existence — or to the New Testament's narration, or the
Church's proclamation, of it.

Modern Protestantism has since the Enlightenment focused upon the
life of Jesus as presented in the Gospels, and has largely ignored the "higher"
Christology of the Fathers. The doctrine of the Trinity with its strange conceptions of *perichoresis* and *communicatio idiomatum* was thought, in the
manner of Harnack, to obscure the moral and spiritually uplifting life of the
man Jesus. Only a Christology from "below" informed by that life was seen as
relevant for the Church's encounter with modernity. The moralisms which
emerged from that view, whether bourgeois, romantic or "realistic," were no
more able than other moral systems to effectively address the crises of modernity. In a cruder form this low Christological ethic is expressed in the popular
slogan: "What would Jesus do?" but that question assumes that Jesus' role in
human history can be understood only in terms of his life in the flesh, and
thus it fails to see the "other factor" involved in his life — namely that it was
and is united with God.

Among the American ethicists of the last century, only Paul Lehmann
seemed to understand that the question is not "what *would* Jesus *do?*" but
"what *is* God in Christ *doing* in the world to make and keep human life more
human?"[22] For Lehmann, the question of what Jesus Christ is *doing* in the
world not only prohibits any restriction of his life to its fleshly occurrence,
but also prohibits any dissolution of Jesus' life into the divinity to which it is
joined. In that unity Jesus does not become a spiritual abstraction by which
one can conveniently identify him with this or that morality. The Jesus who
today converts sinners, transfigures revolutions, and transforms society is the

---

22. The propriety of this question is carefully developed and applied to the presupposi-
tions of ethical enquiry in Paul Lehmann, *Ethics in a Christian Context* (New York: Harper and
Row, 1963), and is applied specifically to revolutionary movements for human liberation in his
The Transfiguration of Politics (New York: Harper and Row, 1975).

same Jesus we meet in the Gospels and in the preaching of the church, so that our ethical judgments concerning what he is *doing* must be informed by what he *did*. While the question before us is not primarily ethical, Lehmann's approach is of interest, because he saw in the Gospel's portrayal of Jesus the hidden factor of a divinity not restricted then by his flesh, or now by his body, the church. He operates in the world of secular politics in a different form than that of his flesh — even if what he does now is consistent with what he did then.

Now the point of all this for our concerns is that this way of considering the life of the living Christ opens the possibility of imagining his work in other contexts than that of the Christian Church, in other ways than those known to the church, and in other forms than those typical of the New Testament witness. This means that Jesus' "other sheep" may hear his voice, and be led into his fold, in a different way. It will, of course, still be the voice of the One revealed in the Gospel — and the way taken will still be that of the crucified and risen Lord. To think in terms of this possibility does not, therefore, permit us to think of Jesus Christ apart from the way he is revealed to faith in and through the scriptures, for it is only there that this possibility comes to light. It is only there that we learn of the mysterious unity and exchange which characterizes the life of Jesus within the Trinitarian life of God. If we say that Jesus Christ "lives," we mean that he lives the eternal life of God, and is thus free to cross the barriers of time and circumstance and "raise up children of Abraham" from any stones at hand.

On the Ascension

Robert W. Jenson

I

Wallace Alston and I have spent five years in vigorous, often loud, and — at least for me — illuminating arguments about Christology. He disapproves of my hyper-Cyrillean (i.e., old Lutheran) positions, and especially my effort to get along without positing a *logos asarkos;* he fears I slight the historical particularity of the Incaration. I disapprove his sliding away (as I see it) from the doctrine, "'Jesus is the Logos' is an identity-statement." I fear he opens the door to speculation untethered from the historical Incarnation. It therefore seemed appropriate that I should contribute to this volume a piece on a similarly controverted and closely related matter, which was on my mind at the time I had to write, and to which I am sure our argument could be transferred without much change of rhetoric.

The creed definitely confesses a specific event that may be called "the Ascension." The direct biblical warrant for doing this may, however, be thought slim, since it consists only of the doubled Lucan account (Luke 24 and Acts 1);[1] and Luke's story itself, in its singularity and oddity, is often discounted as marginal. The entire New Testament, however, either asserts or assumes the risen Jesus' rule from the right hand of the Father,[2] and so from heaven as somehow another region than earth.[3] For Jesus to be there he must

---

1. Perhaps we may abstract from the puzzling circumstance that the two tellings, by the same author, do not seem altogether to agree.

2. For this and much of the immediately following, see now Douglas Farrow, *Ascension and Ecclesia* (Grand Rapids: Eerdmans, 1999), pp. 15-40.

3. So, e.g., 1 Thessalonians 4:16.

somehow have gotten there; and a wide variety of other New Testament passages allude to such a passage.[4] Thus insofar as we entertain the picture of heaven as *above* us, Jesus must indeed have "ascended." This logic is reproduced by the creeds' paired clauses about Ascension and the Session at the Father's right hand, which make the Ascension the precondition of the Session, and the Session the point of the Ascension.

In Luke (24:51) and Acts (1:9) themselves, the needed passage from earth to heaven is pictured spatially: the Lord *lifts up* from the earth and just so is on his way to heaven. In the ancient Mediterranean world and the medieval West, no one could have had any very different picture of a departure for heaven. But for us who envision cosmic topography on the pattern of Copernicus, the Lucan account poses a problem which cannot, I think, be ignored or postponed. If ever a passage of Scripture seemed to need demythologizing, and that very much in Bultmann's sense, it is the Lucan story of ascension; and indeed no theology since Copernicus has gotten by without some demythologizing at this point, acknowledged or not. For can one really — and even if one be the Christ — get to God by space travel?

Within the Ptolemaic and most other pre-modern models of the universe, the answer to that question could in fact be an unproblematic yes, at least so far as the sheer topography is concerned. It is vital to understand that such an answer was not scientifically or otherwise unsophisticated. Ptolemy's cosmology provided not only a plausible and explanatory cosmic topography, but functioned as the medieval world's standard model of physical phenomena generally.[5] According to Ptolemy, the spherical earth is surrounded by a concentric set of crystalline shells, which in their differently vectored revolutions carry the heavenly bodies, and which organize space into concentric regions, each in succession more distant from the heavy and opaque earth and just so[6] more buoyant and glorious.[7] Theological appropriation of this picture could then take the outermost region as a supremely glorious part of creation, made and appropriated by God to be his own fit[8] dwelling place within his creation — to be, if one may put it so, his *pied à terre* with his creatures. It is apparent that this model can easily accommodate the Old Testament's lan-

---

4. Assembled in Farrow, *Ascension,* pp. 275-8.

5. The model accounted for much more than the movements of heavenly bodies. Thus, e.g., very light objects move upward because their entelechy is some heavenly region less dense than that immediate to earth.

6. A la Aristotle.

7. It is worth noting and indeed emphasizing that pre-modern theology's Ptolemaic cosmology thus did *not* make earth the *value*-center of the universe; on the contrary.

8. Analogously, of course.

guage about God "looking down" from heaven, or "rending the heavens and coming down,"[9] and that it provides a route and destination for a bodily Ascension.

By contrast the Copernican universe, while bumpy, is on the whole homogeneous: it is not divided into more and less glorious regions, of which the most worthy might be fit for God. Could indeed one get to God by motion away from earth, even with unlimited time? Could a telescope with unlimited range espy theological mysteries? It is doubtful that even the most ardently anti-modernist exegete will now want to say yes to such questions without considerable hemming and hawing. Medieval iconography of the disciples in a circle looking up at the bottom of a cloud, from which a pair of feet dangle, was not intended to provoke giggles, but invariably now does, also from the pious.

Moreover, the Lukan spatial representation makes a problem within the New Testament resurrection accounts themselves. According to Luke, the risen Lord rose into heaven as the conclusion of his resurrection appearances. But where then had he been located *between* the appearances? It goes against the whole language and tone of the appearance accounts to suppose that with the Resurrection he had simply returned to dwell on earth until the Ascension, and so between appearances was journeying in Jerusalem and Galilee.[10] Rather, he strangely appears to and disappears from "their sight" (Luke 24:31). His belated appearance to Saul/Paul was "from heaven" (Acts 9:3-4), to which he then also withdrew; and that surely offers the most biblically plausible account of the other appearances also. Yet if Jesus appeared from and withdrew to heaven with his appearances to Mary, Peter, and the rest, in no such instance does the account suppose that movement up or down was needed. This observation has led to the suggestion[11] that "the Ascension" was simply the last of the appearances, and that the upward movement was merely a sign in the Johannine sense, to signify that no more were to be expected. The suggestion may be illuminating so far as it goes, but that is not perhaps very far.

It may be thought that the foregoing paragraphs worry too much about Luke's picture, that of course heaven is not literally "up" there and so what? But if we do not construe the ascension as Luke does, we have to construe it some other way, and the history of attempts to do so does not suggest this will be easy.[12] Difficult and in some cases soteriologically weighty questions an-

9. If *we* then *ascend* to heaven, do we have to rend the crystalline spheres on the way? The question worried the mystery-religions and some gnostics.
10. Or perhaps staying with Mary and Martha?
11. Notably by the author's eminently orthodox *Doktorvater*, Peter Brunner.
12. Here again, Farrow provides something like an encyclopedia.

nounce themselves. The one who enters and comes from heaven is the *bodily* resurrected Jesus. If the body did not go up, where did it go? Is it in no region of space? But what would a "body" be that was not in *any* space? If the body is in some plausible sense "up" there, how does it come to be on the eucharistic altar? Or does it? How *is* heaven related to earth? If we are to make Jesus' journey after him, what sort of journey will that be? Where, indeed, is God, with that "right hand" of his? One could go on.

Since Copernicanism's triumph, the most common way of construing heaven has been to turn it into a realm, as Calvin put it, altogether "outside the universe,"[13] into which one could "ascend" by a purely metaphysical journey. "Above" in "heaven above" thus becomes a metaphor for a non-spatial relation between only metaphysically specified realities. Perhaps many readers will finally judge that this particular demythologizing is the best possible. In my judgment, however, it will not do, and in the following I will develop an alternative, also suggested — though perhaps *only* suggested — in the tradition.

One problem with Calvin's — and most other Protestant theologians' — location of the risen Christ outside "the universe" is that this must detach him from space — unless of course Calvin's thinking is still unconsciously parasitic on Ptolemy. What then of Calvin's vigorous insistence that Christ is risen in the body and that a body must have its space?[14] Or if "the universe" does not encompass all places, what other kind of place is there? This, seemingly, would have to be a metaphysical region only analogously to be called a "place," which will hardly suffice for an actual body. And surely this is not the place for cosmological speculation about multiple universes![15] The outcome of centuries of theology on the majority modern line is that most Christians take it for granted that the risen Christ must be a purely "spiritual" entity, even as they verbally confess "the resurrection of the body."

In any case, putting heaven outside our universe seems to undo the biblical notion of heaven, whose presence in Scripture is after all our reason for taking up the matter in the first place. For pre-modern theology had this much right: the Bible does not posit heaven to isolate the God who dwells there from our universe but to locate him in it with respect to us. It is precisely the clouds we see and from which rain and snow descend on us that are the clouds "of heaven" (Matt. 24:30), and it is the visible "sky," carrying the lights and time-keepers God provides for us (Gen 1:6-8, 14-15), which he

13. John Calvin, Ephesians 4:8, cited from Farrow, *Ascension*, p. 175.
14. E.g., *Institutes of the Christian Religion* (1536), iv.122.
15. Wallace will recognize a joint bugaboo.

"rends" when he moves toward us. Heaven and earth are in Scripture the exhaustive two parts of *creation* (Gen. 1:1), one of which he has kept for himself and the other of which he has given to us (Psa. 115:16). We will shortly note that in the Old Testament, the spatiality of God's heaven "above" is not altogether univocal, and this will be a decisive clue; but we will also see that in Scripture heaven is nevertheless always a region to the boundary of which we in our universe can *point*.

The pairing of the two creedal clauses provides, in my judgment, a place to start. Christ ascended into heaven. According to the second clause, the right hand of God the Father is in heaven. Perhaps we should let that second clause tell us what heaven is.

II

It is an ancient theological maxim: God is his own space.[16] However creation may be spatially structured, the space that God is and the space he creates differ as Creator and creature, and so do not themselves overlap. If then God wishes not merely to co-exist with us, but to have to do with us, who are bodies in created space, he must own another space than himself, a created space from which he can come to us and to which he can bring us to be with him.

In the creedal clause, calling God "almighty" presumes a creation on which he may exercise his might; the seat at the "right hand" of this sovereign is then the *locus a quo* of that exercise. Heaven, we may then say, is wherever Christ is when the Father works through him on creatures. And then, invoking another standard theological maxim, that God's work and his presence are distinguished only for our apprehension, we may say that heaven is where God is when he sets out to come to us.

To be sure, I also am now in process of severing "above" from meaning univocally "some distance from earth's surface." It is time to take a closer look at Scripture's language, which turns out not in fact to be so rigid[17] as at first may be thought. Moreover, the complexity sets in precisely at the chief locations at which the Lord comes to Israel.

At Sinai, the people, according to Deuteronomy (4:36), are unproblematically "on earth," gathered before the mountain. But God's part of creation has on this occasion no one geometrical relation to the people. It is simultaneously above them where the meteorological phenomena play, and in

---

16. E.g., John of Damascus, *The Orthodox Faith*, 13, 11.
17. So literal about a "three-story universe."

front of them where the fire burns the mountain. Deuteronomy is especially concerned with the Lord's voice, and this sounds from both locations at once: "From heaven he made you hear his voice. . . . He showed you on earth his great fire, while you heard his words coming out of the fire." Whence the Lord speaks, that is heaven; and if he is in fact heard from two directions at once, so be it.[18]

The Temple with its *shekinah,* with its presence of the Lord in the Holy Place, confuses simple vertical-horizontal coordinates past rescue. Solomon's dedicatory prayer, in the Chronicler's report, begins by locating "highest" heaven as the Lord's abode; nevertheless the new building will set the direction "toward" which prayer to this Lord is directed. The inner sanctuary was occupied by the Ark with its Cherubim Throne. This throne is not literally above the priests and congregation gathered around it, yet can take the place of heaven in the standard pairing of heaven and earth (Psa. 99:1); indeed the Cherubim are *at once* the throne in the Temple and the storm-clouds visibly up there on which "God . . . rides through the heavens" (Psa. 18:9). One great psalm identifies them all, the storm-clouds above and the throne in the Temple and the fire at Sinai: "He rode on a cherub and flew; he came swiftly upon the wings of the wind. . . . Out of the brightness before him there broke through . . . coals of fire (Psa. 18:9-13)."

One more note on this line. Throughout the Old Testament, when "the angel of the Lord" appears (archetypically Gen. 22:9-19), to speak both for and as the Lord, he speaks "from heaven." Yet in the actual accounts, the address of the Angel is regularly face-to-face with those to whom he appears, and in Israel's journey through the wilderness he journeys horizontally "before" them (Exod. 23:20-22).[19]

Such biblical observations can fortify us for Karl Barth's doctrine of heaven, which deserves a key place in our discussion.[20] Both earth and heaven, according to Barth, come to pass in the course of God's movement to be with others than himself. This movement *ad extra* is integrally a movement *to* creation, but since it is also a movement specifically to us, and so to some creatures among the creatures, it is also a movement *within* creation.

---

18. I am of course aware that Exodus's description of the phenomena at Sinai can be picked apart into sources, and all interesting tensions thus removed. Which is nothing to the theological point.

19. NRSV's "an angel" is a mistranslation so blatant it must be deliberate.

20. See esp. Karl Barth, *Kirchliche Dogmatik* (Zollikon-Zürich: Evangelischer Verlag, 1932-1968), III/3, *passim.* For a fuller version of the following report, and for the individual citations, see Robert Jenson, *Systematic Theology,* vol. 2 (New York: Oxford University Press, 1997), pp. 12-121.

Thus a particular coming of God to his people must, according to Barth, start at some created place; and just so a limit is set, *bounding* our place in creation, earth, from God's place in creation. Heaven is "the place in the world from which" God's innerworldly movement begins.[21] So far, in my judgment, so very good.

Barth, however, appears to think that such a boundary is always momentary and so unpredictable.[22] In this we cannot, I think, follow him.[23] For in Scripture, such a boundary acquires a *marker,* so that God's people can thereafter point to it, so that within creation there is in fact a locatable line which is the boundary of heaven. Thus when Jacob awakes from his dream of access to heaven, he says, "Truly this is the gate of heaven," and sets up his stone to mark the spot; therewith "Bethel" became a place one could *find,* to be at heaven's gate (Gen. 28:10-17). When Abraham, at the place the Lord "showed" him, is rescued from disaster by the "Angel of the Lord," Abraham labels the place the "Mount of the Lord" (Gen. 22:1-14); this elevation may indeed be no lesser site than the Temple mount, the supreme place of pilgrimage to be with God.

Such observations may embolden us to press one more step. Martin Luther took Jacob's words in their indeed sacramental sense, and made of them a name for the church: "Go to the place where the word is spoken and the sacraments ministered, and there set up the title 'The Gate of Heaven.'"[24] For Luther, heaven simply *is* what we enter as we live in the church.

If we think along Luther's line, we will say that the consecrated bread and cup on the altar, the mouth of the preacher and the open page of the Scripture, the basin or torrent of water — and however many other sacramental *signa* there may be, for in this matter we can abstract from disputes about their number — mark the earthly places to which we may look to be looking to heaven, to the whence of God's coming; they are the created markers setting the boundary within creation which God rends to come to us. Thus Luther and some of his followers thought there was no explanation needed of how Christ could come bodily from heaven to be available on the table — or to preside at baptism or speak from the pulpit — there being no distance to traverse between heaven and these locations.[25]

Rudolf Bultmann notoriously taught that Christ "rose into the proclamation." There is much to be said against Bultmann's positions generally:

---

21. Jenson, *Systematic,* p. 503.
22. Doubtless in accord with his general lack of sense for the sacramental.
23. Though Wallace may well think we can.
24. Martin Luther, *Enarratio in Genesis* (WA 42), 43:499.
25. For the Lutheran Christology in its eucharistic relevance, Jenson, *Sytematic,* pp. 253-9.

thus, in the present context, he sometimes seems to suggest that Christ rose *in that* the disciples began to proclaim his crucifixion. Moreover, his seeming limitation of the church's life to "proclamation" reflects all too accurately a certain narrow kind of Protestantism. But if we abstract from the wider problems, and if we restore the full Reformation formula and make Bultmann say that Christ "rose into the word and sacraments," we will derive a topography of heaven and ascension into it. In my judgment, it would be the right topography.

At this point I must, however, again point to the choice readers may make. The position just developed begins indeed with a "Reformed" theologian, but is of recognizably "Lutheran" cast. Reformed and Lutheran versions of Reformation have from their beginning been divided about the Ascension — among other things — driven by two apparently incompatible general construals of reality. There seems to be no knockdown argument for either construal.[26]

III

Why is it so important to vindicate the Ascension, in either of the ways sketched above? Why go through the conceptual agonies of either my or the more standard position? For agonies they are; no one would suggest that either offered construal fits easily in the mind.

The question: Of what import is the Ascension? has three components. The first: Why could the creed not just stop with the Resurrection? The second: Why does the continuation have to be precisely an "ascension"? The third: What is the ascended one doing "at the right hand" of the Father? We can be brief, since many elements of the answers are already before us.

To the first question. Some theological construals of "atonement" or even of "salvation" not only have not continued to "ascended," but have effectively stopped with "crucified."[27] That the creed, in contrast, does not stop its christological narrative there reflects the New Testament "gospel" itself, which in shortest statement is not "Jesus was crucified for us," but "Jesus is risen." Paul indeed wanted to know none but "him crucified" (1 Cor. 2:2), but

---

26. For a vigorous, not to say pugnacious, assertion of the Reformed view, Farrow again.

27. Anselm of course comes first to mind; Anselm's total theology incorporates the Resurrection, but his specific theory of why Jesus' death was atoning could just as well work if the story stopped there. But remarkably, the school of Bultmann makes the same error: confession of Jesus' Resurrection is according to them the *response* demanded by a proclamation that itself stops with the Crucifixion.

the referent of "him" is precisely the risen one. It is the fact that the Lord of Israel has raised this one of his servants from death — a death indeed decisively determined as death on a cross for us — that is the saving fact proclaimed in the gospel.

But now the creed continues its narrative yet further, and talks about an Ascension. If we abstract for a moment from the full biblical context and conceptual consequence of "rose from the dead," we may see why. Those bereft by Jesus' death were not given new life by a sheer fact that he was alive somewhere and somehow, but by the fact that he was alive to be their Lord as before. The disciples' faith that Jesus of Nazareth lived beyond death meant that they could resume their conversation with their master and their reliance on him, and even resume their fellowship with him at table; this was their atonement and the present fact of their salvation.

But where were they to turn with their address to their newly living rabbi? Or to invite him to their table, with their primal Aramaic invocation *Maranatha*,[28] "Come, Lord"? Necessarily, to heaven, which the appearances revealed as his dwelling. An invocation of "lord" addressed to heaven cannot, however, remain merely an address of disciples to their own mortal master; the lord who dwells in *heaven* must be Lord of all. The disciples' inquiry of their master, addressed to heaven, became prayer. The *risen* Lord could not be his disciples' master *only* "as before." The risen Lord's universal lordship, his rule from God's place, is an inner consequence of his Resurrection — if, that is, his Resurrection means something to anyone but himself.[29]

To the second question. Jesus' move to be Lord in heaven must be an "ascension," because it is a bodily risen human person who enters heaven from earth. The entering of an earthly body into heaven must be an event within creation and occur at a boundary locatable from within the earth-part of creation. However drastically we may have to rethink inherited topographies of creation — and some readers may well think my proposal is too daring altogether — the notion of a locatable boundary on earth, which is "the gate of heaven" and so is the gate for the risen Christ's bodily movement between earth and heaven, is not theologically dispensable.[30] If readers prefer another mapping, they have this author's blessing to develop it, so long as they do not under the hand construe a disembodied risen Jesus.

---

28. The oldest item of Christian liturgy known to us.

29. Indeed, if a resurrection were of consequence only to the one raised, it would be meaningless for him also. But showing why that is so would burst the limits of this essay.

30. This, I take it, is much of the burden of Farrow's argument, with the affirmations of which I heartily concur.

To the third question. We already have part of the answer before us. A Lord in heaven is a Lord of the universe. From the right hand of the Father, the man Jesus of Nazareth rules all things. The claim is outrageous, but faith in the gospel can rest with nothing less. The claim is outrageous for two reasons.

First, it is the extreme form of what has been called "the scandal of particularity." Humanity's religiosity seeks the general and abtract: "the all," "the One," "universal Reason," and so on. The gospel, to the contrary, proclaims a particular male Palestinian Jew, born of a particular woman to be the Christ of the particular nation of Israel, as the meaning of all things. In all times and places, human religiosity has taken offense at one or another part of this particularity, in the modern West usually by calling it irrational or hegemonic. That a particularly embodied human is now Lord of all things, is for natural religiosity the last straw.

Second is consideration of what continues to happen under Christ's supposed rule. How can "the friend of publicans and sinners," the one who died for love of his enemies, possibly be thought to rule a world so full of evil? In my judgment, at this point one simply clings to God's final goodness or does not; if a reason for disbelief is needed, the so-called problem of evil will indeed provide it. Luther recommended contemplation of the cross.

Throughout this essay, I have spoken of Christ mostly in terms of his lordship. But of course in the Gospels and the tradition he appears also as prophet and priest. The phenomena of prophecy and priesthood are both enormously complex, but for our concern one factor is central: in Israel, prophet and priest are to intercede with God for the people. The writing to the Hebrews can develop its entire soteriology from that observation.

The Truth . . . and the Spirit of Truth:
The Trinitarian Shape of Christian Theology

Colin Gunton

It is difficult to exaggerate the importance of what Wallace Alston has achieved in recent years through his ministry in the Center of Theological Inquiry. There is more to the church than theology, and yet it remains the case that without a living theology, rooted in the gospel, the church becomes a mere shadow of what she is called to be. In that light, let me develop something of the nature of the theologian's calling as part of the ministry of the church.

A Theological Basis for Theology?

Christian Theology is a discipline which seeks to speak the truth, to tell things as they are. It is the church's intellectual discipline, but one which is at the same time spiritual, because it can be truly itself only through what the Holy Spirit gives. We can, therefore, adopt something like Barth's definition of theology as the church's self-examination as to the truth of her message.[1] The church has things to say, both to herself and to the world — or rather, she has but one thing, *res,* reality, and it is called the gospel. The gospel, we must remember, is about God's love for the world, and so it is "about" everything, because the message promises the reconciliation of all things in Christ. Theology's task is to examine that message, to test the spirits to see whether they be

---

1. "Dogmatics is the self-examination of the Christian Church in respect of the content of its distinctive talk about God." Karl Barth, *Church Dogmatics* I/1, ed. and trans. G. W. Bromiley and T. F. Torrance (Edinburgh: T&T Clark, 1957-1975), p. 11.

of God or simply the product of wish-fulfillment or, indeed, of sin. There will, to be sure, always be an element of both of the latter. Theologians are as prone to sin as anyone, perhaps especially the sin of intellectual arrogance, and history reminds us that the councils of the church are as prone to sin as individuals. This is especially the case now that we cannot in that respect say church, but must say churches, in all their partiality and division. And yet we can remain with something like the notion Barth learned at the feet of Anselm of Canterbury, that theology's task is to inquire whether reality is as the Christian believes it to be.[2]

If, then, theology is an intellectual discipline, we must ask about its basis: What makes it what it is, gives it the right to claim, even in its limitations and brokenness, to be telling something of the truth? This in turn divides into two other questions, which we shall take one at a time. The first is this: What gets us into theology from the outside, so to speak? Is it *only* the gospel, or need we also appeal to something more general? And the second concerns the internal bases of theology; what from within our community and history gives the discipline its shape? We shall reach that question only after a long consideration of the first, the crucial one.

First, is the external basis of theology. This is traditionally treated under the heading of prolegomena: things written before the actual task begins. As Robert Jenson has recently written, we live in an era of inflated prolegomena, so much so, it might be added, that some theologians never far get beyond them.[3] The need to provide external supports for theology has become, for some people, pressing in the modern age because of the fact that so many reject theology's claims to truth. Attempted enterprises have included the philosophical and the experiential, but Barth has famously and, I believe, successfully assaulted both. Both Kant's agnostic negative theology and Schleiermacher's appeal to experience are in his sights. Barth's, as hardly needs to be repeated here, is an appeal to revelation that seeks to found theology on God's being as it is made known in his acts. To understand the historical significance of his achievement, we need to go back a long way, indeed to the time when Christian theology first encountered the theology of the Greeks. Various pressures from heresy led to a strong stress on what came to be called the negative theology: the erection of the knowledge of God on a denial of the supposed characteristics of createdness. Much was made of the first half of John 1:18: "no

---

2. Karl Barth, *Fides Quaerens Intellectum. Anselm's Proof of the Existence of God in the Context of His Theological Scheme*, trans. I. W. Robertson (London: SCM Press, 1960), p. 27.

3. Robert W. Jenson, *Systematic Theology*, vol. 1, *The Triune God* (New York: Oxford University Press, 1997), p. 9.

one has seen God," and progressively less of its second half, that his only Son has made him known. To paraphrase Aquinas, we know of God only what he is not; otherwise, our knowledge is restricted to the way in which we know God and the way in which our language characterizes him.[4] It could be said that the philosophy of Kant and the theology of Schleiermacher represent the nemesis of this view, a transition from "we know of God only what he is not" to "we do not know God at all *as he is in himself.*"

Barth's achievement is to deny this, absolutely, on the basis of revelation. God is known in the church: "God is actually known and therefore God is obviously knowable."[5] It is important to see what Barth makes of this. It is not, as has been foolishly suggested, revelational positivism, but an inquiry into the possibility of the knowledge of God on the strength of its actuality. A basis for what is actually known in time is discovered by theological inquiry to be rooted in the eternal being of God, so that the reasons for its actuality can accordingly be spelled out. This is of a piece with the theological method Barth learned from Anselm: theology is faith seeking understanding. Faith — the actual knowledge of God rooted in the life of the church — seeking a basis in the God in whom that faith rests.[6] Revelation means, as Barth repeatedly affirms, that we "can perceive and consider and conceive God." In all of this there is no suggestion that this is due to any intrinsic human capacity, for it is a form of knowledge in which God "raises up man really to be a knower of Himself."[7] Nor is this a form of what might be called brute objectivism, the appeal to some merely external fact. Theology does not operate with a brute *given,* but from God giving himself to be known. Because faith is a form of relation to God in Christ, this kind of knowledge is relational, arises out of a personal relation, in which God moves into relation with his people, and they respond in faith.

Barth distinguished between what he called the secondary and primary objectivity of God. The secondary objectivity is God mediated through creaturely reality, and this is "historical" or relational objectivity — God in relation to us in Christ whose creaturely reality is the vehicle of the knowledge of God.[8] This secondary objectivity is based in the primary objectivity,

---

4. Aquinas, *Summa Theologiae,* p. Ia.2, conclusion.

5. Barth, Church Dogmatics II/1, p. 64.

6. Karl Barth, *Dogmatics in Outline,* trans. G. T. Thomson (London: SCM Press, 2001), p. 15.

7. Barth, *Church Dogmatics* II/1, p. 32. [Further references to this volume will appear in parentheses.]

8. Secondary objectivity is that which is mediated through creaturely reality, Barth, *Church Dogmatics* II/1, p. 17. We might call this 'historical' or relational objectivity.

the fact that God knows himself in the fellowship of the Trinity. "The Father knows the Son and the Son the Father in the unity of the Holy Spirit" (p. 49). Our knowledge of God comes therefore from our being taken up to share something of God's knowledge of himself. There is in this no abrogation of human cognitional faculties (p. 181), but rather their elevation to their proper state, of knowing the truth. This is essentially a christological form of knowing, according to which "Jesus Christ is the knowability of God on our side, as He is the grace of God . . . and therefore also the knowability of God on God's side" (p. 150). Indeed, the work of the Spirit seems almost to be assimilated to that of Jesus Christ, so that Barth can say that "the Holy Spirit is the temporal presence of Jesus Christ . . ." (p. 158). We shall return to the doctrine of the Spirit below.

A number of criticisms of this enterprise have been made over the years, the important ones concerning the dogmatic shape of the proposal. Pannenberg, for example, has criticized what is in effect Barth's over-realized eschatology of revelation, and there is indeed something of an immediacy to Barth's concept of revelation which leaves out other steps which need to be taken.[9] Thus, while charges of a positivism of revelation are indeed foolish, there is something underlying them, suggesting that somewhere the concept of mediation is rather out of kilter in Barth's theology. This raises our central question: granted that theology has its basis in the triune being of God, how — by what means — does it then take shape in human words? There is surely no going back on the fundamental trinitarian proposal. The question is surely, what Trinity and how? Let us examine one essential biblical source for our concept of the knowledge of God.

A Biblical Basis for Theology

Among the series of magisterial "I am" claims which it records as coming from the lips of Jesus, the Fourth Gospel includes, "I am . . . the truth" (John 14:6). Clearly basing the form of the sayings on the revelatory divine "I" of the prophet called the 'Second Isaiah', John is using the form to convey something of the revelatory character of Jesus, whether or not that abstraction called the 'historical Jesus' can be supposed to have spoken in that way. The first neces-

---

9. Wolfhart Pannenberg, *Systematic Theology*, vol. 1, trans. G. W. Bromiley (Edinburgh: T&T Clark, 1991), pp. 226-8. See also Alan Spence, "Christ's Humanity and Ours," in *Persons, Divine and Human: King's College Essays in Theological Anthropology*, ed. Christoph Schwoebel and Colin E. Gunton (Edinburgh: T&T Clark, 1991), pp. 74-97.

sary observation is that Jesus claims or is claimed to be many other things as well as the truth, so that this saying must be interpreted first of all in the context of the other "I am" statements. The immediate partners in the affirmation are "way" and "life," both of them suggesting a direct relation to human being in the world. We have then a propositional claim — to the effect that x is y — but one whose truth is bound up with life and action. "I am the bread of life" (6:48) and "the resurrection and the life" (11:25) similarly make the sayings speech-acts of a definite kind, not so much self-involving as other-involving. The sayings are not merely revelatory, but *saving;* they involve those who acknowledge them in a new relation to God the Father. The "I am" sayings of Jesus are truth-claims which take their hearers up into the world they express. The broader context of John's Gospel indicates something of the way others are involved: above all they are loved and judged by the love and judgment of God by virtue of the fact that Jesus is the love and judgment of God in action.

Such other-involving statements are, therefore, first of all ways of bringing their hearers into a new relationship with God; but second, and consequently, they serve to indicate a truth about the nature of Christian theology. On the one hand, they cannot be reduced to their effect. Theology is not merely a series of moral exhortations or pious exclamations. The statements make propositional claims, claims about the way things really are. They affirm that certain things are the case; are true in the most straightforward and obvious sense of the word in corresponding to the way things are "out there," beyond the words of the propositions and the experience of those who wrote them. But, on the other hand, the fact that they involve the other means that they are not neutral statements of fact but the kind of factual claims that involve not action in a narrow sense — like a series of moral exhortations — but action of a kind more broadly involving life in all its dimensions. This, remember, is also the one who claimed in the same gospel that, "Before Abraham was, I am," indicating that the kind of truth claim he makes is both factual in the broadest sense and complex to a degree. The complexity lies above all in the fact that it is not only a claim made by and about a human being — complex enough in itself — but one which also involves his eternity and therefore his relation to God the Father in the Spirit.

And there, in a nutshell, are the mystery, appeal and difficulty of that discipline known as "Systematic" or "Dogmatic Theology." Its possibility, promise, and mystery are, as we have seen, first christological, but, as our gospel shows, also pneumatological. For theology is also made possible by the sending of the Spirit, the one whom Jesus will ask the Father to send, the other "paraclete." The Holy Spirit is described in the same chapter as the Spirit of truth (14:17; 16:13), and the Spirit of truth is not first of all the spirit of the truth in general, because he is the Spirit of Jesus who is the truth. Among the gifts promised to the messiah in Isaiah 11:2 is the "spirit of understanding," possibly taken up in Ephesians 1:17, "the Spirit of wisdom and revelation." Similarly, 1 Corinthians 14 makes much of the intelligibility of churchly speech as central among the gifts of the Spirit, while right knowledge, understanding, and wisdom are repeated themes of the letter to Colossae. But what does the "Spirit of understanding" enable us to understand? And what in particular is the meaning of such a claim for theology? "[T]he Holy Spirit . . . will teach you all things and will remind you of everything I have said to you" (John 14:26; cf. 15:13). That is almost certainly, as they say, context-specific: the "all things" is explained by "everything I have said to you." To teach the truth is to teach the truth about Jesus and his Father. The function of the Spirit's work is in this context resolutely christological, or rather patrological: for the one who comes into relation with us through the Son and the Spirit is not any God, but the God and Father of our Lord Jesus Christ.

What bearing does all this have on the discipline of dogmatic theology? Let me begin to seek an answer by looking a little more broadly at the Jesus who is the truth. For the writer of our gospel, it is clear that this Jesus, the one who is the way, the truth, and the life, is all these things because he is the one through whom God created the world; he is, in the words of another John, the first and the last, the one in whom all things have their being. The gospel, that is to say, is not proclaimed into a world like an alien landing from another planet, but into one created and loved by God already, upheld from day to day through his Son in his Spirit. And this means that although the gospel is utterly simple and straightforward, the province of the poor and ignorant more easily than of the rich and learned, it is also the case that the position of those whose task is to commend it is complex, always changing, and requires sustained intellectual engagement.

Let us look briefly at aspects of the complex situation. First, because Jesus is the universal creator, the Christian gospel claims to be true in the same way that other things are true: that is, to correspond with the way things actually are in the world. But that is not the same as saying that its truth is transparent or assimilated in one moment of illumination or conversion. This has, it seems to me, implications both inside and outside the walls of the church. Inside, it is clear that the biblical writers expect their flocks to grow in learning, not merely "spiritually," whatever that may mean. The author to the Hebrews, for example, writes that "though by this time you ought to be teachers" — and presumably he is addressing the whole congregation — "you need someone to teach you the elementary truths of God's word over again" (Heb.

5:12), and one could quote other texts. Whenever the church has been confident in its gospel, a commitment to learning has followed, with all kinds of results outside as well as within the life of the church itself. And the converse is true. About thirty years ago, the Russian theologian Georges Florovsky, in a paper entitled "The Lost Scriptural Mind," spoke of the theological crisis in the churches, a crisis that has surely worsened:

> What we need in Christendom "in a time such as this" is precisely a sound and existential theology. In fact, both clergy and laity are hungry for theology. And because no theology is usually preached, they adopt some "strange ideologies" and combine them with fragments of traditional beliefs. The whole appeal of the "rival gospels" in our days is that they offer some sort of pseudo theology, a system of pseudo dogmas. They are gladly accepted by those who cannot find any theology in the reduced Christianity of "modern" style. That existential alternative which many face in these days has been aptly formulated by an English theologian, "Dogma or . . . death."[10]

In what way might theology serve this need? Barth's answer was that dogmatic theology serves the proclamation of the church, that he was writing primarily for preachers. There is something to be said for that view. Theology's calling is an essentially modest one: to serve the gospel rather than to storm the citadels of culture — even though it will hope to have much to say also to those occupying the latter.

And yet that does not seem to me to exclude an orientation outside, as a form of mission, which is not necessarily the same thing as apologetics. The question of how this might engage with other truth, also validated by the creator Son and Spirit, can never be far away, simply because it follows from the nature of the Christ with whom theology is called to concern itself. I have so far resisted seeing the Spirit as the Spirit of truth in general, because for the Fourth Gospel that is not what is meant. And yet there are indications in scripture, including that same gospel, which suggest that this might be part of the matter. Christ is the one through whom all things are created; equally, he is for the letter to the Ephesians (1:10) the one to whom they all move: "to sum up all things to himself . . ." (see also Col. 1:19-20). Could we not therefore say that theology's task is to articulate the particular claims of the creed in the service of a wider vision than the inner-churchly alone? Here we must beware of over-inflated pretensions, such as, for example, have helped to discredit the

---

10. Georges Florovsky, *Bible, Church, Tradition: An Eastern Orthodox View* (Belmont, MA: Nordland, 1972), p. 15.

discipline in some of the more notorious episodes of church history, that between the papal authorities and Galileo above all. What does it mean to see all things as they will be reconciled in Christ?

For this, we need to distinguish theology from other disciplines, and that takes us to the second main point. I have said that it claims to speak the truth in the same way as other disciplines in speaking about what is really there. Yet there is another factor which changes the nature of that claim, for the object of the truth claimed by theology is distinctively different from the objects of all other forms of human speech. As we have seen, the mystery of theology is centered on the source of all things in the God and Father of our Lord Jesus Christ. In what way then is theology unlike other pursuits of truth? In it, we are concerned with the basis of truth in the one — or rather three-in-one — who is essentially other than those things which he has made. Two implications can be drawn. First, "All true knowledge of God is born of obedience"[11] and therefore takes form in a unique relationship between the creator and the creature. The fact that it is the Spirit who leads into the truth means that we are here in one respect entirely passive; or, better, that our activity can flow only from a divine action which empowers it. The second implication is that the purpose of the gospel according to John is that men and women may know the Father through the one he has sent, and through him alone. As we have seen, a particular form of knowing is implied in this gospel: a relational knowing that involves redemption from sin and its moral implications, or, more broadly, its implications for a particular form of life in relation to God and to others. It may be the case that the gospel does not come into a world that is essentially foreign to it; and yet that is what seems to be the case to "the world" in the second meaning that can be given to that word, the world which has set itself in enmity to God. This gospel and its form of life are foreign to "the world" in this sense, and therefore imply a different form of intellectual response from those of other forms of knowing. To see the world in the light of the promised and initiated reconciliation of all things is first of all to see it through the lens provided by the reconciliation of *particular* men and women to new forms of relation with God and with one another. It is to focus theology in the life of the community of faith.

11. John Calvin, *Institutes of the Christian Religion,* vol. 1, ed. by J. T. McNeill, trans. F. L. Battles, Library of Christian Classics, vol. 20 (Philadelphia: Westminster Press, 1960), 6.2.

A Churchly Setting for Theology?

That necessarily takes us to the place of the church in our understanding of theology. Recall for a moment the problem I identified in the case of aspects of Barth's theology, with its apparently rather over-realized eschatology. That is the theological problem underlying this aspect of our topic, which concerns the second of the main themes I articulated at the beginning of the chapter, the question of the internal shaping of theology. We must return to the problem of the christological immediacy which is often charged of Barth. As we have already seen, for this theologian God is known in the church. Barth had a strong sense of theology's rootedness in the church and her traditions. The conversational pattern of much of his theology, and especially the famous excursus in small print, make it an education in the history of theology, and of much else. But so far as the contemporary church is concerned, the impression is sometimes given that he speaks to it rather than from it. (It sometimes appears to be a rather one-sided conversation.) Cautious, with some justification, of attributing too much to any human institution, he underplayed a number of features of theology whose greater stress should enable us to seek an account of what it might mean to do theology from within the community of faith. The point is to stress what happens in the present, to view faith as the relation to God which gives a particular shape to the life lived, in the fellowship of the people of God, between baptism and death. Might that not root it more firmly in the concrete present? And that naturally takes us to the answer to our second question, about what from within our community gives the discipline its shape.

There are three places where, traditionally, a basis has been sought. There is no problem about the first, despite differences about its uses and status, and that is scripture. All the churches of divided Christendom claim to base their teaching on the scriptures of the Old and New Testaments, though some may wish to add what is called the Apocrypha. The differences come when we mention the second source, tradition. Tradition is primarily an activity, the activity of handing over teaching from one generation to another, just as Jesus was handed over to death and the gospel handed over to Paul (1 Cor. 15:3). We are all creatures of tradition, at least in the respect that we learn from teachers who have themselves been taught in a great chain going back to the Apostles and even, as Calvin says, to the patriarchs.[12] Where differences arise is in estimates of the nature and capacity of the transmitters of tradition, and in particular whether the teaching authority has the right to add things not directly claimed in scripture.

12. Calvin, *Institutes*, 6.2.

Third, there are the creeds, secondary sources in that they claim to summarize the teaching of scripture. Creeds and the confessions of the Reformation churches arose out of crises in the church's life, and were centered on doctrines whose distortion perennially threatens the integrity of the gospel. Insofar as they claim to be authoritative summaries and are acknowledged as such, they form part of the basis for all succeeding theological enterprises. Creeds seek to concentrate, distil, or summarize the teaching of scripture, so that later theologians must view scripture through the lenses provided by the creeds and confessions — for example in treating the person of Christ as both human and divine — simply because of the focus they provide. The importance of the creeds is seen in the distinction often drawn between dogma, on the one hand, and doctrine or theology, on the other. Dogma in general refers to the universal and generally accepted teaching of the church, and in particular to the ecumenical creeds; and, for the churches of the Reformation, to the confessions which have served to clarify the creeds in the light of the urgent questions consequent on the reform of the church.

The varieties of teaching about all three of these bases for theology — scripture, tradition, and confession — have one thing in common: a reference to the action of the Holy Spirit. And where there is speech about the Spirit, there also must be the consideration of eschatology. Insofar as we make claims to knowledge in the Spirit, we seek to anticipate that time when we shall know as we are known (1 Cor. 13:12). All theological knowing takes place in anticipation of the last days, and by gift of the Spirit alone. Despite all the worst efforts of a certain type of biblical critic, the belief of those who continue to confess Christ is that the Holy Spirit has at least something to do with the form of the words we read on the page. Scripture is realized eschatology; that is, it is in some way or other revelatory. There is, as we are all too aware, a wide range of views about how this should be understood. The Council of Trent affirmed on behalf of what had become the Roman Catholic Church, now a self-consciously different body from both the Orthodox and the churches of the Reformation, that scripture was written *Spiritu Sancto dictante,* at the dictation of the Holy Spirit, and similar conceptions continue to prevail in Protestantism, though not everywhere in it. All such differences center on differences about the doctrine of the Spirit, and in particular about how he acted in relation to the biblical authors.

So it is also with the workings of tradition and of the Councils. Both the Orthodox and the Roman churches express a confidence in the infallibility of the succession of bishops which owes much to a confidence that the Spirit leads the churches into all truth. This has, to be sure, often expressed itself in a wooden way, leaning on a crude conception of historical succession, as the Orthodox theologian John Zizioulas has argued. His contention is important, because it shows how differences about pneumatology are at the heart of this matter also. Too rigid a view of historical succession in effect excludes the rest of the church from the agency of the Spirit: "we cannot speak of apostolic succession when there is only episcopal succession while the rest of the ministries, including the laity, are not participating in it." If we place too much trust in history, claiming that the Spirit is automatically at work in what has been done, we lose that most important feature, the Spirit's *eschatological* action.[13] Similarly, we have to ask of the councils, while confessing their authority, in what ways they might in places claim an authority which forgets the eschatological reserve in which all human works must be held.[14] Thus Calvin would speak of the relative authority of the Councils, which must always be second to the primary authority of scripture.[15] Scripture, accordingly, has a measure of eschatological status that all other authorities lack, even though we need the authority of creed and tradition if we are to be able to focus our thinking. The reason is that Jesus Christ, for whom the scriptures serve as the swaddling clothes (Luther), is the one realized eschatological reality, the one whose resurrection from the dead places him at the center of all things, theology especially.

What all this must teach us is that theology is not the work of individuals but of those who have been called to be members of the *koinonia* of the church and in *koinonia* with God the Father through the Son and in the Spirit. The writers of the scriptures and the great tradition of their interpreters remain living voices in the fellowship of the Kingdom, so that such knowledge as theologians claim is not theirs individually, but only right theology as it participates in the knowledge of the community of worship and belief. The Spirit of truth is the Spirit of him who was lifted up to gather around him the church which exists for the glory of God but also for the reconciliation of all people and things. In so far as theology serves that mission, its particular teachings become the mediators of God's universal gospel.

---

13. John Zizioulas, "Apostolic Continuity of the Church and Apostolic Succession in the First Five Centuries," in *The Practice of Theology,* ed. C. Gunton, et al. (London: SCM Press, 2001), p. 95. Zizioulas claims that "every local Church is equally apostolic by virtue of the fact that it is the image of the eschatological community" (p. 96). Although Zizioulas does not mean by local church what a Congregationalist would intend, such a point can still be taken.

14. Until quite late in the patristic era the creeds retained the status of 'opinions' — the original meaning of 'dogma': official and authoritative opinions like those handed down by a supreme court of law, but in some sense provisional none the less. U. Wickert, "Dogma I. Historisch," in *Theologische Realenzyklopädie,* vol. 9 (Berlin; New York: W. de Gruyter, 1977), p. 29.

15. Calvin, *Institutes,* 4.9.

The Spirit of Reformed Faith and Theology

Daniel L. Migliore

My title, "The Spirit of Reformed Faith and Theology," suggests two distinct but closely related topics. By the "spirit" of a group or movement we ordinarily mean its dominant tendency or character, its animating features, its distinctive traits, its peculiar emphases. In the first section of my essay I will have this common use of the term "spirit" in mind as I attempt briefly to portray the spirit of the Reformed theological heritage in its relative distinction from the Roman Catholic tradition, on the one hand, and from the Lutheran and other Protestant confessional traditions on the other. But my title suggests another topic as well. It invites exploration of the significance of the doctrine of the Holy Spirit within Reformed faith and theology. The thesis that I wish to propose is that the reclaiming of a strong, trinitarian understanding of the Holy Spirit is vital to the life and mission of the Reformed church in the twenty-first century. This thesis will be developed historically in the second section and constructively in the final section.

I

If we ask what is the distinctive spirit of Reformed faith and theology, we might well respond by saying simply, God is God. This brief but apt summary of the Reformed spirit — a favorite of Karl Barth in his early writings — may seem austere and even offensive. As Barth admitted in his first lectures on dogmatics in 1924, the distinctive Reformed emphasis on the sovereignty of God and the radical difference between God and creation may not be everybody's cup of tea, but it has to be sounded somewhere within the ecumenical church if the witness of Scripture is to be taken with utmost seriousness.[1] The spirit of Reformed faith and theology is a spirit of zeal for the glory of God and of thanksgiving for God's sovereign grace. It is a tradition of faith that acknowledges the greatness and majesty of God, whose holiness and mercy have been manifested to the world in the mighty deeds of creation and redemption. Such faith finds expression in a life of joyful praise and courageous obedience. God is God — the triune God, Father, Son, and Holy Spirit — and all creation finds its fulfillment in the praise and service of this God.

If God alone is to be acknowledged and worshiped as God, it follows for Reformed faith and theology that idolatry, or the substitution of some person or thing or cause for the one and only true God, is the root of all sin. Accordingly, the spirit of Reformed faith is a tirelessly prophetic spirit that struggles against idolatry in all its manifold forms both outside and inside the church. That is the meaning of the familiar motto of the Reformed churches: *ecclesia reformata semper reformanda secundum verbum Dei*, "the church reformed always in need of being reformed according to the Word of God." The Reformed spirit resists every effort to make God into an idol that serves our own interests and purposes.

Corresponding to its understanding of God as the living, active, holy, and gracious creator and ruler of the universe, the spirit of Reformed faith is dynamic and active rather than static and passive. It opposes all calcifications of the life of faith. With the other churches of the Reformation, the Reformed churches confess that salvation is by the grace of God alone *(sola gratia)*, that Christ alone is our Savior and Lord *(solus Christus)*, that we are justified by faith alone *(sola fide)*, and that the primary norm of our faith and life is scripture alone *(sola scriptura)*. A distinctive mark of the Reformed tradition, however, is its emphasis on the transformation of life and its doctrine of Christian vocation. Grounded in the Word of God, confident in the lordship of Jesus Christ, assured of God's forgiveness of sins, and convinced that God has graciously elected in Christ a people to render faithful worship and service, Reformed believers have understood their primary vocation as the call to participate in God's reconciliation and renewal of the world. They have affirmed, in the words of the Westminster Catechism, that the chief end of human life is to glorify and enjoy God forever. As Ernst Troeltsch noted, for Reformed Christians the calling of God is not exercised *in vocatione* but *per vocatione*.[2] In

---

1. See Karl Barth, *The Göttingen Dogmatics: Instruction in the Christian Religion* (Grand Rapids: Eerdmans, 1991), vol. 1, p. 396.

2. Ernst Troeltsch, *The Social Teaching of the Christian Churches* (London: George Allen & Unwin LTD, 1931), vol. 2, pp. 610-11.

other words, obedience to God is not simply a matter of remaining *in* an occupation or social role and of doing one's God-given duty there, but of serving the purposes of God *through* one's occupation or role, and if that proves to be impossible, to work to alter the social order to make it possible.

Acutely aware of the depths of human sinfulness, the Reformed faith has a realistic view of the world rather than seeing it through rose-colored glasses. Yet it is far removed from a Manichean hatred of the world or a quietistic indifference to it. Because the Reformed spirit considers the power of God's transforming grace to be far superior to the power of sin and evil, it calls the church to be courageously engaged with the world rather than abandoning it. In the political realm, this conviction has inspired prophetic political activity and has contributed to the development of modern democratic states. It has been a factor in the formation of the American Republic, in the opposition to Nazism in Germany during the 1930s, and in the long struggle against apartheid policy in South Africa where the Reformed church had to recognize its own complicity in racist attitudes and policies before it was able to bear a clear word of judgment and grace to the South African people. In the ecclesiastical realm, the Reformed spirit has developed a form of church polity that is deeply suspicious of the concentration of power in the hands of a few, that believes in the equality of clergy and laity, and that looks for the guidance of God's Word and Spirit in the prayerful deliberation and debate of the people of God.

Many commentators have expressed puzzlement at this world-transforming drive of the Reformed spirit. They have assumed that an emphasis on the sovereign freedom and especially the electing grace of God would lead necessarily to an apathetic or passive attitude on the part of Reformed Christians. What these commentators have failed to understand is that the Reformed affirmation of the free and gracious sovereignty of God has generated neither indifference nor resignation, but the passion to express gratitude to God and to do all that is possible to reorder life according to the purposes of God attested in Scripture and decisively revealed in Jesus Christ. As Michael Walzer and other historians have argued, there is a revolutionary energy present in this Reformed spirit, a denunciation of disorder — whether the personal disorder of an undisciplined life, or the social disorder of injustice and oppression.[3] It is a spirit filled with passion to participate in the sanctification or new ordering of God's creation by bringing all dimensions of life into correspondence with the purposes of God manifest in the new humanity of Jesus Christ crucified and risen.

3. See Michael Walzer, *The Revolution of the Saints: A Study in the Origins of Radical Politics* (Cambridge: Harvard University Press, 1965).

Because it looks for the renewal of this world, the spirit of Reformed faith is fearlessly contextual. If the world is to hear God's word and be summoned to repentance and new life, the word must be concrete rather than abstract, particular rather than general. Reformed Christians take up their responsibility in every particular time and place to bear witness to the lordship of Christ and give glory to God in the power of God's Spirit. The *Book of Confessions* of the Presbyterian Church (U.S.A.) reflects this dynamism, contextuality, and world-transforming drive of Reformed faith. While respectful of the witness of the church in the past — and most particularly of the trinitarian and christological creeds of the early church — the Reformed tradition, unlike other Reformation confessional traditions, has not been content simply to repeat the confessions produced in the Reformation period. It has celebrated the contextual particularity of its confessions because it understands the church to be responsible in every time and place to bear faithful witness to the living Word of God that addresses people in judgment and grace here and now. The spirit of Reformed faith is the spirit of a great passion for the honor of God and the manifestation of God's reign throughout the creation. This spirit cannot be contained in the life of the church; it impacts the wider society in which the church bears its witness and carries on its mission. Grateful for the mighty acts of God in the past, the spirit of Reformed faith is nevertheless predominantly forward-looking, and is characterized by a restless and creative hope in God for the transformation of all things in correspondence with the purposes of God disclosed in Jesus Christ.

The world-transforming zeal of the Reformed spirit has no doubt taken on distorted forms at times; it has sometimes given in to legalistic, exclusionary, and coercive impulses. It has sometimes turned the authority of the Word into biblicism; the importance of proclamation into didacticism; the call to responsible Christian life into moralism; the concern for sound doctrine into dogmatism; the passion for the public service of God into religious zealotry; and the message of God's sovereign grace into oppressive rule. Such distortions notwithstanding, the spirit of Reformed faith has its ever disturbing center in the awesome holiness and grace of God incarnate in Jesus Christ the servant Lord and active by his Spirit in the renewal of all things. God is God, and to God alone be the glory: that is the spirit of Reformed faith and theology.[4]

4. For other discussions of the Reformed tradition from which my own depiction has benefited, see John T. McNeill, *The History and Character of Calvinism* (New York: Oxford University Press, 1954); John H. Leith, *Introduction to the Reformed Tradition: A Way of Being the Christian Community* (Richmond: John Knox Press, 1977); Douglas F. Ottati, *Reformed Protestantism: Christian Commitment in Today's World* (Louisville: Westminster/John Knox Press, 1995).

II

Having briefly portrayed the "spirit" of Reformed faith in the broad sense, I turn now to the second and more specific meaning of my title, viz. the person and activity of the Holy Spirit as experienced and understood in the Reformed tradition. All that I have previously said about the spirit of Reformed faith is in fact very closely bound to the doctrine of the Holy Spirit in the Reformed tradition. When this connection is lost, the reforming spirit that drives the church is all too easily identified with the spirit of restoration, or the spirit of progress, or the spirit of modernity, or the spirit of individual freedom, or the imperial spirit, or some other Zeitgeist. For the Reformed faith, however, it is not just any spirit but a very particular Spirit that animates the life of the believer and empowers the life and mission of the church. It is the Spirit of the triune God — Father, Son, and Holy Spirit.

It is the Spirit of the triune God who opens the Scriptures to us and illumines our minds to their life-giving Word. Without the Spirit, the written words of the Bible remain lifeless and ineffective. It is the Spirit of the triune God who binds us to Christ and rouses us to faith, hope, and love; otherwise our justification, sanctification, and vocation might be claimed as our own achievements. It is not any spirit but the Spirit of the triune God who gives gifts of service to all members of the church and empowers them for mission; otherwise the church would be its own source of life and its members dependent on a clerical hierarchy. It is the Spirit of the triune God who makes the proclamation of the Word effective in the hearts and lives of its hearers and who is the power at work in the breaking of the bread and the drinking of the cup to make the celebration of the Lord's Supper a communion in the body and blood of Christ; otherwise preaching would be useless and sacramental practices an idolatrous claim of the church to have control over the grace of God. The strength of Reformed faith and theology, I submit, is directly proportional to the clarity and vigor of its affirmation of and openness to the person and work of the Holy Spirit who leads us to Jesus Christ as attested in Scripture.

Paradoxically, however, although the Reformed tradition has confounded historians and commentators by its world-transforming spirit, it has not always given the doctrine of the Holy Spirit the attention it deserves. In this respect Reformed churches have shared in the neglect of the doctrine of the Holy Spirit that has marked much western Christian theology. Commenting on this anomaly, some Reformed theologians have referred to the doctrine of the Holy Spirit as the "orphan" of the theology of the western church. The powerful appeal of the Pentecostal church world-wide should be a reminder to Reformed Christians that the Spirit has often been neglected in the piety, theology, and life of the classical Reformation traditions. Moreover, a good case could be made for the claim that many of the internal battles of the Reformed churches up to the present have been related to the neglect or misunderstanding of the doctrine of the Holy Spirit. Happily, the recent "Brief Statement of Faith," adopted by the PCUSA in 1991, gives the Holy Spirit a very prominent place in its affirmations about the life and mission of the church.

Despite the unfortunate marginalization of the Holy Spirit in certain periods of Reformed church history, in its piety, and even in some of its confessional documents, there are richer resources in Reformed pneumatology than is sometimes imagined. Several distinctive Reformed emphases in the doctrine of the Holy Spirit can be seen in the work of four leading representatives of Reformed theology: John Calvin, Jonathan Edwards, Karl Barth, and Jürgen Moltmann. Since the pneumatology of each of these theologians is very rich, I cannot do more here than mention a few characteristic themes in their writings.

First, according to John Calvin, the Spirit of God binds us to Christ through the proclamation of the Word and the celebration of the sacraments. As Calvin writes at the beginning of Book III of the *Institutes*, "As long as Christ remains outside of us, and we are separated from him, all that he has suffered and done for the salvation of the human race remains useless and of no value for us. Therefore, to share with us what he has received from the Father, he had to become ours and to dwell within us." This dwelling of Christ in us and we in him is accomplished, Calvin emphasizes, by "the secret energy of the Spirit."[5]

Calvin teaches that the Spirit leads us to Christ attested in the written word. He is emphatic that Word and Spirit are not to be separated in the understanding of the authority of the Bible and the power of proclamation. "The Word will not find acceptance in our hearts," Calvin writes, "before it is sealed by the inward testimony of the Spirit."[6] It is the same for Calvin with regard to the sacraments. Calvin is far from being indifferent to the sacramental life of the church, let alone being anti-sacramental. Instead, his point is that there is no inherent power in the sacraments in and of themselves; they are effective only as the Spirit works in and through them to bind us to Christ.

5. John Calvin, *Institutes of the Christian Religion*, ed. John T. McNeill (Philadelphia: Westminster Press, 1960), III.i.1.
6. Calvin, *Institutes*, I.vii.4.

Thus, for Calvin the Spirit is understood primarily as God's power at work uniting us with Christ and enabling us through Word and sacrament to participate in the new life established by his ministry, cross, and resurrection. While Christian life as described by Calvin always bears the mark of the cross, it is also a life empowered by Easter and Pentecost. Calvin devotes an entire chapter to the gift of new freedom in Christ that comes from the Spirit.[7]

Second, for Jonathan Edwards, America's greatest Reformed theologian, the Spirit of God issues from the mutual affection between the Father and the Son who infinitely love and delight in each other. "The Holy Spirit," he writes, "is the harmony and excellency and beauty of the Deity."[8] This Spirit of harmony and beauty is at work throughout the creation, but the Spirit of God is especially lavish in giving gifts to all members of Christ's church.

Edwards was one of the leading preachers and theologians of the Great Awakening in eighteenth-century America. He understood the transforming power of God in Christ by the Spirit to include the whole of human personality: the mind, the will, and the affections. He insisted that the realm of feelings, affections, and dispositions was in need of redirection and renewal if there was to be genuine conversion of life. Life in Christ for Edwards is no mere acceptance of beliefs; nor is it simply the adoption of certain patterns of behavior. It is also and primarily a transformation of the basic dispositions and desires of human beings, a conversion of what the biblical writers call the "heart." Edwards writes, "A man's having much affections don't prove that he has any true religion; but if he has no affection, it proves that he has no true religion."[9] According to Edwards, it is the Holy Spirit who communicates true religious affection, that new "sense of the heart" in which we are captivated by the beauty of God's holy love. The fruits of the Spirit are such virtues as humility, kindness, sincerity of heart, beauty of character, and above all, love. Just as the Spirit of God is the harmony, excellency, and beauty of the triune God, so "'twas his work to communicate beauty and harmony to the world."[10]

Hospitable to the outpouring of the Spirit in the churches of his time, Edwards was also alert to the need to wrestle with excesses and distortions. He called the church to engage in a testing of the spirits to see which are indeed from God. This is a central aim of his *Religious Affections* and of his sermons on charity in which he undertakes to show that the true gifts of the

7. Calvin, *Institutes*, III.xix.

8. Thomas A. Schafer, ed., *The Works of Jonathan Edwards*, vol. 13 (New Haven: Yale University Press, 1994), p. 293.

9. John E. Smith, ed., *The Works of Jonathan Edwards*, vol.2 (New Haven: Yale University Press, 1959), p. 121.

10. Smith, *Jonathan Edwards*, p. 121.

Spirit are those that are Christ-like, that partake of and reflect the temper and disposition of Christ, that are directed to the excellency and loveliness of God in Christ rather than being focused on the believer's own experience of God, and that are expressed in the concrete practice of love of God and love of neighbor.

Next, for Karl Barth, the premier Reformed theologian of the twentieth century, the Spirit of God is the awakening, enlivening, and enlightening power of Jesus Christ that enables the gathering, building up, and sending out of the church. It is the power of the Holy Spirit that enables persons to become subjects of faith, love, and hope. As an heir of the Augustinian trinitarian tradition, Barth was a vigorous advocate of the *filioque* doctrine.[11] He defended this doctrine not because of speculative interests in the inner life of God but because the *filioque* affirms the eternal communion between God the Father and God the Son without which our communion by grace in the life and love of God would lack an objective ground and guarantee.

A repeated emphasis of Barth's doctrine of the Spirit is that the Spirit of God is not to be identified with the human spirit. Because God is always altogether Other, because the Spirit of God is the free gift of God and never to be taken for granted, the donation of the Spirit must be received by us again and again. We never take possession and become masters of the Spirit. So Barth writes, "*Veni Creator Spiritus:* Always and everywhere this must be prayed afresh."[12]

Barth's pneumatology unfolds in close relationship to his doctrine of the nature and mission of the church. The Spirit of God for Barth might aptly be called the missionary Spirit. It was Barth who recovered for Reformed faith and theology a strong trinitarian understanding of the person and work of the Spirit and developed a theology of mission on this basis. According to Barth, the Spirit unites us with Christ and enables our participation in the missionary work of God in the world. In the power of the Spirit the church "is not led out of the world but into the world."[13]

Barth speaks of a deep solidarity between the Spirit-empowered community of Jesus Christ and the world. This does not mean, of course, a mimicking of the ways and attitudes of the world, but an assumption of responsibility for the world and its future. United in solidarity with the world, Christians "are made jointly responsible for it, for its future, for what is to become of it."[14]

11. Karl Barth, *Church Dogmatics* (Edinburgh: T&T Clark, 1975), I/1, pp. 466-89.

12. Barth, *Church Dogmatics*, IV/4, p. 38.

13. Barth, *Dogmatics*, IV/3.2, p. 776.

14. Barth, *Dogmatics*, IV/3.2, p. 776.

Fourth, according to Jürgen Moltmann, a leading Reformed theologian of our own time, the Spirit of God is the Spirit of life in community, where diversity enriches, strangers are welcome, and eucharistic joy is shared. For Moltmann, the Spirit is the Spirit of trinitarian communion who works to liberate and unite all of life in new community. "Wherever community of life comes into being, there is also community with God's life-giving Spirit. The creation of community is evidently the goal of God's life-giving Spirit in the world of nature and human beings."[15] The Spirit of God is the power of new community in which hospitality and friendship are extended to all people in the name of Christ.

In his pneumatology, Moltmann offers a great variety of metaphors for the Spirit drawn from Scripture, tradition, and contemporary life. He contends that the western theological tradition has left the image of the Spirit as a mother undeveloped, despite the fact that the Spirit is described in scriptural passages like John 3 as the one who gives birth to believers. An impoverishment of theological language occurs when experiences of the Spirit are described with the use of only masculine metaphors.[16]

For Moltmann a primary work of the Spirit is doxology. The Spirit glorifies the Father through the Son, and enables our participation in the trinitarian history of self-sacrificial love through our joyful praise and our service of others. According to Moltmann, it is above all in the Lord's Supper or eucharist that the church takes part in the divine drama of self-giving and the doxology that it evokes. The eucharist is the anticipatory realization of God's new world of freedom, justice, peace, and friendship for the whole creation. "The eucharist reveals to the world what it is to be."[17] The Spirit is at work, both inside and outside the church, "groaning," as the Apostle Paul says, in solidarity with all creatures in bondage, and awakening the creation to new hope in God's coming reign. The Spirit aims at a new community of creatures, reflective of God's own trinitarian communion, in which unity does not suffocate diversity, and diversity enhances rather than destroys unity.

Moltmann differs in one major respect from the pneumatology of Calvin, Edwards, and Barth. He challenges the western doctrine of the *filioque* and explores ways of taking up the concerns of the eastern churches that have long rejected this doctrine. The crux of Moltmann's argument is that the *filioque* clause, added later to the Nicene Creed, tends toward a subordina-

15. Jürgen Moltmann, *The Spirit of Life: A Universal Affirmation* (Minneapolis: Fortress Press, 1992), p. 219.

16. Moltman, *Spirit of Life*, p. 273.

17. Jürgen Moltmann, *The Church in the Power of the Spirit* (New York: Harper & Row Publishers, 1997), p. 256.

tionism of the Spirit. As a result, the trinitarian relationships can no longer be understood as genuinely mutual and reciprocal relationships of love. For Moltmann, the trinitarian persons abide in perichoretic unity, and human relationships in the *imago trinitatis* are to reflect the trinitarian perichoresis. "The perichoretic unity of the divine Persons who 'ek-sist' with one another, for one another and in one another, finds its correspondence in the true human communities which we can experience — experience in love, in friendship, in the community of Christ's people which is filled by the Spirit, and in the just society."[18]

All four of these Reformed theologians look upon the doctrine of the Holy Spirit as of great importance, and all set their understanding of the Spirit in an explicitly trinitarian context. For each, the work of the Spirit in the economy of salvation is grounded in and corresponds to the activity of the Spirit in the eternal life of the triune God.

III

I have briefly portrayed the spirit of Reformed faith and theology and have reviewed several characteristic Reformed accents in the doctrine of the Holy Spirit as found in four premier theologians of the Reformed tradition. In this final section, I want to suggest that Reformed emphases in the understanding of the work of the Holy Spirit need to be reclaimed and restated for the church and its ministry today. This is a task far too large to be completed here. I can only briefly mention four areas in which attention to the person and work of the Spirit is of special importance for the renewal of the Reformed churches today: worship, spirituality, mission in a pluralistic world, and encounter of the world religions.

The first area is *the Spirit and the renewal of worship.* As many pastors and lay people alike would readily admit, Reformed worship is suffering from a drought of the Spirit. Worship, no less than theology and mission, matters, and Reformed worship today needs to recover a new openness to the activity of the Spirit in every aspect of worship. Such a recovery would be consistent with Calvin's emphasis on the indispensability of the Spirit in proclamation and sacrament.

At the heart of Reformed worship, in its proclamation, sacrament, prayer, and hymn, is the act of praise. An urgent need in Reformed worship today is the recovery of the Spirit of whole-hearted praise and celebration. In

---

18. Moltmann, *Spirit of Life*, p. 309.

praise we give ourselves entirely to God who is praiseworthy and in whom we find endless delight. The act of praising is a defining act for both persons and communities.[19] Praise is both person-forming and community-forming. The giving of praise to God not only defines who we are as persons but also carries tremendous political implications. A community of praise declares that God and God alone is worthy of our praise and unconditional allegiance and thus commits itself to oppose all the lesser gods that clamor for our attention both in the life of the church and in the wider culture. A community of praise is a community that obeys the first commandment from the heart; in its praise of God alone it shows that it is a community of faith moved by the Spirit.

But if the practice of praise is not to decline into arrogant triumphalism or become merely perfunctory ritual, it must include rather than exclude honest lament and bold protest. When praise and lament are separated, praise becomes spiritless and lament becomes hopeless.[20] Since the world, as it is actually experienced, is afflicted with sin and evil, suffering and oppression, the praise that we render to God cannot be separated from lament. The Psalms, which have always been of great importance in Reformed worship, combine lament and praise with astonishing boldness: "How majestic is your name! ... How long, O Lord?" For the Psalmist there is no need to try to cover up the misery of sin and suffering in our own life or the outrageous evil and injustice in the world. The Psalmist knows that there is no hell in which we might find ourselves where the Spirit of God is absent.

I would contend that we will not recover this crucial linkage between honest lament, outrage against injustice, and authentic praise until we learn to pray with the boldness of the Psalmist and until we restore the Lord's Supper to a central place in all Reformed worship. As no other element of Christian worship, the Lord's Supper acknowledges the brokenness and misery of a world of sin and suffering and yet also proclaims the dawn of God's new world in Jesus Christ. With simplicity and power the Lord's Supper proclaims that Christ is crucified, Christ is risen, Christ will come again. It invites all manner of people from east and west and north and south to an open banquet in anticipation of the completion of God's purposes for the whole creation. Celebration of the Lord's Supper is an anticipation of God's new world

19. Patrick D. Miller, ed., *The Psalms and the Life of Faith: Walter Brueggemann* (Minneapolis: Fortress Press, 1995), pp. 112-32.

20. Walter Brueggemann has led in the recovery of the significance of the lament psalms for Christian theology and ministry. See his essay, "The Costly Loss of Lament," in *The Psalms and the Life of Faith* (Minneapolis: Fortress Press, 1995), pp. 98-111. See also Kathleen D. Billman and Daniel L. Migliore, *Rachel's Cry: Prayer of Lament and Rebirth of Hope* (Cleveland: Pilgrim Press, 1999).

that is coming. I am convinced that practice of the Lord's Supper should be set again at the center of Reformed worship in union with proclamation of the Word and should be made an integral part of the weekly worship service.

The next area is *the Spirit and the cultivation of embodied spirituality*. If the transformation of all of life is a characteristic impulse of Reformed faith and life in the power of the Spirit, Reformed spirituality is necessarily concerned with embodied existence and not merely with the redemption of souls. Far from disregarding the body and the material world, a Reformed spirituality is remarkably inclusive in its understanding of the renewing activity of God.

Embodied — or as we might also call it — worldly spirituality, encompasses every aspect of our life as physical-spiritual creatures. It encompasses the way we treat our bodies and the bodies of others. It embraces our sexuality. It includes our life in relationship with others in our everyday work, in our civic responsibilities, in our cultural life, and in all that makes up our common human existence. It includes our attitudes toward and interaction with the natural environment and our respect for forms of embodied life other than the human. Mark well: the real threat to the Reformed tradition of faith and theology at the beginning of the twenty-first century is not the loss of members that we have experienced in the last quarter century — however disquieting that is and should be to us — but the loss of Reformed nerve, the loss of the spirit of world formation and worldly spirituality.[21] And that can happen either in the form of a sectarian spirit that insulates itself from the world, or in the form of an accommodationist spirit that caves in to the priorities and ideals of secular, consumerist society, a society bent upon merely using other human bodies and all other creatures of God for its own self-aggrandizement.

Edwards's appreciation of the place of sensory delight and the joy of beauty in a Christian understanding of spirituality can contribute to Reformed faith and life today. The Spirit of God is the Spirit of harmony, joy, and delight, the Spirit of holy love that liberates and reconciles us and that creates beauty. Nicholas Wolterstorff, a Reformed Christian philosopher, writes about the importance of the aesthetic dimension of human life, so long ignored in both theology and piety. In one particularly striking passage, he laments the ugliness of many of our metropolitan centers and reminds us that the Christian hope has as one of its seminal images the coming celestial city. Aesthetics and ethics are not mutually exclusive. Reformed Christians should

---

21. See Douglas Ottati, *Reforming Protestantism: Christian Commitment in Today's World* (Louisville: Westminster John Knox Press, 1995), for an eloquent development of this thesis.

certainly enter into solidarity with the poor and struggle against structures of injustice that create poverty. But our understanding of poverty is frequently very narrow. Reformed Christians should also be dedicated to preserving the beauty of nature and to encouraging cultural creativity that brings delight to our common life. "Could it be," Wolterstorff asks, "that living in a city devoid of sensory delight is itself a form of poverty?"[22]

The third area is *the Spirit and the mission of the church in a pluralistic world.* According to the biblical witness and the trinitarian faith of the church, the Spirit of God empowers the church to include and welcome the other, the alien, the stranger. Translated into terms that speak to our contemporary situation, the Spirit of God is the Spirit that is genuinely gender inclusive and that welcomes people of all colors, cultures, classes, and sexual orientation. The Spirit of God is the Spirit of diversity in unity and unity in diversity. Reformed Christians owe much to the work of twentieth-century Reformed theologians like Barth and Moltmann as well as to many liberation theologians who have developed this theme.

A new awareness of the wealth of the gifts of the Spirit must be recovered today. All members of the body of Christ are given gifts to share with others. A strong theology of the Holy Spirit forms the foundation of a robust theology of the laity and of an understanding of ministry as the ministry of the whole people of God. A Spirit-filled church will acknowledge that we are profoundly interdependent and that our lives are impoverished without the gifts offered by men and women who are racially, culturally, and ethnically different from us. According to the story of Pentecost recounted in the Book of Acts, the coming of the Spirit is accompanied by new bonds of community and new opportunities of communication between those who previously were cut off from each other. The Pentecost story will be a crucial biblical paradigm of the work of the Spirit in our midst in our pluralistic age.[23]

In particular, the rich contributions that women have made and will continue to make to Christian ministry and witness will find support and guidance in a more fully developed doctrine of the Holy Spirit. One of the major themes of feminist and womanist theology is the importance of the concrete experience of women for the reform of piety, theology, and ministry in the church today. Many women and men today speak of the experience of grace as an experience of God's friendship in which new freedom, creativity, and solidarity are born. Although some theologians are inclined to dismiss

22. Nicholas Wolterstorff, *Until Justice and Peace Embrace* (Grand Rapids: Eerdmans, 1983), p. 140.
23. See Michael Welker, *God the Spirit* (Minneapolis: Fortress Press, 1994).

the category of experience as incompatible with the Reformed emphasis on the normativity of the Word of God, I would consider this a serious mistake that betrays the lack of an adequate doctrine of the Holy Spirit. A theology of the Word that ignores or denigrates concrete and differentiated experiences of God's Word is a spiritless theology.

The final area to be discussed is *the Spirit and the encounter of the world religions.* The mission of the church in a pluralistic world includes encounter with a plurality of world religions. A trinitarian understanding of the Spirit as mediated through the Reformed tradition makes possible fresh approaches to the question of the relation of Christianity and other world religions. This is a difficult topic and one surrounded by many dangers, but it is a top priority for a courageous, Spirit-guided Reformed faith and theology as we stand at the beginning of the third millennium.

The encounter of Christianity and other religions has frequently been discussed in terms of positions labeled exclusivism, inclusivism, and pluralism. Unhappily, these positions have often been described without attention to the trinitarian faith of the church. Within a full trinitarian perspective, the work of God as our creator, reconciler, and consummator must be taken into account. Christian faith is assuredly Christocentric, but Barth himself recognized that Christocentric faith must not be equated with Christomonism. Exclusivism in the meeting of world religions is inadequate because it sees the person of another religion as a total outsider; inclusivism is unsatisfactory because it relates to the person of another religion only as a kind of anonymous Christian; and undiscriminating pluralism is flawed because it abandons the truth question in the encounter of world religions and thus falls into relativism. Beyond these positions, trinitarian faith and theology provide a distinctive framework for discussing the issue of religious pluralism. The triune God is creator of the heavens and the earth, reconciler of the world in Jesus Christ, and life-giving Spirit who works freely both to bring God's redemptive purposes to consummation and to prepare the way for the reception of Christ. Trusting in the triune God, Christians are called to be honest, open, and expectant in their interactions with people of other religious traditions.

The Spirit of God who hovered over the chaotic waters of creation, energized leaders of the people of God, spoke through the prophets, empowered the ministry of Christ, enabled new understanding and new community between strangers at Pentecost, led Christians of every age to recognize Jesus Christ as the way, the truth, and the life, and filled them with burning desire for the coming of God's reign throughout the creation — this Spirit of God is at work in the world in ways we cannot imagine and cannot contain. While Christians confidently and unashamedly affirm that Jesus Christ is the way, the truth, and the life, this affirmation need not be understood in a way that builds barriers between Christians and others. On the contrary, if we make the necessary distinction between the reality of Jesus Christ and our always incomplete and inadequate christologies, we will remain open to new light from whatever source it comes, even as we continue to bear faithful witness to the light of life that shines in Jesus Christ.

In faith we approach people of other faiths not fearfully, but expectantly, eager to share with them the good news of God that we have received, and ready to listen to what they may have to tell us of God's working in their lives. This is not relativism, and it is not a betrayal of the finality of Jesus Christ and the importance of Christian mission. It is a recognition that the Spirit of God, who is none other than the Spirit of Christ, works freely and is always a step ahead of us in God's mission to redeem and renew the whole creation.

In summary, I have contended that the spirit of Reformed faith and theology is bound up with its understanding of the identity and work of the Holy Spirit. A recovery of a fully Reformed understanding of the Spirit is crucial for the renewal of Reformed worship and spirituality, for energizing the church for its mission in a pluralistic world, and for guiding Christians in their encounter with people of other faiths.

Wallace Alston, to whom this essay is dedicated, writes, "Who is the Holy Spirit? . . . Our understanding of the church today depends on the answer we give to that question."[24] As I have argued — and I am certain Wallace would concur — the answer of Reformed faith and theology is that the Holy Spirit is the Spirit of the triune God. But the answer cannot be separated from the hope and the prayer: "Come, Holy Spirit!"

---

24. Wallace M. Alston, *The Church of the Living God: A Reformed Perspective* (Louisville: Westminster John Knox Press, 2002), p. 36.

The Theology of Worship
within the Reformed Tradition

David Fergusson

Despite frequent lip-service to the principle *lex orandi, lex credendi,* the theology of worship is often a marginalized topic in textbooks. Several causes for this neglect may be suggested. As a minor dogmatic theme, it has been treated as an addendum to discussions of ecclesiology. Often consigned along with the theology of ministry to courses on practical theology, it has been regarded as of second-order importance by systematic theologians. An aspect of ministerial formation or specialist liturgical study, reflection on worship has been dominated by historical and practical approaches to the neglect of the dogmatic. Nonetheless, if the subject of worship has traditionally suffered from theological marginalization in the past, this is less true today. It is cited frequently in an American post-liberal context, and in the recent work of Geoffrey Wainwright there is even an attempt to construct an entire systematics from the perspective of worship.[1] There are several reasons for this and by inspecting these under four headings — history, philosophy, ethics, and ecumenism — some initial insight into the theology of worship can be gained.

The Study of Doctrine in the Context of Worship

History

The study of the history of doctrine reveals the way in which doxological practices preceded and shaped the formation of dogma. Without asserting an

1. Geoffrey Wainwright, *Doxology: A Systematic Theology* (London: Epworth, 1980).

absolute priority of doxology over dogma, one can acknowledge the importance of worship in shaping Christian belief. This is already true of Hebrew
religion where, in the Psalms, the celebration of salvation history, law, divine
rule, and wisdom all contribute to the shaping of Israel's faith. Similarly, the
elaborate sacrificial system and holiness code reveal long-standing practices
which, for example, condition faith and belief in atonement for sin. New Testament scholarship has also made us aware of those credal fragments in the
letters of Paul and elsewhere which reflect established usage in early Christian
worship, for example the Christ-hymn in Philippians 2.[2] Theology was decisively shaped by a range of practices such as praying to Jesus, baptism in the
threefold name, and the celebration of the Lord's Supper as recorded in 1 Corinthians 11. In the patristic period, the development of dogma was also influenced by established practice.[3] Thus in the Arian controversy, Athanasius
could appeal to the widespread practice of addressing prayer to Jesus. Against
Pelagius, Augustine could cite the practice of baptising infants for remission
of sin. Anselm's theory of the atonement invoked the categories of the
church's penitential system, while eucharistic controversies in the middle ages
were determined by the language of the liturgy. One would also have to view
mariology and the subsequent dogmatic definition of the immaculate conception and bodily assumption of Mary in light of entrenched practices of
devotion that first emerge in the patristic period. In all this, however, it is not
merely a matter of doctrine tracking widespread practice. Critical doctrinal
reflection can act as a corrective upon our doxological habits.

Philosophy

The work of the later Wittgenstein has been interpreted and deployed by
theologians in a range of ways, not all of which are consistent. But one widely
recognized contribution of Wittgenstein is the stress on practice and forms of
life in the acquisition of meaning. When a builder shouts "slab" to his colleague he is not engaging in a simple act of naming, as Wittgenstein's earlier
work had suggested.[4] Instead he is issuing an instruction about how and
when to deliver the next slab to his colleague who is laying them in a particu-

---

2. For discussion of the significance of worship in the New Testament, see Larry Hurtado,
At the Origins of Christian Worship (Carlisle: Paternoster, 1999).

3. This is revealed for example in Jaroslav Pelikan's *The Emergence of the Catholic Tradition (100-600)* (Chicago: University of Chicago Press, 1971).

4. This example is drawn from Ludwig Wittgenstein, *Philosophical Investigations* (Oxford: Blackwell, 1953), pp. 8-10.

lar order. The salient point of this illustration is that meanings are only acquired through initiation into the practice and forms of life that shape the world of the building site. Words are not learned by looking out at the world and receiving examples of how to label the objects of experience. Learning takes place through action, exchange, and participation in a complex set of rule-governed practices. Instead of a detached visual recognition, meaning is grasped through touch and sound in complex, communal activity.

These observations about meaning are significant for an account of theological knowledge. We know God not so much by attaching labels to experiences, events, or phenomena, but through participation in a range of rule-governed practices and forms of life. An alternative way of expressing this is to say that we can speak of a knowledge of God only in terms of exposure to and immersion in the life of the community. This will typically require catechesis, baptism, and commitment to regular practice in the love of God and love of one's neighbour.

On this account of meaning, we now become better placed to appreciate the integral connection of worship to a practical knowledge of God. The worship of the community informs our knowledge of God. We are initiated into ways of seeing the world, ourselves, and other people that are theologically significant. Without the regular patterns of worship, the language of faith and its modes of perception will make little or no sense to us. This is a central theme of George Lindbeck's *The Nature of Doctrine,* one of the most influential texts of the last twenty years.[5] We learn faith in a way analogous to a child learning its first language. Experience and belief, too long abstracted from worship in theology, are now perceived to repose upon the practices of the worshipping community.

Ethics

Recent return to Aristotelian virtue ethics in both philosophy and theology has brought a renewed stress upon the importance of habit in the moral life. We act well typically through the development of good habits. These require formation through acknowledgement of the texts, authorities, traditions, and practices of the Christian community. The most important single voice here is that of Stanley Hauerwas. Training in the Christian life, he argues, requires induction into the practices of worship, familiarity with the examples and stories of the saints, and the reorientation of one's life by the claims of Christ

5. George Lindbeck, *The Nature of Doctrine* (London: SPCK, 1985).

and his church. This is stressed in a counter-cultural spirit. The distinctiveness of Christian living requires attention to the ways in which the worship, fellowship, belief, and moral witness of the church reshape our lives.

It has been pointed out that there is a Catholic moment in the ethics of Hauerwas. The attention given to the authority of the church, the lives of the saints and the Aristotelian-Thomist tradition positions this style of Christian ethics much closer to Roman Catholicism than the neo-liberal Protestant views it typically criticises. On the other hand, the writings of Hauerwas need also to be seen in the context of Reformed emphases upon personal holiness, the Christian life, the discipline of the church community, and the transformation of society. The influence of John Howard Yoder and the radical reformation is also apparent and enables him to describe himself as a high Church Methodist with Mennonite leanings. Many of Hauerwas's recent essays are published sermons. These reflect a commitment to the power of the preached Word to change the lives of its hearers. It is through the regular practice of communal worship that we are trained to live as God's people in the world:

> The church is the visible, political enactment of our language of God by a people who can name their sin and accept God's forgiveness and are thereby enabled to speak the truth in love. Our Sunday worship has a way of reminding us, in the most explicit and ecclesial of ways, of the source of our power, the peculiar nature of our solutions to what ails the world.[6]

The work of Hauerwas should be seen in the same post-liberal paradigm as Lindbeck. It is developed by others from a range of perspectives. In a discussion of pastoral care, Willimon points to the importance of worship in consoling, healing, and renewing us amidst the crises of life. He appeals to worship as central to what distinguishes Christian pastoral care from secular forms of counselling and therapy.[7] Miroslav Volf, in a recent collection of essays, speaks of belief-shaped practices and practice-shaping beliefs to describe the integrity of doing and believing in the Christian life:

> Christian practices have what we may call an "as-so" structure: *as* God has received us in Christ, *so* we too are to receive our fellow human beings. True, the way in which Christ's life is exemplary has to be carefully speci-

---

6. Stanley Hauerwas and William H. Willimon, *Resident Aliens* (Nashville: Abingdon, 1993), p. 171. In similar vein, Sam Wells has sought to describe the range of ways in which worship is ethically formative, "How Common Worship Forms Local Character," *Studies in Christian Ethics* 15 (2002), pp. 66-74.

7. William Willimon, *Worship as Pastoral Care* (Nashville: Abindgon, 1979).

fied. Above all, the important difference between Christ and other human beings should counter both the temptation to supplant Christ and the presumption that human beings can simply "repeat" Christ's work. But in an appropriately qualified way, in relation to the practice of hospitality as well as in relation to all other practices, we must say: "As Christ, so we."[8]

Ecumenism

The ecumenical movement has also made a contribution to the renewed sense of the importance of worship for Christian doctrine. Through study of shared practices a greater sense of ecumenical convergence has been achieved, even where there this has not yielded structural unity. This has been fostered by biblical scholarship and historical study of church traditions.

The process leading to the formulation of "Baptism, Eucharist and Ministry," the Lima document of 1982, is instructive in this context. In particular, the section on the eucharist makes significant ecumenical progress by shifting attention away from rival theories of the real presence by focussing on the wider context of eucharistic worship. This was achieved in part through the liturgical reform movement and the creation of an ecumenical order of service for sacramental celebration. The eucharist is set within the context of divine worship broadly considered. It contains most, if not all, of the following elements: praise, confession of sin, declaration of pardon, proclamation of the Word, confession of the faith, intercession for church and world, words of institution, *anamnesis, epiklesis,* commemoration of the faithful departed, prayer for the coming of the kingdom, the Lord's Prayer, the sign of peace, praise, blessing and sending. The stress on the ecumenical sharing of these aspects of eucharistic worship has contributed to a process in which historical differences are minimized, though not overcome.

Theological Description of the Forms of Worship

Attempts to define worship as if it were one single thing or activity, and then to organize everything else around this, are liable to cause distortion. This is a mistaken strategy for it will tend to miss vital elements. Instead, the task is better conceived as offering a description of worship which is informed both

---

8. Miroslav Volf, "Theology for a Way of Life," in *Practicing Theology,* ed. Miroslav Volf and Dorothy C. Bass (Grand Rapids: Eerdmans, 2002), p. 250.

by its centrality for Christian belief and practice, and also by the central creedal affirmations of the faith. We should think in this context of "description" rather than "definition."

Attention to linguistic study of the various terms for "worship" in its Biblical and post-canonical usage is necessary, but not sufficient for the construction of a theology of worship. The Hebrew verb *chawah* is most commonly used to describe the activity of divine worship. It refers to the act of bowing down or rendering obeisance to whom it is due. In the Greek New Testament, the verb *proskuneō* is used in many places with much the same sense of bowing down. *Latreuō* is also employed several times for public worship, and denotes the idea of offering service. Church worship is thus described as service; we still refer to the church service in English or the *Gottesdienst* in German. The English term "worship" itself derives from an Anglo-Saxon word for "honor" *(weorthscipe)* suggesting again that worship is an action of honoring one who is worthy. It can be used of persons other than God in different contexts. Thus, using archaic English, we might address "the Worshipful the Mayor." A better known example is found in the order for the solemnization of matrimony in the Book of Common Prayer (1662). Upon placing the ring on his wife's finger, the husband says, "With this ring I thee wed, with my body I thee worship, and with all my worldly goods I thee endow."[9]

In much confessional writing, the Biblical sense of honoring the divine majesty is prominent. The description of God in the Westminster Confession of Faith is characterised in the following terms: "To (God) is due from angels and men, and every other creature, whatsoever worship, service, or obedience he is pleased to require of them" (III.2). In the Reformation criticism of idolatry in the church, the honoring of God alone is frequently stressed in the exposition of the first table of the Decalogue. So the Shorter Catechism informs us that "The First Commandment forbiddeth the denying, or not worshipping and glorifying, the true God as God, and our God; and the giving of that worship and glory to any other which is due to him alone" (Answer 47). All this must find a place in a theology of worship, yet the honoring of God is neither a necessary nor a sufficient condition for an adequate description of worship. There are several reasons for this. We can honour and acknowledge God in ways that extend beyond worship, for example in our daily work, in the life of the household, in political and social activity. It is the particular

---

9. Despite its archaic usage, the Book of Common Prayer in this respect does not reduce the marriage bond to proprietorial terms. One may "worship" one's partner in marriage, but never one's worldly goods.

form that this honoring takes which requires articulation in a theology of worship. Worship, moreover, involves a wide range of activities not all of which are entirely captured by the notion of acknowledging or honouring God. The range of forms cited in the New Testament recalls us to this diversity, as does the practice of the synagogue. Indeed the Psalms already attest the variety of functions fulfilled by public worship; these include praise, thanksgiving, celebration, recounting, proclamation, confession, petition, instruction, and lament. While Christian practice has sometimes found difficulty in accommodating lament and complaint, all these other themes are generally present in the worship of the church.

Worship as an Action in Which God Is Both Subject and Object

As an event in which God is not merely a passive recipient of our praise, worship creates an exchange between the divine and the creaturely in which God is the subject as well as the object of worship. The dramatic character of worship has often been portrayed by the Protestant account of preaching and by the Catholic description of the eucharist. The preaching of the Word is an event in which not only the preacher speaks, but God addresses the people. It is this that bestows upon worship both a gravity and a joyfulness. Whatever our theological evaluation of the medieval and Tridentine doctrine of transubstantiation and its accompanying account of ordination, we can recognize that in the description of the fraction at the altar there is an acute sense of the continual action of God in the regular worship of the church across space and time. Christ is re-presented to his people each time the sacrament of his body and blood is celebrated. In this same context, note should be made of the action of the Spirit in public worship in recent charismatic traditions. The criticism of mainstream western theology that it was too binitarian is not without force at this point. A fuller account of the person and work of the Spirit should enhance the sense that the Spirit is active in prompting, guiding, and enabling worship in all its dimensions.

Here worship might be described as a performative action in which both the church and God participate. It is not merely a human acknowledgement of who God is or what Christ has done. Worship is an event by which God is known and Christ communicated; it is not of our own making for it is dependent upon the grace of God. In this regard, the act of worship is not merely a human recollection or bearing witness although it includes these. It is also an event in which God's grace works for us in repeated, regular, and dependable ways, albeit in a manner that refers us to the once for all action of Christ. Appeal can be made in this context to the priestly theology of the Hebrews and the claim that the ascended Christ is seated at the right hand of the Father. Though difficult to formulate conceptually, this language implies that Christ continues through the Spirit to intercede on our behalf. He continues to pray for and with us, even as we pray through him and in him. Worship here becomes the coincidence of divine and human action together.[10]

This can be a powerful and liberating insight, particularly at those moments when faith falters and prayer becomes fitful. Simon Peter is told that though his faith will fail, Christ has prayed for him. So also the ascended Christ continues through the Spirit to intercede for us. The awareness of Christ as the one who perpetually prays for us and also of the company of the faithful who surround us is a source of pastoral encouragement and liturgical strength. In reflecting upon the theology of Easter Saturday in the midst of his own terminal illness, Alan Lewis has written these moving words:

> It was surely a terrible mistake of our fathers and mothers in the faith to make a person's deathbed state of mind the sole criterion of how he or she would stand beyond the grave before God's supposedly terrifying judgement. We face suffering, distress, and death with courage, faith and trust, not by maintaining serenity of psyche or buoyancy of soul within, but precisely by casting ourselves in all the times of emptiness, aridity, and wordlessness — as well as those still more spiritually dangerous times of optimism or elation — upon the gift of grace outside us and around us. God promises to do what we cannot do, and go where we need not go, to enter the dark valley ahead of us and defeat on our behalf the frightening foe. And the Spirit undertakes to pray for us, and stirs others to intercede on our behalf, just when we feel awful, overwrought in body or in spirit, when faith eludes intellect or consciousness and our tongues have lost all utterance.[11]

In stressing the ongoing action of the Spirit in relation to the priestly office of the ascended Christ, we can understand worship as God's action in our midst without compromising the once-for-all character of the work of Christ. In stressing this point, however, we should not overstate it so as to present worship as something that we do not do. Worship is not an intra-trinitarian

---

10. This is developed by James B. Torrance, *Worship, Community and the Triune God of Grace* (Carlisle: Paternoster, 1996). See also Graham Redding, *Prayer and the Priesthood of Christ* (London: Continuum/T&T Clark, 2003).

11. Alan E. Lewis, *Between Cross & Resurrection: A Theology of Holy Saturday* (Grand Rapids: Eerdmans, 2001), pp. 430-1.

transaction that takes place over our heads, unrelated to the practices of the visible, empirical congregations to which we belong. An over-stretched christomonism will lead to the enervating and implausible conclusion that in worship there is nothing much left for us to do.

To illustrate the performative character of worship, we might consider further the Psalms. It is generally assumed that these were memorized and recited in worship before being committed to their present literary form.[12] In celebrating the kingly rule of God, the Psalms not only attest that rule, but also contribute to it and participate in it. In part, it is through the praise of Israel that God's rule over creation is exercised. Through a covenant partnership, expressed in the forms of worship, God wills to be known and obeyed. Thus in Psalm 24, though the ark of the covenant is no longer present, the enthronement of God in the praise of the post-exilic people is enacted. Here we see why worship must have a public character. Israel and the church are called into covenant partnership with God not as an aggregate of disconnected individuals, but as a people which, in its corporate, social existence, worships together. This does not exclude private acts of worship and devotion, but it seems to demand the centrality of the regular, public diet of worship on the Lord's Day in fulfilment of the fourth commandment. This public event has a dramatic quality by virtue of its character as both a divine and a human action. In his Aberdeen Gifford lectures, Barth once insisted,

> [T]he church service is the most important, momentous and majestic thing which can possibly take place on earth, because its primary content is not the work of man but the work of the Holy Spirit and consequently the work of faith.[13]

Reformed Exposition of Worship Under the Rubrics of Word and Sacrament

In much Reformed writing, the topic of worship is dealt with by reference to the two "notes" of Word and sacrament. What takes place in worship is expounded by reference to the reading and preaching of God's Word and the right administration of the sacraments. Set out in confessions, catechisms and theological textbooks, much of the exposition is located within an initial context of sixteenth-century polemics.

12. E.g., Claus Westermann, *The Living Psalms* (Edinburgh: T&T Clark, 1989), p. 4.

13. Karl Barth, *The Knowledge of God and the Service of God* (London: Hodder & Stoughton, 1938), p. 198.

The need to reform the life of the church according to the Word of God entailed a good deal of attention to the range of activities that took place in worship. Thus Bullinger's *Second Helvetic Confession* engages in a patient description of the tasks of the minister, the sacramental relation, baptism and the Lord's Supper, religious meetings, church architecture, the language of prayer, singing, canonical hours, holy days, fasts, catechizing, pastoral care of the sick, burial of the dead, ceremonies, rites, and *adiaphora* — the things of indifference. In the *Second Helvetic Confession*, we have something akin to a comprehensive description of worship:

> Although it is permitted all men to read the Holy Scriptures privately at home, and by instruction to edify one another in the true religion, yet in order that the Word of God may be properly preached to the people, and prayers and supplication publicly made, also that the sacraments may be rightly administered, and that collections may be made for the poor and to pay the cost of all the Church's expenses, and in order to maintain social intercourse, it is most necessary that religious or Church gatherings be held. For it is certain that in the apostolic and primitive Church, there were such assemblies frequented by all the godly. (Chapter 22)

Although this is a rather low-key and urbane account of worship, it is to be commended for its attention to detail and its strong sense of the local, empirical and visible congregation. It is broader in its scope than most Reformed accounts of worship which focus more exclusively on Word and sacrament. These require some comment.

The attention to the preaching of the Word reflects several features of Lutheran and Reformed worship. These include the return to Scripture alone over against tradition as the supreme rule of faith and life; the importance of a right understanding of the faith, reflected also in the translation of the Bible and the liturgy into the vernacular; the commitment to education shared with renaissance humanism; and also a polemic against the medieval notion of the sacraments as effective *ex opere operato* (by the sheer performance of the act) without reference to the faith of the recipient. In the response to all these concerns, the regular preaching and hearing of the Word became of paramount importance. In much Reformation theology, the preaching of the Word is characterized in sacramental language. For Luther, the Word of God could be described as present in, with, and under the words of the preacher. Within the Reformed tradition, the relationship is not described in terms of a consubstantiation, but in terms of the capacity of the Spirit to speak through human words that have been properly applied to the proclamation of the

Scriptures. Here there is an indirect identity of human and divine speech in a manner that again recalls sacramental language. By contrast, the Roman Catholic tradition has tended to construe the sermon more as a homily, a piece of instruction, subsidiary to the celebration of the mass.[14]

This account of the Word contributed greatly to the dramatic and performative character of worship. Where the preacher speaks, there God too will address us. This attaches to preaching, together with the training and preparation invested in it, the highest seriousness. In both Lutheran and Reformed writing this is evident:

> We may well be amazed, but the concrete situation for the preacher actually is that when he goes up into the pulpit, a printed book lies before him. And that book must be the basis of his preaching, exactly as if it had "fallen from heaven."[15]

One can find Scriptural support for preaching in the ministry of Jesus himself and in his command to preach the gospel. Yet the isolation of the sermon from other forms of oral communication has arguably become problematic in Reformed worship. In particular, the relative loss of both instruction and discussion has caused an undue constriction of worship, and an isolation of the preaching of the Word that does it no service.[16] From the beginning of its history, instruction in the faith was important for new converts. The risen Christ bids his disciples not only to preach, but to teach all that he commands. Jesus himself had been called a teacher, a rabbi, by those around him. And this didactic task was taken seriously by the early church in instruction about the foundational events of the faith and the catechizing of candidates for baptism. Instruction never assumed sacramental status, yet it is as prominent in the New Testament as either baptism or the Lord's Supper. Whether it takes place in or alongside the weekly diet of worship, it is clear that it is closely associated with the building up of the community. Similar remarks can be made with respect to discussion. Conversation is a means of grace in the ministry of Jesus. One thinks of his private exchanges with the disciples, Nicodemus, and the Samaritan woman. Moreover, empirical research suggests that many more people come to faith through personal con-

---

14. More recently, post–Vatican II pneumatology has stressed the importance of preaching and the need publicly to invoke the Spirit at its outset.

15. Rudolf Bultmann, "On the Question of Christology," in *Faith and Understanding*, ed. Robert W. Funk and trans. Louise P. Smith (London: SCM, 1969), p. 131.

16. Here, I am indebted to Hendrikus Berkhof, *Christian Faith* (Grand Rapids: Eerdmans, 1979), pp. 352ff.

versation, discussion, and exchange than through listening to sermons.[17] In this respect, we should not discount the role of para-church organizations where the faith was actively discussed. These complemented and enriched the preaching of sermons. Their decline in some quarters must be viewed with some concern, particularly at a time when we have become conscious of the counter-cultural significance of Christian formation. The ministry of the Word is not to be constricted, but should be set within wider patterns of communication in the church.

In the traditional exposition of the sacraments, we often find a generic definition of a sacrament followed by exposition of baptism and the Lord's Supper. This is true both of confessions and catechisms. These begin by defining what a sacrament is, before expounding the different senses in which both baptism and the Lord's Supper are sacramental. Despite their lucidity and precision, these statements also have their drawbacks. The generic account of a sacrament tended to emerge from eucharistic controversies about the nature of the real presence. The effect was somewhat Procrustean when baptism was presented as another species of the genus. Here, despite disclaimers, the effect of baptism was too tightly tied to the action of immersion or sprinkling in the threefold name. Thus the act of initiation became too easily detached from the context and subsequent activities which also mediated divine grace and without which the language of baptism made little sense. In the case of the Lord's Supper, attention to and disputes over the sacramental nexus also contributed to a loss of the wider ethical significance of the sacrament, the "as-so" connection described above. The regular reception of God's hospitality in the supper is closely linked in the New Testament to the hospitality that we are called to display towards others. Thus the link between eucharistic celebration and *diakonia* was arguably obscured in formal accounts of worship, but is robustly present in works such as Wolterstorff's *Until Justice and Peace Embrace*. This narrowing of sacramental focus may have been compounded by the tendency to infrequent celebration of the Lord's Supper, the arguments of Calvin and others notwithstanding. In the modern-day Church of Scotland, though not perhaps in other traditions, we have a situation in which we can celebrate baptism too often and the Lord's Supper with insufficient frequency.

---

17. E.g., John Finney, *Finding Faith* (Swindon: British and Foreign Bible Society, 1992).

The Aesthetic Dimension of Worship

Any theology of worship which ignores the significance of the aesthetic is deficient. We worship God not as angels, far less as discarnate souls. Our worship is that of embodied, social persons for whom communication takes sensory forms. These include the visual, the verbal, and the musical. In celebrating the beauty of creation, many of the Psalms pass effortlessly into celebration of the beauty of Israel's praise. This aesthetic requirement directs our attention to church music, the use of language in prayer and preaching, the lay-out of the church building, lighting, and even public address systems. One sometimes assumes that the Reformed tradition is hostile to the intrusion of the aesthetic in worship, yet this is hardly true. It has its own distinctive aesthetic forms.

In the sixteenth century, the reform of church life involved in part an enhanced commitment to preaching, congregational participation, forms of language capable of universal comprehension, recitation of the Psalms, and exclusion of all that diverted the attention of minister and people from the gospel represented in Word and sacrament. While this may have led to some iconoclastic excesses and a deprecation of the visual arts, it nonetheless represented a prioritizing of key aesthetic forms as most appropriate to the communication of the evangelical faith and the glorifying of God. In a discussion of the role of singing in worship, Calvin writes of the power of music to move and inflame hearts. Conscious of its capacity to function in different ways, not all of which are virtuous, he insists upon the need for musical forms which display a weight and a majesty worthy of God. These qualities pertain to melodies that Calvin describes as moderate *(moderée)*. Moreover, our singing should be of words reflecting sound doctrine so that there is a unity of the heart and the understanding. The Psalms are given to us for this purpose:

> [A] linnet, a nightingale or a popinjay will sing well, but it will be without understanding. But man's proper gift is to sing, knowing what he says; after understanding must follow the heart and the affection, something that can only happen when we have the song imprinted on our memory never to cease singing it.[18]

18. Ford Lewis Battles, trans., "John Calvin, The Form of Prayers and Songs of the Church 1543: Letter to the Reader," *Calvin Theological Journal* 15 (1980): 164. For the original French text, see P. Barth and W. Niesel, eds., *Joannis Calvini Opera Selecta*, vol. 2 (Monachii: C. Kaiser, 1952), pp. 12-18. I am grateful to John de la Haye for drawing my attention to this article.

Rather than eschewing aesthetic beauty, the traditions of the Reformed church reflect qualities embedded in its theological convictions. In characterizing its worship, the poet and scholar Donald Davie has spoken of the simplicity, sobriety, and measuredness of its style which provide a particular type of exquisiteness.[19] This is exemplified *inter alia* in the felicitous language of prayer and preaching, a commitment to intellectual precision in the service of the Word, the use of verse and musical forms, and the wearing of unostentatious vestments. Perhaps it had its limitations, particularly with respect to the visual arts. Yet at a time when worship is threatened by a loss of beauty and the incursion of forms which merely represent the personal preference of those leading it, we might do well to study more closely the aesthetic values of our tradition. These deserve not only historical respect, but renewed appreciation for their contribution to the worship of God.[20]

19. Donald Davie, *A Gathered Church: The Literature of the English Dissenting Interest, 1700-1930* (London: Routledge and Kegan Paul, 1978), p. 25. Nicholas Wolterstorff points out that loss of interest in these aesthetic dimensions of worship was connected to the exclusive position assigned the sermon in Protestant worship with the consequent overwhelming of the liturgy, *Until Justice and Peace Embrace* (Grand Rapids: Eerdmans, 1983), p. 159.

20. An earlier version of this essay appeared in the *Scottish Bulletin of Evangelical Theology* 21, no. 1 (Spring 2003): 7-20.

Contributors

DENISE M. ACKERMANN, Professor of Practical Theology,
University of Stellenbosch, Stellenbosch, South Africa

MILNER S. BALL, Professor of Law and Religion,
University of Georgia, Athens, Georgia

DON BROWNING, Professor of Practical Theology (Emeritus),
University of Chicago Divinity School, Chicago Illinois

BRIAN E. DALEY, S.J., Professor of Christian Dogmatics,
University of Notre Dame, South Bend, Indiana

DAVID FERGUSSON, Professor of Systematic Theology,
New College, University of Edinburgh, Edinburgh, Scotland

BOTOND GAÁL, Professor of Christian Dogmatics,
University of Debrecen, Debrecen, Hungary

THOMAS W. GILLESPIE, President and Professor of New Testament
(Emeritus), Princeton Theological Seminary, Princeton, New Jersey

NIELS HENRIK GREGERSEN, Professor of Systematic Theology,
Faculty of Theology, University of Copenhagen, Copenhagen, Denmark

COLIN GUNTON†, Professor of Systematic Theology,
Kings' College London, United Kingdom

CYNTHIA A. JARVIS, Pastor, Presbyterian Church of Chestnut Hill,
Philadelphia, Pennsylvania

ROBERT W. JENSON, Senior Scholar for Research,
Center of Theological Inquiry, Princeton, New Jersey

L. ANN JERVIS, Professor of New Testament,
Wycliffe College and Trinity College at Toronto School of Theology,
Toronto, Canada

JOHN S. McCLURE, Professor of Homiletics,
Vanderbilt University, Nashville, Tennessee

J. HAROLD McKEITHEN, JR., Interim Pastor,
Williamsburg Presbyterian Church, Williamsburg, Virginia

A. J. McKELWAY, Professor of Religion (Emeritus),
Davidson College, Davidson, North Carolina

ALLEN C. McSWEEN, JR., Pastor, Fourth Presbyterian Church,
Greenville, South Carolina

DANIEL L. MIGLIORE, Professor of Systematic Theology,
Princeton Theological Seminary, Princeton, New Jersey

PATRICK D. MILLER, Professor of Old Testament,
Princeton Theological Seminary, Princeton, New Jersey

JÜRGEN MOLTMANN, Professor of Systematic Theology (Emeritus),
University of Tübingen, Tübingen, Germany

JOHN POLKINGHORNE, Past President and now Fellow of Queen's College,
Cambridge, United Kingdom

FLEMING RUTLEDGE, Episcopal priest, Rye Brook, New York

GERHARD SAUTER, Professor of Ecumenical Theology (Emeritus),
University of Bonn, Bonn, Germany

WILLIAM SCHWEIKER, Professor of Christian Ethics,
University of Chicago Divinity School, Chicago, Illinois

DIRK SMIT, Professor of Systematic Theology,
University of Stellenbosch, Stellenbosch, South Africa

Max L. Stackhouse, Professor of Christian Ethics,
Princeton Theological Seminary, Princeton, New Jersey

Virgil Thompson, Pastor, Bethlehem Lutheran Church,
Spokane, Washington

Carver T. Yu, Professor of Systematic Theology,
China Graduate School of Theology, Hong Kong, China

Michael Welker, Professor of Systematic Theology and
Director of the Internationales Wissenschaftsforum,
University of Heildelberg, Heidelberg, Germany